CRAZY HORSE

The Strange Man of the Oglalas

THIRD EDITION

A biography by MARI SANDOZ

INTRODUCTION TO THE BISON BOOKS EDITION BY
Vine Deloria Jr.

University of Nebraska Press
Lincoln and London

© 1942 by Mari Sandoz
Introduction © 2004 by Vine Deloria Jr.
Glossary © 2008 by the Board of Regents of the University of Nebraska
Discussion questions © 2008 by the Board of Regents of the University of Nebraska

Manufactured in the United States of America
∞
First Nebraska paperback printing: 1961

Library of Congress Cataloging-in-Publication Data
Sandoz, Mari, 1896–1966.
Crazy Horse: the strange man of the Oglalas / Mari Sandoz; introduction to the Bison Books edition by Vine Deloria Jr.—3rd ed.
p. cm.
Includes bibliographical references.
ISBN 978-0-8032-1787-4 (pbk.: alk. paper)
1. Crazy Horse, ca. 1842–1877.   2. Oglala Indians—Kings and rulers—Biography.   I. Title.
E99.O3C728   2008
978.004'9752—dc22
[B]
2007041558

INTRODUCTION

Vine Deloria Jr.

A classic book in the publishing industry usually means longevity in sales and positive reviews in the right places. Often a title has a prolonged shelf life simply because it covers a topic on which few writers are willing and able to devote their time and energy. Other times a book deserving benign neglect is embraced by an authority in the field because it promotes his or her personal point of view and thus preempts better, more thoughtful work. It is a classic in the sense that it becomes immune to criticism because of its sponsor. A better criterion might be whether or not people continue to keep the book in their library after the periodic culling of titles and read it again, even if with some irregularity. But perhaps the best description of a classic is a book that can withstand our ignorance about the subject and offer us a continuing dialogue as we age and become more familiar with the topic.

I first read Mari Sandoz's *Crazy Horse: The Strange Man of the Oglalas* nearly fifty years ago, as a young man, rushing through it on my way to learning all there was to know about the Sioux Indians. It was one of many books available and seemed to tell a good story, but due to my hasty read it did not impress itself upon me. In retrospect, I understand that I failed to savor the words, sentences, and paragraphs so carefully crafted as a seamless document. At my tender age they seemed to blend together into a homogeneous mass containing many extraneous details but difficult to use because of the lack of footnotes. Facts were my quest in those days.

At that time, as a callow and ignorant youth, I was a little offended that a non-Sioux had written a biography of one of the legendary personalities of my tribe. Surely, I thought, she could know little of the nuances of meaning that characterize Indian communities. I was suspicious of the sometimes awkward sentences that seemed to parody reservation English and detract from the straight historical narrative I had encountered in other books on Indians. On the whole I could not see the book as distinguishing itself from other popular histories of the Sioux.

Sandoz's background did offer some comfort of her knowledge of the Indians about which she was writing. She lived in the northwest corner of Nebraska, adjacent to the two largest Sioux reservations, and was intimately familiar with the peoples, red and white, who lived in the desolate Sandhills country. There was never a question of her personal credentials; but the social relations between the Indians and the settlers were not always admirable, and like some readers of literature on Indians, I read the book initially against the backdrop of conflict and suspicion that I had experienced growing up in the area. Yet I had to admit that prejudice had increased since Sandoz's time, and the intermixing of red and white, as she describes it in the book, had been far more positive then than what we see today.

Rereading the book after nearly fifty years was as traumatic as my first encounter with the text but for entirely different reasons. My first response was again to look for footnotes, as scene after familiar scene unfolded in my mind. Surely I had read many of these things before—but where? I certainly couldn't say I had retained much from my first reading. As each chapter chronicled the story of the Sioux wars to their tragic conclusion with the assassination of Crazy Horse, I began to see something entirely different emerging. Mari Sandoz had presented a masterful and wholly authentic account of the struggle for the northern plains during the 1850s through the 1870s in which almost every line rang true.

I was stunned at the wealth of detail contained in each line of text—material that must have come from her conversations over time with a large number of elders, filed then in some great and efficient memory bank, and later skillfully woven into a chronicle of the times that overflows with authenticity. Indeed, reading quickly became a game in which I sought to cross-reference some of the tiniest details in Sandoz's book with statements made by Luther Standing Bear, Charles Eastman, and Black Elk or found in army reports and frontier diaries. I wondered how the book would appear if one took the time to compare and document what Sandoz had written with what we have been told by other writers who were in a position to know the truth.

For example, one short paragraph describes Crazy Horse, brooding over the changing circumstances of his life and worried for his people, as resembling an old buffalo bull, mean and grumpy, standing on a hillside, so fired with the desire to be alone that even the birds dared not land on his back to pick insects and worms. The picture Sandoz creates of the buffalo and the birds is memorable from a careful reading of Standing Bear's *Land of the Spotted Eagle* and gives the book an authority that cannot be dismissed. It is a tiny and superfluous detail but one that rings so true that it is almost as if Sandoz had been present. And how else could this greatly distressed Indian—regarded as unique among his people and focused entirely on issues that we can only guess—be adequately described except through the unforgettable picture of a raging old buffalo bull?

What had happened during the intervening half century that made this reading of Mari Sandoz's *Crazy Horse* so memorable and exciting? For one thing, I had finally learned to read. Instead of rushing through the book, I had learned to pick up ideas, quickly process them, and compare them to other parts of the book and to the mass of information I had gathered during fifty-some years. I realized that through many careful readings of Standing Bear and Eastman I had gathered a formidable knowledge of Sioux life and practices. They had become the standard against which I was now judging other books; and using this criteria, Sandoz's account represented a work of real genius.

Sandoz had an amazing ability to identify and develop themes and issues that plagued Indians during her time and that continue to disrupt us today. It was as if she had looked deep into the hearts of the people, recognized that certain character flaws would always inconveniently appear—no matter what generation of Indians might be involved—and told the story straight so that Indians reading the book a century later might recognize familiar tendencies in the behavior of their people and might finally take steps to remedy the situation.

Foremost among the character flaws she identified was the constant jealousy displayed among and between leaders of the bands that rendered large-scale cooperative efforts useless and prevented the kind of response to danger that one would ordinarily expect from a society under extreme yet identifiable pressure. Those bands living in the Platte River valley became familiar with the attitudes and erratic behavior of U.S. officials through their contact with the whites along the Oregon Trail. These Indians in turn often received more care and respect than the groups to the far north, in Wyoming and Montana, who remained largely unknown to the Americans at that time. With leaders of the southern groups able to manipulate the traders and government officials, the traditional manner of choosing leaders withered; tribal members began to follow those leaders who could produce benefits, even if at the cost of reducing the lands on which all the Sioux hunted. The same practice holds today, unfortunately.

Sandoz also identifies behaviors that prevented war parties from accomplishing their goals. In particular was the tendency of young warriors, eager to make their mark according to the old ways—counting coup and stealing horses—to thwart the battle strategies tediously developed by older, wiser men. The Plains wars would have lasted considerably longer and perhaps resulted in more negotiating power for the Indians had the chiefs been able to spring ambushes in several of the battles. How many times does Sandoz discuss the complex and clever battle strategies the chiefs designed to give the soldiers a sound thrashing? The old men understood the psychology of war—that the arrogance of inexperienced officers, such as Fetterman, could be used to lead the U.S. Army into neatly laid traps. But often young Indian men bolted into action just prior to closing the trap in order to win honors that were inconsequential to the kind of warfare being waged.

Also notable is the framework of the story, which focuses on the difficulties the Indians encountered on the "Holy Road" (the Oregon Trail) along the Platte River. Sandoz leaves no doubt that the transcontinental trail, which enabled the United States to become the continent-spanning nation it is, was the death of the Sioux. The trail became the lifeline for immigrants moving to the coast, and trading posts and forts along its path attracted the Indian fur and hide trade away from the Missouri, where there were few whites, to the southern plains, where thousands of immigrants crossed the plains every year. These points of contact offered too many opportunities for mischief. Once caught in the nineteenth-century version of the consumer society, Sioux society and solidarity shattered, and Indians eventually became dependent on the traders not only for manufactured goods but also for interpreting their attitudes and actions to the increasingly powerful government forces.

Sandoz's account of the Plains Indians during the 1850s through the 1870s surpasses other such works in terms of its accuracy and clarity. Thankfully, Sandoz clarifies the relationship among the various bands of Oglala and Brule Sioux that led to the eventual capitulation of the Tetons. Other historians tend to describe these tribes as if they were a unified group capable of responding in a unified manner. Sandoz divides these tribes into their respective bands and families and demonstrates that there was a considerable difference between, for example, the northern and southern Oglalas. This distinction then enables the careful reader to discern the northern bands of these groups from the extreme northern Sioux, such as the Hunkpapas, Blackfeet, and Yanktonais, who were closer to the Powder and Little Missouri rivers and thus concerned with entirely different intrusions into their hunting lands. It was these northern tribes of Sioux that refused to sign the 1868 treaty and demanded that steamboats be prohibited from coming up the river beyond Fort Union, a major point of contention when Father DeSmet tried to convince Sitting Bull and others to agree with the government's demands. Without Sandoz's identification of the general areas controlled by the respective bands and tribes of the Sioux Nation, one cannot begin to make sense of the story and of the Peace Commission's reports.

Sandoz similarly paints a clearer picture of events on the northern plains. Other historians seem content to describe the Fetterman battle as the most significant conflict on the Bozeman Trail and then jump straight to a discussion of the peace treaty; Sandoz ensures that the reader understands it was the nature of the constant conflict on the trail, not one battle, that finally forced the United States to abandon the line of forts established in the best Sioux hunting grounds. These frequent skirmishes, led primarily by Crazy Horse, made the trail so hazardous that it became a road of almost certain death. Mercifully, Sandoz does not describe the practice of the northern Sioux (the Hunkpapas, Blackfeet, and Yanktonais) after the Sand Creek massacre in mutilating the bodies of people found on the trail as a warning that atrocity would be met with atrocity.

Sandoz also thoroughly discusses Crazy Horse's affair with Black Buffalo Woman, and her explanation clarifies much that is lacking in other accounts. We are told in other books merely that Crazy Horse "stole" the woman from her husband, leading us to believe he was a home wrecker. In fact, the woman left her husband and willingly went with Crazy Horse. Within its cultural context, the domestic conflict is not nearly as heinous as historians have led us to believe. Sandoz slips a bit in describing the aftermath of the incident and fails to give us more background on Black Shawl, the woman who took up with Crazy Horse shortly after he was shot and disgraced as a "shirt wearer." Perhaps the circumstances of that marriage were unknown to the elders Sandoz visited or it was still too painful to discuss.

We often believe that warfare during this period was restricted to fights with the army since intertribal warfare is usually cited briefly and not discussed adequately. Actually, battles with the army were not as frequent as raiding parties of different tribes against old enemies. The conflict involved, as usual, tribes stealing horses from each other or fighting over hunting grounds. Crazy Horse was prominent in these activities. Sandoz suggests that he sought to dispel his anger over losing the woman he loved and the loss of his brother Little Hawk and Hump, the beloved elder who had protected him when he was young, by increasing his raids on the Crows and Shoshones. If anything, Crazy Horse's constant expeditions to the camps of other tribes greatly enhanced his reputation as a warrior and contributed to the sense of confusion that characterized this period of Plains life. Fighting between tribes actually lasted well into the 1880s, long after the tribes were confined to the reservations, and reflected the old patterns of intertribal warfare that the 1851 treaty had sought to eliminate. Whether the deaths of all the many white men killed near the Oregon Trail can be attributed to Crazy Horse is a matter of speculation. He certainly had the capability of clearing the road of whites if he had the mind to do so.

Red Cloud is a figure who receives rather harsh treatment from Sandoz.

Though her description of the Sioux leader may anger some Indians to-day, we must assume that Sandoz drew the unflattering picture of the old chief from remarks and memories of the old men at Pine Ridge while gathering materials. Since so much of her description of the Sioux people and their feelings holds true in other respects, we have no reason to doubt her portrayal of Red Cloud. The fact that he was one of the Bad Face band bolsters Sandoz's interpretation since those people were known to be jealous and disruptive even before contact with the whites. Indeed, the various conflicts reported of the Red Cloud camp—particularly jealousy among the leaders of the various bands—can still be seen in modern-day Sioux politics at Pine Ridge. Once removed to the reservation, where skillful diplomacy was the only weapon available, Red Cloud did a credible job of protecting his people. Over the years his reputation grew more positive. For example, we know Big Foot and his band were fleeing from the soldiers and headed for Pine Ridge to seek the protection of Red Cloud when they were overtaken and slaughtered at Wounded Knee.

Nothing seems so accurate as Sandoz's description of the mood of the hostiles beginning in 1875, however. Isolating themselves from the southern people and dependent on news from only the spies they sent to Fort Laramie or half-truths told by mixed-blood sons of traders, the northern bands were filled with despair at the reported cooperation of the Oglalas and Brules with the U.S. government. The optimism generated by the national camp gathering at Bear Butte in 1858, which encouraged the various bands to recognize and renew their kinship and return to ancient ways, had become badly eroded by the actions of the southern Sioux. Crazy Horse, Sitting Bull, and others were outraged that Red Cloud, Spotted Tail, and the lesser chiefs purported to speak on behalf of the whole nation let alone that they would cede the nation's lands and agree to the construction of forts for a few gaudy presents. The northern Sioux interpreted Red Cloud's trip east after the 1868 treaty as a surrender to the whites, and they thereafter understood their relations with the United States in stark terms: keep the old ways and die fighting or surrender and starve at the agencies.

Sandoz's description of the gathering of people at the Little Bighorn follows a somewhat traditional format and does not shed much light on the events leading up to the battle. There has always been a debate concerning the number of Indian warriors engaged in the conflict, and Sandoz is quite orthodox on this point in particular. Certainly many young men left the agencies to join the hunting tribes in the Bighorn area. But Sandoz's descriptions of the magnitude of the Indian camp leave us breathless; it seems nearly impossible that so many single men might be encamped with the northern Sioux without their dependents. How many women were in the camp to cure the meat from the hunt? If there were thousands of people there, how did the Indians feed themselves for any length of time?

Censuses taken later that fall by agents suggest that very few people actually left the reservations to join the hostiles. And we cannot suppose that Indians wearing cavalry uniforms and sporting new rifles were welcomed at the agencies that fall or were inconspicuous when they did return. Sandoz tells us that there were bad feelings between the northern Sioux and the reservation people, so it is not likely that many warriors left the agencies to join the camp. Some accounts from soldiers of Reno's command report that as his troops approached the Indian camp they found a horse herd being watched over by two teenage boys. It could not have been a very large horse herd if these youngsters were its sentinels. If we accept traditional accounts of the magnitude of the camp, we have problems explaining how so many war horses, accommodating thousands of warriors, along with a much larger number of hunting and pack horses to transport the meat, did not graze down the available grass in a very short time. There are some impossible logistical requirements for such a large camp that many authors, including Sandoz, simply do not recognize. Every description of the battle by Indian participants recalls immense concern for the Indian noncombatants, suggesting that figures for the participation of Indian warriors have been grossly overestimated.

Following the battle at Little Bighorn the various bands of Sioux dispersed, knowing that they could travel faster and sustain themselves easier as small groups. Sandoz gives a magnificent description of the gradual and inevitable erosion of the numbers of people in the hostile bands and the dreadful feeling that Crazy Horse and others felt when messengers arrived from the agencies asking them to surrender. We look at the earlier life of Crazy Horse and his closest friends, remembering the solidarity they once enjoyed, and discover that many former allies are now working for the government. Each visit from the agency Indians must have cut deep into the resolve of those remaining free. To have former friends enticing people in his band to come to the agencies must have been an excruciating experience. There was no doubt that the Great Sioux Nation was dissolving, leaving the rank-and-file warriors to grow old telling stories about the days of freedom, the chiefs to fend off possible retaliation on their own.

The burden of maintaining some semblance of a nation fell to Crazy Horse, though his own band suffered dreadfully as the army pursued them throughout a brutal winter that took a heavy toll even on the soldiers. A sense of utter hopelessness pervades these pages. If one is searching for historical authenticity, can it be anywhere but here? Even the effort to rescue the people trapped at Slim Buttes was beyond the capability of the remaining warriors and failed. Yet Crazy Horse and his followers would have fought on were it not for the suffering of the women and children. So finally in May, after defying the United States all winter, Crazy Horse led his people to the Pine Ridge agency—it was a parade of the proud and unconquered, a people sure of themselves but logistically unable to continue resistance under the relentless pressures of the army. Sandoz only briefly mentions the reaction of the agent and army officers, who were outraged on seeing the exhibition of pride Crazy Horse and his people displayed. I believe it was this triumphal march that led to his assassination. Surely both white officials and reservation Indians must have been jealous when seeing a leader and a people of much higher and more admirable character than they march in that day. One thing the winter resistance ensured was the elevation of Crazy Horse in the eyes of the American public. Anyone who showed such stubborn courage would certainly be endowed with mythical status, as was Chief Joseph that same year. Rumors that Crazy Horse would be recognized as the chief of all the Sioux must certainly have rankled the chiefs who had earlier bowed to the inevitable power of the military.

During his few remaining days at the agency, Crazy Horse experienced a strange fate. His former adversaries became quite fond of him, and his relations with the government were positive. But the rules of the game had changed. Now those chiefs who embraced the reservation way of life found accommodation profitable and, with no way to determine status in war or hunting, their primary means of maintaining their place in Lakota society was to ingratiate themselves to the agent. New reputations had to be established and, following ancient ways of jealousy and personal conflict, the tendency was to discredit one another. The reputation of Crazy Horse could be sullied only by lies and distortions, and quickly his alleged views and motives became grist for the mill. Had Crazy Horse demonstrated even a slight thirst for political power, there is no question that the majority of the Sioux would have joined him. People cannot be subdued unless they lose belief in themselves, and it is dangerous and disruptive for anyone to have such personal charisma that they must be included as a mysterious force when discussing the future.

Sandoz points out a factor leading to the sad conclusion of the story of Crazy Horse that most historians miss completely. When the people arrived at the agency, there was nothing for anyone to do. The women had no hides to cure or cloth to sew. Beef was delivered on the hoof and often eaten on the spot with little thought of preserving food for the future. Men could only visit each other. They had no arms for hunting. War with other tribes was severely restricted. No person or group could move around without triggering rumors of rebellion. The blizzard of false rumors blanketed the reservation, and groups were frequently told to move closer to the agency when irresponsible stories about them created fear in the minds of white officials. A disaster of major proportions hung over everyone's head. This legacy continues to the present time.

In summing up Mari Sandoz's portrait of the strange man of the Oglalas we find that her description is the most accurate of all. She clothes historical facts with a sound knowledge of the culture and beliefs of the Sioux people and thereby brings the reader into the emotional universe of these turbulent decades. It is not just battles or the shifting movements of the Sioux bands that are important but also those intervals between historical events, the understanding and emotions of the people and their leaders, that make the book great. What would any of us feel, sitting in a worn-out tent in freezing weather, hearing the cries of malnourished children, wondering when the soldiers would strike next? Across from us is an old friend and companion, his spirit broken, his vision fixed on mere survival, and he now represents the government who is relentlessly pursuing and needlessly killing the helpless. What emotions would sweep over us in this moment? Would we be submerged in a tidal wave of despair? Would we direct our anger at our old friend? Would his counsel make sense so that we could transcend the traditions of a lifetime and surrender to the inevitable? Once brought into this emotional world by Sandoz, we come to understand Indians then and now, for much of that grief has never dissipated.

The fate of Crazy Horse seemed to be preordained. We are not dealing simply with his vision here. Sitting Bull during these years was a charismatic leader who had an immense following based on his visions and generosity, values not recognized by white society. When he became a headline celebrity in Buffalo Bill's Wild West he was often introduced as the man who killed General Custer—a fact that though patently false generated excitement among white audiences in the show. How much more explosive would the show have been if Crazy Horse—a hero with an impeccable military reputation—had become part of the Wild West show? Indeed, some rumors after the Little Bighorn suggested that Crazy Horse had studied at West Point, implying that white military instructors alone could have developed such a devious strategy to defeat America's favorite soldier—as if responding to an attack on one's home required immense military planning.

I doubt if anyone else could tell the life of Crazy Horse as well as Sandoz does. She must have known many Sioux people during her formative years, and memories of those people must have come flooding back when she began writing. How else can we explain how her writing captured nuances that only a few would know and understand? How unfortunate that reviewers and scholars lacking any experience of the western lands have missed the real genius of the book. Although it has withstood the test of time, it has not received the acclaim that is its due. Perhaps it speaks primarily to those people who, like Sandoz, have their roots in the plains and their peoples. Or perhaps it is the careful reader who savors the well-written word who can see in this book history as biography and biography as history.

Dedicated to ELEANOR HINMAN, *who spent many faithful months on a biography of Crazy Horse and then graciously volunteered to relinquish her prior claim to me.*

FOREWORD

THE home of my childhood was on the upper Niobrara River, the Running Water of the old-timers, at the edge of the region they called the Indian Country. It was close, or what seemed close in those open days, to the great Sioux reservations of South Dakota, to Fort Robinson and the Black Hills—the final places of refuge for many of the old buffalo-hunting Indians, the old traders, trappers, and general frontiersmen who looked with contempt upon the coming of the barbed wire and the walking plow. Such men, with their heroic times all in the past, are often great story-tellers, and these my father, Old Jules, drew to him as a curl of smoke rising above a clump of trees would once have drawn them, or the smell of coffee boiling at sundown.

So, around our kitchen table or perhaps at the evening fires of the Sioux often camped across the road from our house, I heard these old-timers tell many and wonderful stories of hunting the buffalo, the big-horn, and the grizzly, and of Indian fights and raidings all the way from the Arkansas to the Musselshell, from the Missouri to the Green. But most often they talked of the battles in what the whites called the Sioux wars, from that climactic summer day on the Little Big Horn all the way back to the beginning, when, in 1854, the young Grattan with a few soldiers, a drunken interpreter, and two wagon guns foolishly pushed his way into a peaceful Sioux encampment and never came out again.

As I listened to these stories it seemed that through them, like a painted strip of rawhide in a braided rope, ran the name of one who was a boy among the Oglalas the day the chief of his people was shot down. He must have been twelve then, quiet, serious, very light-skinned for an Indian, with hair so soft and pale that he was called Curly or the Light-Haired Boy. But by the end of those wars, twenty-three years later, he was known as the greatest of the fighting Oglalas, and his name, Crazy Horse, was one to frighten the children of the whites crowding into his country, and even the boldest warriors of his Indian enemies, the Snakes and Crows.

And once, while my father was talking to some strangers, Brule Sioux from the Rosebud agency, an old man among them, noticed me sneak up to listen. Reaching out, he took my hand and walked beside me to the top of the ridge above our house. There he shaded his whitish, fading eyes and looked slowly all up and down the river valley and the bluffs and ridges along our side, making a few low Sioux words, annoyed words, his grandson told me, over the white man's way of changing the face of the earth. But after a while he was satisfied. Down there, about where our old Dyehouse cherry tree grew, they had built the death scaffold of Conquering Bear, their peace chief killed by the whites. And later I knew that if this was not the exact spot, it could not have been far from there, and that our gravel-topped Indian hill must be very much like the one to which young Curly fled for fasting and guidance in the confusion of his heart over this shooting by those who called themselves the white brothers of the Indian. Certain it was that the young Oglala had often walked this favorite camping ground of his people, perhaps thrown plums at the pretty girl for whom the great warrior would one day risk everything he knew of this earth.

Yes, truly this was a fine story and evidently many others thought so too, for often I heard of this one or that, sometimes a professional writer, who was working on the life of Crazy Horse. But nothing seemed to come of these ventures, perhaps because there was so little in print about the hostile Indians that held up under investigation and nothing about Crazy Horse that bore much resemblance to the gaudy, blood-thirsty Sioux warrior of popular notion. It is not only that the man was pale-skinned and had little interest in the things that delighted most of his brother Sioux—paint and feathers, singing, dancing, and recounting the honors of war—but that the name by which he was often known, Our Strange Man, seemed to mean just that to many of his followers, and in retrospect, to many descendants of his enemies. I found a strong suggestion of this in the army reports, dated 1876–7, giving the accounts of the spies returning from his camp. Even those sent out from the Missouri River forts felt it, men who had never seen Crazy Horse rally the warriors fleeing from a hard, uneven fight or stand off a Snake charge alone, never watched him walk in silence through his village in peacetime, every face more alive for his passing.

Then came the opportunity to write the story of Crazy Horse myself. I had worked a little in frontier history, been a member of the staff of our State Historical Society some years and associate editor of the *Nebraska History Magazine*. Now I put in much of two winters in the archives in Washington, going through the AGO Records and the files of the Indian Bureau for the trans-Missouri country from 1840 to 1880; I looked into all the published material on the subject in the historical repositories of Nebraska, Colorado, and Wyoming and the Library of Congress, and all the available documents, letters, and manuscripts, including the interviews of the Ricker Collection at the Nebraska State Historical Society.

In 1930 Eleanor Hinman and I made a three-thousand-mile trip through the Sioux country, locating Indian sites and living out among the people, their wagons stopping at our camp much as they once did at my childhood home on the Running Water. We interviewed the few old buffalo-hunters still alive, including such friends and relatives of Crazy Horse as Red Feather, Little Killer, Short Bull, and particularly He Dog, his lifelong brother-friend. It was well that this was done then, for now He Dog is dead. The last time I saw him was in a thundershower in 1931. It delighted the blind old man to pretend that I had brought the rain. "You will come again in the dry time, my granddaughter?" he asked. "Your step is good for the ears of an old man—" There have been many dry times since then, but I did not get back before He Dog died.

And now my book of Crazy Horse is done. In it I have tried to tell not only the story of the man but something of the life of his people through that crucial time. To that end I have used the simplest words possible, hoping by idiom and figures and the underlying rhythm pattern to say some of the things of the Indian for which there are no white-man words, suggest something of his innate nature, something of his relationship to the earth and the sky and all that is between. I hope I have not failed too miserably, for they were a great people, these old buffalo-hunting Sioux, and some day their greatness will reach full flowering again in their children as they walk the hard new road of the white man.

M. S.

Acknowledgments

For assistance with material: Dr. A. E. Sheldon and the Nebraska State Historical Society, of which he is superintendent; the staff of the National Archives, Washington, D. C., particularly those in charge of the War Department and the Indian Bureau records; the Western History Department of the Denver Public Library; the Bibliographical Center for Research; the State Historical Society of Colorado; Lawrence K. Fox of the South Dakota State Historical Society; the Wyoming Historical Department; Dr. Larson of the University of Wyoming for the opportunity to look through the Grace Hebard Collection; the late Helen Blish for visits and notes about her Bad Heart Bull manuscript; and many, many others who are not forgotten.

Contents

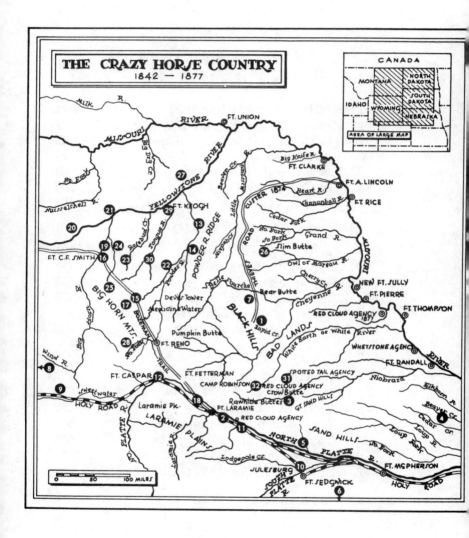

THE CRAZY HORSE COUNTRY
[*Key to figure*]

1. Crazy Horse, called Curly throughout boyhood, born on Rapid Creek, about 1842 (authorities vary from 1840 to 1845).

2. Young Curly sees Conquering Bear shot, August 19, 1854, by soldiers under Lieutenant Grattan.

3. Wounded Conquering Bear dies. Other sites given are mouth of the Snake and above Box Butte Creek, all on Running Water.

4. Brule war party kills Logan Fontenelle, chief of Omahas. Young Curly kills an Omaha woman.

5. Battle of Blue Water, September 3, 1855. Young Curly finds a Cheyenne woman left behind.

6. Sumner's saber attack on Cheyennes, July 29, 1857, on Solomon River.

7. Great council of Teton Lakotas (Sioux), summer 1857.

8. Young Curly helps in fight against People Who Live in Grass Houses and is given name of Crazy Horse for strong deeds.

9. Fight with Snakes, June 20, 1861. Washakie's son killed.

10. Cheyenne-Lakota attack on Julesburg, January 7, 1865.

11. Uprising of peace Indians at Horse Creek, June 14, 1865.

12. Crazy Horse leads decoys in attack on Platte Bridge, July 25–6, 1865.

13. Attacks on Cole's column, September 1, 4, 5, 1865, along Powder.

14. More attacks on Cole's fleeing soldiers, September 8 and 10, 1865.

15. Crazy Horse helps decoy Fetterman and his men to their deaths, December 21, 1866.

16. Hayfield Fight, August 1, 1867.

17. Wagon-Box Fight, August 2, 1867.

18. Crazy Horse, American Horse, and Little Big Man attack old Horseshoe Station, March 19, 1868.

19. He Dog and Crazy Horse carry the Oglala lances in fight called They Chased the Crows Back to Camp.

20. Fight with Major Baker, escorting survey party for Northern Pacific Railroad, August 14, 1872.

21. Fight with Stanley's troops under Custer, August 11, 1873.

22. Camp of He Dog and Two Moons struck by Reynolds, March 17, 1876. People fled to Crazy Horse camp.

23. Crazy Horse helps plan attack that drives Crook back from Rosebud, June 17, 1876.

24. Battle of Little Big Horn or Little Horn, June 25, 1876.

25. Sibley Scouts attacked, July 7, 1876.

26. Iron Plume village struck at Slim Butte, September 9, 1876.

27. Miles attacks Sitting Bull while counciling, October 21, 1876.

28. Dull Knife's village struck, November 25, 1876. People come to Crazy Horse camp.

29. Lakota peace men, carrying white flag, killed by Crow scouts at Fort Keogh, December 1876.

30. Miles attacks Crazy Horse, January 8, 1877.

31. Crazy Horse takes his wife to her people at Spotted Tail for safety, September 4, 1877.

32. He receives bayonet wound through back, September 5, 1877.

BOOK ONE

The Light-Haired Boy

COW TRACKS *on the Holy Road*

THE drowsy heat of middle August lay heavy as a furred robe on the upper country of the Shell River, the North Platte of the white man. Almost every noon the thunders built themselves a dark cloud to ride the far crown of Laramie Peak. But down along the river no rain came to lay the dust of the emigrant road, and no cloud shaded the gleaming 'dobe walls and bastions of Fort Laramie, the soldier town that was only a little island of whites in a great sea of Indian country two thousand miles wide.

On the broken plain around the fort there was a clutter of soldier, trader, and trapper outfits, Indian travois and lodges, and freight and emigrant trains nooning at this western outpost of 1854, much as they nooned here five, ten years ago, and more. But then the fort had still been an Indian town; the white traders who owned it were married to the women of the Lakotas, as the Tetons, the western, buffalo-hunting Sioux called themselves, and their people were almost as free to come and go through the wide gates as they were free to camp and trade and hunt and war as they liked. From the first there had been a white man's road past the fort, and once in a while even soldiers came riding on it, their swords bright in the sun. But they had always gone on, and there was plenty of water and grass and buffalo for all.

So the trail had started, with just a little stream of white men coming through, and the Indian lifted his hand in welcome and went out to smoke and watch this lengthening village of the whites that moved past him day after day all summer, always headed in the same direction. He wondered that he never saw them come back, yet they must be the same ones each year, for there could not be that many people on all the earth. At first he wondered at the women and children too, for he had long thought of the whites as only men, although he had heard stories of the families that had been seen, the women with the pale, sick skins and the break-in-two bodies, the young ones pale too, with hair light and soft as the flying seed of the cottonwood that tickles the nose in summer.

Even when there were quite a few on the trail the Indian had let the whites use his trader town while he sat with his pipe and blanket looking on as they bought perhaps a handful of gunpowder or the last cup of flour for a sick woman, or had their footsore oxen shod at three dollars a shoe. Often they left more wagons behind with the many already standing dead as old bones around the fort because the animals that were to pull them over the far mountains had been worn out.

Puffing at his long-stemmed pipe of stone the Indian had watched all these things and found them very new and strange. But soon the little stream of whites grew into a great river, wider than a gun could shoot across, and the grass and the buffalo got so used up that the Indian ponies were poor far into sundance time and the hunters had to travel many days, sometimes clear to the Crow country, for a kettle of fresh meat. There was uneasiness about this, and much talk at the councils. The younger chiefs and warriors from up on the Cheyenne River or down in the Smoky Hill country and other places back from the white man's road were angry at the things they saw happening. And when the trader chiefs like Conquering Bear and Bull Tail and old Smoke made strong talk for continued peace with the people on the trail, the others called them Loaf About the Forts and said they had sold their tongues to the white man for his sugar and coffee and whisky.

But before the young warriors could do much more than demand tobacco and a feast now and then from the travelers, or drive off a few mules, the soldiers came and bought up the Indian trading town on the Laramie, and while the traders did not leave, only moved down the road a little way, the soldiers stayed. The wilder young men of the Lakotas stood off watching this thing that was happening, talking about it among themselves in growing anger. They had seen the white man's wheel tracks and his guns drive the game away, his stock eat their grass, his breath scatter diseases among them so thousands died. Now his soldiers had the fort right in the middle of them all.

At last a young Minneconjou of great war honors rose to speak. "My friends," he said, "these soldiers of the whites who have pushed into our country with their wagon guns are not many. They are really only a very few, a puff of the breath in the middle of the dark cloud that is our warriors."

"Hoye!" the others cried in the sign of agreement. "Hoye, hoye!" It was true, and a good day to gather up the arrows, to sharpen up the knives for war.

But before they could carry the pipe to the other bands, for their help, the whites made the Big Council of 1851 on Horse Creek, with much feasting and dancing and presents for everybody, a wagon train full. And if the chiefs would touch the pen to the peace paper, there would be more presents every summer, for fifty-five years, the age of a strong man. Even so some spoke against this thing right in the council.

"We have nothing to sell for the presents of the whites!" they cried.

But with all the goods of the government to help them, the trader chiefs, those who sat around the places of the white men, were very strong and the feasting made even some of the wilder hearts tame as winter colts. They could see now, as the old men had said, that peace would be good, that the trail was only a little thing as wide as the ground between the wheel tracks, and that the soldiers were really too few to hurt, many of them acting like friends, taking women from among the Lakotas as the traders had done.

But as soon as the Big Council was finished the gates of the fort were kept shut against the Indians, with only a few of the relatives of the women allowed to pass through together. Every little while part of the soldiers went away and others came, and each time some of the women of the fort returned to the villages of their people, carrying their white-man babies in their blankets. Then once more new soldiers would come to the lodges where the games were being played. Sitting on the men's side they would throw the parched mule corn over the fire to the daughters of the Lakotas, and some of the girls, even after seeing what had come to their sisters, threw the corn back. Soon these were living at the woman's camp beside the fort, and their people had new presents to show.

That was how a handful of the walking soldiers with three or four wagon guns, the cannon of the white man, were still in the Indian country. It seemed that the white paper said they were not only to protect the travelers on the trail from the wild young men but also to keep the peace on the great buffalo plains stretching from the roaring Yellowstone to the sandbars of the Smoky Hill, keep the peace between the Lakotas and their allies, the Cheyennes and Blue Clouds, and the Pawnees to the east, the Utes and Snakes and Crows to the west and north. The soldiers were also the protectors of the rights and ponies of the Indian, and of his yearly issue of goods sent by the Great Father to pay him for giving up the honors of the war-path and for the trail that cut his country in two, the trail called the Holy Road because its people must not be touched.

Now it was once more far past the time for the goods and presents. The Oglala and Brule Lakotas [1] had come in long ago to camp on the broad bottoms of the Platte, seven-eight miles below the soldier fort. There were over four thousand of them, and their pony herds had spread like cloud shadows over the far breaks, eating the grass roots from the bare earth, and in the three circles of their painted lodges stretched out between the river and the emigrant road the ground was footworn and tired.

[1] The two southern camps of the seven that made up the Teton circle of the Sioux. The others were the Minneconjou, Hunkpapa, No Bows, Two Kettles, and Blackfoot.

Today the great encampment was quiet, a few strings of smoke from the cooking fires twisting into the air, the feathers of the spears and war shields on their stands outside the lodges hanging still. Here and there a horse stomped flies at his picket, a dog snored, or a baby made soft noises in his cradleboard. Most of the children were off along the sandy river, the bigger boys farther away on their ponies. Many of the women, neat-haired, in their doeskin and calico working dresses, were away too, some spreading robes around ant hills to rid them of the lice and nits from long camping among the whites, a few in the chokecherry patches stripping the bushes once more for a little fruit for the kettles. Others were scattered out on the bare bluffs catching rattlesnakes, using forked sticks to hold them down while they cut the heads off with the butcher knives and slipped the writhing bodies inside the blankets around their waists. And from a little gully filled with brush a woman came alone, walking slowly, carrying a new Lakota in her blanket to be hung in a cradleboard in a day or two as his cousins were.

Some of the men were over at the Bordeaux trading houses across the emigrant road, pounding at the blacksmith anvils, cutting frying pan and hoop iron into arrowheads for the buffalo hunt to come, their lean bare backs bent over their work, their braids hanging down before them. Most of those standing around visiting were bare to breechcloth and leggings too, a few of the younger men with shells or silver disks tied into their scalp locks and perhaps beads or a little looking glass hanging on their breasts that were new-scarred from the sundance.

As the shades moved into the lodges and lengthened on the other side, most of the Indians came back to the camps. Some of the women worked with awl and sinew at the moccasins or brushed summer flies from the nursing babies, making drowsy little talkings among themselves, like prairie chickens feeding. The younger ones, with their faces vermilioned and beaded bands hanging from their braids, sat around in circles playing the plum-pit game, tossing the baskets, laughing a little over the counting for the strings of beads and the brass rings and ribbons piled in the center.

The men, too, found little for their hands. Some squatted cross-legged in the shade of the lodges rolled up to coax the dry August whirlwinds through or loafed under the few pine-bough shelters. Some rubbed lazily at arrow sticks with the straightening stones, drew pictures in the dust for the boys they had taken as sons, or played with the naked, strong-legged younger children. Many of the older men sat in little circles, moving their eagle-wing fans slowly, the red willow bark in their pipes fragrant on the air. Here and there one sat off alone, perhaps to sing his holy song against some perplexity of the heart or the uncertainty before his people. Many slept, except down in the lower camp circle, where a medicine man shook his rattle and chanted his songs, working over the dying Bull Tail, one of the old-man chiefs of the Brules.

"Ey-ee!" the women of his relations were crying, and some who were not related but with hearts on the ground from the long waiting and the emptiness of the parfleches, the painted rawhide boxes that held the dried meat, for now the children were getting hungry. The new agent-father was to have been here long ago to give out their goods so they could go to the buffalo ranges, fill the drying racks with meat, make robes for the winter already spreading its snow over the peaks of the White Mountains, the Big Horns. Soon others besides the old men would be dying if the agent didn't come.

At first the waiting had seemed good, with a few late winter robes to trade to the Frenchmen, where there was often a little of the black medicine, the coffee, and sometimes music of fiddles and flutes and the traders' children of their Lakota women making the dances of their fathers. There had been time, too, for watching the whites on the trail. Some of the people had not been down from the buffalo ranges since the sundance and the annuities of last summer, some had not seen each other since the Big Council, three years ago. So there was much visiting and recounting of gossip, and many stories of the great hunts and wars of the people to be retold by the picture writers. There had been dancing too, of vows and ceremonials and of the joy of being together once more. New horses had to be tried out in the races, with Lakota wealth thrown in bets at the foot of the old cottonwood where the stakeholders sat, or where the horses were tied. In the evenings blanketed braves stood in line for a word with some young Lakota woman who perhaps last year had been only a shy little girl beading her first robe but was now suddenly worth much time and many gifts and horses.

But the trading was long finished, with scarcely an extra robe left to be sneaked out for a little whisky while the women were away. The visiting, too, was done, and the dancing and courting; the grass so worn out that the race horses were poor as emigrant mares. It was time to be getting away to the buffalo range, to a little forbidden warring and horse-stealing against the Crows or the Snakes or even the Pawnees, who had very good horses. For it was these things that made a man of a boy.

Towards the cool of evening, when the women were stooping over the cooking fires and the men were out talking and smoking, some of the older ones went to sit along the trail for a while, to beg a little tobacco or to brood within their robes as they saw more whites come through their country. All, even the busy women, stopped to look to the east for the fast wheels of the agent's prairie wagon, with horse soldiers in blue riding in front and behind. It would not be their old friend Broken Hand, Fitzpatrick. He had gone to the white man's town and died of their diseases. So they would have a new father, and surely he was a slow man.

With winter already coming to the mountains, there was less travel along the Platte, mostly freighters and a few small emigrant trains. Far behind one of those that the whites called Mormons, hurrying fast because they were so late, walked a man driving a foot-sore cow, pounding her along with a thick club. As he reached the lower lodge circle of the Brules, a pack of boys came running their ponies in from the south towards the trail, whooping and yelling, for the race was close. At their noise the old cow threw up her tail and bolted off the Holy Road before them, right into the camp circle. Ducking under the lifted skins of the first lodge she came out on the other side with a bundle caught on her horns.

Upsetting a shield stand into the dust, she galloped on, falling into kettles and parfleches, tangling in the picket ropes. Old women ran chattering and screeching after her, boys yelled and dogs barked, the men, too, going to see about the commotion; the warriors of the Fox society, the *akicita* keeping order in the village, hurried from their lodges. The man of the cow followed her to the edge of the camp but the sight of hundreds of Indians scared him and he began to wave his club at them, walking backwards, one step after another, as a *heyoka* dancer sometimes does, after the wagon train. When a shot came from somewhere deep in the camp, he turned and ran, falling over the deep wheel tracks almost as the cow had done, the women laughing loud to see him go.

Out at the trail the old men of the Brules lifted their heads at the gunfire, taking their pipestems from their mouths, listening. Then they put their pipes away in the long, fringed buckskin bags and, stretching their stiff knees, drew their robes up and went to see about the cow. There might be some trouble.

The next morning the wife of Conquering Bear saddled his horse, and with several of his headmen the chief of the Lakotas started for the soldier fort. It seemed like a great foolishness, this getting out on a hot, dusty day just for an old cow, but Bordeaux had come from his trading houses to tell them the Mormon white man was making bad talk about reporting the loss of the cow to the soldiers at the fort. "We'll have them Injuns cleaned out like a nest a snakes!" he kept saying.

Bordeaux, long trader in the Indian country and married into the Brules, had pumped the man a cold drink of water and offered him ten dollars for the cow that was so poor he could never have driven her over the mountains to Salt Lake. But the Mormon wanted twenty-five dollars and said he would still complain at the fort about the thieving, depredating Indians. Of course it was all a great foolishness, the Frenchman admitted, but perhaps Conquering Bear should go up there to see the soldier chief.

So he and his followers rode out of his camp and up the trail towards Laramie. The sun was hot and the Brule wore the officer hat that the Great Father had sent him at the Big Council, with the top cut out for air and the one feather standing up. He had on the officer coat given him then too, full of cricket holes by now, and hanging loose as a bear's skin in the springtime on the lean, strong Indian, but the soldiers seemed to like it. Across the front of his saddle was a fine blue chief's blanket with the white beaded banding and on his breast hung two long braids, so heavily wrapped with panther fur they scarcely stirred as he loped along between his subchiefs on the silver-maned buckskin.

At the Bordeaux stockade and all along the big encampment there were many out to see him go, to give him a friendly sign, and some, too, who told each other he would make something for himself from the ride, papers of vermilion for his women, of course, and coffee and sugar to feast his friends, and who could say what hidden favors besides from the white man?

Conquering Bear of the Brules, often called Bear chief or just the Bear, was one of the first Lakota chiefs in the Shell, the Platte River country, to help the traders of one fur company against the others, in return for goods and favor. Soon there were complaints to the Great Father from the opposition company about Indian trouble, horses and robes stolen, white-man lives endangered, and they blamed the American Fur Company and their hired chief. So the Bear got his name known as one who could be made a friend of the whites even before they came to the Big Council and asked that the Indians make one head chief for the Lakotas, as the Great Father was the head of the whites, so the two men could talk together for all their people.

The Indians had held their eagle-wing fans between their faces and the one speaking, not wishing to hear these words. It was not so easy to do this thing that was asked. The Lakotas were not the men to follow like pack mares as it seemed the whites did. Today they might listen to this one, tomorrow to that, or to none at all, for they were free men.

But when it was plain that the Great Father would have this

thing done, the twenty-four chiefs of the buffalo-hunting Lakotas, including those from up on the Yellowstone and the Missouri, seated themselves in a circle to see what could be done, each with his painted stick to put into the hand of the one he wanted for the place. They smoked and counciled for a long time, but it was as wind in the tree-tops, bringing nothing. With the Oglalas it was the old trouble that sat between them ever since old Smoke's nephew, the young Red Cloud, and his followers killed Bull Bear, chief of the Bear people. The northern Indians, the Minneconjous and the Hunkpapas and the others, said they had no sticks for any Loaf About the Fort trader chief. Even some of the Brules tried to say this making a head chief was all foolishness, that they would only follow when it seemed good and turn their backs when it did not.

So at last the soldier chief who was called Mitchell said that if they could not make a head chief he could, and it would be Conquering Bear of the Brules.

The words fell past the ears of the Indians like rain that comes but hits nothing. The northern people were too far away to care, the Oglalas sat divided, like a great rock broken in two, and those of the Brules who didn't like trader chiefs knew that Conquering Bear was very powerful of voice and arm, with many strong brothers of both blood and adoption, good men like Red Leaf and Spotted Tail and Long Chin, big in the *akicitas,* the warrior societies—thirty such brothers.

So the whites had a paper chief and the Lakotas went on much as before, even down here along the river they called the Shell where the soldiers were, and few seemed to remember that when the big treaty was finally signed no Oglala touched the pen.

It was darkening, the lightning in the northwest like far guns shooting in the night when Conquering Bear came back from the soldier town called Laramie. He stopped at the Oglala camp and followed the old herald to the council lodge in the center where the headmen sat at a smudge fire built to keep the mosquitoes ·

away. The chief was quiet tonight, heavy with things to happen, and wanted to talk particularly to Bad Wound of the Bear people and Man Whose Enemies Are Afraid of His Horse, called Man Afraid, head of the Hunkpatilas, to whom most of Smoke's followers once belonged. But there were older men there, like Smoke himself, and these had to be given respect, so Conquering Bear let his lean body down in the place made for him in the circle. When the silent pipe was done he spoke to them of the day at Fort Laramie.

There were some foolish things being planned at the soldier town, he said. They all knew of the cow Straight Foretop, the Minneconjou, killed last evening? She had run into the Brule lodge circle, and when the man who had been driving her started to go away, the cow was killed by him and some others, and eaten, as an old moccasin can be eaten but not much better, so poor was she, and full of years. But they ate her anyway, for there had been little fresh meat here during the long waiting for their father, the agent.

"Hou!" the voices rose around the circle. It was true that the time had been long, and the game so far out that they had to dry the meat to bring it in less than rotten.

Today Conquering Bear had been up to talk with the soldier chief, to tell him the young Minneconjou of his village had meant no harm. The man with the cow had run away and left her, so the Indian made meat. But as it said in the peace paper that whenever there was trouble between the Indian and his white brother, the Bear was to help make peace, so he had come in, even though one of the old-man chiefs of his village was dying and it was not good to council when such a thing was happening.

At first the officer had talked like a friend, given out tobacco to smoke, and had bread and molasses and coffee set before them. He laughed about the cow. Many like that one left their bones for the wolves along the emigrant road. If this time the Indian found her first it was a little thing and could surely be made good with a couple of robes or some pay-money.

But the soldier chief also had his wild young men, it seemed, talking big of shooting and of war. Worst of all these, as some of the men about him knew, was the one they called Lieutenant Grattan, he who had only bad words for the Indian ever since he came from the eastern soldier town of the whites. Then, too, the interpreter spoke with the crooked tongue, twisting the words of the chief as a bad horse can twist the best rope.

"It was Wyuse?"

Yes, it was still Wyuse, the trader's son from the Iowas, called Lucien. Even though he was married to a Lakota woman, they had asked many times for another interpreter at the fort, one who knew their language and had a good heart for them. A man like Antoine Janis, or his brother Nick. But always it was Wyuse, with only a few Lakota words that they could understand—a drunken man, and mean as a thorn in the heel of a moccasin. Today he had twisted the words of both Conquering Bear and the soldier chief they called Fleming until the white man became red-angry, saying all at once that pay was not enough. Straight Foretop must be brought in and locked up.

Bear chief tried to say that the man was not of his people but a guest, with the sacred rights of a guest. The Minneconjous were of the northern Lakotas; they did not know the white man and were afraid of his iron house. Hot-tempered and scared, Straight Foretop might make trouble. Why not wait for their father, the agent, who would say what was right to do?

When the officer would not wait, Conquering Bear suggested that the man of the cow come out and take his pick of the best of the chief's own herd of sixty horses, young and strong, many of the best Pawnee stock.

But the officer would not have this either. The Indian must be brought in. Tomorrow ten or twelve soldiers would come to the village and Conquering Bear was to help them arrest the young man and take him away.

"Ahh-h!" The sound of surprise and concern went around the circle and over those sitting behind it, back to the women and children scattered in the smoky darkness. Soldiers coming to a camp of Lakotas, and over a cow, a poor cow, with blood in her tracks and meat like rawhide!

When the Bear finally started home, Man Afraid got up too and rode down the storm-dark trail with him, their horses seen to be close together in a brighter flash of lightning, their hoofs slow and soft in the dust of the emigrant wagons.

When they were gone the Oglalas scattered to the smaller grass smudges, making a few words between the little whistlings of their pipes, heavy words with some, like Smoke and the other old men of his band. It was those wild young warriors from the north, the Minneconjous—they must be driven out before they brought the good people into trouble. If a strong man from the Oglalas had been made the paper chief of the Lakotas at the Big Council instead of the Brule, that would have been done long ago. There were not twenty lodges of the visitors.

They talked like that, knowing there was no man of strength among them, for the Oglalas were indeed as a rock broken in two. Behind them the women sat silent, here and there one tucking the blanket over the sleeper at her breast and looking away towards the dark river and the buffalo grounds beyond, far from the Holy Road and the soldiers. It seemed their father, their agent, was truly a slow man.

There was much talking among the young men about these Minneconjous too. While they of the Oglalas and Brules had to slip out in the night for a little enemy raiding so the chiefs could say they had not seen them go, the Minneconjous were still warriors and went gaily and openly against Crow and Snake, Hohe and Blackfeet, starting away with the old-time parade through the village in their paint and feathers, singing their war songs, their lance points flashing in the sun for all the women to see. They had even exchanged a few shots with the soldiers of the fort last summer and were the envy of every Lakota who had not yet struck an enemy. But they made the old ones, those very fond of the sugar and coffee and whisky shake to the heel fringe of their moccasins, so afraid were they of losing those soft, white-man things.

Some of the boys of the Oglalas, like young He Dog and Lone Bear and the son of Man Afraid—mostly those who had killed their buffalo but had never struck an enemy—lay on the warm sand of a knoll at the emigrant trail where the smoke of the camp smudges rolled over their bare backs and kept the mosquitoes off. As the lightning neared and the thunders made themselves heard the boys talked of the visitors down in the Brule camp too, and of the time when they, themselves, would be doing great things, stealing Pawnee horses, counting coups on Crow and Snake. Then their deeds would be sung through the villages as were those of men like Red Cloud, Pawnee Killer, Black Twin, and the one called Hump. The old women would cry out their names as they passed in their war glory, the girls looking shyly down.

"Hoye!" they agreed, like warriors giving their approval. "Girls—!" nudging each other, laughing, thinking perhaps of this one or that, perhaps of the daughter of Yellow White Man, or Many Antelope, or the niece of Red Cloud. But none made words of these soft things, covering them under more talk of war.

One among them, the son of Bad Face, sitting up to keep his buckskin shirt clean, took no part in these plannings. They were just talking big, he told them. They could never do any of these things because it was against the white paper signed at the Big Council. No horse-stealing, no warpath at all, just peaceful living with their friends, the white men.

"Hear the Pretty One!" they roared out in an old joke against their companion, pounding one another, rolling over on the sand in their laughing. "Hear the pretty words he makes!"

It was true that the boy's speech was much like the things he wore: paint and quilled buckskin and beads every day, like the show-offs from the woman's camp at the fort, or the young Pawnees that the boys had heard about, dragging a whole skunk skin, striped tail and all, behind each moccasin on just any day in camp. But these were not the men who carried off Lakota scalps, or the ones the boys planned to strike.

So the talk went past the Pretty One, as it always did, even though he was Smoke's grandson. There were still some great warriors in that family, like Red Cloud, the son of the chief's sister, who brought in many horses and counted coups as boldly as the old chief himself ever did. But Smoke's own son did not need the sundance or the wars to learn fortitude. The tongue of his wife was like a buffalo-hide whip across the cheek, shaming him before all the people, so they called him Bad Face until his right name was almost forgotten. Now it seemed that his son, the Pretty One, was also turning from the warpath. Turning from it before he had ever struck an enemy.

As the other boys planned the great things to be done, he waited for a hole in the wall of talking to wonder whether the soldiers coming tomorrow might wear the coats with the fine bright blue trimming, as when they made the walking lines up at the fort. Maybe there would be even some with red, as he had sometimes seen.

No, there would be no red, the son of Man Afraid told him. That was for the men of the wagon guns, for big fighting, not just for taking one Indian from the camp of a white man's paper chief. He had once seen the soldiers fire a shot into a herd of antelope moving past the fort. Just one shot from the big gun and the plain was full of dead and wounded, many trying to crawl away with legs broken or shot off, some so torn and scattered that there was no picking up the pieces. Much meat, for just one shot. He would like to have such a gun for his people, but the ammunition would be hard to get, and could not be made by the Indians.

No, it could not be made, the others agreed.

Through all this talking there was one among them who made no words at all—Curly, son of Crazy Horse, the Oglala holy man. Although his top lock scarcely came to the medicine bundle behind his father's ear, Curly had already killed his buffalo and had been the first on a wild horse caught up in the sandhills, after which his childhood name of Curly had been thrown away by his father for a new one, His Horse Looking. Crazy Horse used this name and so did High Back Bone, called Hump for short, the warrior who had made the boy's first bow. But many of the younger men and all the women, even those of his home lodge, still called him Curly, after the way of women. They were very slow to see that he was growing big and should have a growing-big name.

As Curly lay in the flickering darkness of the knoll with the others from his camp, he let sand run from one palm into the other and said nothing of the things he wished to do. Although he lived with the Oglalas, his mother who had died was a Brule and the sister of Spotted Tail, as was his second mother, in the custom of the Lakotas. And yesterday, when the boy was visiting his Brule relations, he was given a piece of the Mormon cow, not meat but a piece of the fresh hide for a war club. He needed it, for the last time they went to the soldier town the Pretty One grabbed his club from his belt and threw it into the Laramie River. From near noon to the sunset gun at the fort Curly had searched under the swift current because it was the club Hump had made from the hide of the boy's first buffalo. But it was gone and so today, with strips of green hide to fasten the handles and the pointed stone heads together, he made two new ones, for himself and for his friend, He Dog.

Tonight, in the storm-flashed darkness, young Curly thought about the rawhide drying tight about the head of his war club. It seemed good that it should be making itself strong when the lightning was moving over them out of the northwest, the thunders shaking the earth with their great wings. The boy liked storms coming upon him like this. They made him feel hot and alive and filled with sacred things unknown.

But into these thoughts came the little earth-beatings of far pony hoofs. Pressing his ear closer to the ground, the boy knew they came from the south, two horses, one ridden, the other led, and probably loaded. At the rhythm of the feet Curly slipped away, the others watching him run through the red of the heat lightning over their heads. Although there were many hunters out for meat they knew who this would be. All day Curly had watched the south for High Back Bone, not only because he wanted to tell him of the Mormon cow and the trouble it was making but because the one called Hump was his warrior friend.

At the mouth of a dark gully young Curly waited and when the two horses came out of it he leapt up behind the rider as he used to do when he was a small boy hanging to the lean warrior's waist with both his short arms until the two on the galloping horse really seemed to become one, as the old people say happens to those who ride together so.

Hump showed no surprise. "Hou, younger brother!" he said. "The gaunt belly truly sharpens the ear—"

"Yes—and makes the hunting medicine very strong, it seems— to help you find two antelope, young ones, and not far out," the boy answered, making these many words in a rush of joy at the luck of his friend.

"Hoye! You have the ears of the Lakota, and the wolf-sharp nose—" the man laughed in satisfaction. He had spent much time with· the boy from the days of his first bow, watching him as the tree watches his own kind rise from the ground at his feet, taught him the ways of the hunt and the warpath, although it was well known that the Crazy Horse family had long been holy men, good hunters too, and men who fought very well when it was needed, but never the ones to seek out honors for the victory dances. Instead they were known for their quietness and modesty, thinking always of the good of the people, with wise, calm words for those who came to them in bad times, and with the power to see ahead of the next moon.

Many were surprised at the choice made by young High Back Bone, the great Minneconjou-Oglala warrior. He could have had the son of almost any great warrior family for younger brother, as he could have almost any woman for wife, even if she belonged to another man and without foolish talk of trouble or of horses to be paid. But Hump did not spend his time with these things, or with the people who could get him ahead in his *akicita,* his warrior society, help make him a chief, or even carry him from the fighting if he was hurt. He spent much of his village time with this strange boy of the light skin, the hair yellow and soft as a young prairie chicken's, and eyes the brown of a deer's but sharp as the stone arrows from the boiling-water country up the Yellowstone.

As the two reached the lodge of High Back Bone the old woman came running out, making the cry of gladness for the fresh meat to be divided among the hungry. While she took the horses away Curly followed the man inside and watched him settle to his place behind the handful of coals, their glow red on his bare breast, that was deep-scarred from the tongs of the sundance and the wounds of war, on the lean nose and chin of the Lakota. Gravely the tired man made his smoke, and then taking a horn spoon of boiled meat from the kettle, he offered a bit to the sky, the earth, and the four great directions and began to eat with noisy enjoyment.

Sitting back in the duskiness of the lodge Curly was thinking of what the tomorrow might bring, wanting to tell his friend of the cow that was killed, to ask questions, but as always he waited for another to make the words. He wondered if the soldiers really could take a Lakota from his village. Last summer, when the Minneconjous got into trouble, he had heard Man Afraid tell them it could not be done and the man who was the soldier chief then had agreed. The paper of the Big Council said it was only the head chief who could arrest a man for trouble-making between the Indians and the whites. Even that was very hard for the Lakotas to understand, for to them the chiefs were men who led in council or in war if any wished to follow, not people who watched others as the whites did their young ones, to see they made no wrong.

Curly wondered about something else in this peace paper. Who was to punish the white soldiers from the fort when they went out to shoot lone Indians hunting the breaks for deer? Everybody knew this happened, mostly to old men whose ears had grown thick with years, their eyes blurred. Not a month ago it had been old Little Eagle, the Cheyenne visiting with his son who was married into the Oglalas. The people from the woman's camp at Laramie saw the soldiers show his scalp with the blue stone tied into it around among the emigrants, the white women making shaking little cries, their eyes shining. It was said these soldiers gave themselves much trouble in this scalp-hunting. Young Lone Bear, who had relatives at the woman's camp heard that sometimes they borrowed Indian ponies so there would be no iron hoof tracks and wore moccasins so the scalpers would seem to be Crow or Snake. Always, so far back as Curly could remember, the haranguing of the old chiefs for peace had been heard, but some day the young men might turn their faces away. What would happen then? And what would the soldiers do with Straight Foretop tomorrow?

When Hump had finished his pipe and his eating he started away to the council lodge, Curly following out into the storm-brightened camp circle. There was a strong smell of rain, a few drops already falling, one here, one there, lonesome as old buffalo bulls on a hillside. Most of the camp was quiet, with a little drumming at the lower end and a few dark figures moving around a fire, some of the young men and women dancing. Wishing that his father were not at the council lodge, where a boy could seldom go, Curly went home. No light shone through the lodge skins and inside there was the sound of sleeping, his brother near the opening, his sister on the woman's side, but the one he called mother was still up at the back, in her own place. Softly he went to sit beside her, quiet for a time, and when he began to talk a little he wondered about Straight Foretop, what would be done with him for killing the old cow.

"One cannot say," the woman replied, "but he is the son of Iteyowa. He will be brave—"

Yes, he would be brave, but it would surely be something bad, something secret and full of terror. Curly had seen the white soldiers take men, their own people, down the trail with the heavy chains on their hands and feet, and never bring them back. Indeed, as Hump once said, it was better to die fighting on the plains than to live in the irons of the whites.

THE COMING *of the Wagon Guns*

THE morning sun came up over the breaks of the Platte into a sky that was red as the coals of the council fire. It touched the ridge above the Oglala camp, brightened the smoky tops of the lodges, and moved swiftly down their painted sides. Here and there a dog stretched, or an impatient horse pulled at its rope, nickering towards the herds on the far hills. Blackbirds awoke in the rushes of the river, and from the prairie the sky singers rose straight up into the sun, scattering their song as they sloped back to their earth. It was morning, but no Indian stirred into the dew that would soften the soles of his moccasins.

When the sunlight had spread itself well over the worn camp ground, the old women came out to light the cooking fires, the smoke rising straight up and then flattening into a haze that clung along the breaks. Clubbing the dogs from the emptying parfleches of meat, they called the girls to help bring wood and water, the boys to relieve the night watchers of the pony herds. Then the younger women came out of the lodges in their wing-sleeved deerskin dresses, their dark hair smoothly combed, their cheeks vermilioned, to put up the spears and the shield cases or other regalia of their warriors beside the lodges.

Now the day had begun. But the cloud-streaked sky was still red, with the long, late red that speaks of a troubled day. Many of the men looked off towards the west as they lifted the lodge flaps and came out. Crazy Horse, the father of Curly, and several others who treasured the deeds of their people went to sit with Bad Heart Bull, the Oglala historian, one of those who paint the stories of the people on skins, the big things of the winter counts and the little too, for the singing and retelling when important visitors come, or the people are together. There was a bad thing to be done at the Brule camp today and now came this red morning, deeper in foreboding than the one before Bull Bear was killed, making a long fighting in the village, splitting the Oglalas and shaming them before the people. There had been a red sky that morning, a red sky that brought a day from which to count time.

Although it was still early several horses stomped flies beside the lodge of Man Afraid. He was the head of a great family known for their strength in battle, their wisdom in the councils, their fatherhood of the people clear back to the days remembered only in the hero stories, long before the Lakotas had horses, back when they lived beside the great water and fought battles against enemies whose names were now forgotten. Man Afraid was six foot four as the whites named this tallness, and known as one with a straight tongue, one not looking for power or for ponies. So last night the council had chosen him to go to the fort, to see what such a man could do about soldiers coming with guns where the helpless women and children were. He took three or four of the younger headmen with him, riding close together, for there was much that needed talking.

When they were gone, Curly, young He Dog, and the son of Man Afraid followed along the other side of the river, racing their ponies, whooping, wishing for something to happen. They got past the Gratiot stone houses where their government annuities waited for the agent and well into sight of the white walls of Laramie before Man Afraid signaled the boys back, so they turned off into the breaks north of the river, passing and repassing each other as they whipped their ponies, pretending they were winding them for battle. But as soon as they were out of sight they sneaked back to the brush along the bottoms and loafed the hot summer hours away, watching for signals, waiting.

When the sun was past the middle the Indians and several white visitors from the fort started down the trail. There were soldiers with them, an officer on horseback and a wagon full of walking, soldiers with more riding on the two wagon guns, the wheels lifting the thick dust from the earth of the Holy Road. The boys rode for their camp with the news. But it was already known to those at the council lodge. Scouts had reported that the big-talking young Grattan and thirty soldiers were coming, with Lucien, the trader's son called Wyuse by the Indians, along as interpreter. Again he was not right from the white man's whisky and got more of the burning cup at the stone trading houses where the soldiers loaded their guns ready for shooting.

Most of the Indians of the great encampment were out to see the soldiers come over the ridge to the west and stop a little there to look down on this broad valley with its three great lodge circles and probably twelve hundred warriors. Then the dust started again and the women, knowing about the cannons and the long knives, ran to call their children together, take in the spears and shields, and loosen the lodge stakes for swift striking.

When the soldiers reached the Oglala circle, Man Afraid and the others had dropped back to show that they were not in this thing. By now the camp was as sleeping; almost everybody out of sight. Leaving the soldiers in a little bunch at the trail, the officer rode up to the spreading poles of the council lodge and jerking his lathered horse to a stop, called out: "Hey, you! You infernal red devils, come out here!"

But there was no movement in the circle of blanketed backs that he could see under the partly lifted lodge skins, no sign at all, so he called for Wyuse.

"Tell the damn Indians they better stay close to their tipis or I'll crack into them," he ordered and spurred on, leaving the drunken interpreter to repeat the warning in bad Lakota as he clung to the saddle horn with one hand and shook the other in a white-man fist at the empty camp circle. But off to the north the pony herds were coming in fast from the breaks, their manes and tails flying, the herd boys whooping hard behind them as they splashed through the river and thundered over the bottom towards the camp. The soldiers in the wagon pointed to them, shouting something to one another, but the wheels carried them along after the little soldier chief, hungry to take an Indian today.

At the Bordeaux stockade, just above the camp of Conquering Bear, Grattan stopped to get old Jim to help him. But the stocky little Frenchman would not go, although he knew that the officer could make him much trouble, perhaps even have him and his traders driven out of the Indian country. So he talked in slow confusion, making it seem he did not understand, making it take time.

What was this talk of wanting him to go to the Brule camp with soldiers carrying guns? Something about a cow? Whose cow? Oh, the cow! Yes, yes, the Mormon cow. But the owner had been offered good pay for her, much more than the old carcass was worth. It could not be that they were foolishly taking cannons into the Indian camp for this? Somebody would get hurt. There was much mourning in the Brule camp for old Chief Bull Tail, who had died last night; the women and some of the men wild and excited, their arms cut and bleeding, their hair full of dirt. It was not a good time to go to the camp, not even for visiting. No, positively he, Jim Bordeaux, would not go there.

So the whites who came down from the fort stayed at the stockade but the soldiers pushed on, the Indians about the trading houses watching them go. It was a bad thing they were doing, and their friend Jim could smell trouble as far as a horse the coming storm. Always he was a man of peace when it came to shooting-fights, even if he had to hide in the robes of his wife's bed, as he once did. And nothing she could do got him out. So today the soldiers had to go on without him although Man Afraid, who was very anxious to save trouble, talked strong to his trader friend. This day they needed a good man for the interpreting and they had only the drunken Iowa.

It was true that Wyuse was already doing a bad thing, running his horse up and down the road past the Brule camp to give him second wind, as the warriors did before a fight. And as he whipped and spurred, the interpreter slapped his mouth in the war whoop and called out insulting words to the Indians as though they were chunks of green buffalo chips he was throwing at them. So they would laugh at him, these enemy Sioux, set themselves above him as on a snow mountain? He would bring them down, cut their hearts out and eat them! He would give them new ears so they could understand the words he carried in his mouth!

While a few of the Brules stood at their lodge doors watching, the last of the women and children slipped away to the willows of the river. Many of the warriors were going too. Their hands full of the things of war, they came dropping over the bank behind the lodge circle, to the brush where the camp horses were often tied in the shade. Some were already stripped to the breechcloth, others tying their hair in knots on their foreheads, painting themselves in their sacred way. There were not only Brules and Minneconjous but Oglalas, too, who had come down along the bottoms. More of them rode openly on the Holy Road: Red Cloud, Black Twin and his brother No Water, and many others past the first heat of warrior youth, coming slowly, in little talking bunches, as though for a visiting.

Conquering Bear had gone out to meet the soldiers at his camp. His broad, concerned face was free of paint today, his hair loose without fur or feather, a faded old blanket of mourning held around his body with a steady arm. He urged the officer to keep the soldiers out of the camp, as Man Afraid and Big Partisan had done, and the thickset Little Thunder of the Brules. They would sit and smoke as friends with him, settle the trouble like good men.

But the officer would not have the thing done so. Loudly he ordered the soldiers into the center space of the camp circle and down towards the place of the Minneconjous, near the chief's own lodge. There he lined them up, running around to load and aim the wagon guns himself.

While a few of the chiefs and headmen stayed near the officers, standing straight and silent in their blankets, making no answer to his loud threats, more and more of their warriors slipped away over the bank. Even boys came now, and were sent away, all but Lone Bear and young Curly, who was known as the follower of Hump and the blood nephew of Spotted Tail. By keeping quiet, they got to stay, to hear what the watchers told of the things done up in the camp, of Conquering Bear and Man Afraid going back and forth between Straight Foretop and the soldiers, trying to get the Minneconjou to surrender, or the soldier chief to go away until their father, the agent, came and said what must be done. But it was plain that the one called Grattan had come for a fight, although the Bear offered a good mule from his own herd for the cow and sent the camp crier around to collect some horses. When the old man came back he had five marked sticks, meaning a horse each from the herds of five good men. These he laid down on the ground before the soldier chief, saying there were others who would have given but they said it was enough and too much for a poor cow, slow with many far miles and the load of years.

But the officer did not want mules or horses. He would have the young Minneconjou standing there in the door of his lodge, leaning on his gun, a bow and arrow in one hand, his bare breast scarred from the sundance. And Straight Foretop would not go with the whites. Last year the soldiers had killed three of his people over the trouble about a boat on the Shell River and this year, while some of them were sitting beside the white man's road. an emigrant had shot at them and hit a child in the head. The little one recovered, but it was a long sickness and made the heart dark. He would die where he stood rather than go with the people who did these things. Yet he did not wish to make trouble, so he asked that the chiefs take the people away and leave him to the soldiers.

"I am alone now," he said. "Last fall the whites killed my two brothers. This spring my uncle, my only relative, died. Today my hands are full of weapons, my arms strong. I will not go alive."

These were brave words, sent straight as from a good bow, the Indians saw, but the interpreter was not making them right for the soldier chief, or those of Conquering Bear and Man Afraid either. Instead he said something the Indians did not understand but many thought meant that the Bear had refused to give up the Minneconjou. Those were crooked, lying words, but the soldier chief got even redder and roared out that it was enough. The Indian must be brought to him immediately. Against the advice of all the others, Conquering Bear said he would try, but as a Lakota he had no right to do this thing and so must go to the man as an enemy. For that he must get his gun from his lodge.

There was no telling what words Wyuse made of this either, for as the chief turned, the officer gave an angry order. His men jumped up, leveled their guns. A shot was fired and the brother of Conquering Bear fell, his mouth gushing blood. The other chiefs scattered but the Bear stayed, jumping around so he would be hard to hit, calling to the Indians to keep cool, not to charge the soldiers. The whites would probably be satisfied now that they had hurt a good man.

But the one called Grattan was not done. Aiming the wagon guns himself, he ordered his row of soldiers to fire. This time Conquering Bear went down, and then the cannons boomed, the blasts tearing through the tops of the lodges and away across the river.

Now Straight Foretop lifted his gun and shot through the stinking black smoke. Grattan fell, and almost before he was down the Indians were upon him, cutting and hacking him to pieces as, with a whooping, Spotted Tail led the hidden warriors up over the bank, pouring a wall of arrows into the soldiers at the wagon guns as they came. With spears and war clubs they trampled the white men to the earth, grabbing their guns and swinging them like clubs upon the rest. A few of the soldiers managed to get on the cannon carriages and the wagon and whipped the mules towards the emigrant road, firing back until they, too, went down in the charge of warriors. A few who were cut off made a stand, for one breath a brave little island of whites facing the Indians. Then they were gone too.

At the first shot Wyuse and Grattan's horse-holder spurred away up the road, mounted Brules hard after them, the Oglalas from the upper camp cutting them off. As the soldier was struck from the saddle, the horse of the Iowa fell, and kicking loose from the stirrups, he fled into the death lodge of Bull Tail. But the Indians went into that sacred place after him and pulled him out, bawling like a cow-calf. His own brother-in-law struck him down with his war club, tore off his clothes, cut a long gash up each leg from the ankle to the waist, and left him there outside of the death lodge. So it was done to the man who would give the Lakotas new ears to hear with, cut their hearts out to eat. A dozen struck him with their bows or their knives but none would take his scalp.

As soon as the warriors were gone, Lone Bear and young Curly sneaked up. Feeling strange and a little sick under their belts, the two boys stood over the naked, mutilated man, the blood already clotted in the darkening gashes of his legs, the face twisted and afraid, the eyes sticking out like stones. This man, mostly Indian himself, and accepted into the Lakotas as one of them when they gave him a wife, had brought only trouble upon them—many smaller troubles before, and today this big thing.

As the young Curly looked down upon this enemy of his people, his Indian blood rose like a war drum in his ears, swelling hot. For a moment it seemed he must kill, kill whites, many of them to make his heart good after what this man and the soldier chief had done in the Brule camp today. Then suddenly he was big and powerful, so powerful there was only contempt for a miserable thing like this Wyuse, and with a quick motion he jerked his breechcloth away and stood bare before the staring eyes of the dead man, offering him the ultimate insult of the Lakota.

For a moment the boy was dizzy with the boldness of this act of chiefs in the council lodge. Then he was once more just young Curly, the slender twelve-year-old son of Crazy Horse, a holy man, counselor and father to all who came to him. So the boy covered himself before anyone could notice and, running for his pony, headed towards the Oglala camp. There would be trouble from all this killing, perhaps a great war, and he must be with his people to help. Faster and faster he hurried his pony until the little pinto was laying his hairy belly low to the ground.

Behind him came the forgotten Lone Bear, trying hard to catch up with his friend, for already there was nothing else he could do.

As Conquering Bear fell, Man Afraid and Big Partisan and others ran in to lift him, to carry him down over the bank out of the way of the charging warriors. They saw he had many wounds, three bad ones: a shattered arm, a bullet through one knee and another deep through the soft middle parts that would bring down even a buffalo bull. They laid him out straight on his mourning blanket and stood about the Great Father's peace chief who was brought to the ground by the guns of the soldiers, who fell as a great man falls, shielding the people of his village.

In the meantime the warriors who had followed the fleeing soldiers up the trail stopped at Bordeaux on the way back to the camp, demanding the whites who had watched the fight from the flat tops of the houses and were now suddenly gone.

"Where are the rabbits hiding today? Shake the brush, scare them out!" the young Brules cried, going through one house after another, their lean, brown bodies shining in sweat and streaking paint, their faces fierce. Some were blood-spattered; some had fresh, short-haired white-man scalps hanging from their belts or their bow-tops. And beside them ran the little Jim Bordeaux rubbing his hands, pleading. They had done nothing, these whites that they were hunting, only ridden along with the soldiers from the fort as people going the same way on the road often do. They were blameless.

"They are of the enemy!" the nephew of Conquering Bear roared out, plunging his new soldier sword into the bed rolls, one after another. By now Curly and He Dog had slipped back down to follow Hump. They heard Swift Bear and two more Brule brothers-in-law of old Jim talk for him and the other whites, haranguing the wild young men. The warriors were angry at this but they listened because Swift Bear was still a strong man among them, if too much for peace. He was one of the best catchers of the wild horses that lived in the sandhills of the Running Water country, and so they let him say that they were like the foolish white soldiers, coming to kill people who had done them no harm. Let those who would be men go help the fleeing people, Swift Bear said, or had the years of peace they so despised really softened the young Lakotas, made such weaklings and fools of them that they could not see the people were truly in great danger today and needed men to help them, not bush-shaking boys playing at war?

So the wild young warriors went away like dogs caught at the meat racks, some still looking back. But when they turned their eyes ahead they saw that Swift Bear had spoken true. The Lakotas were fleeing as these so young men had never seen them go. The whole river bottom was one great herd of milling people, women, children, and old ones, horses and travois and dogs, all mixed together, with many men among them, trying hard to get everybody to the river, where Little Thunder was splashing his horse through the water marking a path across the quicksands of the Shell with standing poles of willow.

And at the Brule camp it was as though a great wind had come that way, leaving only one lodge standing, that of Conquering Bear, guarded by members of his *akicita*, his warrior society, and a few of those strong in the councils of the Lakotas, like Man Afraid and Big Partisan. And before the door were scattered the naked bodies of the soldiers. These the young warriors charged again, Curly along, jumping them with their horses, driving spears into them and more arrows. They threw their ropes over the wagon guns and dragged them around the camp, upside down, tearing up the worn sod. One they took down into the river and cut it loose in the deepest current, to be lost. Then they piled brush around the gun carriages and the wagons and, firing them, circled the blaze, whooping and riding wilder and wilder as they heard the women along the river make the trilling cry for them.

And when the fire was done they swung around the moving

camp of their people and on up the river to meet some of the warriors returning from a talk with the Oglalas, making the call for charging the enemy, the whites.

"Hoppo!" they cried. "Let us go!"

Now Little Thunder came riding fast to the Bordeaux houses, his heavy face lined with the things of this day. It seemed the warriors were planning to burn the soldier fort on the Laramie.

"Stop them, *sacré,* stop them!" the little Frenchman shouted, sputtering like wet buffalo fat thrown on the fire. "If they do no more damage the Great Father may forgive it. They have some reason for fighting the soldiers who come and kill their chief before their eyes, but if they burn his fort he will send a hundred wagon guns; the soldiers will come thick as the grasshoppers in summer to fight them, to butcher the women and children."

"Hou!" Little Thunder said, making it a sorrowful agreement. He saw that the things their trader brother said were true. They must do what they could. Getting some of the head warriors together, he made a long talk to hold them while Jim and his Brule wife sent tobacco and hard bread and a barrel of black molasses out to the rest, still angry as bumblebees stirred up with a stick. They were all mounted now and new painted, riding in circles, whipping their ponies with the war ropes, sliding down behind them as in attack, whooping. But Little Thunder held their leaders through their respect for a man of years and honor. Besides, it was getting towards the time of the evening meat, the sun near to setting. It would be long dark before they could reach the soldier town, and war at night was not good, as every Lakota knew. Tomorrow they would go.

Ahh-h, tomorrow! And now it was time to eat, so getting off their horses they pushed up to the things the trader had set out. Holding up the long tails of their breechcloths like white-woman aprons, they filled them with tobacco and hard bread; dipping their hunting knives, sticks, or even their fingers into the barrel of molasses, they licked the sweet drippings. Tomorrow was time enough for fighting.

But the trouble was not yet done, not for Little Thunder or for Bordeaux. As soon as it was dark the whites hidden at the trading houses wanted to ride for Laramie, and get killed on the way. And when Swift Bear and another Indian found a wounded soldier hidden in the brush holding his arrow-split belly together with his hands, they brought him to the stockade too. But Jim and Little Thunder ordered him taken away at once, Bordeaux's wife slipping out to help him in her Lakota way, wrapping his belly tight in wet buckskin and giving him a little whisky and a robe and covering him with brush.

Almost before all these whites were hidden again, more warriors, hundreds of them now, were whooping outside, slapping their mouths with their palms, sliding their voices into high, thin cries like the panther in the darkness. They pushed into the candle-lit trading house until it was tight full, many milling around outside, demanding, threatening. To prove that their chief was not dead and so not yet to be avenged, some of their leaders, like Spotted Tail and High Back Bone had been taken into his lodge, lit only by a few coals and the smoldering grass wick in the bowl of the medicine man. Besides, the chief was covered, so they could not see the slow-oozing, yellow-brown blood, almost as yellow as that of the gut-shot buffalo that the hunter need only follow a little way. But the man's eyes had dropped back so deep into his head that they knew how it was, and so once more the ten white men at the trader stockade cowered under the robes of the warehouses while Little Thunder rode back and forth from the people huddled north of the river in their fear of more soldiers and wagon guns to the lodge of the wounded chief and then on to the Bordeaux houses.

"Wait," he kept saying to the warriors everywhere. "Wait—nothing can be done until it is seen what will happen. Making war against the whites is a big thing and not to be decided fast as a lead ball flies from the gun. There must be counciling. Wait!"

Ahh-h wait, wait! That was all the chiefs had been saying for two moons, some of the warriors cried out against him. Their supplies had been used up waiting for their father, the agent, and he had not come. Now they would not get their annuity goods at all, and their children would starve.

"Nobody will starve! We will kill the whites and take the goods for the people!" one among them promised, the others answering him with their loud "Hoye!" pushing closer upon Little Thunder and the French trader, their faces wild in the candlelight, their paint-ringed eyes fierce. The Brule chief saw how it was and moving his eagle-wing fan wearily, advised Bordeaux to give them more goods, anything they wanted, for they were only trying to pick a fight to start the killing.

So Jim Bordeaux gave out tobacco, the sweet lumps, coffee and hard bread, raisins and bacon and beans until these were gone. Then he pulled calico and blue cloth and blankets from the shelves, brought powder and ball from the back room, even gave away his cattle and his horses. Tears running down his dark, hairy cheeks, he gave out all his goods, and when everything was gone and he stood behind an empty counter with only Little Thunder and Swift Bear beside him and the mass of dark-faced warriors pushing against them, he began to talk. One white man, unarmed and alone, he began to talk to the fight-hungry warriors, flattering here, blaming there, bringing up old angers and spites and hatreds among them, dividing them with his smooth trader's tongue, talking long and hard for his life and for the life of all the whites of the upper Platte River country.

Most of the night Curly was with the pony herd, the boys taking turns to slip away to the Bordeaux houses, where there was surely much going on. But it was not easy, with the *akicita* watching the herders very close, for the horses must not be lost this night. After the excitement of the day they were restless and easy to stampede by soldiers or by Indians from up at the woman's camp at the fort, or even from among their own people here.

Curly managed to get away once, sneaking down a gully black

under the late moon. He stopped at the back of the Conquering Bear lodge, away from the guard. A faint redness glowed through the skins between the dark shadows of the men with the chief, but everything was so still he could hear the arrow hawks falling upon the mosquitoes over the river bottoms. There was an owl hoot too, a signal to returning hunters who did not know of this day. And behind all this was the rumbling of the warriors over at the trading houses.

As the boy listened he noticed a dark figure huddled at the lodge of the chief, a woman, probably the old wife of Conquering Bear, with her blanket drawn over her head, sorrowing for the wounded one. It was bad for a woman to see her man dying so, not from battle or even sickness, but by the hand of those who called him friend.

Once more the sun was up, bright and hot in the whitish, wind-streaked sky. Over at the Bordeaux houses old Jim was hoarse, stripped of much of his property, but he had kept the warriors from starting to Laramie until it was too late for a dawn attack on the fort. And now he was stretched out on the buffalo robes behind the counter, snoring. Somewhere the wild young men slept too, making no war and no victory dance with the scalps taken. There was the sign of death over their people and besides, the soldiers had died too easy.

All the night the Indians north of the river had watched for the fire signals from their scouts around Laramie, but there was nothing until the sun came to the hills and brought the mirror flashings of good news. No soldiers on the Holy Road, nothing at all coming from the soldier fort. So the Lakotas moved out on the broad travois trail leading northward over the breaks towards Rawhide Creek, the Oglalas and Brules together, one great camp.

They took the wounded Conquering Bear with them, six of the tallest, strongest Brules carrying him in a buffalo-hide sling between two long poles. Ahead of the chief rode the younger wife leading his favorite old war horse, his shield and spear on one side of the empty saddle, the war bonnet in its case on the other. Before and behind the Bear rode members of his warrior society, a guard of honor among his fleeing people.

Even now the Lakotas moved as always: four old-man chiefs, the councilors, going ahead to select the places for smoking and rest and for camping through the nights. In their hands they carried the fire of the villages and the safety of the people. Behind them rode the other chiefs and some of the *akicita* selected to keep order and to guard the death travois of Bull Tail and the sling of the wounded chief. Next came the people, the older men, the women, the children, and the helpless ones and all the lodge and bundle travois, followed by the pony herds and then more men with war clubs at their belts and bows ready in their hands. A few of the warriors had guns, mostly those taken from the soldiers yesterday. They rode along each side and behind the moving people, with scouts far out in all directions.

Usually the moving of a large camp was a time of fun and visiting, with much horse racing, playing of tricks, and singing of songs; the women gay with talk and gossip, their faces vermilioned, their deerskin dresses fringed and beaded, their saddles fine with hangings reaching past the bellies of the horses, the warriors galloping up and down, sliding from side to side on their horses, springing to the ground and up again, making songs, showing off for the women and girls to see. But today there was little heart for these things, even among the boys along the edge of the great camp. Instead the moving was swift and quiet, with now and then a medicine song from one of the men to lift the hearts of the people.

At the highest ridge beyond the river Curly saw many dark faces turn back to look anxiously over the Holy Road and the trading houses where the government goods were stored. They were moving away from their annuities, a whole year of them, leaving everything behind. Only a few knew that early in the morning a young Indian had ridden up to the Gratiot houses to talk to Salaway, the trader's son working there, and well known to the Indians from his waiting outside of the lodge for Big Mouth's sister all the summer. They were going north, but some would be back for their goods later, and because they didn't want to fight their friends, they hoped they would be out of the way.

But many of the women were looking towards the soldier town on the Laramie, although the scouts had signaled no dust on the trail from galloping American horses or wheels of wagon guns. It seemed, too, that the dead white men were still lying down there with the flies on them and no one coming to carry them away or lay them in the ground. A young Brule riding in from Bordeaux said that Fleming, the soldier chief, had sent word to old Jim to defend himself any way he could, for there were no soldiers to help him. It seemed, too, that the soldier chief called Grattan had been told to be careful, to take only twenty men and no wagon guns, to make no trouble over the Minneconjou if he would not come in peace. And hearing these things the young warriors spoke loud of the weakness at the soldier town. The whites could not carry away their dead; they could not punish the Indians.

"They will come—" some of the older men said quietly, looking down into the fire. Mostly the young men sat silent, but one Brule with a sister in the woman's camp talked very big with knowing. "They cannot chase us," he told all who would listen. "They are very few at the fort—no more than so many—" holding up his two hands, the fingers spread. The others were quick to agree with what they wanted to believe, and so all the day the signal went from group to group: only as many men in the soldier town as fingers on two hands and much plunder in horses and goods to be taken, many coups and scalps for the victory dance, and to help the young warriors get wives.

Hou! It was good. Perhaps one could still be a man.

But all the chiefs were against any raiding now and many others strong with the warriors, too, like Red Leaf and Spotted Tail and Hump. A few of the wilder young men wanted to go anyway, certain that the Minneconjous, who had been driven from the Brule camp by Stabber the night after the trouble, would be glad to help. But the one sent to where they were traveling alone came back with the slow feet of bad news. Straight Foretop and the others were against making more trouble, feeling very bad about what had come from killing an old Mormon cow. After that the young warriors didn't try very hard to sneak away from the watching *akicita*. They were too few to charge the thick 'dobe walls and the wagon guns of the soldier town.

When the village reached the Rawhide, there was more talk of going back after their goods. In this they were many and strong and so they rode away openly into the dusk, some taking pack horses, others skin sacks and extra blankets to bring back the things that were theirs by treaty. At dawn the next morning young Curly rode beside Hump as they splashed into the knife-bright waters of the Platte. The fur-company houses were deserted, Salaway and the rest all gone. But by the time the Indians had smoked and planned the division of the goods, several of Conquering Bear's family came galloping up on foaming horses, Red Leaf at the head. From the stone steps of the big house he looked down upon the Indians gathering below him, a lean, tallish man in a plain blue blanket, his face lined by the hard things of the last few days.

Slowly he began to talk, quietly, a little uneasily, as a young man who has not spoken much in council. But he was the brother of the wounded chief and had ridden hard, so the warriors let it be done. He had come, Red Leaf said, to tell them his brother, the Bear, did not like this thing they were planning to do here because he was struck down by a wild and foolish young man. This place was not of the soldiers but of the fur company, who had been his friends long before one soldier came riding up the Shell, the company standing protector of the annuities as a chief must for the trader goods brought to his camp.

"I am a Lakota warrior like you," Red Leaf told them, dropping his blanket from his scarred breast, "but I am also the brother of Bear chief who is bad hurt and so must speak to you with my tongue. Do not touch these goods, he says. Trouble enough has been brought upon the people. Leave here in peace and go to the hunting grounds; go fast and make plenty of meat and robes against the hard winter coming. So he has spoken."

These were good words, Curly heard many say, and many called out the "Hou!" and then pushed up around Red Leaf, put their shoulders to the door, and when it broke, the leaders crowded into the storeroom and handed out the goods as fast as they could. By mid-forenoon the Indians were gone, heading north towards the Rawhide, the pack horses loaded, the skin bags and knotted blankets hanging ripe and full as from the women's saddles when the village was moving. Behind them the Gratiot houses were clean of everything except the whisky buried in the floor, in a place well hidden.

Day after day the Indians kept going, the Oglalas heading north, the Brules northeast to the Running Water and down it to the mouth of a creek they called the Snake, Man Afraid and some of his best warriors, including Hump, along to help with Conquering Bear. They went as fast as the wounded man could stand, right through the heat of the day, and although he was getting weaker and burning with the fever of powder and lead in the entrails, he hurried them on, wanting to get his people far from the Holy Road and the soldiers that would certainly come against them.

Since the shooting the Crazy Horse lodge was in the Brule camp, for in troubled times it is best that the women be with their own people. Curly helped with the family horses and travois and followed Hump when he could. But he missed his Oglala friends, particularly He Dog and the shy, pretty girl who was the daughter of Red Cloud's brother. Often she had looked up under her lashes as he passed in the village, and it was partly because she had made the beaded band around the war club the son of Bad Face threw into the Laramie that Curly had searched the waters so long.

But some day the people would be together again, and now there was much to be done and his Brule cousins to take up his free time. It was a good fall in the Running Water country, the chokecherry bushes bending like dark plumes in their shining fruit, a few patches of late currants still holding their berries, sweet and blue to the tongue, the wild plums turning yellow. There was small game too for the boys, ducks, quail, curlew, and young prairie chickens, plump and heavy for their short wings and so silly that if one shot the mother the young hopped about her, picking at her curiously, as though her flopping with the arrow through the breast were play. They could be knocked over with untipped shafts or their heads snapped off with a strip of rawhide on a stick. Roasted over the coals they were so tender they almost fell apart before they were done, and afterward their juices ran down the boys' chins. The old hens they carried home for the soup kettle, very good with buffalo peas and wild turnip and onion.

From the high places the boys saw many fine things: the antelope running in waves like wind over the yellow grass; hunters stalking deer in the brush patches and bringing them in across the horses, the heads hanging low to the ground, those with horns cut off, for there was no time in the fast-moving camp for these things.

When Hump could leave his duties with the wounded chief, Curly was hard on the fringe of the warrior's moccasin, and so it happened that he saw Conquering Bear. The boy knew the chief's life was melting as the winter snows from the Chinook's breath and that many waited to see where his robe would fall. There was old Smoke. It was known that he would like the power for the son to whom he had already tried to give his place but found that none would follow this Bad Face who was shamed by his wife before his own people, her tongue so sharp that not even a hungry boy would go near her cooking fire. But others turned their eyes upon the place of white-man chief of all the Teton Lakotas. There were even some among Conquering Bear's own people hoping to profit from his death. Stabber was already talking loud of driving the Bear's family from the camp of the Brules.

"Making the peace sign towards the whites—doing any bad thing he thinks will please them," the others said, their mouths bitter as from dust.

So it was that while many planned for power not even the Bear's closest friends got through the lodge door to see how he was— almost no one except the medicine man, the holy men, and those who lifted the wounded chief in and out of his covered sling. It was one of these times that Curly saw him. The boy was so close at Hump's moccasins that when the warrior motioned him back, he stooped quickly and saw the wounded man between his friend's legs, or what must have been the man but looked like a skull from the prairie with the yellow skin still on it, the eye holes almost as deep and empty, and all around the smell of death.

Far off on the bluffs Curly tried to think of what he had seen that morning at the lodge of Conquering Bear. It had been somehow a sacred thing and made him run to his horse to get away by himself. When some of the boys tried to follow he drove them back in anger. Then he hunted out a high point back from the river, where Roan Mule, the eagle-catcher of the Oglalas, had an old pit he used every year. Here the boy made a walking hobble for his horse so it could move to water and grass, and then he stretched himself, bare to the breechcloth, on the gravel and looked into the deep blue of the sky. There were many things he must think about, things of the Bear's lodge this morning, of the last week, and of the long years at his father's fire, and with Hump. Everything seemed somehow tied together today like beads on a long, long string of rawhide and the glories of the hunt and the warpath might be only a few of these.

All through the day and the chill of the night the boy lay flat on the butte, putting sharp stones between his toes and piles of pebbles under his back to keep awake. When it seemed that even his arms hurt for sleeping he got up and walked around, trying to sing as others did at such times, but no songs came and so he lay down again, all that day and the next too, until his eyes were burning holes and his tongue big as a beaver tail in his mouth and as rough. Yet nothing of the earth came near him, no animal, no being at all, not even a grasshopper or an ant, and no bird flew all the wide sky that he could see. This was a strange thing, the living ones keeping from him when he sought a vision, and so the boy began to wonder about himself. Finally he sat up and looked in the round signal mirror on his breast, seeking out the things in him that made the boys laugh, white-man things, they called them: his narrow face, his light skin, and particularly his hair, still little darker than a new-hatched prairie chicken, and so soft that the Lakotas called it curly. Then there were the things no mirror showed: his dislike of paint or beads or dancing, of many other Lakota ways. Before today he had seldom thought of these things except when he was with the Pretty One, who was always being pointed out by the whites of the Holy Road and petted and given presents by the soldier women and by some of the men, too, because all the year he flowered like the springtime in beads and quills and paint and fringe as no other one among them.

And if Curly was there, these people always looked beyond the Pretty One to the plain, unadorned boy and talked their white-man words among themselves. He had picked up a few of these, including one he heard often, always as a question: "Captive?" It used to seem funny to him, for it was well known that his mother was the sister of Spotted Tail, the Brule. But the last year or so the question stirred anger in young Curly, stirred very much anger, and when the white women saw this they were certain of their mistake, calling him a savage, which seemed to be their way of saying Indian. Yes, he was Indian, Brule, with Oglala and a little Minneconjou on his father's side, even a little Cheyenne, too, he was told. But what mattered was that on both sides he was Lakota.

A third day the boy stayed on the hill, trying hard to lift his mind to the land behind this one as he had so often heard others tell had happened to them. But to him the ordeal brought only weakness and the sick feeling of one not fitted for a vision, so he finally went to get his horse, walking slow and bent as an old man. The pinto was in a low place, near a broad cottonwood that spread its shade in a wide circle. But the sickness and the turning in the boy's head made him sit with his back against the tree, the wind singing a cool little song in the leaves above him and stirring the short hairs that had worked loose from his uncombed braids.

It was almost dark when he awoke enough to know someone was shaking him hard. He struck out with his arms and then saw that it was his father with Hump standing near. They were very angry. Where had he been? This was no time to be running off alone, with probably both Crow and Pawnee raiding parties near, and perhaps even white soldiers coming, everybody worried over the dying chief and no one knowing where young Curly was until his horse was seen. When he told them he had gone out to fast for a vision, they were more angry than before. Out to fast for a vision without making his preparations, without the sweat or the consulting with the wise ones for guidance, or even telling his people where he had gone!

Back at the lodge Curly was given a little soup and sent to the sleeping robes, silent and angry that they all thought him a boy, wondering about a dream he had at the foot of the cottonwood. But he could not ask them about it now. They had not been kind.

Next morning, at daybreak, the herald came for Crazy Horse and for Man Afraid. They had been with the wounded chief until the night hour of dying seemed past. But now it was the time; the other headmen of the Oglalas were there and the Brules. When they came in, Conquering Bear called to Man Afraid in a voice they could scarcely hear, such a small voice from the chief who had often filled the camp with a roaring so even the dogs ran for the hills.

And when Man Afraid was beside him, the Bear told him always to remember the treaty that had been made at the Big Council. It was about things that belonged to them all and to their children, goods to be sent them for giving up the wars on their enemies and for making the emigrant trail a Holy Road. To pay for these things there were to be annuities for fifty-five years and protection by the soldiers for all the people from every enemy, Indian or white.

"It was the white soldiers themselves who came to our peaceful village—" one growled in low anger.

But the Bear had no time for hearing. There had been a mistake made a few days ago and he did not want Spotted Tail and his blood brothers Red Leaf and Long Chin to get angry with the whites when he was dead. There were wild young men who did not do right among the Indians too, and more fighting would only bring trouble—more trouble. After a while the man spoke again, slower, the words little more than his breath. "I am killed now," he said, "and in my place I put one you all know, a good man, with many good fathers before him. To Man Afraid I give my people— all the Teton Lakotas I give to him—"

"No, no, I am not strong enough to carry this thing," the Hunkpatila cried out, the firelight red in the tears that stood like rain on his dark cheeks.

But the wounded chief would have it so, for his ears were closed.

The GIFT *of Ears*

THE death scaffold of Conquering Bear was made of four poles set into the ground with a platform across the top, high as the hand could reach. There, with his bow and his shield beside him, wrapped in his robe as for the sleep of a winter night, he lay on the high place that overlooked the valley of the Running Water and the old camping ground that was pounded hard by many generations of moccasins. When the first few days of mourning were over and the people began to scatter, there was talk that the family of the Bear was to be driven out by Stabber and his followers, with some help from Big Mouth's Loaf About the Forts. It was a bad thing the little chiefs were planning, the others knew, but Red Leaf and his people would go rather than make a trouble to split the Brules as the Oglalas were by the blood of one of their own.

These were times of changing things, unsettled and hard, some of the older people were saying when they saw a winter away from the whites of the Shell River ahead of them. It would be the first one since the Oglalas followed Bull Bear southward from the Black Hills country to his traders twenty years before, the first winter without white men and their goods somewhere in the Lakota country in the memory of the oldest among them. But now it seemed certain that the soldier chiefs were very angry and would not let the Indians come back to the Holy Road or let the traders bring their packs and wagons to the camps. When they thought of this it seemed very hard, for they had forgotten how to live without trader goods, not only for eating and wear, but even the arrows and spears would fail them without iron for the points.

45

With the family lodge back in the Oglala circle and the people coming as always to talk to his father of what was in their hearts, young Curly heard much about these things, and from Lone Bear, with his relatives in the woman's camp at the fort, he got more news of the fighting. It seemed there had been a soldier left from the Conquering Bear killing, and somebody at Bordeaux got him to the fort afterward, but he died, too.

"Hou!" It was good that none was left to say he helped kill a Lakota chief.

Yes, and the other soldiers were still shut inside of their town. They never came out to bury their dead ones at all, but gave Bordeaux pay-money to do it. He rolled all of them except the soldier chief on a big buffalo hide and dragged them with horses to a long ditch and then piled stones on the place to keep the wolves from digging. It couldn't have been an easy thing to do, this burying the whites. They didn't smell very good alive in the summer and these had been dead many days in the heat of the Moon of Cherries Black.

There was waiting, too, among the Lakotas of the Platte country, and watching to see what Man Afraid would do with the new power the dying Conquering Bear had tried to put into his hand. But none could tell how many would have followed him as head chief of all the Tetons, for he was the same as always, a tall, friendly man with nothing on him to show that he was a chief at all, no feather, not even a border on the blue blanket he wore as he went about the village looking after the weak and the old as his fathers had done before him. His herd was never large but he could always find a horse or two for those who had lost theirs, perhaps worn out with the waiting for the agent and the hard traveling to the Running Water after the cow trouble. Truly he seemed the same, a little quieter, perhaps, and saying nothing of the duty Conquering Bear had tried to lay on him when he died.

Often, through these bad days, Curly saw the fine, tall Lakota come to sit in the guest's place in his father's lodge to plan the things to be done for the people when more soldiers came up the trail, as they surely would. Once or twice the boy was sent out to bring in Hump, so they might discover from him what was in the hearts of the warriors. Then their quiet, serious talk went on into the gray light of morning, the son of Crazy Horse listening from his robes as long as he could hold sleep away.

And often he wondered what was to come from the things done down on the Platte, wondering too, if the dream he had under the cottonwood could mean anything. But his father and Hump had been so angry with him that he had not spoken, and now, held up against the troubles of the people, it seemed too little and as mixed up as the wild-horse racings the boys sometimes made.

But with all this uneasy trying to look behind the next moon among the Oglalas, Curly found it good to be in his own village circle once more, with only the earth and the sky and their things around them, to sit in his home place with the lodge goods unpacked and orderly, the painted lining up all around the inside, his father's pipe and bow and sacred things hanging at the back, in the man's place. Evenings he liked to sit beside his brother, who was growing big too, and look across the pan of coals to their sister, a young woman now, and time, for she was two years older than Curly, and he was almost a warrior. Lately she was full of new things, little laughings to herself, little songs she made while she sewed the moccasins and rubbed the deerskin, and at night she lifted her head just a little at footsteps coming to stop beside the lodge, although she did not yet go out. Curly seldom spoke much away from home but in his own place he was less silent, even teasing his sister with look and word far beyond what the old Lakota women thought was good between the young people of a family.

"It seems our sister has the long ears—" Curly said to his brother one night, nudging him and tossing a pebble across the fire to her as he had seen a young soldier do this summer down on the Shell River. It made a great laughing between them because they knew of the young Oglala warrior who would soon come to stand outside of the lodge, waiting, rooted and patient as a cedar on the hill.

But when the others turned the teasing upon Curly he had no more place to hide his eyes than his sister, and the pan of coals was very hot to his face as the others made the throwing motions in his direction. So he leaned back into the shadows and thought of the plum-picking today, where he had seen the niece of Red Cloud. He had gone to the thicket while the women were filling the skin sacks, to get some plums for the boys to eat at their arrow-making for the hunt. He had slyly thrown a few at the girl, and then looked hard to the filling of his quiver with the ripest fruit. He made the game last as long as he could, thinking that perhaps the girl's shy eyes had turned his way a time or two, but he couldn't be sure. Then one hit her right on the cheek and, startled, she clapped her hand to the place, looking him directly in the eyes. Turning a dusky red at her boldness, she dropped her head and worked faster than ever, the women laughing at the two, shooing young Curly away, crying out that he was making the girl put green plums and leaves and everything into her sack.

So the boy loped back to the arrow-making, his heart drumming like pony feet on the hard, dry earth of fall.

The Oglalas were almost ready to leave for the hunt when Richard's men came with two wagons and the usual Richard goods: blue cloth and Mexican blankets on top, whisky kegs underneath. It was forbidden by the soldiers, but none would try to catch them just now, and the traders had to make a living some way, they said. There would be no bringing robes to the Platte for a long, long time.

This day in the camp was always one of joy and playing, the last easy day before they moved to the buffalo range. It started with a clear, bright morning after a line of frost along the river. As the sun warmed, the air began to hum with late insects: flies, heavy with fall, winged red ants crawling, and buffalo gnats in slow gray clouds like biting dust to the face. As the day lengthened, here and there a lone Indian went to stand on higher ground, a feather or two in his hair, his blanket held close about him, singing his songs

of joy and thankfulness, or of supplication for success in the time
to come. Young men ran races or played games, tossing arrows
through willow hoops, throwing the balls stuffed tight with antelope hair back and forth, each side pushing the other hard, for
many people were out watching. Those still boys, like Curly and
the son of Man Afraid, wandered around in bunches, casting arrows from the hand at stumps and sand spots or buffalo chips, the
winner running to take them all. Children dodged between the
lodges and among their elders, whooping as they charged one another with blunt spears of weed. Dogs ran too, getting underfoot,
but without much barking, for a barking dog might betray a village to the enemy and so reached the soup kettle for some unexpected guest or a special ceremony while still young and fat. Girls
paraded in groups in their whitened deerskin, quilled, beaded, and
fringed, the ends of their hair bands hanging well below their
waists, brass and silver rings in their ears and in their hair, too, for
it was a day of celebration, this last one before the move to the
hunt. The women were cooking for the feasts, the older men sitting around smoking and talking, planning the surround, laughing
over stories of other times, as when young Lean Elk tried to show
up big by jumping on a yearling bull and then was afraid to slide
off, so he had to walk back many miles, and none taking a horse out
to him.

Then the creaking wagons of the Richard men arrived. Scouts
had reported their coming some miles off, but at first it was thought
they might be from Bordeaux. Perhaps their father, the agent, had
come and was sending the presents he had promised to bring them.

But it was only Richard's wagons with the hidden whisky
headed for the lodge of Red Cloud, a relative of the trader's wife.
Now once more there would be drunken troubles in the Oglala village, perhaps like those of which Crazy Horse and his brother
Little Hawk sometimes spoke, with a Brule chief falling from his
horse and breaking his neck, or Bull Bear getting killed.

There were no robes yet but the traders would take horses and
any annuity goods that might be sold to the emigrants at the place

called Richard Bridge, on the Platte far above the soldier fort. Or they would take the promise of fall robes, robes to be made and delivered for the marked sticks that no good man denied when once given. So that night there was much laughing and singing and loud talk in the moonlit village. Some of the old women, knowing how it would be, grabbed up the small children and all the weapons they could get, particularly the knives that did so much damage when mixed with firewater, and ran to hide in dark gullies and brush patches along the water. Soon the laughing and singing changed, men stumbling as they moved, swearing in the white man's words because there were none strong enough for this in Lakota, crying, quarreling, fighting, and finally dropping into a deep sleep anywhere.

Crazy Horse, the holy man, sat dark and angry at his fire, the flap of his lodge tied fast, and none allowed out, although Curly wanted to see this thing that seemed like a wild storm sweeping through the village that was to have moved to the hunt in the morning. Several times in the night the noise awakened him and he thought of the niece of Red Cloud, and the whisky-crazy people among her relatives in the lodges all about her. He wished he might slip out past her place to see if it was quiet, but he knew that this could not be done for his father was still sitting in his blanket at the little fire.

Curly's mother, too, did not sleep this night. She was a daughter of the Brules, and ten, fifteen years ago she had seen their villages torn by many nights like this, until even such wild young men as Spotted Tail vowed never to touch this poison water of the whites that was destroying them all. Now she hoped that somehow the village would come through this thing without big trouble, without crippling and death and bad hearts for all the years of a life. She was a strong woman, of a warrior people, and injury and dying she could stand to see, but anger and hot words within the village grieved her heart, as Curly knew, and it made him feel warm towards her, towards this woman that in the Lakota way he called mother. She was silent, sitting in her blanket and lost in the darkness of her place, but her anxieties for the people were thick as the night within the lodge.

And in the morning, when Curly was allowed to go out, the camp was truly as if swept by a windstorm. Robes, blankets, leggings, moccasins, even breechcloths and hair-binders were scattered around. Here a kettle lay, there a war bonnet, the breath feathers blowing in the wind, a woman running to save it. Bows, broken arrows, and war clubs were everywhere. And in all the clutter many men, and some women too, lay as they had fallen, faces to the sky, their mouths open, many showing hurts from the fighting, cut by clubs and knives. And over them hung a stench that seemed worse than that of death.

But there was one orderly place in the morning village, the Richard wagons and the lodges beside them filled now with the goods the Indians had taken from the stone houses after Conquering Bear was shot. And out on the hillside was a big herd of horses and mules no longer watched by the Indian herders but by Richard's men.

As the sun climbed, some who had taken the whisky of the whites began to live again, to look around them with sick eyes. Near the Crazy Horse lodge an old woman was sitting alone, not as a woman sits, but with her legs straight out before her, a shameful thing even for one so old. Every now and then she wiped at her tears with the worn wing of a sleeve as she made a steady droning of complaint against the two sons who squatted sullen drunk, beside the pile of skin covering and poles that had been her lodge before it fell upon them in the night. Suddenly the woman pulled herself up and pointing towards an old man, Two Antelope, walking past, she cried out: "My sons! There goes the bad man who makes me cry, and made you and your sisters cry when you were small. He is the one who killed your father!"

Slowly the two sons raised themselves up to look where she was pointing, and before anyone could stop her bad talking, one of them reached into the lodge pile beside him and, drawing out his bow, shot the old man through the back.

Immediately there was anger and excitement among the people, even the sleeping ones awakening for it. Some of the sobering *akicita* who were to keep the order of the village hurried up with their weapons. The one who shot the arrow saw them come and started to run away, dodging between the lodges, falling, and then running again, out over the bottom land. Relatives of Two Antelope grabbed their bows and war clubs, those of the old woman rising against them, and at once it was a battle fierce as with an enemy come upon the village. Arrows whistled, guns boomed in the valley; then the two big parties came together with clubs and knives, and when they were parted by men carrying the pipe, and the dust and smoke were gone, the fleeing son lay dead and two others with him. Many more were wounded, one with his nose hanging only by a strip of skin about the mouth, while back of her fallen lodge the old woman, sober now, was crying aloud at what she had done. Big Ribs and several others of the grayheads were with her, telling her she was a foolish old woman, reminding her that Two Antelope had always been a friend of her man's, that when he was killed by the Crows, thirty years before, Two Antelope was the one who brought the body all the way back to the camp on the Running Water.

"Ey-ee!" she cried, making the sorrowful sound again and again. "Ey-ee!" It was true, but it had seemed otherwise only a little while ago.

"It was the white man's firewater—"

Yes, the firewater, everyone agreed, as the bodies of those killed were carried to the death lodge in red blankets and the keening of the women grew like a rising storm. In the council the Big Bellies, the old chiefs, were trying with aching heads to think what gifts could be made to the relatives of Two Antelope and the others to acknowledge the wrong done them before all the people, to make it good again. If this could not be done, there might be serious trouble among them for years. Lakota blood had been spilled on the village ground and from it might sprout blackness in the heart and silent scheming long after those here today were gone, making more killings, no one could say how many.

At the first whoop of the fighting the Richard men left. They slipped off into the willows and rode towards the Platte, the Red Cloud people working hard to protect their property, all except the whisky. Two leaders chosen from the *akicita* destroyed that, driving arrows into the keg that was full and holding the Indians off as the earth drank it up.

That night when Crazy Horse came back from the long work with the dead and the wounded he sat silent in his blanket, not leaning against his back rest like a man easy in his heart, but hunched forward, with no word of greeting for anyone. It was a strange thing for the father to do, and young Curly felt many things about him, dark things, unexplainable. The women of the lodge hurried to the soup and brought it to him in a spoon made of the big-horn that lives in the mountains, a spoon holding about four of the white man's cups. He ate, and then with the coffee in his spoon the father began to speak, half to the son, half to himself.

These were very bad times. Some of the things the white man had given the Indian were good, like this black medicine, the coffee, with the sweet lumps in it, he said, warming his chilled fingers around the horn spoon, drinking deep with the good sound. Then there was the blanket the whites made, lighter and easier than the robe for wearing. But the guns and the powder were sometimes bad, helping to destroy the game, and the diseases and the whisky always. In the days long past, the Lakotas had none of the good white-man things but they had been spared the burning cup. It was true there were no horses then, but they did not have to go far for enough meat. They had corn and grew squash as big as the paunch of a buffalo, very rich and sweet from the hot ashes. There were great war parties then, too, and great chiefs to guide the people, and greatness in other things. His mother's mother had been known far among their trade allies for her pottery and even among their enemies, the Chippewa. Today there was probably not one woman among all the Tetons who could make so much as a cooking pot. It was not only the things of this day, which one could see, that were bad, but worse lay under them, like black water under ice—the chiefs running after the white men, pushing for favor and power with them, selling them the daughters who should become the mothers of great men of the Lakotas, giving them the blood and the hearts of their young men to be spilled by the whisky. Honor and the good place that come from a life of work done for the people seemed slow and hard as pulling meat home through the deep snows of winter to these trader chiefs and their followers.

Once more young Curly wanted to tell his father of his dream under the cottonwood, but before he could find the words there was a new keening, the voice rising thin and high, spreading all over the village. Maybe another of the hurt young men had died, rubbed out by the white man's firewater.

But it was the old woman, the one who had started the trouble. She had hanged herself from a tree along the water path. The boys who found her cut her down right away, but her head was like a ball loose in the end of a sack, rolling every way. Her neck was broken.

It was getting late, the geese coming out of the north, heading for the Platte, the whole country full of green-head ducks, juicy from the roasting fire, and very easy to shoot with any boy's arrows if he had learned to make the little duck sounds well. In the higher breaks the bull elk whistled like birds and sometimes in the mornings the lodge skins were frosted white. The women made a loud complaining that the meat parfleches were still folded flat. As soon as the time of mourning was over they should start on the hunt, most of the Oglala thought, without taking time for the ceremonials. But there were others who talked of the killing in the village, saying no good could come from a hunt or anything else until there were the ceremonials of fasting, endurance, and purification. Some of the older men talked still another way. The Richard wagons had stirred their longing for the things of the emigrant trail, their thirst. Not content that the Bear people had been driven out, they began to talk of killing those who had fired on the soldiers, cutting off their heads in the old Lakota way and taking them to the soldier town on the Laramie. War was bad for the people, they said; peace must be made. But the Minneconjous were long gone northward to the Missouri, and it would be hard for the old men to get the heads of Spotted Tail and Red Leaf and Long Chin.

Yes, very hard.

There were others, like Bad Wound, Man Afraid, and Crazy Horse, who heard such words with sorrowful ears and thought that when the Lakotas began to talk of killing their own, it was time they were made busy by war or at least by the hunt, so tomorrow they would send out the scouts.

"Without the fasting and the dance and the purification?" some asked, surprised, knowing that all these were good men, and Crazy Horse a holy one.

Yes, there was no time for these things now, they said. Tomorrow the scouts should go out and the village would begin to move.

That evening some warriors, including High Back Bone with young Curly along, came in from hunting. They had been west, two sleeps' away. "The deer are wild for the bow," Hump told Crazy Horse. "Too many hungry Indians chasing them. The Cheyennes and the Blue Clouds, the Arapahoes, waiting at the soldier fort for the agent are out of meat. But the good ears of our son laid to the earth heard it tremble when we of greater years could only find the wind on the grass. So we rode that way and the second morning we found it was indeed true."

"Ahh-h, the buffalo?"

"The buffalo."

Hou! It was good. And when the guests were gone, Crazy Horse lifted the case of his sacred pipe from its stand and went out into the night. From a knoll he offered it to the great directions that are all things, singing a song of a hungry people who needed a very fat hunt—much meat to fill the stomachs and the parfleches of winter, and all the hard work of it to make the hearts good again. For a long time he had felt that the pale-haired boy in his lodge was a strange one among them, but lately he was seeing some of the things that High Back Bone did when he picked the small, quiet boy as his follower and called him son in the Lakota way. There had once been great leaders in the lodges of his fathers, Crazy Horse knew, but that was far back, when the light on the people seemed clearer. Now, perhaps, there might be another. So once more his voice rose in a song for strength, strength and wisdom to see what should be done for this young one in his lodge, to make him ready for all the hard things that he would need to do. The road ahead was a dark road, and yet it must be walked if the people were to be saved.

At last the man's voice died away and once more he filled his pipe. This time he sat over it until the half-eaten moon rose and brought the quiet lodges of the Oglalas from the shadows of the night.

Early the next day the buffalo scouts were taken out by the councilors and sent on their way. Then the village started after them, the Crow-Owners, the *akicita,* known for its success with the hunts, guarding the moving. The councilors led the people very fast to make them tired enough for nights of sleeping. They stopped only once or twice between the time for smokes and the eating, and barely long enough then to let the women dig a few turnips on the gravelly hillsides. Not even the boys found much time for their racing, or for charging the young antelope, coyotes, or even the rabbits.

Then one morning, when the lodges were still up, the old crier ran through the camp before he got his leggings on, his shins looking very naked and thin and bony in their unusual bareness. It was very funny to see him but soon the laughing was lost in the hurrying and excitement, for the buffalo scouts were coming in.

First two of them appeared on a hill and then on another two more, making the signals for much game found. A trilling of joy went up from the women, and some of the men wearing the buffalo-horn headdresses went to the edge of the village to meet the scouts and lead them to the council lodge, where they were seated in a half circle, the people gathering about them. One of the councilors filled the sacred pipe with the bark of the red willow and set it on a buffalo chip in front of him because the buffalo is the brother of the Indian, giving him food and clothing and shelter. Then he lit it and offered the stem to the sky and the earth and the four great directions. When this was done he passed the pipe to the scouts.

"Smoke," he said, "the life of the people depends on you."

Silently the scouts took the pipe, passing it from one to the next. Then the councilor asked where they had been and what they had seen.

The first scout spoke, the people listening well, for he had smoked, and must tell what was true.

"We went forth over many hills," he said, "to the fork of Lightning Creek and beyond. There we smoked and put our ears to the ground. We found there was a little rumbling and from the next hill we saw a few buffalo."

"Hou," said the councilor, but not strong.

"Ahh-h, we did see buffalo, but they were few and we remembered that the people here are many, and the parfleches flat, so we went down the wind around those and smoked again and put our ears to the ground. This time there was more noise, and over the next hill more buffalo, but still too few. A third time we smoked and now the rumble of their feeding was great and beyond the hill the plain was dark every way before us with buffalo, dark as the winter robe."

"Hoye!" cried the councilor, strong and loud this time, for the word was good. And all the people cried: "Hoye!" with him and then scattered to be ready when the crier came past singing that the knives were to be sharpened, the arrows too, and the hunting horses brought in.

"Get ready! Hurry! All who do these things well will make plenty of meat!"

Soon the people started for the buffalo, the *akicita* going ahead, riding abreast in a long row so nobody could get past to scare the buffalo and lose the meat for the people. There were many foolish young ones along, those who had spent too much time around the whites and did not learn the good ways. But each time they tried to slip away some one of the Crow-Owners saw and whipped them back, or even broke their bows if they would not listen.

Behind the row of *akicita* came the hunters, riding five abreast, a long line of these, each leading his fastest buffalo horse. Last came the people, with a few warriors behind them, so there might be no surprise attack from small parties of enemy Crow or Pawnee, who like to strike the helpless ones and then run away.

As the Oglalas moved upon the buffalo the headman of the council went around picking the best hunters with the fastest horses, calling out that they were strong young men, doing good work in fighting and the hunts, so today they would kill to feed the helpless. There were old and feeble people among them, with no sons or nephews, and women and little children without men. Whatever these chosen ones killed should be theirs. This was a great honor and when Curly saw Hump was selected to be one of the leaders of these he was big inside and proud that this man was his friend, and wished to do something to prove his worth, but he felt so weak and foolish, and Hump was the greatest warrior of them all.

When they were just over the hill from the buffalo the hunters stripped to the breechcloth and moccasins and with quivers of arrows hanging at their sides mounted their barebacked buffalo horses and separated into two parties, one going each way far around the feeding herd. The buffalo were moving slowly, making a thunder of snuffling as they cropped the grass without looking up, their little eyes lost in the wool of their faces, trusting to the wind and to the watching ones on the edges of the herd, the old bulls who had stood off wolves and evaded arrows for many years.

When the hunters had circled the herd, there was a signal and all spurred in, crying: "Hoka hey! Charge!"

Now the buffalo stopped, looked up, sniffing, and, tails up, started to run, but there were the man-smelling things all around them, all riding in sideways as the sun goes. Before their whooping and the sting of arrows the buffalo began to circle a little, slowly at first, then faster and faster as the hunters pushed in past the old bulls to the fat cows and the young. Bowstrings twanged, arrows sank into the young meat behind the left shoulders, some to the feathers and some that struck no bones going clear through. And as the buffaloes went down, the hunters cried out their "Yihoo!" until the air was thick with the noise and the stinging dust and the smell of the dying. Curly got a yearling and then a curved-horn two-year-old that took four arrows and all the pull he could manage on the bow before he added that "Yihoo" to the others. Then he spurred over to where a big cow was charging young He Dog's horse, pawing and bawling as he filled her full of arrows, hoping to get her for the big hide his mother wanted. By the time she finally went down, the boys saw that the men were scattering after the small bunches of cows trying to get away with the bulls. All the flat was dark with dead and dying buffaloes, more killed than the boys had ever seen in one place before. Some of the hunters had got one with each arrow in the quiver, for it had been a long time since the last hunt and the arm was strong and the blood hot.

When the hunters returned and fell to butchering their kill, each to those with his own-marked arrows, the women came running in, making a great trilling of joy as they came, all the men who did not hunt running with them. The long knives glinted in the late sun and the skins rolled back from the fine, fat meat. Boys chased one another over the ground between the butchering, shouting, bragging, getting a little raw liver here and there from some good woman. Even the younger children were around now, chewing at chunks of emptied gut with a touch of gall from the tip of the knife on each little piece. By sunset the butchering was done and the pack horses loaded, the meat hanging over them like thick red blankets between the fresh hides, with the marrow bones tied on top, leaving little for the wolves that followed every buffalo herd.

At the camp the women had cut long poles and forked sticks for the drying racks. When the hunters came in they threw the meat in piles on the leaves and branches saved from the rack-making; the women cut it in strips thin and flat as the hand and hung it up to dry. Then the leaders of the hunt went back to the council lodge and from all directions the people came with gifts of the best meat for them, the men singing to the meat-bearers as they laid the pieces down. All over the camp the cooking fires flared and sputtered from the roasting hump and ribs, and the fine smell brought the lagging boys running to their lodges.

All that night the drums throbbed as the people feasted and danced and sang their joy and thankfulness, with special songs for the *akicita* that had kept the impatient ones from scattering the herd, and then for those who had killed so much meat for the needy.

When this was done High Back Bone came out and went around the firelit circle of the camp singing of one among them who was yet young but already first to find the buffalo. He had counted no coup, this young one, his voice had never been heard in the council, and seldom in the village, but to him had been given the great gift, the gift of ears for his people.

All around the wide hunting camp the warrior sang this song, fine and tall in his dark blue leggings, his red breechcloth hanging in long, quill-worked ends front and back, his voice coming deep and strong from the scarred breast, his eyes and those of all the others seeking out young Curly. But the boy had drawn back into the shadows of the lodges and instead there was the Pretty One, in all the beads and paint of a warrior ready for the victory dance, standing out boldly in the firelight where his mother had pushed him. But the one called Hump was done singing. He gave away three good horses to the needy and then sat down, with many people calling out his name for what he had done and that of the boy who had found the herd for this big hunt.

So Bad Face went out to sing of his son who killed a buffalo calf although none there had seen this killing or the calf, and many doubted that it had happened at all. But with his woman standing close by, Bad Face had to do this, singing it very badly, in a sort of low, angry rumbling, like a nest of bumblebees trapped in the grass cage of a small boy. It was very funny and many laughed, but they soon stopped, for the one they called Bad Face was a good man and there were others in the camp who could understand his trouble.

It was a good feast and a fine hunt, the meat racks hanging heavy and ripe, drawing the long-tailed birds, the magpies, from all the country, the dogs running to growl at them from under the strips of drying meat, hoping to scare them, make them push off a piece or two. But the women were always watching, and as soon as the magpies flew in from the timber, they came with a great shouting and waving of clubs to drive the birds and the dogs both away. The small boys, too, had a game called counting the coup, which meant stealing small pieces of meat from the racks and running away to their hiding-places with them. The women chased them as they did the other stealers, but sometimes a good woman would pretend she did not see when a boy sneaked around the lodge and pushed a piece off the rack with a stick.

All the people were busy now. Much of the space around the lodges was covered by skins stretched, flesh side up, on the ground, the women scraping them, shaving them thin, and rubbing them with tallow and brains and other soft parts mixed together. When they were dry they were stacked in piles in the lodges for the traders, if any of them ever came. One big robe was finely painted and carried to the top of a hill above the hunting ground and there given back to the earth.

While the women tanned the robes and lodge skins, the men made new bows and arrows and spears and war clubs, getting ready to defend the people, and for a few raids too, against Crows and Snakes and Pawnees. They would get some more horses and perhaps a gun or two and a little powder. Then let winter come, and the storms, for the lodges were strong, the parfleches full, the people happy. The bad thing that was done in the Hanging Woman camp was almost forgotten, and the talk about killing those who shot at the soldiers.

But some of the older men spent much time walking slowly over the hunting ground, searching out every broken arrow for its iron point, walking everywhere they went as no Lakota should, with eyes always on the ground. They did something not done since they were boys: picked up every stone arrowhead and lance point that they could find. Although these were heavy and pulled the arrow down in the flying, they were good, for they had been made by the spider and scattered over the ground for the people in time of need, and surely some day the soldiers would be coming.

Nor did the men forget to turn the skulls, bare now and bleaching, towards the west, towards the great sun. They did this last service to their brother, the buffalo, because without him the people would surely die.

SOLDIERS on the Blue
Water

IN NOVEMBER, the Moon of Falling Leaves, the Teton Lakotas sent out their first war party of all time to go against the whites of the upper Platte country. The dying Conquering Bear had asked Red Leaf and the others of his relations to keep their hearts good towards the white man, but they could not do this, and as soon as the people seemed safe, with winter meat made and the ponies fattened, Long Chin, Red Leaf, Spotted Tail, young Conquering Bear, and one or two others rode through the village dressed for war and then started away to the emigrant trail, the women watching them go and singing the strong-heart songs as if for a war against the Pawnees or the Crows.

It was a small party, and not well armed, but they were good men, some of the best among the Brules. Almost at once the Oglalas heard of their going, through the driven-out relatives of Conquering Bear living among them. Now Curly and his friends saw the warrior lodges of their villages full of battle songs too, and preparations and plannings for the time when they knew what the raiding Brules had done, and what had happened to them.

Long Chin, Spotted Tail and the others went along the white man's road a ways before they found anything because there were few wheels to stir the dust so late in the year. At last they saw one of the box wagons, those the whites called mail coaches, coming down the trail. They hid where the banks were high, not far from the camp ground of last summer's trouble, and when the wagon came along they fired down on it, killing the driver and the man with the long mule whip on the seat beside him. They let one from the inside get away with only an arrow in his leg while they divided the money they found in an iron box. There were many small pieces of paper in it too, and with some of these they made cigarettes as they had seen the Spaniards do. The rest they scattered in handfuls on the wind, watching it fly up like snowbirds rising before a blizzard. Some of the gold and silver they spent at Bordeaux, where they found out that the paper used up was money too. It was very funny to see their little Frenchman relation jump around when they said what they had done.

"*Sacré!* Throw away five, ten thousand dollars!"

It was funny to some of the Oglalas too, this big pile of the white man's pay-money blowing away or burning up wrapped around a little willow bark and tobacco. But others had no time for such laughing. They saw that a few young men, not many more than could be counted on one hand, had gone down to the Holy Road, killed the whites, and no soldiers came after them, not even when they stayed around there visiting with Bordeaux and looking at the bones of the whites he had buried last summer already washing out in the fall rains.

The young Oglalas talked about this story and thought of the spring and the many wagon trains of goods that would be on the road. The traders were very disturbed. If the Brules were not punished all the Indians would soon be raiding and nobody would be safe; if the soldiers came and made war there would be no time for hunting and robes, no trade left.

The Oglalas saw these things too, but they couldn't keep their young from visiting Little Thunder's winter village up near the White Earth River, where there was usually a trading camp since back in the days when the Frenchmen first came over from the Missouri. Here the young men saw the guns and powder bought with the money taken from the mail coach, and the many things another party of Brules got in a raid on the Ward and Guerrier trading houses above the soldier fort. Ahh-h, it was good, this trouble the whites had started, the young men told each other, rubbing their stomachs as after a fat meal, and spring would come with grass, and the ponies strong.

Hou! Spring would come, with coups and scalps for everybody. Up north the Minneconjous were already carrying the war pipe among the Hunkpapa and Blackfoot Lakotas. But some remembered other big war talk against Indian enemies that ended in nothing. Perhaps this would be no more than the little wind walking on a hilltop, or the chatter of women sitting together to pound the cherries and the hard-roasted meat for the *wasna* that the warriors carried on their long journeys against the Crows and Snakes.

So the fall moved slowly by, plump and fat as a prairie dog. Although there were none of the white-man things coming in, it was the best fall, many thought, that they had seen in a long, long time. Not only was the meat plenty but there were parfleches of dried plums and fox grapes and buffalo berries and the turnips, too, from the hills, and many skin sacks hung from the lodge poles filled with the sacred herbs the women used for hurts and pains that were very little for the medicine men. They had gathered many other things too, the colored earths and the yellow and brown dusts of the puffballs on the prairie for paints, and all those with small children or with new ones coming collected sacks of the brown sticks growing in the marshes for their soft down that would line the inside of the cradleboards. All these things and many more the earth gave the Lakotas.

The young people, too, seemed new-made, the girls beading fresh tanned deerskin instead of begging for the white man's cloth, the warriors working at new bows, clubs, lances, and shields, training their horses for the hunt and the wars, busier than anyone except the very old people had ever seen young Lakotas before. It was truly good to have no Holy Road and its trading houses for loafing. The *akicita*, who had lost many members through all those years when there was nothing for the warriors to do, made feasts and dances now to get the older boys to their lodges, to fill the empty places. He Dog was often with those of the Fox society, where his older brother, Bad Heart Bull, belonged. Young Man Afraid was already one of the Crooked Lances, a strong lodge with many good members among both the Lakotas and the Cheyennes. The Pretty One, as grandson of old Smoke, was chased by all the *akicita*. Curly still preferred Hump and the open country to a crowded, smoke-filled warrior lodge with big-talking and feasting and songs.

Before the snows came to lay on the ground, several small raids were made against the Crows and Snakes and Pawnees. A few war parties went out, too, with women and lodges along, hunting a little on the way. Sometimes the relations of Smoke or other Loaf About the Forts started out with them and then sneaked away to the Holy Road, a few at a time appearing at the woman's camp until there were many, and it seemed nobody tried to hurt them. Most of the Oglala headmen, even Red Cloud, who had grown up around Smoke's lodge after his father died, did not like this. It was weakening their camps and so might make the soldiers less afraid to come out upon the women and children. Besides, those down there who belonged to their relatives would be helpless before the guns when the soldiers came. But others said the whites at the fort were still so few, not enough to do anything but make the walking patterns and to shoot the boom gun at sunset. Anyway, the soldiers were not angry, the Pretty One told the other boys. He had three big silver disks in his hair from a soldier he knew to prove that he had been down there. This soldier liked him as well as before the trouble; his heart was not bad at all.

Lone Bear and Curly and the son of Man Afraid looked at each other and laughed a little as they walked away, leaving the Pretty One very angry behind them, and without words.

"You—Lone Bear, you are nothing!" he finally called out, throwing chunks of earth after them, as a small boy would. "And the curly one, he looks like a white man, or an albino—" using a word the soldier had made when the Pretty One complained about the boys to him, not knowing its meaning but saying it as he had thrown the dirt. The son of Man Afraid knew what the word was and told the others. He had heard the traders call the white buffalo robe his grandfather had an albino and offer a great deal in goods for it, but the old chief would not trade because it was a holy thing.

Perhaps Curly's hide would be worth much too, he said, pretending to examine his friend more closely, holding his own brown arm alongside the one so light, and as smooth as the seat of a saddle. Lone Bear laughed. It was fur they wanted, not rawhide. Not even Curly's scalp was the holy color, which was white, or nearly so, the eyes with it red.

No, they decided between them, the skin of the son of Crazy Horse would really be worth very little at the trader's, and when that foolish talking was worn out, they got their bows and went to a knoll to test the strength of their arms once more. They got more distance than last week but still too little for real warriors. They did know how to drive the arrows far—by lying on their backs, putting their moccasins against the bow, and pulling the arrow back with both hands. That made the bowstring sing. But an enemy couldn't be fought like that, by warriors on their backs on the ground, their feet in the air. It would be shameful.

And when the Pretty One followed them to the knoll to make more of his white-man talk, they got their horses and started the knocking-them-off-their-horses game. That sent him back to the village. It was too rough and somebody might get hurt, he said.

With more of the people living down along the Holy Road and the soldiers' eyes not turned that way, many came to visit and to eat the hump roast in the northern camps. They brought news. Their father, the agent, who had finally come when the trouble was all made, looked at what had been done in the Brule camp and wrote to the Great Father against the Indians. A few days later he became angry with the soldiers and wrote against them. There were some trying to make trouble for their friend Jim Bordeaux, too, the white man's newspapers with their little black talking signs dark with stories about him, saying he helped Conquering Bear catch the soldiers in the Brule camp as in an antelope trap, to be butch-

ered. Even some of the other traders were saying things like that.
Perhaps they were afraid that the strong talking by Bordeaux that
kept the warriors from killing all the whites in the country, would
make things too good for him with the Great Father.

These were some of the stories the Loafers told, and always they
made talk of many soldiers coming in the spring, enough soldiers to
give the warriors a bellyful of lead. They said this with the words
rolling on their tongues like sweet lumps, and when Curly spoke
of this joy they took from the bad predictions, his father made the
whistling sound of thinking in his pipestem. "The coyote is pleased
to snap at the heels of the wolf when he can," he said.

The winter was a good one, with the camps scattered along the
sheltered water, plenty of wood close, the lodges glowing a fine red
in the early night as Curly and his father rode in from their many
hunts together. Young Little Hawk hunted too, but he liked the
winter games, the buffalo-rib sled races down the hills, the ice
pulls, with the two sides tugging at the rawhide rope sliding, falling down in laughing piles, the snow snakes that whistled as they
skimmed over the ice or frozen snow.

Few whites except trappers came into the Indian country this
winter, and they traveled in bunches, getting to the lodge of Man
Afraid or Sitting Bear or Brave Bear right away because these
men were strong in the old way of protecting the visitor in the
village, even if he was an enemy Crow. As always the trappers
made little presents to the women and the girls, sometimes taking
one away as wife. The man who tried to get the sister of Curly
found that her eyes were turning strong towards a young warrior
called Club Man, and that her father saw it as better so.

The whites even left a few iron traps with those who had learned
this way of catching otter and beaver and mink, the traps to be
picked up in the spring, with a share of the skins for their use.
They also left a little of the white powder that sickens the wolves
to dying when they hang around the horse herd too much in colting
time.

"Use their own kill, rabbit or colt or anything, for bait," Old

Garnier said, showing the Indians how much of the poison to bury in a hairy piece somewhere—just a little on the tip of the knife blade and pfuu!—making the snapping-away motion with his fingers.

But even with all these things of friendship done in the village some of the young men stood off from the white trappers, holding their blankets up just under the eyes in the look of warning and suspicion.

The winter passed, the grass started, and the horses grew strong, and still there was peace with the whites, no parties taking the warpath, no soldiers darkening the Holy Road, and so the Indians made their sundances and scattered to the summer camps. The last of the Loafers had gone from them now, the women of the white men back with them along the trail, Big Mouth's sister with Salaway at the Gratiot houses. Everything seemed as before.

In the Moon of the Cherries Reddening, July, a raiding party of Brules went down to the lower Platte country. It was the time when the Omahas usually left their cornfields along the Missouri for the summer hunt on the buffalo ranges of the Loup and the Elkhorn, and there might be a good fight or two. Some of the party, like Spotted Tail and Iron Shell, had their wives along, but most of them were young men and boys, including a few Oglalas drawn by news of the expedition and the hope of good horses. Curly, who was visiting his mother's people, went along. It was his first opportunity to see the enemy country to the east, and his first trip with his far-traveling Brule relations.

While some of the warriors went down the Loup River to the big Pawnee earth-house village to get a few horses; the others found the night camp of the Omahas and, cutting the hobbles of the best horses, got away with them. The next day, when many of the warriors were following the trail of their stolen stock, the Lakotas swooped down on the camp.[1] Three Omahas fell in the attack and then Curly got one that he saw sneaking through a brush

[1] Sioux attack on the Omahas, summer 1855.

patch. He knew he had made a good hit because the Indian straightened up and fell forward. Feeling fine over his first enemy killed, the boy jumped off, his knife ready to lift the warrior's scalp, when he saw that there were only braids. He had shot a woman.

For a moment the boy hesitated. He knew that the scalp was a good one, for it is a greater shame on the warriors to let their women be killed than to die themselves. So he tried to cut through the braided hair, but when he saw that the woman was young, the hair neat and shining and brown as his own sister's, it made him a little sick. So he went away and let another take the scalp.

By now the Lakotas had withdrawn to higher ground, all except Spotted Tail. On a very fast horse, well painted in his sacred way, he charged right up to the Omaha camp, their guns booming hard as he swung past them. He did this more than once, riding into the blue smoke while his wife made the trilling and many of the other warriors swung their blankets in warning, calling him to come back. There would be better days to die, against a stronger enemy than corn Indians. But others saw that the Brule's medicine was good today and whooped and shouted him on.

Finally he came back and they all started home, the Omaha scouts following them to see that they left the country. The Lakotas felt good, with some fine horses, both Pawnee and Omaha coups, and four Omaha scalps. They teased Curly about losing his.

"You'll never get anywhere with the people that way, or with the girls," they told him. They made a little song about it, singing it as they rode along:

> *A brave young man comes here*
> *But a foolish one,*
> *Without a good knife.*

It made him hot all over at first, but they laughed like friends when they sang it, the women joining in too, and so he felt easier. It was not as bad as when those of the Loaf About the Forts made up songs and jokes about him, the Pretty One singing:

We have a poor relation among us;
He goes plain as naked.
He has no fine things.

Once his father heard this and calling the boys to him, told them
a story of the old times, a good story of the nation in danger that
was saved by a poor man. It was long ago, when the Oglalas did
not have herds as today, with horses to give to everybody. Because
this man was poor he had to walk and was far behind the rest of
the people when the enemy came. So it happened that he saw them
following the trail and threw himself in their way, instead of hiding, and the noise the warriors made charging him let all the others
know of the danger, and while he was scalped and cut to pieces,
the women and children were all saved.

"It is better to be a good man than to darken the hills with your
ponies," he told them. They thanked him as was customary and
went away, but Crazy Horse knew how weak his words were
with many of them, for he was only a holy man, and most of the
Loafers were interested in the white man's way of power and
ponies.

As Curly thought of these things, the Brule war party was getting farther and farther from the place of fighting. When their
scouts reported that the Omaha scouts following them had all gone
back, the whole camp moving down Beaver Creek for the hunt, the
Lakotas swung around ahead of them. They found two of the men
out for elk. One fled but the other was very brave. Although he had
a fast bay horse, he dropped down into the high grass and fired
upon the charging Lakotas. The first shot missed but there was a
second one right away and a young Lakota who tried to ride him
down before he could reload was hit. The others got the man and
his good twice-shooting gun. Now they saw that he was not a full-
blood Indian but probably a trader's son and surely a big man in
the village, by the things he wore. With his scalp and his horse to
show, the warriors rode against the Omaha camp, and when the

people saw these things in the hands of the enemies, they all cried out, pointing, and the women raised a loud keening. But the men kept shooting and so it was a long fight, lasting three hours. The Omahas all had guns, and the one who escaped had warned them so the women dug ditches and holes around the camp to protect the fighting warriors. One more Omaha was wounded and some horses, while several Brule horses went down and a man was hurt. It was enough.

When the Lakotas got back to their camp, Iron Shell and Spotted Tail made a talk to the party. It seemed they had not only killed a trader's son, which was bad, but it was the son of Fontenelle, who had once lived at the soldier fort on the Laramie when it belonged to the traders. Through his mother the son was a big man among the Omahas; he had gone to the place called Washington last year and was made a chief there. His killing might bring trouble with the Great Father, with the soldiers and the traders and their sons, too.

So they started home, making up what they would do as they rode along. When they were brought in and feasted at the Brule camp in the good way, they told of the horse-stealing and the counting of a couple of Pawnee coups, and then gave away some of the captured horses. They talked of the Omaha attack to only a few, to none who might carry it to the traders or the woman's camp at the fort. And even then they didn't tell of the trader's son killed, saying instead that Curly had brought down an Omaha woman with an arrow in the brush, making much of it that she was of a reservation, with brown hair that had the look of a trader father. If this were known there might be trouble in the Brule camp and the Oglala too; it might perhaps bring a driving out of Curly and his family to please the whites, for there were Lakotas among them who followed the white men like a buffalo calf his mother.

So the four Omaha scalps were destroyed. The fine bay horse of Fontenelle with the hot iron mark of the white man on it had already been turned loose for someone's finding, with a front hoof split for a short laming so it would not return to the lower country.

The bellowing of the buffalo bulls in the west country drew the Brules to a hunting, Curly going along, very quiet as always, but treated as a warrior by Spotted Tail and the others. Then, as the cherries blackened, visitors from the Loafers brought news—who was born, who died, word of Blue Robe, who came to those around the soldier fort after being driven from her village for trouble-making, for going behind the lodges as everybody's woman. The old men laughed a little over their pipes at this. Driving such a woman to the soldiers was like the Cheyenne custom of giving her kind to the warriors. Either way protected the people and kept their meat safe, for it was well known that when the women lose their virtue the buffalo go away. But there must be nothing unjustly done, for if the people try to deny a good woman the right to leave one man for another, the calves come weak or not at all.

"Ahh, yes, that is also known as true," the old men said, their ears sharp for word of the Fontenelle shooting. But there was nothing more except news of another agent, another father at the Holy Road, one called Major Twiss, a tall man with hair like the snows of the White Mountains. He said he knew who attacked the mail wagon and who were hostile and these must keep away. All the others who were for peace must move south of the Platte River and wait there until they were told what else was to be done.

At first the wilder young Brules wanted to kill the messengers with this word and go north to join the Minneconjous, making a great noise about it until Little Thunder went out and quieted them. It was said that Man Afraid had moved his camp down to the white-haired father, but most of his warriors stayed out after coups and horses. A few Brules went too, including the Stabber, who was shunned like bad medicine since he drove out the Conquering Bear people. But most of the others remembered the last time they went down to meet a new agent, and lost a chief.

Little Thunder was camped on the Blue Water, a creek flowing southward into the Platte far below the Laramie, when a runner came to say that many soldiers had started up the Holy Road. The

Brules had made a good hunt; the racks were full of drying meat, the women busy tanning robes and pounding the *wasna*, and everybody knew that Little Thunder was for peace, had worked hard all the night after the shooting of Conquering Bear to quiet the warriors, to keep them from firing the whole upper Platte country into war. So when the agent's messenger came he said it would be foolish to move his people so far from their own country to show again that he was for peace.

Jim Bordeaux, who had been on both sides of the great salt water, sent word to his friend Iron Shell that the whites were very many and they could not all know the same things. Now many soldiers were coming, foot and horse, with wagon guns, making a big dust up the Platte, and the Brules better come in or take their women and children far from the trail.

But Iron Shell was a calm, quiet man, not excitable like their Frenchman friend. It was well known that his heart had always been good towards the whites, too, and so he gave Goose presents to carry back, and good words. Jim tried once more, this time sending his clerk, a white man married into the Brules, to make a strong talk to the chief. The Indians listened to him, counciled, and decided to stay on the Blue Water a few more days to finish their work. It is not good to pack meat or robes half-dried in the heat of this moon. Just a few more days and all would be away in the sandhills where no soldiers could follow.

So it happened that, early in the Moon of Calves Growing Hair, old Tesson found the Brule village for the soldiers.[1] He had lived a long time with the Indians and knew all their favorite camping grounds. In the night the horse soldiers crossed the high prairie above the creek and hid in a gully to wait for the daylight attack while the walking soldiers moved up from the Platte towards the sleeping village.

Through a storm-clouding afternoon young Curly rode in from the northwest towards the camp on the Blue Water, pulling the

[1] Battle of the Blue Water, September 3, 1855.

wild buckskin yearling he was leading along as fast as he could. He had worked hard to get the colt because it looked like the fine buffalo horse Long Spear had lost in the hunt last week, such a fine one that he was having his woman tan the tail for the dance stick he rode like a boy's play pony in the ceremonials of the old Horse-Owners society. Perhaps this colt would make a good hunter too.

Curly was riding alone. Earlier there had been four other young Lakotas with him, but when they saw a big smoke climb up the sky in the direction of Little Thunder's village, they were afraid and cut around to the west, heading for the agent's camp near Laramie. Curly went on, keeping away from the old travois trail that led down from the Running Water, watching it for enemies. As he came closer to the camp he picked up the smell of gunpowder smoke, of burning skins and meat. It made his empty belly move in sickness, for this smell could only come from the village; it must have been struck and destroyed.

The lightning had brightened in the evening sky by the time Curly neared the Blue Water. Hiding his horses in a washout, he crawled to the top of a hill that overlooked the Brule camp. There was a fog of smoke in the valley, but not of cooking fires burning or of the sweet red willow from the pipes. It was the bad smoke of man-things destroyed, but not here, for the village place was deserted, the lodges gone, travois, parfleches, and bundles scattered around and away along the path up the creek left by the fleeing people. And when the boy laid his ear to the ground he could hear the feet of marching soldiers down towards the river, marching soldiers and riding ones, but nothing of the pony drags of his people. He slipped down to look at the trail and saw there were many moccasin tracks with the whites, mostly women and children, Lakota moccasins and a few Cheyenne—many of the people captured.

A moment the boy who had grown up in the peace of the Holy Road hesitated, not sure what should be done here. But people were in trouble, and so he left the weary colt tied with a walking hobble and rode after them, keeping to the gullies and canyons out of sight of any soldier scouts. Once he crawled to the top of a ridge and looking over saw the dark moving line his ears had heard, a long, thick line of soldiers marching through the dusk towards the Platte. He could hear the blurred sound of many feet, the grind of the wheels of wagons and wagon guns on the hard, dry earth, and over this the far laughing of white men as they laugh when there are women around, young Indian women. Now it made a drumming in the boy's ears, a new kind of hot, angry drumming, so he wanted to cry his "Hoka hey!" and charge straight into the soldier guns.

Then came a cooler, slier Lakota thought. It was true there were many soldiers down there, but the warriors should be firing into them from the darkening gullies and brush patches, trying to cut off at least some of the captured people. Perhaps there were other soldiers still chasing the Indians, killing more of the helpless ones. Running to his horse, the boy hurried back up the creek to find his people.

By the time he reached the camp ground again it was dark night between the lightning and the rumble of thunder. Letting his horse pick the way, he followed the trail of the fleeing village, the tracks of wheels and iron hoofs and soldier shoes mixed thick over those of the moccasins and ponies of the Indians far up the Blue Water. At the foot of a sandstone bluff his pony stopped, snorting at the smell of burning and of blood. Here, with the help of the great spears of lightning that were brighter than the sun, the thunders shaking the earth, the boy saw that the Indians had made a stand and that it had been a very bad and desperate thing. Scattered along the rocky slope were lodge rolls, parfleches, robes, cradleboards, and many other village goods, all trampled and torn and burnt, and among these lay dark places that were blood and darker ones that were the dead of his people.

By the light of the storm the boy pulled his uneasy horse up the slope through these things, looking at them like a stranger, recognizing no face among those turned gray as stone towards the sky. At the shallow holes along the top of the bluff the dead lay thick, children hacked and gashed through with swords, many shot and blown to pieces, women cut up too, or with their bodies torn as the earth and the rocks around them were torn by the exploding balls of the wagon guns. And among them an animal cowered like a frightened coyote, but in the lightning the boy saw that it was a dog, the old worn-out dog of his grandmother. Now he realized that these dead ones with their faces open to the storm were his people, and suddenly he was very sick and stooping over himself, his belly came up again and again.

When at last it seemed worn out he began the search among them, waiting at each one for the lightning, pulling down the dresses of the women that the soldiers had thrown over their heads, leaving their dead bodies bare and shamed. And each time he was afraid that it might be a relative, perhaps even the mother of Spotted Tail, his own grandmother. Then he saw the blue-painted dress of the young girl sister of Long Spear, one of the maidens chosen to chop down the sundance pole this summer, her wide sleeves like flying wings. The skirt of her dress was pulled up too, and she was scalped in a bad place.

Now all the sickness in the boy was past, and the heat of anger too, leaving him cold, as a man is cold when planning a fight years ahead, waiting, thinking how he would make it come out; as one would set an ambush for a Crow who had killed one's father.

And as the young Curly stood there with the roar of the storm coming in over the prairie, the sky and the ground and all the things between were suddenly something he had seen before, something holy and of the world behind this one. Now the dream he had at the cottonwood a year ago was with the boy once more, not as a dream but as a vision of the sacred circle of the earth around a man riding through gunfire and thunder, a vision pointing a way young Curly must follow.

Then the air filled and darkened, the flaming braids of lightning whipped the earth, the thunders falling upon it. Before the wind the small pines along the ridge bent down and let the storm sweep over them like a buffalo herd moving fast. The boy might have crawled into one of the shot-torn caves and kept dry but he had to find his people. So he jumped on his tired horse and going with the storm that was cold as hail water he followed the path of the fleeing Indians across the Blue Water creek and through the broken country eastward. The soldiers had chased them hard, walking soldiers on one side of the trail, riding ones on the other, but after four or five miles they seemed to drop behind and finally only the tracks of the people went on, washed by the driving rain, with here and there a robe, a broken travois, or a dead horse left behind to tell where they had gone. But they were safe now, if no more soldiers came, or those of the tracks did not swing around ahead.

In a gully Curly found a small boy dead beside the trail, his wet body gleaming like brown metal in the lightning, the blood washed clean from a hole in his breast. Beside him lay a robe-covered pile with a soft keening sound under it. Curly lifted the edge and saw a woman with a new baby. Seeing the dark figure over her, she cowered down like a prairie hen, covering the child with herself, shaking and silent, making no begging for life as she waited to die. But at the good Lakota word of sister, used towards a woman in trouble, she looked up.

"The white-haired one!" she said softly, knowing no name for the boy. She was Yellow Woman, a Cheyenne come to visit the Brules not long ago. Her man lay back there at one of the caves, where he had tried to shield her and their son who was shot there too. She had carried him as far as she could before the new one came, following the trail of the people. Now he was dead.

And when the woman had spoken this she started her little keening again, softly, for the night might be full of enemies, rocking her body back and forth in her grief under the lightning and the driving waves of rain.

Curly put the robe over her and, forcing his horse back against the storm, picked up one of the lost travois. With the woman in it, the robe tied over her against the wind, he started away on foot, leading the tired horse that had load enough with the drag. He had to leave the little boy where he lay in the gully, and all night the soft keening of Cheyenne grief was in Curly's ears, and in his heart the heaviness of all the things he had seen.

Towards day the rain stopped. Letting his horse eat a little he studied the trail. It was freshening, and breaking up, the people scattering as was good when they had to flee. After a while he located some broad, deep hoof tracks that seemed to be those of the American horse of his uncle, Spotted Tail. These he followed until the scouts watching the trail saw them and sent for help.

At one of the many little fresh-water lakes of the sandhill country the trails came together once more like the wing-tip feathers of an eagle. There they found the village, well guarded, sorrowful, angry. Young Curly was fed and rested and then they told him the story of the many good people hurt and captured and rubbed out.

Early yesterday morning the walking soldiers, with the shining bugle and the striped flag, had been seen coming up the Blue Water. Some of the women were afraid and, striking their lodges, started up the creek towards the hills. One, going very fast, saw more soldiers, horse soldiers with wagon guns, already ahead of them to cut off the escape. In the meantime, the chiefs had ridden out with white flags in the hands of Spotted Tail and Iron Shell to meet the soldiers. On a knoll across the Blue Water the white-bearded soldier chief, who said he was called Harney, smoked and counciled with them, and while this was done, his men moved up from all sides upon the people.

But the chiefs did not know this, making their speaking as though the council were to be a good one. Little Thunder said once more that he was not for war and that he had talked peace even when Conquering Bear, the white man's chief, was dying from the soldier bullets; he had kept the warriors from attacking the fort, from making war against all the whites of the upper Platte country.

But this was a new soldier chief, and all he could say was that he had come for those who had killed Grattan and his soldiers. They must be given up right now. The Brules told him they could not do this thing, for the Minneconjous had been driven out and gone north to the Missouri country and no one could say who among the Brules had helped kill the whites. After they saw their chief fall in the center of their own village everyone who was a man was fighting, all mixed together. But White Beard roared that the killers must be given to him, and so Little Thunder went back to tell his people to get ready to fight, and found the soldiers already in line. They fired and the chief went down and many of the women and children behind him. Some were shot, others were trampled by the horse soldiers charging them with swords and guns.

When they saw this, Iron Shell and Spotted Tail threw away the white flags and fought side by side, holding the soldiers off with their bow-armed warriors until the people could gather up the killed and wounded and fall back to the rotten sandstone bluff, about three miles up the creek. There they stopped until surrounded and charged again by the horse soldiers. Then they broke, running across the creek and east through the breaks where Curly followed their trail. But many died back there in the little caves that were shelled by the wagon guns, and many were taken prisoner.

Curly knew this; he had seen the things that were done.

Ahh-h, it was very bad. Some of every family, almost every lodge taken, even from those of the headmen. Brown Hat, the one who kept the history of the Brules, was captured; the pretty young wife of Iron Shell, his five-year-old son, and his mother-in-law, too, and one of the small daughters of Spotted Tail. The warriors had to see these things and could do nothing. Even without guns many had talked of going down to attack the soldiers while they crossed the Platte in the night storm, but their people who were prisoners would have been killed in the fighting. There must be nearly one hundred of these captured ones, as the white man counts, and almost as many dead. A bad day for the Lakotas.

But there were stories of brave things done, too, particularly the fighting by Spotted Tail. He had given his horse to his younger wife, telling her to save herself, but instead of following the rest of the family, she stood on the hill and watched the fight. Her man had gone unarmed to the council, as one does, and so he had to face the charging soldiers with nothing in his hands. The first one tried to use his sword, but Spotted Tail, who was over six feet tall and powerful, jerked it from the soldier's hand, and knocking him from the horse, leapt into his saddle. With the sword he struck more and more soldiers to the ground, as fast as they rode against him. Some said it was thirteen he knocked down, and each time his wife gave a trill for her warrior man from where she was watching. Now Spotted Tail lay in his lodge, wounded in four places, two of them pistol shots through the body. But he was hot to live, to avenge the loss of his small daughter, the hurt and grief of the people. The Brules knew then that there was a great man among them.

Soon it was plain that Little Thunder would not die and that Spotted Tail was healing as from scratches. By now many had gone back to care for their dead, and come home with their hair loose and tangled, crying their sorrow. There was news, too, of the captives taken up the Holy Road. Spotted Tail's little girl had been wounded but was living, and Iron Shell's mother-in-law. The old woman had bound up her split belly with a wet skin and followed her daughter's moccasin tracks. The prisoners had been taken to Laramie, the soldiers marching on all sides of them, singing:

> *We did not make a blunder,*
> *We rubbed out Little Thunder*
> *And we sent him to the other side of Jordan.*

By the time they got to the fort twelve of Little Thunder's warriors were already there, pretending to trade. When the column marched in they stood under the 'dobe walls and as the herders passed, they swung the blankets and stampeded many of Harney's horses. This was good to hear, but perhaps it helped make White

Beard talk even bigger over the Brules and Oglalas waiting so quietly for him there. They had listened quietly too, but it had taken hard work to hold the warriors when the woman-killing soldiers came so close to their camp and when White Beard scolded their chiefs like children. He said nobody could come to the army post any more except by permission of the soldier chiefs and that no Indian must go near any trading houses anywhere. No trading was allowed. And until those who had robbed the mail coach were brought in they would all be considered hostile.

It was hard talk, and the motionless Lakota chiefs had looked to each other under their heavy lids. The mail-coach trouble was made by relations of the dead white man's paper chief. Besides, nobody believed that the soldiers would stop their warring on women and children if they brought those men in. The soldiers and their wagon guns had come into a peaceful, waiting Lakota camp long before that trouble, back when it was only a dead cow.

Other news, too, was brought to Little Thunder's camp on the Running Water. While most of the whites, including a few of the traders, said that the soldier chief had stopped the fighting too soon, some of the newspapers called him Squaw-Killer Harney, their way of saying that he did wrong when he rubbed out women and children.

Hou! the headmen agreed, but Brule people were locked up down there in the fort, the soldiers taking the younger women, including Iron Shell's pretty wife, for themselves. Yet what could be done? Some of the young men would die rather than give themselves up to the soldiers as White Beard wanted. They had seen what was done to innocent ones, people accused of no wrong. What would they do to the young men who had shot whites?

"But they have our helpless ones in the iron house—" some pleaded.

Ahh-h, that was true, and the winter was coming, the soldiers many, the women and children afraid. So one evening in the Moon of Falling Leaves some of the young men, painted as for war or death, walked gravely through the village to the council lodge, the people watching them go in wonder. The next day a runner was sent to the soldier chief, and most of the village started down towards Laramie, but not as always before, in a gay traveling to visit relatives around the woman's camp and the trading houses, to eat and wear the white-man things again. Now the people came uneasily towards the soldier guns. When they were near, Spotted Tail and Red Leaf and Long Chin rode through the camp in their finest ceremonial clothes. Singing their death songs they circled the camp and swung off towards the fort. They were going to the soldier chief to say they came in for those that the agent wanted. They were not whipped, but they wanted to die with their locked-up women and children.

As they rode away from the people watching silent and dark on the plain at Laramie, their women came out too, riding in a little row, following their men into captivity to comfort them to the end. And now it was truly seen that these young warriors were going away to die and a great keening went up all over the plain.

Not long afterward Curly once more stood with the people of his mother outside of the fort on the Laramie, on ground that was all their own only a few years ago, with no whites stirring up dust on it or spilling Lakota blood. They had come to watch Spotted Tail and Red Leaf and Long Chin again, this time to be taken away down the white man's Holy Road. And among those watching was Iron Shell, who had always worked hard for peace until the son and the beloved young wife were lost to the soldiers. But the whites had lost something good that day too, the friendship of a Làkota strong in the hearts of the young warriors. So now, arms firmly folded on his breast, he watched the soldiers bring out the wagons and his Brule brothers with the iron chains on them, balls bigger than those for the cannons on their feet, their women going sorrowfully behind them. When this was done Iron Shell turned his back on the soldier fort and the Holy Road and stalked through the waiting people, a long, long enemy of the whites.

As the wagons started away, a keening went up from the women

for those going to the unknown land of the whites from which
no prisoner had ever returned, and a keening, too, for all the captives taken at the Blue Water. Not one of them had been given
back to their people as had been promised if the young men would
come in. It was a keening made by Little Thunder's Brules but it
echoed over the breaks beyond the Platte and farther out to their
relatives scattered on the Cheyenne, the Powder, and the Yellowstone, out to every Lakota whose blood still ran hot. In the ears
of the warriors, even of the young ones like Curly, it throbbed like
the war drums: Better to die fighting, better to die fighting—

And when the wagons were gone down the Holy Road young
Curly turned his horse north towards the village of his uncle and
his father's lodge. He had been away a year and it would be good
to see his family again and to visit with the other Oglalas. Perhaps
Hump would have returned from his Minneconjou relatives by
now with stories of some good Crow fights while he was up in
that country. Young Curly wondered, too, how it was with the
niece of Red Cloud, how much she would have grown, how long
her fine braids would be, and if she would still wear them hanging
behind her like a child or on her breast like one growing into
womanhood. It seemed a very long time since the day of the plum-
picking when he had struck her round cheek with a plum stone
and brought the reddening to her face. Many things had been
done since that time, many things that could not be finished.

But he was going home and this was not the time for thoughts of
anger. He was leading the buckskin colt caught in the sandhills.
Little Deer, the medicine man, had gelded it, and now Curly was
taking it as a present to his brother, who was already known as a
good hunter and so brave that their uncle gave the boy his own
name, Little Hawk, and took for himself an old one, Long Face.

As Curly neared the smoke streak that hung above the evening
village that was his home, his mother, out for wood, saw him and
ran like a plump crier between the lodges, calling out the boy's
name all the way. Everybody came forward to greet him, to see

that while he was still not very large he had grown much this year with the Brules. It was noticed that he talked a little more, too, perhaps because there was so much that needed saying now. And beside the fire that night the father felt something else in the boy that was new—something that one could know without seeing, as the sap that rises in the tree is known long before the leafing.

The Great Teton COUNCIL

TO the Indians of the upper Platte and Missouri River country the news of the attack on the Blue Water was like a war whoop
in the stillness of a winter night. Never had the Teton Lakotas
been whipped like this—a whole camp in the hands of the enemy,
nearly one hundred left dead on the ground, their women and
children carried off to the iron house of the white man. This thing
had happened not to the wild Minneconjous or even to the people
of Conquering Bear but to Little Thunder, the great friendly, and
after he had taken his headmen out to smoke with the soldier chief.
And now Lakota blood lay like a great red blanket on the ground.

In the Oglala camps many came to sit at the fire of Crazy Horse,
to smoke and to eat from the guest horn spoon, to wonder what
must be done, with no one to lead them. After the council at
Laramie White Beard had marched right through their country
up to Fort Pierre on the Missouri and they held their warriors
back, thinking that if he found nobody to shoot he would go away.
But he didn't, and now he sent runners saying the chiefs must
go clear up there to hear him talk again. Even Twiss, the new agent-
father, could not help them, for the officers at Laramie were saying he advised the Indians to close their ears to the soldiers and
was trading with them, taking robes for white-man goods. When
they ordered him to live at the fort it came out that he belonged
to another chief, not to the soldiers at all. So now they were trying to take his power away with the Great Father. There was word,
too, that while the whites were talking peace to the chiefs at
Laramie, they were making many travois to carry soldier ammu-

nition and wagon guns into the Indian country as soon as spring came.

The winter was a hard one, the snow too deep for visiting, so the people went back to an old way almost lost around the Holy Road—they sent out news walkers, young men who liked to travel, even if it had to be on snowshoes.

Curly was glad to see the one from the Brule camps come in, saying they were wintering well up around Hat creek, with elk in the hills and the frost cloud of a buffalo herd plain in the mornings to the southward. But there was no news of what had been done to Spotted Tail and the others, and the soldiers were making trouble about the two young men with them in the attack on the mail wagon. Both lay in the robes now, one with the coughing sickness of the whites and the other with frozen feet. The soldier chief sent Swift Bear out to bring them in immediately, although the snow was so bad that the soldiers waiting to go to Fort Pierre could not start. Even Iron Shell was helpless in this, for they had almost no guns or powder and their captured people were still locked up in White Beard's new soldier fort on the Missouri. So they had to help Little Thunder get the young men to surrender. The brave warrior son of Black Heart went in the place of the sick man, and the one with the frozen feet was carried in a hide sling by a hundred men and women afoot through the eighty miles of deep snow and storming to Laramie.

"Is this thing that the whites call peace worth so much?" Hump demanded.

It seemed the Brules were wondering, too, while up north the White Beard was still thundering that the Indians must come to the Missouri instantly, no matter how bad the trails or how weak the ponies. At last Little Thunder said he would go, fat and old as he was for such walking, but they must have the Frenchman, Janis, married into their people, as interpreter. They had seen enough trouble started by a bad man of the soldiers.

So in the winter moon of the Dark Red Calf they went to the Missouri, Bad Wound swinging around by way of Man Afraid's camp to say he must come, that the soldier chief had ordered it. But few of the Oglalas went up, and when the new treaty was signed not one of their names sat on the paper. It was as well, Crazy Horse and his brother Long Face thought, with the treaty good only for the whites, saying they could make another Holy Road through the Indian country to Fort Pierre and that the chiefs must tell the soldiers all the bad things done by their young men and bring them in to be punished.

"Like children—"

Yes, like white-man children, and if these things were done the Indians could trade again, but only in the fort, or with Ward, a man not liked even by his Brule wife. Bordeaux and the other traders could do nothing with all the goods hauled up from St. Louis on the promise of peace. No one was allowed at their houses and no whites were to go to the Indian camps.

Ahh-h, the trading would be like hunting with a single arrow—and that a weak one.

White Beard had made a lot of new paper chiefs, too, putting Bear Ribs of the Hunkpapas over all the Lakotas, although everybody knew that it was not good to have a man's name spoken too often, particularly by the tongues of the whites. The last paper chief was soon used up. But the Hunkpapa let it be done, and because this seemed to make no difference to Man Afraid, he was more than ever called Our Brave Man, one who did not reach out for power.

It was true that Bear Ribs was only another trader chief, this time from the Missouri, but it was said he had acted like a good man at the council, speaking strong to Harney through Janis, saying that the friendly Indians were starving around the forts, the agents stealing their goods, and if the traders were taken away their children would all go hungry.

"The White Beard is a bloodthirsty man to be a soldier chief, killing helpless ones while he is angry," Bear Ribs told him. "When the whites shot my brother my heart was bad too, but I am a chief; I must think of the people, so I let it pass."

The one called Harney got very red from these words but he admitted he was so mad when he came up the Platte that he struck the first Indians he could find.

Ahh-h, even after he knew they were of the friendly Little Thunder, the chiefs told each other, speaking within the mouth, so none could see who made the words. It was truly bad to put the great power of the wagon guns into such hands.

But all this good talking made no difference. The treaty was the same as when first read to them, so the Indians let the things in it be done, for the soldier guns were all around them and around their captured people. In the evenings they counciled quietly among themselves, and when those taken on the Blue Water were back in the home village and the troops were scattered again, a pipe was sent around. It was not a war pipe but a bigger thing, the great Teton council pipe, sent around for a meeting at the north edge of the Black Hills near Bear Butte twelve moons from the next summer, in the year 1857 of the whites.

So passed the winter called White Beard Is Holding. Late the next September, the Moon of Calves Growing Black, Spotted Tail and the others came back from the far place called Leavenworth, where they had been locked up. The soldier chief called the people in to Laramie to hear the talk the Great Father sent. Quite a few went, mostly relatives and those living close, for it was the time of the fall meat-making and who could believe that the young men would really be brought back? Some of the soldiers said that one of them had killed himself down there. So they would say of the rest too.

But the Brules came back and the news of it spread fast through the fall camps of the Oglalas, and something else too, of how it was with them.

"The warriors that went away are lost and in their places sit people who are fat and soft, young men suddenly become as Big Bellies," those who had seen them said. And it was true that one of them did not return.

It seemed that Spotted Tail and Red Leaf wore the blue soldier shirts and listened quietly to the talk of the Great Father telling them that when a white man kills another who has not wronged him, he is lifted up to a tree with a rope around his neck. That could have been done to the Indians, for they had killed whites who had done them no harm. The Great Father was very powerful. He could send many soldiers—enough to hang all the bad Indians —but the Great Spirit had told him to have pity on these red children who said they were sorry and would kill and steal no more. So now their feet were free of the chains and they could go home to their people and tell them all to do right, for the Great Father would not always be so kind.

These words sent to them were good ones, many thought, including those who hoped for the old days back, the high-piled trader carts in the villages, with feasts and presents for the chiefs and perhaps a keg of white-man whisky under the trader blankets. But some, and not only the wild young warriors, were asking who was to punish the whites for all the Indians killed who had done no one any harm.

After the fall hunt, when the bears were getting fat and sleepy, the Oglalas moved down to Rawhide buttes where a temporary agency had been set up to distribute their goods. Few had believed that the annuities would ever come again and so there was much good feeling, except that the driven-out Brules had to go to their people on White Earth River for their goods. Curly and his brother went along. Young Little Hawk was thirteen now, brave to recklessness and making uneasy nights for their mother. Three times he had been sent back from war parties and once he tracked some Minneconjous clear to the Crows, keeping hidden until the enemy charged him. The warriors drove the Crows off and then whipped the boy with their bows, but he only laughed, for they could not send him back alone through enemy country. So he brought home three Crow horses and some great stories to tell those who stayed around the lodges.

At the Brule village the boys saw Bordeaux with his two-wheeled Red River carts, trading much as in the old days. Curly wondered how this happened, and was told that the law-makers of the Great Father did not like the White Beard peace paper, so everything was as before.

But Curly saw that the people were not as before. Troubled and uneasy, they sat around, talking, talking, when there seemed much to be done for the winter. And those who should be leading them were caught in the net of words like all the rest, caught like fish in a net of sinew that could not be seen in the water. Little Thunder had lost much of his power since the Blue Water fight; Iron Shell was bitter as sage dust, and the younger men were making strange, played-out words. Everywhere he went Curly heard this, even in the lodge of Spotted Tail—his own uncle talking of the many, many whites on the earth, and that their soldiers were thick as the clouds of grasshoppers in the bad years.

"It is useless to fight; they are too many. We must keep the peace," he said.

Sitting back in the duskiness of the lodge young Curly had to hear this and remember that the man making the words had knocked thirteen soldiers from their horses with one of their own swords. Perhaps it was as Hump and Crazy Horse had said; perhaps Spotted Tail must sweat off all the fat of the soldier food before his heart was his own again. But it was hard to see a good man so, and as soon as he could the young Oglala slipped out and went to the shelter, the wickiup where he and his brother slept.

"Tomorrow we go home," he said.

"Hoye!" young Little Hawk agreed, saying the words as his Minneconjou relatives would. He was ready to go. The village of the Brules was like the lodge of an old man where no warrior lived.

All the past year the Lakotas had heard that the soldiers were making trouble for the Cheyennes, although they had worked hard to keep their young men quiet through the slow coming of their goods, through all the Grattan and Blue Water troubles.

Then the soldiers at the Richard Bridge above Laramie ordered them to bring in four stray horses some emigrants claimed had got away. The Cheyennes turned in three, Little Wolf saying he had had the other one a long time, long before those emigrants set their crazy wheels on the road they called holy.

"If we give up what is ours for the emigrants' claiming, then nothing will be left to us," he said.

And when the soldiers tried to lock up the Cheyennes who came in to the counciling, the people ran away, leaving their lodges standing, although Wolf Fire was captured and another man wounded. That night the angry young warriors killed Garnier, the old trapper with an Oglala family, a man they had known for years.

Then there was more foolishness at a place called Fort Kearny, many hundred miles down the Platte. The Cheyennes there did not know that the soldiers were making war and let the whites shoot six of their people, the others running away to save trouble, even leaving their horses behind. But the relatives of the dead men went out and killed some emigrants and so the chiefs, saying that it was a lot of mistakes by wild young men on both sides, took their people south to the Solomon River, away from the soldiers.

Ahh-h, it was indeed better to keep the people far from the whites. The Cheyennes had tried staying near the forts as their agent and the officers asked and so were easy to reach when the soldiers wanted some shooting.

"It is a strange way for the white chiefs to do, with their mouths full of talk about good hearts and making the young men do right. Truly one cannot hope to understand them!" Crazy Horse said.

"Ahh-h!" the Cheyennes living among the Oglalas agreed. They must go down to help their people on the Solomon.

Young Curly went along. He had a few relations among them there and many who were his friends since the night he found Yellow Woman on the fleeing trail from the Blue Water, for it turned out that she was a niece of Ice, one of the strongest medicine men of the Cheyennes.

The camp on the Solomon was a fine, orderly one, and the people made the young Lakota feel very good, with none of the looks and words sometimes thrown his way by those who were against him or his people in the Oglala camp, mostly by the sons of the Loafers, or the Pretty One and his friends. Here he was a guest. In the dances the shy young girls barely looked his way, as was proper, but he saw he was welcome when he moved in their direction at the drumming. There was much that was new in that south country, plants and animals and even the winds and the clouds. The hunting was good until very late, and young Curly brought in many of the birds the traders' sons called wild turkeys—a bird very scarce in the north country, and very good to eat from the roasting fire.

With the ground not frozen, there was horse racing far into the winter, and when the snow finally came the Cheyennes made many fine, fast games. They even got him to try the snow snakes, teaching him how to skim them along until he was so good that many wanted him on their side for his true eye, if his arm was less powerful. And here he found that he liked to be with the people, for no one seemed to notice his light hair or his pale skin, and none thought it strange that he spoke so little.

And if he got lonesome for his home village, Yellow Woman would see and send her brothers to bring him to the big, friendly lodge where they lived, or come herself, for it seemed that a Cheyenne woman could do many things more freely than the Lakota. Curly knew there had been a few women warriors among his people, and now and then one who took part in the sundance, but almost every Cheyenne band had at least one or two women who had been in the sacred ceremonials or who had counted coup or borne an injured brother or his friend from the battlefield. Sometimes they even brought back a staked-down Crazy Dog warrior, sworn never to retreat, to die there if the fight went against him unless someone dared ride in and pull the stake of his warrior rope. Cheyenne girls went about much more without an old woman along than the Lakotas, always wearing the binding rope, of course, as Ice, the medicine man, explained to young

Curly. The boy knew most of the women of his people wore the rope too, when their men were gone, or if they were not married, and the man who violated its meaning was punished, usually by being driven from the village. Sometimes this was not necessary because the woman had used her butcher knife so the man could never trouble another. That was said to have happened to old Little Badger, who lived alone at the edge of Man Afraid's village and was pitied by everyone who knew what had been done.

Among the Cheyennes the man who broke the meaning of such a rope might be cut to pieces and the bones scattered. But there was little trouble, Ice told Curly. They were good hunters and brave fighters, counting their coups early and so could marry early, as was best in all but those specially chosen for some sacred work, as was Roman Nose. It did seem a good way, Curly thought, seeing the women and the girls walk proud and free as any warrior through the spring village of the Cheyennes. He liked them so and often at sundown he sat in his blanket among the young men waiting along the water path for a friendly word.

"A few more years of meat on your ribs," Ice told him, "and we will make you a good Cheyenne—" meaning give him one of their fine young women.

The boy laughed, thinking he didn't need so much more thickness on his ribs. He had widened out and lengthened too, this winter on the Solomon. When several of the young Lakotas came down with the son of Man Afraid for the early hunting, they looked upon him with surprise and hurried to test their wrestling against him. Now young Curly won more often, for he was no longer only quick and tricky; he was strong too, not only in the strength that comes from the heart but also from sinews lean and tough as rawhide.

But summer brought an uneasiness to the village, the people like horses before a storm, with always more soldiers marching into the Indian country, shooting anybody they found. Wolf Fire, the Cheyenne captured up at Richard Bridge over the horse trouble, was dead from the coughing sickness and the irons on his legs, although their father, the agent, had tried hard to get him free to die with his people. And when some of them went for his body, they were driven away with the guns.

Truly the whites would have war.

But Ice and Dark, the two strongest medicine men of the camp, talked comforting words to the people, saying they could be saved. It was the lead balls flying from the guns that did the hurting, as everybody knew, so they would give all who wished it the power to stop them. A council was called and with the two medicine men leading, some of the old Cheyenne ceremonials were made to give the people strength and courage. They were good ones, young Curly saw, with everything done well and carefully, the people watching, hungry for the sacred help. And after a while the dancers truly became of another world, and then the drummers, the helpers and the people melted into one power, and finally the circle of the earth and sky about them too, all becoming one sacred whole, as many small rivers give themselves to one great roaring stream.

Then the two medicine men, each painted and dressed in his own way, led the people to a little lake and, with everybody watching, dipped their hands into the water while they sang their medicine songs and made the medicine gestures. Now a warrior was called out to shoot at them. He did this, shooting first at one and then the other with a good gun from very close, but both of them held up their hands that had been in the water and neither was hurt. Seeing this, a trilling of joy went up from the women, and when the men picked the lead balls from the folds of their belts, all the people, the warriors and everybody, sang songs of praise and thankfulness and went back to the village to make a long feasting and dancing.

Now let the soldiers come.

Curly had watched all these sacred things done and then went away into the hills. A long time he sat in his blanket, even when the village below him was lighted red from the great fire in the center, the dancing people dark against its burning, the drums beating like the feet of many, many horses running on hollow ground. He was thinking of the Cheyenne ceremonials he had seen, and the great surging of power through the people that seemed to come from the earth and the air into them. If this could be brought to others, to the Lakotas—ahh-h, if some man could make the great circle of the Teton Lakotas as he had seen the Cheyennes today, of one body, one heart beating! Yet it might make the strongest man afraid, lighting the fire of such power, setting it moving.

But perhaps nothing could be done so long as those who were the little rivers would not bring their strength together, for without them there could be no great stream. Tomorrow he must return to the Oglalas and his father, make his vision, if it was even a little one, make it become of the solid world around him for all the people to see so others might do the same.

But in the clear light of morning Curly was less sure of himself and besides, the brothers of Yellow Woman were going for antelope in the Cheyenne way, making a great pit drive. When they returned there were other things to do and before he finally got started it was nearing the end of the Moon of Cherries Reddening, July, and bad news came to the Solomon. It was brought by several lodges of their people hurrying in from the north with a story of Cheyennes killing many emigrants and soldiers, hundreds of them. A trader's son in the camp read the white man's paper they brought aloud in the council lodge, turning the story into words they could understand. But nobody could understand about the killing or the other news of Cheyenne depredations along the Holy Road. None of their people had been around there since the trouble at Fort Kearny. It must be an excuse to kill more women and children.

Perhaps this was true, for the newcomers had seen soldiers not far away, and the next morning the scouts reported that a big bunch of them was coming fast, straight for the village. So the medicine men led the Cheyenne warriors and the visiting Lakotas, Curly, Young Man Afraid, and the others, out to the little lake and made the shooting-proof ceremony. When all had dipped their hands into the water, they were drawn up in a deep line of battle between the river and the bluffs, waiting with empty hands, the great warriors of the Cheyennes in the front line, and far behind them the youngest ones, with the Lakota boys beside them. The horse soldiers came as the scouts said, riding fast in three long strings, the wheels of the wagon guns behind them raising a thick dust from the prairie. Farther back were the walking soldiers, many of the walking soldiers who could not run away. It would be a good fight, with coups for everybody.

When the cavalry got close they made a wide marching line and the Indians moved slowly ahead to meet them, singing strong-heart songs. The soldiers got their guns ready and the warriors held up their palms to stop the lead balls, knowing they would drop like little stones to the ground.

Then something happened. Instead of the booming of the guns, there was a loud calling back and forth and a bugle sounding. The whites were doing something with their guns, the sun shining on the long knives, the swords, as they jerked them from the scabbards. Holding them straight out ahead, the soldiers charged the Indian line. A warrior was knocked from his horse, a sword sticking through him, and the line behind him broke, the Cheyennes scattering in all directions, helpless, for there was not a gun ready or an arrow at the bowstring. Young Curly and some of the others had to go over seven miles to get away from the soldiers. The ponies were lean from the hunt and fresh, and the soldiers couldn't catch them but four Cheyennes were lost, four good men lying back there on the ground.

At the camp the women left the lodges standing and fled with only a few packs, going south very fast, looking back now and then to the cloud of black smoke rising where the soldiers had fired their village.

As soon as they could, the young Lakotas started away north-ward, stopping at Swift Bear's lodge for coffee and to tell of the Cheyenne trouble. Curly sat back in the darkness, saying nothing. Three times in four years he had seen an Indian village scattered, each time much of the goods and lodges lost. This time he had seen a powerful medicine destroyed, there seemed no telling how. Perhaps someone slipped away to the Indian scouts of the soldier chief, telling them of the protection the Cheyennes had made against the guns. Curly knew now that some of the Brules had let White Beard know where Little Thunder's village was, and that the man Tesson, married into the Lakotas, had taken them there—always men of their own people helping the soldiers.

The next morning Curly started north towards the Bear Butte and the great council already gathering. Here the seven people of the Teton Lakotas were moving into one great circle camp that seemed wide as the horizon, their pony herds making all the higher ground dark as the *Pa Sapa*, the Black Hills that rose be-yond the foothills, their warriors like a great forest, like many, many tall, straight trees standing thick.

The Lakotas looked around them and saw their strength with swelling hearts. They had been giving up too easily. With all this power they had let their women and children die before the guns of the whites in their own camps, seen their friends, the Cheyennes, killed in small bunches, because they were few and nobody helped them. Soon it would be here as to the east, where the whites were pushing in over the waters of the Missouri, driving the Indians into reservations—little patches of ground like islands in a great lake, with nobody allowed to go away to hunt or even to visit a relative when he liked. Some of the Lakota chiefs had been down as far as the great trading town called St. Louis. They knew what had happened to the Pottawatomis, the Delawares, and others moved far from their homes and fenced in with white-man lines that must not be crossed. They knew what was being done to the Kaws, and the Otoes and other Missouri tribes, the people poor and miserable, the game going, and the white man's poison whisky like the flood waters of spring through their villages robbing them even of their war bonnets and other sacred things, all going for the burning cup.

So a big double council lodge was made of many painted skins laced together and stretched over special poles from the tall pines of the Black Hills. Here the headmen gathered, the great pipe of the Tetons was filled, and the long smoke begun.

Through all the wide camp the people feasted, danced, and courted, with much visiting and exchange of news about the old ones known to all the Tetons from the trading days on the Missouri River and about the people killed by the soldier fights over the country.

For the first time Curly saw the great ones of the northern Lakotas that he had been hearing about at the winter fires: old Four Horns, the Hunkpapa, and his warrior nephew, Sitting Bull; Long Mandan of the Two Kettles; Crow Feather of the No Bows. And standing beside these some from his own country still seemed great to the young Oglala: their own chief, Man Afraid; Lone Horn of the North, the Minneconjou; and the rising men like Red Cloud and Lone Horn's seven-foot warrior son, Touch the Clouds. Spotted Tail was there, too, known everywhere as a brave man, but now as one returned from the death scaffold, older, quieter, and talking for peace even here. Not that he liked the white man's peace, it seemed, but because the whites were so many.

Quietly these men walked through the great camp of their people and young Curly's heart was big for them, and big, too, because it seemed that his friend Hump was as strong a warrior as any of the Tetons.

There was something else that Curly and many much older than he had never seen before, the seven great camps of the Tetons together—Oglala, Brule, Minneconjou, No Bows, Blackfoot, Two Kettles and Hunkpapa—all in the sacred circle. It was really the way Crazy Horse had told his son. As their own Hunkpatilas were one of the seven bands of the Oglalas, the Oglalas were one of the seven camps of the Tetons. And bigger yet, all the Tetons

together here were one of the seven great council fires of the Lakota nation. It made the boy feel a part of something holy to think
of the repetition of this sacred number, each one a part of seven
in a circle which was one of seven in a greater circle, and that a
part of the greatest, the whole.

Ahh-h, it was plain now that the Lakotas were still the same as
in the old days, everyone was saying as the chiefs came in a great
row from the last council, walking firm together, their moccasins
strong on their earth. They had vowed resistance to every white
man who pushed in anywhere on Teton lands. They would get
guns and powder; they would stick together, for they were many.

Young Curly saw them so, and in him grew again the feeling of
power he knew that first day when he looked upon the great camp.
Let the whites be even as many as his uncle said. Some day the
Lakotas would rise as a storm cloud piling high over the Black
Hills and, sweeping out over the plains, would shake all the earth
as far as the muddy waters of the Missouri.

Perhaps he, still called by his childhood name of Curly, would
live long enough to see this done.

The SONG of a Good Name

WITH the first noisy gathering of the mountain jays for their flight south, the people began to scatter from the great council at Bear Butte. The Oglalas and Brules of the upper Platte country started first, moving off westward around the Black Hills, to separate later at some fork in the travois trail or to make their winter camps together. Then the Two Kettles and the No Bows left, and the Blackfoot and the Hunkpapas, until only the poles of the great council lodge stood on the sacred place, to fall under some far-off winter storm, back to the earth from which they grew.

Crazy Horse and his son went out from the butte in a direction that had no trail. They rode alone, each leading a pack horse, and several times the father stopped to smoke and consider, the son quiet beside him. Finally he picked a high point and when they climbed to the top it was as he had wished: a place that looked far over a country stretching away in the sun like the shadow-marked flank of a buckskin horse, while just below them lay a sheltered little valley, with trees and a stream. Here the Lakota father sat and made a long smoke. And as he smoked he remembered many things of this place, and many things of his young Brule wife who bore him two sons before she died, sons that seemed like no others among the Oglalas, particularly this first-born beside him, whose eyes and whose way had long seemed chosen for sacred things, not only to him as the father but also to him as a holy man. He had waited several years for this son to speak of what was within him and now, because it seemed that he must make the words soon or lose his power, the father had brought him up here, for

101

as the tree that does not leaf in its time, so it is with the man who
does not use the power that rises in his youth.

When the father's pipe was out, he scraped it carefully and put
it away in the beaded bag with the four fringings of pale hair
from the horse like the one in his vision that gave him the powers
of a holy man. He got the hair from the mane of a wild sorrel mare
who had long led her bunch with great cunning and wisdom into
the Bad Lands whenever the horse-catchers came. But Crazy
Horse had finally walked her down in a deep-snow winter and
cut off this much of the mane hanging between the eyes, where lies
the power to see beyond the things that are. She had never become
gentle for the packs or the travois but she brought him colts in
years too hard for any other, and always strong ones. When his
young wife died he had led the sorrel mare out and shot her at
the scaffold. It seemed good that the mother of his sons should
have the proud red mare beside her.

Quietly, thoughtfully, the father stroked the hair of his pipe
case for the wisdom he must have to speak to this son. Finally
he began.

There, in the little valley below them, was the place where
Curly had first come into the sunlight of a fall day like this. It was
during the very bad times for the Lakotas of the Shell river, for
all their relatives. The Brule camps were crazy from the white
man's whisky, the lodges old and torn because the new skins were
made into robes to trade for the burning cup, and many children
went hungry because none would go far enough to make a good
hunt. Many young Brules ·died; others, like Spotted Tail, vowed
never to touch the whisky. Among his own people, the Oglalas,
there was even greater trouble, with much quarreling and fighting,
the blood of their brothers spilled on the ground. Since then there
had been no man strong enough to bring them together. Now it
was not only the Oglalas that must be brought together if their
lands and people were to be saved, but all the Tetons, all brought
together and held against the guns and the presents of the whites.

"Somewhere a good man must rise from the young ones among

us," Crazy Horse told his son. "One who has had no part in the old troubles. It will not be enough for him to speak words of wisdom if he cannot give the people ears to hear and hearts to make them strong against the power of the white man's favor. He must be one who does great deeds for the young to see, great deeds for the people. It will take a very big, a very strong man, one the people can see standing above the others."

So the father spoke to young Curly, and because the boy could not bear to look into his face he got up and walked to the edge of the little hill, hot and ashamed under his blanket that he was not a big man, big as his uncle, Spotted Tail, or his cousin, Touch the Clouds, the man who stood tall as a tree among the warriors.

But his father was not yet done. "Strength of arm and heart, even with every wisdom, will not be enough," he said. "The man must have the help of a great vision, one that drives him straight as the bowstring sends the arrow, one that brings together in him all the powers that are in the people."

The son looked out over the yellow plain below him and now it lay wide and far and empty as the whole earth and before it he was indeed small and weak, his heart as snow water. His father saw this happen and came to stand by the side of his son. "It is true that it will take a great man to save the people now," he said softly, as though speaking to himself, "a very great man, and many will hate him, and many try to get him killed—"

Still young Curly made no words of reply, but slowly his lean, sharp face lifted, his eyes looking beyond the fall-shadowed plain to the place where the earth and the sky meet, the earth and the sky and everything between, and suddenly now he was a part of them, a part of all things that are, and as he saw this, power surged through his breast.

Turning, the boy dropped his blanket and stood straight before his father, waiting.

So they built a sweat lodge near the creek and took a fast and a sweat and then they talked, young Curly telling all he could of the vision. At first it was pale as an old dream, fogged in forgetting. But it became much clearer in the stinging breath of the sweat lodge, plainer even than when he sat under the cottonwood after the long waiting on the bluff the day before Conquering Bear died. So he made the words for it, keeping back only what he thought the man of the vision would not have told, only the little about things that would make for sorrow before it must be. He told his father of seeing the dead-alive chief between the legs of Hump and then running away to the high gravel hill, of the fast and the long wait, the hard work to keep from sleeping, the feeling that he was not fit for a vision because nothing came to him, no vision and no living thing, and then the giving up and going down to where his hobbled horse was feeding. But by then it seemed that all the earth was shaking around him, with a great sickness sitting in his belly, and because he was afraid of falling from his horse he waited a little in the shade of the cottonwood.

It seemed he must have slept because he had a feeling of giving up and letting himself go, and almost at once his horse that was hobbled out there eating started towards him, his neck high, his feet moving free. A man was on his back, sitting well forward, only the heel fringe of his moccasin stirring as he rode. It was not like the world the boy knew but the real world behind this one, the sky and the trees in it, the grass waving, but all in a strange and sacred way. Then he saw that the horse the man was riding changed to a bay and then yellow-spotted and many other colors too. And always it seemed to float, so light, and the man sitting on the horse seemed light too. He wore plain blue leggings and a white buck-skin shirt, with no paint and only one feather in his long brown hair that hung loose below his waist. There were a few beads in his scalp lock and a small brown stone was tied behind his ear. He spoke no sounds but the boy heard him clearly, saying things that have no words.

And all the time the enemy shadows kept coming up before the man, but he rode straight into them, with streakings all about him, like arrows and lead balls, but always disappearing before they struck him. Several times he was held back, it seemed by some of his own people who came up from behind and caught his arms, but he shook them off and rode on, while behind him a storm cloud rolled and thunder was in the air and on the man's cheek a little zigzag that seemed of lightning, and a few hail spots on his body that was stripped to the breechcloth now. Then the storm faded, the spots too, and he rode on, the people closer around him, making a great noise, some grabbing, grabbing, while over him flew the small hawk with red on his back, making his killy-killy crying.

Curly stopped and was silent, and when his father urged him on, he said that was all. Suddenly the man had faded, and everything of that other world with him. Out on the bottom near the cottonwood his horse moved slowly about, awkward as before in his eating hobbles, and on a purple thistle, swaying with its weight, a small red-backed hawk was saying "killy-killy" and beside him, looking at him with impatience, were Hump and his father.

A long time Crazy Horse, the holy man of the Oglalas, sat silent over this. Finally he spoke to his son.

"Hou! It is as I saw it that day. You have been given a great vision, and you cannot move the load of it from you," he said. "The man on the horse is what you must become—did you not see his hair, how bright and long—or how he thought—?"

Yes, how he thought— It must have been himself, Curly saw now, for he knew what the man was thinking without any hearing of words at all.

So it was, the father agreed. And when young Curly went into battle he need only think of this vision to be like the man, unhit by enemy bullets. At all times he must do as the man did, dress like him, have a hawk over him, and the small stone behind his ear. He must be the first in the fighting, as the man was, and in the leading of the people, and he must do these things although often the road would seem dark and dangerous, the right way

not clear. It would take much thought, and much trusting in the
power of his vision, for it is only from the very high hill of death
that all the rivers can be seen to run to the salt sea.

After the great Lakota council at Bear Butte broke up, some
Minneconjous and Hunkpapas hunting buffalo west of the Black
Hills found a soldier chief with many wagons along who said he
was Lieutenant Warren, going through their country for the Great
Father. The Lakotas were very angry, the warriors hot to kill them
all. Bear Ribs and the other chiefs held them back and told the
officer he must leave at once and tell everybody to keep away
from the Indian country. If their annuities were to pay for the
whites coming into their lands they did not want the goods, and
if they were given to stop the fighting against the Crows, they
didn't want them either, for the war was to go on.

So it seemed that the northern Lakotas might be strong, but
there was no heart in the Oglalas, with many still thinking about
the little troubles of their own villages. Old Smoke lived down
near the soldier town with the Loaf About the Forts, but his band,
called Bad Faces now, was up north around the headquarters of
the Cheyenne River, near Red Dog's Oyukhpes, Sitting Bear's True
Oglalas, and the Hunkpatilas. White Beard, angry at the inde-
pendent way of Man Afraid, had made Bad Wound of the Bear
people the paper chief of all the Oglalas. The old Indian let it be
done, but he did not try to come near the councils of the northern
Oglalas; instead he went south to Little Wound, the son of Bull
Bear, hunting with the Brules in the Republican River country, still
claimed by the Pawnees.

There were more soldiers coming up the Holy Road, not only to
fight the Cheyennes but going against the whites of the Salt Lake
country. So the Mormons who had built houses and fields up where
Deer Creek joins the Platte hurried away west to their people at
the lake. As soon as this place was empty, Major Twiss moved the
agency and his young Oglala woman up there. Janis, the trader,
visiting with Man Afraid, said that the officers at Laramie were

very angry with the agent for this. But he had been a soldier chief himself and knew how to talk to them.

"You cannot come corporaling it over me!" the major had told them. And they let him go.

Crazy Horse and some of the others wondered about the story Janis told. They had seen soldiers do very hard and foolish things because a man they called their officer told them to.

Oh, but this was different, Janis said. The major belonged to another branch of the government, as though to another *akicita* among the Indians or to another band. Perhaps someone from the Brules or the Minneconjous would come to tell Man Afraid to do something?

That made the Indians laugh, the women too, sitting back from the fire, softening deerskin between their hands, their small children beside them. It was funny. Not even the greatest chief among them told anybody what to do.

But it was good to have an agent like that, the older men said, between the whistlings of their pipes. Good to have their annuities given out near the buffalo ranges, and the traders once more coming to their villages with the coffee and the sweet lumps, the guns and the powder, as they did in the old days, before the Holy Road of the whites cut through their buffalo herds like a knife gash down the middle of a robe.

Hou! And it was good to be far enough from the soldiers so that they could not be counting everything that came in, every barrel hoop for the arrow points or palmful of powder for the guns. Even Richard was back at his bridge over the Platte, and that meant the good Spanish blankets and other things from the people to the south.

Yes, and a little whisky for the belly cramps. As the stocky Richard with the many sons always said, no man was strong enough to keep him from selling anything he liked. Certainly it would not be the white-haired father at Deer Creek or the soldier chief down on the Laramie.

So that winter and spring the Oglalas scouted out new camping grounds along the headwaters of the Powder and the Belle Fourche and began to hunt in closer alliance with the Minneconjous and No Bows of the Black Hills, and with the northern Cheyennes of the upper Platte. The meat was fat up here, and the camps full of the roasting smells. They had sent word to the Crows to make all the arrows they could, for the Oglalas were coming, openly this time, and strong with men. The peace paper signed at the Big Council was forgotten by the Indians as it had been forgotten by the soldiers when they brought wagon guns into the Brule camp to kill their chief, more than four winters ago.

Some of Curly's friends had gone against the Crows last year, He Dog among them. Because the chiefs must pretend not to see, they could not make the war party parading through the village but had to slip out and back in the night-time, bringing in some good Crow horses and a couple of the white blanket capotes with hoods for the winter storms. Best of all were the two new guns that the Crows dropped as they ran away. Even young He Dog got a horse and a Crow spear with an old Lakota scalp tied to the end. But nobody had been hurt and no coups were counted, so it was nothing compared to the fight with the Omahas where Fontenelle was killed and Curly shot the woman, or to seeing the strong medicine of the Cheyennes against the white man's guns broken by the charge with swords. But it was better than anything the boys of the Loafers had to tell, and it made the waiting for the next expedition seem very long.

Finally the sundance and the summer hunt were done and a party got ready, openly, as agreed in the council at Bear Butte, with He Dog, Young Man Afraid, Lone Bear, and Curly along. Crazy Horse and Long Face had made a medicine bundle for the boy, and got him a brown stone to tie behind his ear and a red-backed hawk to put on his head for the fighting. The other warriors seemed as anxious as Hump to have him along now, for it was said he had been given a very strong medicine, and they wanted to see it tried.

But just before the party started, something bad happened. Curly was shot in the knee, not by an enemy, but by an Oglala in his own village. It was an accident and so to be forgotten as the water that falls on a stone is forgotten, but some saw it as part of the sacred vision come true. It was only by his own people that the son of Crazy Horse could be hurt.

The war party went out anyway, although it was considered a bad sign if anything happened to one of the warriors before they started. But Curly was only a boy, and so he had to listen to a night of drumming and dancing and the noise of the party leaving the next morning, the women calling out this name and that as the warriors rode by, making the trilling as the party started away. Curly buried his ears in the wolfskin pillow. He could bear the staying behind with a good face, but he disliked the noisy joys and griefs of his people more and more. Sometimes it seemed they must be as bad as the Crows, whose men, it was said, cried loud as the women for the dead. It made the Lakotas seem not brave, this noise over everything, and that Curly knew was not true.

Before the next moon the party was back, sneaking into the village in the night. They had found no coups and no horses, only big travois trails going north, beyond the Yellowstone.

While his knee was healing, young Curly limped around with the forked end of a long stick under his arm, what the traders' sons called a crutch. He spent much time listening to the father of Bad Heart Bull, the band historian. From him he learned the history of his people, the keeping of the winter counts and the picture histories that helped this man sing the great deeds of the Lakota heroes at the ceremonials and councils.

"A people without history is like the wind on the buffalo grass," the old man said over his paint stones and his quill and bone brushes.

"Hou! That is true!" Crazy Horse agreed.

As the geese and sandhill cranes went south and then came back, the Oglalas followed the path laid out through their new country the year before, every camp with wood and water close, the moves often enough for good grass and cleanness, everything done in the good way, without confusion or trouble. Now that there was no hanging around the whites of the Holy Road, no begging or grabbing at anything they could get, like dogs around the meat racks, Curly saw that many of his people were still the same as in the stories of his father and the band historian. Perhaps old-time white men like Le Beau and Bridger who knew the Lakotas before the days of the whisky wagons and the Holy Road spoke true when they said the Indian got lazy, dirty, and lousy from the whites. It was strange that the lazier, lousier ones were given presents and that those who would hunt for their living were chased by the wagon guns.

So the buffalo dropped their red calves, the fork-tail bird, the swallow, came back from the south, and the eagle-catchers cleared out their pits. With the summer's passing there were stories of the buffalo gone from up around Heart River, where many Hunkpapas and Minneconjous lived, the people eating ponies. So a party of Oglalas went up with old Lone Horn of the North, taking pack horses of meat and robes, and invitations to their relatives to come visiting. Some men who had been far down the Missouri for a little visiting said they found not one buffalo all the way, or any chips. They found wheel tracks all the way up the Running Water too, right over the old camp ground where Conquering Bear died, and through all that country where so many of their dead ones lay. Here, too, the buffalo were leaving before the lengthening shadow of the whites.

Ahh-h, it seemed indeed so, the old ones agreed, and down along the Holy Road there was a cow-dying sickness this summer, one the Frenchmen called bloody murrain. Many wagons were left standing where the cattle fell down. The trail from Laramie far into the west was lined and stinking with the carcasses, particularly around the agency at Deer Creek, where the slopes above the road were yellow with fall flowers as if nothing at all had died. Some said the sickness might do like the others brought by the whites, spread through the Indian country. It might kill the horses or even the buffalo. There was a story of so many antelope already dead on the northern ranges that the sunburnt prairies were dark with them, and the wolves so fat they lay down to eat.

But in the new Oglala hunting lands the summer had been a good one, hot and a little dusty, with many of the sky pictures that the traders called mirages—pictures of shaking little lakes and green trees. In the nights there was the star with a long white tail to speak of good things, and it was true that the buffalo were plentiful clear down to the forks of the Platte, where the Bear people lived. When the wolves cleared away the stink of the dead cattle it was pleasant around the agency at Deer Creek, with always a few Indian lodges pitched near, the people trading, visiting, and then going away with their annuities. When the snows made the robes thick and the fur of the beaver and otter, too, the traders came to the villages as in the old days. There were several in each camp, for the white-haired agent had licensed enough to make the trade good again. Big Bat and a helper came with eight pack horses to Red Cloud's winter camp far west on the Wind River and took a full load, twenty robes to the horse, back to Richard. It was so in every village, clear up towards the Yellowstone, where Guerrier let a spark from his pipe fall into an open keg of powder he was measuring out for robes. When the Oglalas heard how he was blown to pieces they felt bad, but he was one of the soldier traders and so not like their own.

Towards spring Curly and Lone Bear found a white man dead in the Sweetwater country. He had no gun and nothing along to eat, but in a dirty little sack that smelled of tobacco hung around his neck were two stones of the yellow stuff, the gold that drove the whites crazy. Curly had seen great trains of these people go west when he was a small boy, all headed over the mountains to the salt sea, Bridger told them. Damn fools, he called them. Many came back and some, they heard, got caught in the snows and ate one another. Truly these whites were a strange people.

Lately they had started to run down into the mountains in the country of the Black Men, the Utes. Even some of those married into the Oglalas went, like the Janises. The Cheyennes had found many of the gold-chasing white men lost and starving along the Smoky Hill River. They fed them and showed them how to get back to their people, but they would go on, although some of the wisest chiefs said that the yellow earth was not worth as much as the turnips the women dig, for those a hungry man could eat.

Now some of the gold-crazy ones must be coming to the Sweet-water, for where there is one, even a dead one, there will be others, bringing the bad things of the whites, scaring the game, scattering sickness. Already people were dying of the stinking spots over in the Beaverhead Valley, where a camp of trappers and traders' sons were living.

Yes, there would be many gold-hunting whites around, but the Crows and the Snakes were better fighting, the warriors said.

Up in the north country there was a stranger thing—several white buffaloes had been shot this fall, more than were sometimes seen in all the days of a man's life. Nobody understood this and so the robes were painted and given back to the earth, as was good with such sacred things. Then, the evening of a thawing winter day, Curly saw one. He was coming in alone from the mountains, his horse loaded with fresh elk. The buffalo stood on a south slope, almost as white as the snow patches about him. Curly was near enough for a good shot but before he raised his gun the animal threw up his fine, curly head, sniffed the wind, and was gone over the ridge, his hoofs throwing snow and pounding on the dark, freezing earth. The boy whipped his loaded horse after the buffalo but he found nothing except tracks leading through a dusk-filled little valley. In a bare place they ended, as when the long-eared rabbit doubles back on his trail and then jumps to the side to sleep with his eyes open and watching. But the buffalo is not small and helpless and has no need for such tricks. It must have been a holy animal, so instead of searching for more tracks, the young Oglala hobbled his horse, made a wickiup of cedar branches where the trail ended, and spent the night there, hoping to dream. He slept well, awakened only once or twice by the howling of wolves drawn to his fire by the smell of the fresh meat. In the morning it was snowing, soft, warm, with the promise of a spring sun to break through and free the bowing cedars of their load. All the tracks were gone, everything covered, and he had dreamed nothing he could remember. So he started home.

The day he got back to the big Oglala village a crier went around calling everyone to the woman feast for the niece of Red Cloud, Black Buffalo Woman as she was now called. Young Curly looked out to make certain he had heard right, and then hurried to dress himself for the feast. It was lucky he had not tried to hunt for the white buffalo or he would have missed this great time in the life of the pretty Oglala girl. He had not seen her very often the last few years, with all his visiting among the Brules and the Cheyennes. But she was always in his heart, as surely in a certain place as a warrior's weapons are, so even while sleeping he can grasp them at any strange thing in the night.

Curly had been a small boy when Black Buffalo Woman was born. He remembered it because the one he called mother had stayed back with a woman one day when her people were moving with them. Later the two came into camp with one who hadn't been with them before, a new little daughter for the brother of Red Cloud. Young Curly looked upon this small thing as somehow belonging to his own lodge, and when she got bigger he often stopped his playing to chase flies from her face as she swung in her cradleboard from a branch or leaned against the lodge while her mother scraped the hides. With the long spear of grass he used for playing he tickled the corners of her sober little mouth until she awoke and laughed, learning to look around for him with her round black eyes before she could make words. She had been one of the little girls in the ceremony when he was given the name of His Horse Looking, which no one used, although it was done with the parading through the village, the feasting, and the horses given away. Then there was the time he threw plums at the girl, his sister and brother teasing him about this, making him so warm and happy in his blanket. Since then he had been much away from the Oglalas, and often when he was home the Bad Face village of her people was not camped near. But the last year the girl had grown tall and was much alone. When the people were close together Curly sometimes loafed along the water path to walk a little with her, but the old woman of her lodge always chased him with such loud shouting and abuse that he ran, laughing much and pretending to be afraid. But sometimes it seemed the soft eyes of the girl sought him out, even in the daylight circle, where many were ready to see.

Now the old camp crier was running through the village announcing that the niece of Red Cloud had become a woman and that all the people were invited to visit her father's lodge. There was much excitement, much dressing up by the young men, much noisy moving down towards the lodge, for there would be feasting and ponies given away and a fine first woman-dress to see.

When Curly worked up through the crowd of men, women, and children, he found that the whole front of the lodge had been thrown open and behind the coals of ash wood, on a pile of robes, was Black Buffalo Woman. She was sitting in the woman's way, her feet to one side, and her hair smooth and shining, the part vermilioned, her slender young face too. Her dress was of white buckskin with a deep beaded yoke of blue, the wing sleeves and the bottom fringed, the leggings beaded too, and the moccasins. On her breast hung many strings of beads, blue, red, and yellow, and on her arms were bracelets of copper and silver. Beside the girl stood an old man of the village, shouting advice in a voice loud enough for all to hear, earning the good pony he would receive for his work. He spoke first of her duty to her father and her brothers, to honor them by bringing a strong man into their family and giving them good sons, to hear them in all things.

"A Bad Face is speaking," some of the women of the other bands whispered, laughing a little among themselves, remembering the troubles of the son of Smoke. But the old man had words for the other things, too, the old, old things that make a good Lakota woman—diligence, modesty, virtue, and the mother heart for the people.

"Follow Mother Earth in all things," he counseled. "See how she feeds her children, clothes and shelters them, comforts them with her good silence when their hearts have fallen down. Be like Mother Earth in all things and so be a good woman of the Lakota!"

Hou! the people agreed, while the girl sat with lowered eyes. Once she looked up and, seeing young Curly so near, her cheeks turned ruddy under the vermilion as she dropped her head.

When the talk was done and the people crowded around her to see the fine new clothes, the young men passing before her in their best regalia, Curly pushed his way out, not waiting for the feasting. At the lodge he threw himself upon his bed, buried his face in the wolfskin that was his pillow, and thought of things that filled his breast hard with strength and greatness.

The next day Curly and Crazy Horse rode off into the hills for a smoke. There he told his father of the white buffalo and the way that it was lost. A long time the holy man of the Oglalas sat silent.

"It seems there are many sacred things happening to you, my son," the father said. "It is hard to tell what they will bring, but it seems they will be good things if you work alone like the buffalo you saw and do not try to carry anything back for yourself."

The next day Hump led a party out to raid a small tribe of Indians said to be relatives of the Snakes, but speaking a changed tongue. The Oglalas knew little of them, for they had seldom camped as far west as the Wind River country but the scouts said they lived in grass houses, so they would not be a fighting people like lodge Indians, and they had some very good horses. The warriors were hot to try their hearts against these strangers.

But the people of the unknown tongue evidently had scouts out and long before the Lakota party reached their houses their warriors started shooting from the top of a hill. It was a good fighting place they had selected, high up, covered with big rocks, and there seemed to be many guns among them. Hump and his warriors circled the place several times, whooping, shooting under the necks of their horses, but it seemed these people had seen such fighting before and did not waste much powder on running horses so far away. Then Hump led his warriors in a crawling up the hillside, but there was little to hide behind and some good men might be lost before they got into bow range, so they gave that up too, and tried charging a few times and more circling, still hoping to waste all the enemy powder.

It was a hard two-hour fight, the Lakotas losing some of their horses and getting a man hurt. They killed one or two men but couldn't drive the others from the rocks. Finally Curly's horse went down, and as he jumped from it, he remembered his vision and, catching a loose one of the enemy, he got on and was waiting for another circling when somebody behind him fired a shot. The horse was young and wild and it charged straight ahead, up the hill into the enemy. As in his vision he rode light and safe through the arrows and bullets that flew all around him making a wind past his bare breast, hitting stones and spurting up gravel. Flat against his horse he managed to draw his bow and drive an arrow into a warrior rising with a gun from a gully before him. The man fell back, the horse jumped him, and shying sideways from another one, swung off down the hill. There was a great whooping over this strong medicine from the Oglalas. Hump rode out to meet the boy, but before the warrior reached him, Curly had turned the horse and charged up the hill into the wall of shooting again. Once more he got a man, this time with the revolver from his belt, dropping him lower down in the gully, and as the whoop of approval went up from the Lakotas, Curly's heart swelled. Forgetting all his vision, he slipped off to take the scalp, and the other man's too, in full sight of the enemy. Just as he ripped up the second lock he was hit in the leg, the wild horse jerked loose, and so he had to flee down the hill afoot, jumping this way and that, the ground and the bushes on both sides cut by the flying lead.

The Oglala warriors were in a half circle watching this thing—those with guns firing at the enemies who looked from behind their rocks at the boy getting away through all their shooting.

Only when the boy was back among the others did he remember about the hair he held in his hand. He should not have taken it, and because he did he was wounded. So he threw it away and sat down behind a rock to stop the bleeding. Hump looped the scalps under his belt, cut the iron arrow from the boy's leg, and tied it tightly with a fresh piece of skin from a dead horse. It was enough for today, the warriors said, and leaving the enemies in the rocks they started home.

Outside of the village the party stopped and sent a man ahead to announce their return. Then they came in, the two shield men leading, their spears bright in the sun. Behind them came the warriors in rows four abreast, their weapons in their hands, the war-bonnet men in their feathers. And in the back was the boy the village knew as Curly, without paint or feathers, only a red-backed hawk in his hair and the small brown stone half hidden behind his ear.

That night there was a big victory dance, for they had killed four, counted eight first coups, got some good horses, and lost no man at all. One after another the deeds were told, the people cheering each man for what he had done. Only Curly would not tell of his exploits. Twice he was pushed forward into the circle and each time he backed out. So they went on to dance the scalps, the mother of Curly, the only woman with two on her staff, leading them. Many eyes were on the boy, seventeen now but still small among the warriors, many eyes that were friendly—Hump's and his father's proud, his brother's excited and adoring, and those of Black Buffalo Woman soft and no longer so shy. But there were some eyes that were envious of this light-haired one and these, too, young Curly could not forget.

That night the boy did not sleep. His leg pained very little in its wet bandage of herbs that his father had cooked in a stone bowl in the old way, touching no iron or other metal, but there were so many things to think about, particularly his forgetting about the scalps. What good was a strong vision to a man if he forgot it in the first fight?

The next morning he still felt bad and so he lay still on his side of the lodge, so still that even his brother thought him sleeping. As his people got up they went out quietly, and finally young Curly slept. When the sun stood almost straight up, he awoke and was given a horn spoon of soup. Then Crazy Horse came in and took his ceremonial blanket from its case, the one with the beaded band across the middle showing all the sacred things of his holy vision. With this blanket about him, his braids long and fur-wrapped on his breast, the father walked slowly through the village, making a song as he went, singing it so all might hear:

> *My son has been against the people of unknown tongue.*
> *He has done a brave thing;*
> *For this I give him a new name, the name of his father,*
> *and of many fathers before him—*
> *I give him a great name*
> *I call him Crazy Horse.*

And behind the father came all those of the village who wished to honor the young man among them who had done a brave deed. By the time they came to the lodge where the boy sat, there was a mighty double line of the people until it seemed that everybody was walking in it: young men, old men, great men, wise ones, and all the women and the children too, all singing and laughing.

Then there was feasting and dancing all that day and late into the night, for among the Oglalas there was a new warrior, a warrior to be known by the great name of Crazy Horse.

BOOK TWO

The Glorious Warrior

FAT TIMES *for the People*

FOUR winters had passed since the Oglalas left the soldier fort on the Laramie and its Holy Road worn to dust by the wheels of the moving whites. They were good years, with a new strength running through them, the strength of fat hump ribs roasted over the coals and war whoops echoing free in the country of the Snake and the Crow. When the agent, Major Twiss, first came, he had tried to turn the soldiers from the camp of the Brules on the Blue Water, and later he stood beside Man Afraid and the others as the one called Squaw-Killer Harney brought in the walking herd of captured women and children, sorrowful, sick and hurt from the fighting; he heard the White Beard talk loud over the head-men of the Lakotas, and saw the biggest among them sink his face deeper into the blanket and hold his silence. But soon there had been dark words enough against both the soldier chiefs and the Indians who would sell their people for the white man's favor. Stabber, the one who had driven out Conquering Bear's family, could not live among the people any more, and a man who was only a warrior jerked his breechcloth before the Brule in council, waving his nakedness in the Stabber's face with both Indians and whites there to see.

But now the northern Oglalas were away from the soldier chiefs and all the big-talking. The agent had really become their father, one of their people; the high-piled trader wagons stood in the villages, and the Crows were being thrown back from the fat buffalo ranges of the upper Powder River towards the Yellowstone, war parties always out against them, keeping them moving, giving them no peace for making the meat and robes. But some good Lakotas were lost too, like Big Crow, who got his name from a brave thing done against them long before, and when the year of mourning was done, his father, Black Shield, led eighty lodges of Lakotas deep into Crow country and wiped out an entire party. Young Crazy Horse brought back a medicine lance and a good bay war horse but what he liked most was the way Black Shield carried the pipe. Although avenging a favorite son, he joked, told stories, and sang songs to keep the warriors encouraged on the long trail. And when they came back they had guns, horses, fine bead and quill-worked ceremonial shirts, war bonnets, even the medicine man's wooden bowl and his badger bundle.

"A bad day for the medicine of the Crows," some said.

Hou! the others agreed, with their warriors scattered like poisoned wolves on the prairie, and none to tell their people how they fell, no one to do as much for their bones as is done for the skull of the buffalo, the eye holes turned towards the sun.

Through all the telling of the fight young Crazy Horse sat back in the shadows and felt good for the things that had been done in the way that his father might have, or others who had given up their warrior places. Maybe he should be more like the other young men, all hungry for honors to win higher places in their *akicita,* to get wives. Coups, particularly the good ones of enemies touched before shooting, Crazy Horse had, but the horses he usually gave away, never keeping more than two good hunters and two or three for war. It was true he could use those of his father, now called Worm, and those of Long Face, his uncle, but their herds were never large, with so many from the woman's camp at Laramie coming north after the soldiers left them without even a travois horse to pull the patched old skins they used for shelter.

The young warrior knew there were some who thought he should be getting more of the things that make a man big in the villages, particularly with the Bad Faces, the people of Black Buffalo Woman. Already his mother and others were telling him that there was one who often went right past the young warriors into the lodge of the girl's people. It angered those waiting, but he was a man of many horses and honored connections—the brother of Black Twin and a relative of old Smoke. One like No Water could not be thrown into the ice-trapped current of a winter stream as a common warrior might be if he would not wait.

But it seemed that Black Buffalo Woman kept her young face turned from No Water, and that her father and her brothers were in no hurry to send her from their lodge. So when the camps were close, Crazy Horse still went to watch the pretty girl in the dances, to walk past when she worked with the women at the robes or sat in a game of the plum stones with some friends—not playing noisily, as the women did, but as was becoming in maidens of good Oglala family. A time or two he had been in the hand game in the big lodge of her father. There he heard her laugh clear and free in the excitement of guessing the hands, and then drop her face when she recalled herself. A few times Crazy Horse had a moment with her in the circle of his blanket, not saying much, perhaps asking if her brother was back from the Brules and receiving only a soft "no" spoken so low he could scarcely hear it. Mostly it was just having her close, the smell of the sweet-grass on her dress, feeling her shy, quick breathing inside the dark folds of the blanket he held about them with his bow arm.

Yes, he must work for horses, too, and honors, all the honors his medicine allowed, even if they were the quiet, hard things that made no showing.

With several Oglala villages near the country of the Snakes, a few small raiding parties went against them. Then, late in the Moon of Making Fat, June, the scouts came flying in to say they had found a big hunting camp on the Sweetwater—Washakie and all his people, with several whites along, killing buffalo. The Lakotas started out right away, with only a small party because so many were hunting or at the trader houses, but getting a few young men from the Blue Clouds and Cheyennes. Young Crazy Horse, visiting with the Cheyennes, went along. The mixed crowd of warriors, anxious to get ahead of each other, gave the *akicita* hard work to keep them hidden in the breaks until the scouts returned to say the village was still there, the horses in close, with few watchers, perhaps because the whites were along. So they ate of the *wasna* to save making a fire smell, slept a little, and then when the night thinned in the east, moved out against the Snakes.

The morning sun coming up over the village on the Sweetwater glanced bright along the spears of the line of advancing Lakota warriors. The lodges were still night-closed but some old women out to start the early cooking fires saw the enemy and ran through the camp crying: "The Sioux! The Sioux are upon us!"

But the warriors charged on past the village to the grazing horses and with whoops and waving blankets cut off four hundred before much shooting from the awakening Snakes could reach them. While the raiders pointed the running herd towards the ridge and the Lakota country far beyond, Crazy Horse and seven or eight others dropped behind rocks and trees, to hold the Snakes off as long as they could, slowly falling back before the increasing boom and powder smoke. Several times the young Lakota charged them, always jumping from his horse to shoot. The man beside him was hit, but his knees under the war rope held him on out of range. A Cheyenne who lost his horse caught another and got away before the Snakes brought him down. Then the herd was out of sight over the ridge and they could follow, leaving the camp in the valley below them swarming like an opened ant hill, the warriors running to get ready for the chase, the women keening for their fallen men.

Soon Crazy Horse and the other watchers saw small puffs of dust start after them, stringing out along the trail, the Snakes not keeping together, each one coming as fast as his horse could go. The big herd slowed up the raiders and a few miles out a lone warrior caught up with the eight men behind. Instead of running from so many he whipped straight on, and as the warriors closed in he drew two revolvers and killed an Oglala with each before

their lances met and he went down. The first man off to strike
him saw that it was the son of Washakie, head chief of the Snakes.
He had died well.

Yes, a brave young man, and a good scalp for the dancing, with
more Snakes sure to follow, hot for revenge.

It was true that more came, the old chief himself leading what
looked like the whole Snake nation, making a three-hour running
fight. Several times they caught up with the tiring herd and once
they cut in from the side and recaptured some of their horses, but
along in the afternoon the raiders reached a thick grove of the
rustling trees on the Little Beaver. Here the Snakes charged several
times but they couldn't do much except show off and dare the
enemy to come out. A Cheyenne went first, but a cross-fire of good
guns dropped his horse. Another bullet cut the string of his breechcloth and so he came bounding back like a long-tailed antelope,
holding the loose strip of red cloth up in front, the other end flapping along behind. It was very funny, but a finger's length closer
and they would have been dragging him in to save the scalp from
the enemy.

Others charged out to hold the Snakes beyond gun range, but it
was young Crazy Horse who did the unusual, the foolish thing, as
the older men shouted to him in anger: "Come back!—It is bad
medicine!"

But he had to go on because out there in a buffalo wallow was
a wounded horse. It had made a noise like a keening woman when
it was hit, and then kept kicking and trying to get up. When the
Snakes saw the young Oglala charge out afoot, they seemed to
think he was going to stay in the hole to pick off their circling and
charging warriors. So they began to crawl up on him, the other
Lakotas calling out more warnings. But it took only one swing with
the war club to finish the horse and then he started back, running
in a zigzag way, like the lightning's trail, bullets hitting all around
him. A Snake warrior on a fine sorrel was circling the trees on a
run, close in, very brave, clinging by a foot to the far side of the
horse, aiming his gun over the back and not seeing the Oglala

behind him. A swing of the war club dropped him, and grabbing the sliding war rope and the gun, Crazy Horse was on the sweat-slippery sorrel and headed hard for the trees, leaving the scalp for another to take. He hadn't even drawn his revolver.

"Your medicine is strong today," an old warrior told him, "but it should be used for bigger things than killing a crippled horse."

Silently Crazy Horse took his place among the fighting, and when a cloud came up to darken the moon they all slipped away. There was mourning in the villages, with three Lakotas lost and one each from the Chevennes and the Blue Clouds, but there were many fine horses and the scalps for the victory dance, including the hair from the head of a chief's son.

When another moon stood in the evening west, thin as a drawn bow, two whites from the Snakes stopped with the Bad Faces on their way to Richard. They told that Washakie had been impatient with his oldest son, a war chief, the day of the fight because he was waiting for a few good men to gather instead of rushing out to meet the raiding Lakotas as soon as they charged.

"What is this son I have fathered," he roared out, "that I find him hanging around the lodges while others are fighting off the raiders? Even I, the old-man chief, have killed one!"

The words were so loud and strong that the son, shamed before all the people, whipped his horse out alone into the dust of the fresh trail. The old chief tried to call him back, rode hard after him, in time to see the spears of the Lakotas cut him down.

Ahh-h, some of the older men said, making a pitying sound among themselves. So they sent word to Washakie with the whites that the scalp had been red-painted in the honor color and was being saved for him. It was hard to lose a son so.

Crazy Horse heard the story of the young war chief told in his father's lodge, Worm saying that he did not think it good to try to heat the blood of youth with shaming words. "It inflames the proud and the brave like red coals thrown into the grass of fall; the coward it leaves cold as the wet stone."

But Worm was thinking more of his own son, wondering why he had not waited in the Bad Face camp for the dancing, or at least a little visiting. It might be his dislike for the mourning, the noise of the victory dance, or perhaps, in his strange way, it was because he had done nothing he wanted told before Black Buffalo Woman, he, with more honors in his eighteenth winter than most men carry to the death scaffold. Besides, there was the new gun and the sorrel war horse he brought in. These must be from the Snakes.

Another thought kept rising in the breast of the father, one not new to him: perhaps through some sacred sign that he had not told it seemed to the son he must remain without a wife. Worm was not certain that he could see this as a wise thing, and yet Roman Nose, the great Cheyenne warrior, was said to have his power from a vow to take no woman.

Or perhaps it was again as with his son's vision—a waiting overlong to speak.

Stories of the fighting, of scalps and coups and horses counted, drew many young men from the camps of the Bear Oglalas, the Brules, and even from the Loafers to the northern villages, until they were over three hundred lodges, seven or eight people in each, and many visiting warriors sleeping in wickiups, ready for the warpath.

From these visitors they heard that the southern traders were saying the white-haired agent turned the face of the Great Father from the war made on the Crows, afraid the northern Oglalas would lose their goods and the agent would get none of them. Deon, who had been long with the Indians, said that the southern traders were angry because the agent had reported that they were trapping robes with the whisky cup, even using blackened tallow hardened in the bottom of the second and third one to shorten the measure.

Anyway, it was plain to the Loafers that these people up here were richer than any other, the parfleches bursting with meat, the hills dark as burnt land with their horses, the camps full of white-man goods. And to those from the southern camps the new, bright-painted lodges, the many good bows and guns, the fine blankets, and the stacks of beadwork in almost every lodge spoke even more of good living. Truly, the man who follows the buffalo eats well if he eats, while he who chases the whites is like the one who chases the rabbit: even when he eats he is hungry.

Yes, the northern Oglalas were living fat, and if the Great Father cut off their annuities that were to pay them for keeping the peace, the warriors would take what they wanted from the long rows of wagons passing on the Holy Road.

But while all this talking was going on, it was said another Great Father had been made. No, the old one was not dead, nor was there a fight among the white men. They just wanted a new one. This sounded strange to Crazy Horse and the other young warriors, but not to Worm or his brother Long Face, wearing the silver medal given out forty years ago by still another Great Father. Since then there had been many. The whites were very changeable.

Yes, and the new Father did not like their agent, so he had sent another man, one the Lakotas did not know, who wouldn't come above Laramie. But their old friend Major Twiss stayed. He brought his Oglala wife and children to the Powder River and lived among the people in quiet honor. It was funny to remember now that when he first came to the Lakotas he talked of settling them on reservations and teaching them to grow corn, to dig up the earth.

Dig up the earth! The Oglalas pulled the fat, juicy meat from the roasted ribs with their teeth and laughed.

So came the winter of Plenty Buffaloes, the one the whites called 1861, the year that saw the Holy Road dark with moving men, many going to the places of the yellow metal, many running away to the mountain diggings to keep out of the war parties the whites seemed to be raising against each other. But there was something really new and strange along the Holy Road that year, the talking wires. The Indians had seen the tall poles put up, with the wires strung along the tops, and heard the singing that was in them. At first they whipped their horses along underneath, trying to get ahead of the good sound, and when it was always there, they cut down a few poles with their war hatchets to find it. But as soon as they were down there was nothing. The song had died.

The soldier chief was very angry over this. The talking wires and everything about them was very strong medicine and to be left alone, he said. At Deer Creek there was a house with a thing that made a tapping like the red-headed bird that runs up the trees. It was worked by a white man called Collister, small as a boy, but liked by the Oglalas. He even let it be tried, let Man Afraid try the talking wires by asking a question of old Smoke, living down in the woman's camp at Laramie. The Hunkpatila got something good to ask, something only the two chiefs knew: Where did they once find a little cache of trader goods when they were out hunting together? And he was stunned as though struck between the eyes with a war club when the answer came in about an hour: "On the Running Water, at the mouth of Box Butte creek."

"The little man and his wires are indeed powerful medicine," the chief told the others around his fire that evening. He said it good and strong, and a little uneasily too. There was no telling all the magic these white men might know.

Young Crazy Horse sat beyond the shadows and heard his words and wondered if their Brave Man should be with the whites, even these good whites, so much.

When the longest night of the winter was past, Bissonnette came up from Deer Creek to open the season's trade. As usual, one of his men went back to the trading houses often with the packs of robes and brought the extra things that were wanted, more red ribbon for a young wife, or silver dollars to make the hammered disks for the hair of the warriors. Often it was Sitting Bull, the Oglala, wanting the man of the talking wires to send more of the papers with the little black marks, the newspapers, for he was learning to read. He even learned to write his own order with a lead bullet on a strip torn from the edges, saying: "Want the black and white papers" and signed it with a picture of a man's head with a buffalo on his haunches floating above it—the Indian way of writing Sitting Bull.

Many traders, like Bordeaux and Richard, sent their children down the Missouri to the white-man schools. Those who returned sometimes came to the villages to make the counting of robes and goods. They had wonderful stories to tell of that far country and liked to help with the newspapers. It was from these that the Indians knew of the fight between the whites, a big fight, with very many getting killed.

Ahh-h, perhaps that was why most of the soldiers had marched away, Man Afraid and Worm told each other, leaving too few of them along the Holy Road to break the peace again. But the young warriors saw something else—an opportunity for a little raiding like the Snakes and the Utes as soon as spring came, saying it even in a council with Bissonnette, Deon, and Collister there. But this time they had one strong with the wildest young men against them, old Lone Horn, the Minneconjou. It was true that the emigrants and the soldiers came shooting but there were bad Indians too, some who would bring soldiers charging the women and children. The whites were very many, their rifles shot farther than any arrow a man could make, and their wagon guns shook the earth.

"These white friends sitting among us are also of the others, relatives of those you wish to kill!" the chief said.

The warriors listened quietly, not understanding this about the white men. To them the ones here were as different from the soldiers and the emigrants as the Lakotas were different from the enemy Indians. But they listened to the old chief and remembered that there were still plenty of Snakes and Crows to fight.

Yes, these were still good times for the young warrior, with so many horses to get, many coups to count, good times even for one who could not scalp. And between hunts and raidings Crazy

Horse cast bullets for his gun from the lead of the traders, made iron arrowheads for the feathered shafts, tying them with the head set in the same direction as the bowstring notch for the hunting, across it for war, so the arrow would slip easily between the ribs. And in the evenings, when the bands were close enough together, Crazy Horse rode over to the Bad Faces and waited in line with a dozen others at the lodge of Black Buffalo Woman. Always he remembered that first time she stood such a little while inside his blanket. And always it seemed that now he could not let her go.

But there were others waiting, making loud and unmannerly complaint.

"Hoppo! Let us rescue the Lakota captive in the blanket of Crazy Horse," they cried. But none dared charge the young warrior until the time the old woman of the lodge tore the blanket aside. This was very shaming and caused a laughing at the young warrior who took so much time that she would dare to do this. But Crazy Horse came again, quieter, now saying almost nothing at all, the girl content to stay only a little while, so there would be no more shaming.

Soon after this Red Cloud sent word around that he would lead a big party against the Crows. With such a strong man to carry the pipe many wanted to go and Red Cloud picked Black Twin and No Water and their followers from the Bad Faces, and Hump with some Minneconjous and Hunkpatilas. Young Crazy Horse and Little Hawk went along, the older brother leading the sorrel horse he had got from the Snakes, the tail tied up for war with white buckskin, the other leading a fast bay. They made a fine pair, these two, the reckless Little Hawk, his skin smooth, his weasel-wrapped braids smoky brown, a little paint on his face, beads around his neck, and a silver band high on his arm; the slighter, lighter-skinned brother with one feather standing over his long, loose hair, his face unpainted, serious as ever, yet learning to joke a little and to tell stories to shorten the long path to war. But he would never need to do this for his brother; it was well known that Little Hawk's heart was never down.

Worm stood at his lodge looking with pride after his sons as they rode behind their leader through the camp, the women making the trilling as they swung out on the trail, their guns steady across their saddles, the bows and quivers swaying hardly at all at their sides—truly a fine pair of young Lakotas for the girls to see, and lately even Crazy Horse seemed to have eyes for them.

When they met the Bad Faces, there was rejoicing at this help, for Hump brought some good men, including his younger warriors, Young Man Afraid, Lone Bear, and the sons of Worm, one so daring it stopped the heart, the other already a well-known warrior with more coups than many older men of the party, his medicine strong enough to make a good day for everybody. With young Crazy Horse along nobody was afraid of being left wounded or dead to the enemy.

So they sat in a big double circle to smoke and talk and eat a little from the *wasna* bladders and to promise themselves a great fight. But when they were ready to go on, No Water was holding his face with his hand, saying there was a great paining in his tooth. That meant he could not go into the battle, for his medicine was the two fierce teeth of the grizzly, and this was a warning. Everyone knew of the man who went into battle with a bad pain in his hand and got killed because his medicine was the forefoot of the spotted tail, the raccoon.

So No Water took the back trail and the others went on, Red Cloud leading, with his Bad Faces about him. He was a great warrior, usually bringing in more horses than any other, and so the younger men pushed up close to hear what he was saying, the songs he sang, for it would be good to know the ways he used.

Two weeks later the party was back, with coups and scalps and great stories to tell. They had struck a large hunting village of the Crows, killed one of the old-man chiefs, and followed them deep into their own country, the people driven away beyond the Powder and the Tongue and the Little Horn.

But Crazy Horse did not stay in the Bad Face village to be feasted, to be asked about the warriors he killed, the coups he counted, or of the wounded Lakota he and Little Hawk had dragged back to safety. Instead he slipped off into the willows and followed the river out of sight without even a word to Hump or to his brother. At home he buried himself in the sleeping robes, and none was allowed to come near him with food or with questions. His mother and the old woman of the lodge took their moccasin-making to a relative, and Worm went too, crossing a few pieces of brush before the lodge door to show that none was at home there.

So they left the young warrior alone to think about this thing that had been done. It was bad, and almost any other Lakota would have gone out to a hill to sing his sadness and his sorrow to the sky. But Crazy Horse could only bury his face in his wolfskin and remember over and over that while they were away against the Crows, Black Buffalo Woman had married. It was No Water who had done it, he who sneaked back, naming an aching tooth as the cause for his return. He it was who had taken the girl from her lodge.

Crazy Horse had heard it even before they got back to the village, heard it from her cousin who was among those out to meet the returning war party.

"Somebody has been walking under the blanket," Woman's Dress, the one they used to call the Pretty One, said, and while it was nothing that the son of Bad Face had done, Crazy Horse could have killed him for bearing this bad news, could have slit his throat with a knife and warmed his hands in the rush of blood over them.

Now there was the crossed brush of a lodge that is to be left alone at the door of young Crazy Horse, and around the camp many stopped in their work and their playing to talk of what had been managed while their young warrior was away.

"Ahh-h, it is not for wondering," one who had unmarried daughters in the lodge said. "No Water is a coming man, one who will bring power to the family of Black Buffalo Woman."

"Hou!" some agreed. "But she is the niece of Red Cloud and

carries much in her own hand."

"*Phah!* She is truly the niece of Red Cloud, one of the pushing Bad Faces herself, and carrying the itching for power in her palm," old Makes the Lodge said, and went away for wood, leaving the others to look after her broad back.

On one thing the women agreed. This was the meat of one man's making. All had seen that Red Cloud was reaching out to strengthen himself every way he could, slyly, as a tree that sends its roots into the ground that others have kept shaded. He was drawing everybody he could to the people now called Bad Face. Even the lodge of young He Dog was seldom near his friends any more. Of course his mother was the sister of Red Cloud, but his older brother, Bad Heart Bull, long making the picture history of all the Hunkpatilas, seemed to be leaving too.

And how cunningly these things were done! Red Cloud got up a great war party, and when he returned, No Water, brother of Black Twin, a man who was strong in the councils, belonged to him. Now Woman's Dress was loafing in the shade of the Red Cloud lodge on a painted robe in his fine village-man's clothes, loafing at the lodge of a great warrior for all to see just because he was the grandson of old Smoke.

So the women spoke and among the men were some who thought these same things but their words were different. The chief killer was learning to do his work without spilling the blood out on the ground, they said.

But young Crazy Horse knew nothing of the words of the village. He lay on the robes in the lodge of Worm and thought about what had been done, thought about it days long, it seemed, but at last he had to notice that there was no stirring around him, and getting up, he stumbled into the crossed brush at the door and saw what had been done. Tears, strange to the eyes of this Lakota, ran over his lean brown cheeks. It was an unusual thing for a father to leave his lodge like this, a real Lakota thing to do, and he must act like the son of such a man.

Packing bullets and powder into his war sack, he got on his horse and started north, once more going against the Crows. No one ever heard him say what was done, but he came back with another gun, which he gave to Little Hawk, a pair of the far-seeing glasses that the soldier chiefs carried, and two Crow scalps that he threw to the dogs to worry about the camp. After that he went to the hills with the robes for a sweat lodge, and when he came back he slipped into his old place in the village and none seemed to see anything different in him. But No Water kept out of his way and kept Black Buffalo Woman out of the young warrior's way, too.

Then one evening, coming home from a hunt, Crazy Horse found the young wife out alone gathering herbs and the strong-smelling silver sage plant. Seeing him from afar, she threw her blanket over her face, but when the horse had stopped beside her and no words of anger or contempt were made she dropped her blanket.

"I had my duty to my father and brothers," she said slowly, twisting the sage plant in her hands, not looking at the young warrior. "You remember the first thing the old man adviser told at the woman's feast—to hear them in all things—"

Young Crazy Horse remembered another thing too, something the women said that day: "A Bad Face is speaking." But he must make no hurting words about this, not against anybody. "I would have everything good between us," he said. "I have made a vow that it should be so. There can be no anger in my heart, even against myself."

This he said and rode away, leaving the woman standing to look after him. Suddenly she threw everything from her blanket as far as she could, the fragrant plant too, and went home to tell No Water she must have new things from the traders—silver rings for her arms and blue cloth for a dress and many, many elk teeth for its decoration; these things she must have right away.

WHITES *Like Rising Flood Waters*

IT SEEMED that the wild, free times away from the white men were over for the Oglalas. Messengers came to say they must move down to Laramie for their goods and for a talking by the soldier chief, so once more they went to wait for an agent who would come up the Holy Road, sit among them a few days, and then run away with his pay-money like a coyote that has been among the chickens of the whites.

And while the Lakotas waited they saw the dust clouds of many new soldiers going through to the west where the Snakes were raiding the trail and its talking wires, the few warriors in the Oglala camps around Laramie wishing they could be out too. But most of them had stayed north with the Minneconjous, keeping the Crows from their buffalo herds. As always, some of the soldiers came to visit the camps, among them one called Caspar Collins, the son of a soldier chief. He went up north to the warriors, and Crazy Horse and the others liked him, took him on hunts, showed him the game wisdoms and some of those of the Indian, for he asked not to laugh but to know their people. So they told him of the men's ways and of the women's ways and those of the lodge, and many he found good, as that a man never made direct words to his wife's mother, or she to him.

"That might be a good way for the whites too," he said, and the Indians asked why it was not done so, if it seemed better.

136

"You don't know our women!"

"But it is a sign of great respect," they told the young soldier chief, and now he laughed, as a friend.

So it happened that he seemed almost one of their own to the Oglalas, learning much of their speech and the signs before he had to go to the Sweetwater to chase the Snakes. The trouble out there had been used by Holladay to pull his fast-flying mail wagons off the Holy Road all the way through the Lakota country, although the mountain men and others who knew the Indian said both they and the Cheyennes were peaceful, that the stopping was made because Holladay's horses were played out. Hadn't the wagons been dumping newspapers and letters in big sacks and bundles all along the trail for the Indians and the wind? It was true that a few horses turned out loose had been run off by wild young Indians or by the white thieves the Lakotas called the Gray Men. Anyway, the trail was soon open again, but the warriors watching it from the high places had seen this easy stopping of the whites by such little raiding as the Snakes could make. It was a good thing to remember.

There were other things for the Oglalas to remember that year. Bear Ribs, Harney's chief of all the Tetons, had been killed. The treaties had been broken, the Missouri Indians said, and they would have nothing more of the peace paper, not even the goods. The agent talked the old chief into taking a little for his own Hunkpapas, trying to make the others feel jealous and hungry. So the No Bows killed him.

Truly it was not good, this having one's name made big by the whites, the Oglalas said. Their Brave Man had been wise to turn his back on the power laid before him.

There was also a bad story of soldiers going against their far relations, the Santees of Minnesota. Soon some of these people came to the Missouri, proudly showing their camps full of white-man goods and captive women and children. But they had lost all their country; many of their own people were killed or captured, and the soldiers were hard after them. Knowing no difference between the Santees and the Tetons, they were now shooting the Missouri friendlies. The Oglalas were far from this trouble, but they could see that the whites among them knew about it, and that even some long in the Indian country looked about them with a new uneasiness that made much excitement among the wilder young men.

So young Crazy Horse went down to visit with the Loafers as far east as the Bordeaux houses, to smell out the wind in that country himself. More soldiers were coming, the old Frenchman told him, meaning not where the Santees were hiding, or down where the Cheyenne troubles had started again, but here, to the Lakota country.

On the way home he found little bunches of the soldiers already scattered at the stations along the Holy Road, even small places like Deer Creek, where he stopped for a visiting with Two Face and his friendly Oglalas. While Crazy Horse was in the chief's lodge and a trader was making a feast, their little man friend from the talking wires came visiting too. It was cold and Collister wore a cavalry overcoat that he had got from the soldiers because his own was worn out. But when the warriors saw him come among them so, they drew their blankets up to their eyes, giving him no word of greeting. Not noticing this thing, he went to the chief's lodge, but there even the trader refused to see him, looking down instead, his sunburnt cheek suddenly pale as a sick white woman's as Two Face and those about him made the angry sound in their throats and reached for their weapons, the warriors pushing in at the lodge door with guns in their hands.

It seemed that the little man saw now he had done something bad, but he did not try to run away. Instead he stood up very straight before the angry chief—no bigger than a boy, but stood up like a man.

"Hou, *cola!*" he said, loud and strong for all to hear, calling Two Face his friend as though everything were as any other time. It was a brave thing to do and slowly the anger and hatred slipped from the Oglala and he began to laugh a little, answering: "Hou, *cola!*" Motioning the white man around to the back, he took both his hands, making the crossed-arm handshake of respect, first the right one of the chief on top, then the other way.

With this good sign upon him the little man went from the lodge into the waiting warriors. But now they were laughing, too, white teeth shining, ready to visit. Soon the trader came out, and Crazy Horse with him.

"A white man could have been foolishly killed in there today," the trader said. There had been trouble at the little army post just an hour or so ago between an Indian and a soldier. Others joined in, and some Indians were struck with fists and gun butts.

When Crazy Horse went home he spoke of what he had seen to his father, the warriors leaping like fire in a cedar gully against a friend because he came in a soldier coat. Worm did not like such excitement over the things a man puts on. But young Little Hawk laughed to hear the story and made the scalping motions with the knife he was sharpening on his whetstone. Great times were coming, and he would be ready.

Crazy Horse, who had seen the helpless ones of his people scattered over the ground, blown to pieces by the wagon guns, looked down to his feet folded close to him. He had on Cheyenne moccasins, sent him by Yellow Woman, the one who had been left behind on the Blue Water fleeing trail because her time was upon her, with her son dead beside her, a hole in his young breast. Even Spotted Tail's little girl had finally died, although the soldier who found her had been very good.

Yes, the warpath was a fine thing for the young warriors, Crazy Horse thought, but he would try to make it so Little Hawk need never see the women and children lying on the ground like animals butchered in the hunt.

When the last trading was done, the Oglalas spoke more about taking their young men from the Holy Road. The soldiers brought in since the white man's war started in the south were different from those in the country before. Talking like Grattan, the little soldier chief that got killed, they threw away or traded their uniforms as fast as they could and wore fringed buckskin and Spanish spurs; riding Indian ponies they stirred up a big noise about taking scalps and making redskins bite the dust.

"Like the Indians were wolves—" the little man of the talking wires at Deer Creek said. The Indians made the sign of disagreement. To them the wolf was another brother, one who used up the dead things that would poison the air and helped make their old camping grounds clean again.

But plainly these new soldiers were a strange people, even for whites, the Indians said, telling one another the story of a woman at the Deer Creek trading houses. Her baby had died of the little spotted sickness, the measles, and she was sitting on the ground outside rocking it in her blanket, crying over it, as women do. Some of the soldiers passing saw her.

"Well, I be damned," one called out to the others. "Look at that there Sioux squaw a-tryin' to act like she was a white woman—" saying this openly as they did other things, not thinking that there were Indians who knew many of the white man's words.

Ahh-h, these new soldiers were indeed not to be understood, unless it was that they all had no parents, and none to bring them up. They were very foolish too, going out from the fort alone, or in twos and threes, and so it happened that many of those who talked big of getting scalps did not return, and if their bodies were never found who could say that they had not done like many others, deserted and run away to the gold diggings?

The older men saw these things and took the Oglalas away up to the Belle Fourche, to winter camps strung along the sheltered stream. Just before the snows came, five Crows sneaked up and scalped a boy alive. The warriors followed them and got three but the others were lost in a blizzard that came up swift as the snow lightning that flashed in its blowing. Crazy Horse did nothing; his medicine was weak ever since he had gone out for scalps after No Water got Black Buffalo Woman. And taking them hadn't helped, for his heart was still on the ground.

But on the way home he found himself suddenly shut away

from the others, with only whiteness about him and a warmth as if the storm did not touch him. And now he saw that a strange thing was true—no snow came near him. It lasted only a little while and then there was a bolt of the winter lightning, a thundering that was half wind, and the snow whirled over him again, while straight ahead was the blurred rump of the war horse he had been following. But inside he was still warm, his heart good again.

When they reached the camps, Deon was pulling in against the storm to Red Cloud's lodge with five big wagons, and just in time or he would have been snow-fast on the trail by what must be a medicine storm, for not even the weather woman among them had foreseen its coming. But now everybody was in camp, all the warriors and hunters, and the winter traders. Man Afraid had Hank Clifford and Brave Bear Nick Janis, so, with the trading prices already settled, Deon sent the crier around to call the men to Red Cloud's lodge to feast and see his goods.

Crazy Horse didn't go; he was seldom in a Bad Face lodge now. It wasn't because of the woman, who had been like a star seen in water and gone in the wind's first rising, but because there was a new dividing among those Oglalas who had stood with Smoke in the Bull Bear troubles, a slow separating as might come to a herd of wild horses, with the more pushing men going to the Bad Face camps. Instead Crazy Horse was often at the fire of Clifford or Janis, listening to the older men of his people tell stories of the wars and the hunts and the long-ago times, or else he was out in the snow, looking for the breath cloud of a buffalo herd or the tracks of elk. Several times he made the snow-thunder medicine, a secret thing, Worm said, going back to the old, old days, for the thunder was always a strong help of the people, but given to a very few by the winter storms, which were like those of the summer, killing too, with their smothering snows, but bringing all the new life of the spring that was coming.

"Go out, my son, into the snow and you will know what to do, for none can tell you—and none can say what your work will be except that you have had your sign. You belong to the people."

The midwinter thawing brought visitors, a few Santees and Minneconjous from the north and several Cheyennes up from the Smoky Hill. They carried bad word of the soldier plannings for the spring. Crazy Horse heard these things and then went down to the Little Wound and the Spotted Tail people below the South Platte to see how it was for himself. When he came back his father listened and then took him to the lodge of Man Afraid.

There, talking low and quiet as always, he told of the uneasiness of the southern people. In the summer the whites were moving like ants on the Smoky Hill road that went through the middle of their buffalo ranges, and in the season of the robes the hunters came with their big guns, shooting with forked sticks to hold up the barrels, from down wind, until whole herds lay dead. Then they drove stakes through the noses and pulled the hides off with horses, leaving all the meat, even the hump and the tongue, for the wolves.

Ahh-h, he had heard of this thing, Man Afraid said, and it was a bad way to do to their brother, the buffalo.

Yes, and at the soldier towns, young Crazy Horse was told, the dried skins were piled up long as the ridge standing beyond the Belle Fourche, waiting for the freighter wagons to take them away east, where all the good things of the Indian country seemed to go—the beaver, the buffalo, and perhaps the land too, for now the warriors had found out that the old Cheyenne chiefs had signed a paper two winters before giving most of their hunting grounds to the whites. So the smell of hot lead hung strong over the villages down there, and the young men were carrying the pipe around, although the old ones still said the whites were many.

"But if we do not fight we will be dust under their wheels—"

Ahh-h, it was true, and perhaps down there the soldiers would try to make that happen very soon.

The Oglalas heard, too, that the soldier chief at Laramie was trying to get new rifles, the kind the traders called breechloaders, like the ones carried by the hunters coming to carry away big heads with horns.

"Hoye!" the warriors had said when they saw these used. With such a gun one could reload from the running horse. It seemed there was complaining, too, about the soldiers taking Indian wives. Collins, the father of the young Caspar who liked to visit in their villages, was sending orders against this thing to Deer Creek and the other little forts, so once more the women would be carrying their white-man babies to their people.

When the days lengthened into heat, the Oglalas came together for the sundance, and once more there was feasting and visiting with much work for the advisers and the holy men like Worm and Black Elk, helping with the purification of those who had vows to be fulfilled or ordeals to be endured, and with all the preparation for the great ceremonial of the Lakotas that was to strengthen the people and bring them plenty of buffalo and scalps.

Crazy Horse still took no part in this dancing, his breast smooth and unscarred as ever. But he was there and saw Black Buffalo Woman almost every day. Sometimes her young son was in the blanket at her back or in the cradleboard hanging from the tall horn of her woman's saddle. Many watched her pass on her spotted horse that was rubbed to shining, her buckskin dress the whitest, her beaded leggings the finest in the camp. She had grown into a tall, proud-walking woman and now her eyes met the brown ones of Crazy Horse straight and open for all about them to see. Once when there were many around a dancing fire, she teased him that he had still no wife.

"Hou! It is not good that he live the free, easy life always. He must work to pay for the trader things of a woman too," No Water laughed. "Come to my village, we have some good ones there."

Crazy Horse let it pass in silence, but the gayer young Little Hawk took it up, asking the women if they would not have him instead of the silent one. He would make someone a very useful husband.

Ahh-h, so he would, the women agreed, crying it out so strong that the young Lakota moved a little closer to his brother at this open speaking.

When the moon was still bright so those from far could see to
ride home, the sundance crowd scattered. The Oglalas had to go
down to wait on their agent again. But not the young warriors; they
had other plans, with the soldiers themselves so busy. In the
south they chased the Cheyennes, keeping them moving and making even the women angry as grizzlies with wounded cubs. In the
north the soldiers looking for the Santees found the friendly Yanktonais at White Stone Hill and fell upon them. And at Bear River,
beyond the west mountains, they struck the midwinter camp of
Bannocks and Snakes, killing over two hundred, many of them
women and children, leaving only a few to hide out in the snow.
Big Bat, the trader, knew that country and said it was claimed
some people pushing into the Bannock lands had been shot and
so it was done as on the Blue Water, the soldiers saying afterward
that it ought to teach the Indians a lesson.

"Teach the lesson never to let the soldiers get near our women
and children!" young Crazy Horse said in hot anger.

Worm looked up from his long pipe. "My son has a loud voice
in the lodge of his mother," he said quietly. The young warrior
drew back into the shadows, the women making the murmur of
comfort for him across the fire.

But it was true there was soldier trouble on every side of them,
like flood water rising all around an island. Here in their own
country one called Bozeman had driven stakes in a row from above
the Yellowstone down to the Platte, straight as a bullet through
the heart of their hunting grounds. Then he gathered up a big
train of wagons and horsebackers going to the northern gold diggings beyond the Crow country and started them up the old
traders' trail to the Powder River, following the fresh stakes instead
of going by Bridger's road through the Snake lands.

The Indians had let this man go down in peace because he was
alone and seemed to be leaving their country, not understanding
his sticks in the ground. But now smoke signals were sent up against
the sky to call in warriors from the great bands of the Oglalas,
the Minneconjous, and the northern Cheyennes. At Lodgepole

Creek, one hundred and fifty of the white-man miles above the Platte, the Bozeman train awoke one morning surrounded by Lakotas. Out of gunshot, the warriors sat on their horses, motionless as the buttes, and when one had to leave the line another took his place, for there were many hundred waiting and many older men sitting along the ridges, smoking.

Young Crazy Horse saw this and once more he felt strong in his people. There was no hostile move against the whites, just the standing in the way in the daytime, the circle of little fires burning around then in the nights. After almost a week of this, the white women crying, the men shouting their angry words to the wind, two of them started to sneak back towards the Platte. The Indians let them go and got signalings that they had reached the Holy Road and used the talking wires. But now sixty horse soldiers were starting out to take the emigrants through to the Yellowstone, and so the night fire signals called more warriors together. They came from everywhere, riding hard and openly, the puffs of dust they made moving like far whirlwinds over the sun-baked country. Around the corralled whites the ridges darkened with mounted Indians, and many more were hiding along the trail of the soldiers.

Then a Lakota runner came from the forts saying that the soldiers were ordered to bring the whites back to the Platte. Some among the Indians believed this a trick to make the warriors scatter to their camps. When Man Afraid said that honest ears hear only the straight tongue, Red Cloud, Hump, and Big Road made a plan to please everybody.

"Let us believe the soldier chief and withdraw the warriors so he can get to the whites. Let us withdraw them up along the staked trail; then if they try to go on, we will be ready."

So it was done. The soldiers came and took the people back. Bozeman and seven others slipped out on horseback towards the Yellowstone in the night. The Indians let them go; they would not give the soldiers an excuse to stay in their country for eight foolish men.

When the summer hunt was done the Oglalas and some Minne-conjous under Touch the Clouds went against the Crows. They got away with three hundred good horses but the Crows still had enough to follow. Crazy Horse was, as usual, with those protecting the rear, and several times he turned back alone to charge the warriors. The first time they shot his horse, but he landed on his feet, his gun ready with the Crows whooping upon him. He aimed at the one ahead, but not into the place where a man sits, as was good in a running fight, for he wanted the spotted horse that had carried this warrior so fast into the battle. At the crack of the shot the Crow threw up his hands and slid off backward, the war rope uncoiling from his belt. Crazy Horse ran for the trailing end, got it, and in a hail of bullets and arrows was off after his friends. And when he turned back after that, the Crows stopped, afraid of his medicine. But some of them cut in ahead to a place of rocks and picked off five Lakotas before they could be driven out, so when the party reached home eight were missing from them.

In a few days Crazy Horse began to see why the Crow he had shot was so far ahead of all the others. The spotted horse left dust in the face of every other in the Oglala village, even winning a good revolver from No Water when he came down to try to beat the young Oglala's horse with his smoke-blue racer gelding.

Crazy Horse tried not to race, but he had to, and then not to take the revolver, but when some of those standing around said: "Are you the man to let the Bad Face carry everything from you?" saying it in an angry way, he slipped the revolver into his belt and led his horse to his lodge.

Soon there was no more racing, for the snow came early and lay so deep and white none dared to go into the open without the face dark-painted against the sun. And in the Moon of the Tender Grass Coming there was news that trade was to be stopped again with all but the Loafers, although the northern Oglalas had been far from any white-man fighting. Even the trader at Laramie was locked up in the iron house, it was said, and all the arms and am-munition taken from the others.

It seemed the officer called Mitchell was back in the country. He sent for the chiefs of the southern Oglalas and the Brules, but when they came to the Platte he was not there, only a little soldier chief who made the roaring sounds like a gutshot charging grizzly. But his roaring was no more than so much noise in the canyons because they roared too.

"The Smoky Hill trail through our buffalo country must be stopped, the hunters driven out, the soldiers taken away!"

Nothing was done, so they must all come up to Laramie. It was a very far road for the people, yet Spotted Tail and the Cheyennes went. Three times they came to council and nothing was done. But something else was done by the warriors. The young Cheyennes had started raiding the emigrant road, and with a few of the Lakotas they had killed people at Plum creek and taken captives.

In the summer called 1864 the northern Oglalas were far from these troubles, up around Bear Lodge, the Devil's Tower of the whites, but they heard that some Cheyenne people had been killed by the soldiers and that the emigrants were afraid and shooting anybody with a feather in the hair, even the friendlies.

The soldiers were still out in the Missouri country too, and a big party of Minneconjous and Hunkpapas trying to keep away from them came to the Oglala country and went down to see the Holy Road they had heard about. There they found an emigrant train, smoked and ate with the whites, who seemed good people but a little afraid. While they were eating, a messenger came riding in from the north, saying the soldier chief on the Missouri had killed some of their relatives and set their heads up on poles.

That made their hearts very bad and so they shot some of the emigrants, burned some wagons, and taking the goods they wanted and two women [1] and a little girl, they started back north, fast, to help their people.

This troubled young Crazy Horse. More soldiers would surely come now and he didn't like this capturing people. Ever since he was a boy and the emigrant women used to look at him and ask

[1] Mrs. Larimer and Mrs. Fanny Kelly, June 1864.

the white-man word "captive" he had hated it.

Soon more soldiers came, bringing enemies of the Lakotas to fight them, many Pawnees in soldier coats with breechcloth tails hanging below, and so when about thirty of Lone Horn's Minneconjous started down towards Laramie, Crazy Horse went along.

One day the Indians saw a large soldier party come in from a hard scouting and leave their horses on the sandy parade ground of the fort, to roll awhile. It was a quiet, hot day, the sun straight up, most of the whites in the buildings and the watching ones standing in the shady places. So with Crazy Horse and several others who had known the fort as boys leading the charge, the Lakotas raced down on the post and through it, waving buffalo robes, firing guns into the air. Almost before a shot could be returned, every horse was stampeded and headed away towards the north in a great whirl of whoopings, dust, and pounding feet.

It was over an hour before the scouts left behind saw the soldiers start after the horses and then they took a wagon gun that had to be sent back because it couldn't keep up. All afternoon and night the Indians whipped northward, holding the herd close together, the soldiers coming fast too, but never catching up. By the second night the Indians were in their own country, so they scattered, knowing that the soldiers, afraid of ambushing, wouldn't break up to follow. Now and then a scout on a high place lifted a few arrows to drop among them, to keep them reminded. At last they turned around, going back much faster than they came out.

In the Moon of the Cherries Blackening, August, their old white-haired agent, Major Twiss, stopped at Man Afraid's lodge on his way home from the soldier fort on the Laramie. He had his women and children along, all in new clothes, looking fine. He said he had talked of the white man's war in the south and the soldier chiefs had looked at him in astonishment that he understood these things —thinking him an Indian from his dress and his sunburnt face. The old man laughed hard to remember it, wondering what they made of his beard.

He laughed, too, over these new soldiers who had taken women from the Lakotas, for the old-time presents to the fathers. But it seemed the girls were not the old-time daughters. Some wouldn't go as wives to these wandering whites, and others did not find it to their liking. One Oglala father saw how it was and took his daughter to the northern camp—the soldier's gift horse too. Another girl scratched and fought her man so he let her get away, right out of his quarters, and had to stand much laughing. He went to complain to the interpreter.

"There she sits on the floor, that goddamn blanket over her head and pulling away when I tried to touch her," he said. "So finally I jerked the blasted blanket off and then she scratched and bit like a goddamn wild cat—"

The Indians made the low, laughing noises in their chests at these white men who could not give a maiden a little time. Man Afraid laughed too, recalling a trick he had played on his elder wife. He took her right off on a little hunt and by the second day she was so lonesome away from her noisy home lodge that she followed his tracks to the beaver traps, standing before him with her face uncovered, but her eyes down in shame.

At this there was a mumbled protest, not loud even now, so as not to shame her man before her friends, but a mild complaining against the telling.

"Did I say she was not modest?" the chief asked the others. "You know how she keeps herself back, not like some whose scolding voices are heard through all the village, even in the blizzard's roaring."

Hou! the others agreed. There was the wife of Bad Face, nor was the wife of Red Cloud silent as the winter mole. It was true that many a man planted his moccasin firm and long on the warpath because there was no peace in his lodge.

But it was not only the young women who did not like this marrying with the soldiers, Major Twiss said. It seemed that the soldier chief was making it hard too, letting no more goods be carried out to the woman's camp, so it was almost deserted.

It was as well, for these young men of the whites who knew only the killing were no fit fathers for a great people.

With all this trouble around them, most of the Oglalas were still peaceful by the time the Indian scares of the summer were past and the emigrant trails opened again. They even let a wagon train of people go up over the Powder River road, where they had turned Bozeman back. But things were not good in the country to the north of them. Man Afraid came back from there with word of much fighting, the soldiers chasing everybody and the warriors rising hot. A big train was surrounded a long time east of the Little Missouri. They had a wagon gun and made a fort of earth but had to go back anyway because the Indians were very angry. The whites had left a box of hard bread on the trail with wolf poison in it, and many had died of the cramping pains.

Man Afraid had gone to get the captive called Mrs. Kelly that the Minneconjous and Hunkpapas had carried north from the Holy Road in the summer. But the whites at the northern forts wanted her turned in somewhere up there because those forts were much nearer, and the trading places of her captors. From what he heard and saw of her, it seemed that the women of the whites were indeed weak and foolish, and the Indians who wanted them seemed even more foolish.

"Perhaps they are not all like that one," his wife was moved to say.

"I can hope for my friends, the whites, that your words are true."

But suddenly now there was news so bad that all the old things were forgotten: a big trouble in the south, where it had been hanging like prairie smoke for a long time. There had been three great peace men among the southern Cheyennes. One was shot last spring while shaking hands with a soldier chief. The other two, Black Kettle and White Antelope, tried hard to forget and keep the peace, but every time they got their young men quiet the soldiers came to shoot some more women and children. Finally, in the fall hunting time, the two chiefs slipped away with their friendly Cheyennes and Blue Clouds to the place their agent marked on the ground for them, a place called Sand Creek. There the soldiers found them.

First the Oglalas heard only of all the people killed and then they heard the names of many they knew, and of the shameful things done—men, even old ones, with their man parts cut off, women scalped in a private place and the scalps showed around in the whisky houses of the white man's town called Denver, others cut open and the babies they carried laid out beside them. Among them was Yellow Woman.

Crazy Horse heard these things told and they made a firing in his breast. All the peace things done in the ten years since Conquering Bear was killed, the treaty papers, the moving away from the whites, everything, had come to this end. And when the runners were done speaking, the young Oglala went out alone into the cold hills of winter and walked by himself. Once he saw the spotted eagle soar over him and then swoop low, yet there was nothing, only one broken feather drifting down.

But today they needed no sign to show what must be done, with the things so plain before the eyes. At Fort Laramie old Smoke, so long for the crackers-and-molasses peace of the whites, lay in his blanket on the death scaffold. And from the south people, Cheyenne and Lakota, all of Spotted Tail's Brules and the Bear Oglalas too were coming towards them for help, not as dogs whipped from the meat racks but as men angered at last beyond all talking, coming burning and killing along the way. So now it was war for them all, a war to the end. Down there in the camp below the hill where Crazy Horse stood were many helpless ones who might fall on the ground before it was done, and off down the river a ways lived No Water with Black Buffalo Woman and a new son on her back, and this one too was not the son of Crazy Horse.

But today he was a Lakota warrior, one among so many that they stood like a forest, as he had seen them at the council up at Bear Butte. Truly their number was great and their hearts were strong.

Let the soldiers come.

The BIG YEAR

NOW there was a great thing happening, such as no man had ever seen, but the Indians of the north knew it was true, for the runners brought the news, and a runner who does not carry the straight word will fall as a horse that is worn out, and his bones will be left to whiten on the prairie.

So the truth-bearers came with the word that the southern people were moving up towards the Powder River—all the people, the Cheyennes, the Blue Clouds, and all the southern Lakotas. Even the long-time peace chiefs, like Black Kettle, were coming north, and at the head of the great camp moved the councilors carrying the pipe of war.

Ahh-h, now there would truly be blood in every track!

Every day they watched the big village come nearer, moving up from stream to stream as though climbing the branches of a great tree. At the head were the Lakotas, honored guests because they had been the first to accept the pipe, leading the nine hundred lodges, the six thousand people, through the cold time of January, the Moon of Frosting in the Lodge. There were whites along too, and the Bents and other traders' sons, for now it seemed that their place was surely with the people of their women.

The first big attack these Indians ever made on the whites was by a thousand picked warriors sent against the soldiers near the place called Julesburg [1] after the trader they used to know there.

[1] January 7, 1865.

The war party moved out in the old, old way with its pipe-bearers, scouts, and the marching *akicita* to keep the wild young warriors quiet, just as the Lakotas once went against the Rees and Hohes and Mandans, and even against the Chippewas back in the walking days, when there were few horses, and dogs pulled the travois.

At the little stockade place the decoys drew the soldiers out and towards the ambush in the hills. But the young men could not wait until they were close enough for arrows or their poor guns. Charging out, they spoiled a good surround and got only fourteen of the soldiers and four other whites with them, instead of all. Afterward while the Indians broke into the warehouses at the station and loaded their pack horses so they could hardly move, some of the younger warriors galloped out across the prairie unrolling bolts of red cloth to blow far behind them in the wind, drove off big herds of stock, or threw their ropes up over the talking wires and, whipping their ponies away, dragged the wire and the singing poles behind them. But no more soldiers came out of the stockade to fight.

When the northern chiefs heard of the surround spoiled, they made a complaining over their pipes. The young men of today knew only of raiding for horses and scalps and coups for themselves, nothing of fighting for the people. And behind the headmen the warriors looked down, for the arrow of blame sent against those of the south struck them too.

It seemed now that the Indians had been almost peaceful at first, the anger over the killing at Sand Creek hidden under the mourning blankets. The whites among them said that the attack had not been by soldiers like those they knew in the forts but by short-time ones, soldiers who stirred up Indian troubles so they need not go away to the big fight, the Civil War. But the warriors caught some of these soldiers on the emigrant trail and in their goods they found scalps taken at Sand Creek, and some of the private things too, and so they chopped the soldiers up with their war hatchets. All that night there was a new keening among them and the next day the big killing began.

Now it was war against every white they found and so Black

Kettle, still a peace chief, turned back south with what was left of his band. The rest struck through the Platte country like three great spears, the Cheyennes pointing northwest, the Lakotas northeast, the Blue Clouds between. Killing, scalping, burning, they swept over the ranches, the stage stations, and the Holy Road, the soldiers running back to their forts or hiding in a circle under the mouths of their wagon guns until they could get away. Every night the victory drums throbbed in the great camp and the light of the dance fires stood red as burning prairie against the sky. At the Platte River the Indians moved across the sanded trail on the ice, followed by the big herds of horses and cattle they had picked up, so much that they took only the best, leaving the poor and the wild behind.

Young Crazy Horse saw this thing. He went down with several others related to the southern people to help bring them to the north in the good way and found that Worm had spoken true about Spotted Tail. Now that the Brule's white-man fat was really gone the warriors once more followed upon the heel fringe of his moccasin. Crazy Horse rode with them in the second attack on Julesburg, helped load the pack horses and saw the houses and haystacks left burning, sending up smoke clouds great as the thunderers make for themselves in the summer.

In March, the Moon of Snowblindness, they reached the Oglalas on the Powder. Then there was the offering of the war pipe and the feast of welcome, with a big showing of the things they had brought —not everything, some said, not the captive or two kept hidden in the Cheyenne lodges because the northern Indians seemed not to like them. It was these Cheyennes who once asked the peace men of the Great Father for some white women along with their coffee and flour promised in the treaty.

As soon as the first visiting was done the great camp scattered into smaller circles down along the river, the young men building log corrals to keep the good horses close at night, the wild stock and the pack animals sent out with herders to watch against the Crows, who would remember that a village is often careless in its bigness.

The raiders did come several times and were followed, the Cheyennes getting four that they chased into a hole and then smoked out.

"Like the skunk, or the winter bear!" they said, laughing as they told of it.

The great camp spreading so far along the river was truly fine and brought a rush of spring power to the young warriors, to all the people, many riding from circle to circle just to see it, to feel its number. Crazy Horse was often with his Brule relations and with the Cheyennes too, now that the little sister of Yellow Woman had grown tall as the young rustling tree, with many moccasin tracks outside her father's lodge, and many offerings of strange horses tied there, to stand unaccepted. The girl had been hit in the face at the Sand Creek fight, the scar a small dent like the tip of a finger pressed into her round cheek, deepening when she laughed. The young men liked it, called her Pretty Valley, and made a long waiting line for her, but if Crazy Horse was among them she had no eyes for the others.

"He gave our sister back to us once," she told them, not laughing now. "He must be first."

So it happened that she often stood in the blanket of the young Lakota. Crazy Horse even got so he went to watch her in the dances and loafed around the family lodge as he had eight years ago, down on the Solomon. Many saw this, the older people saying it was time the light-haired one took a wife; it is not good for a man's feet to be as free for roaming as the winter wolf's. But why not an Oglala woman, or at least a Lakota?

To the light-haired one this talking was no more than the wind over the buckbrush. It was true he was often with the Cheyennes, perhaps the relatives of Little Big Man and Black Twin or in the lodge of Pretty Valley, the girl a good friend, one with whom a silent man could walk across the village circle, sit at a lodge fire, or stand in the dark of the blanket in a moment of kinship. But he found no desire for her as a woman.

"The bad things done by the soldiers—they geld the good man so

long as the remembrance lays cold in his heart—" a Cheyenne medicine man told him one evening, seeing how it was.

Perhaps that was true, for not even the eyes of Black Buffalo
Woman brought a rising fullness to him now.

Close as the herders watched, there was still news of Crow
horse-thieving. The Black Twin family lost some of their best
hunters and racers and were getting up a revenge party, with
He Dog and Crazy Horse asked to go along. There would be a
feasting at No Water's lodge the day before they started, all done
in good heart, and so the young Oglalas went.

When Crazy Horse got back from the Crow country the camps
had scattered for early grass; the Cheyennes moved two sleeps off
and with them the sister of Yellow Woman. But it did not matter,
for in the lodge of No Water the young Oglala had heard Black
Buffalo Woman sing a little sleeping song to her two children. He
had seen the red glow of the fire on her face, saw her straight-
looking eyes as she put the spoon of the big-horn sheep into his
hand. She need not have bent over the kettle at all, but she took up
the duties of the old woman of the lodge as a compliment to the
guests, to make them welcome. It was good that she did this,
No Water said, for the spotted horse she rode in the woman's line
at the ceremonials, the finest woman's horse among the Bad Faces,
had been taken by the Crows.

They didn't get the stolen herd back, but after that Crazy Horse
often visited in the No Water camp. Chips, the young medicine
man there, a stone dreamer, was working on something for the
protection of his war horses, to keep them from being shot under
him.

Because the Indians knew there would be trouble from the raiding that lay like the wide black path of a prairie fire across the
white man's Holy Road, the Hunkpatilas sent some ears to listen
around Laramie, particularly among Big Mouth's new Indian
police, Loafers with soldier coats over their breechcloths, and with
soldier guns to chase their own people. The spies brought word
that the big war between the whites in the south country was done,

and that the officers around Laramie were talking of pushing the Indians all north of the Missouri and building forts through the country where they now lived, right through the middle of their buffalo ranges.

The young warriors did not wait. Already a few were down at La Prelle Creek, on the Holy Road, shooting at the soldiers. When a big party with the back-loading guns came to chase them, the Indians rode for the breaks and the soldiers went back to Deer Creek. Maybe they were not the ones who wanted to push the Indians across the Missouri.

Early in May, the Moon of Shedding Ponies, the Indians came together on the Tongue for buffalo and for a big council to make the war planning of the summer. There was a shield dance at the camp of the southern Cheyennes with the *akicita* of both tribes helping. They gathered around the great fire in the center of the camp, each society painted and dressed and dancing in its own way, the Foxes making the little trottings, looking slyly from side to side, the Dogs, the Bone-Scrapers, the Crow-Owners, and the others in their own way too, whooping, stamping to the drums, the hawk bells at their ankles jingling.

And afterward the headmen of the societies told them there would be a great attack on the Platte Bridge stockade in mid-summer. Until then no more big parties could go out, for the horses must get strong. Besides, the officer called Moonlight was coming from Laramie with over five hundred horse soldiers and several wagon guns to look for the Cheyennes. The old mountain man Bridger was guiding him, and the Indians better look out.

A scouting party went down, Crazy Horse with them. They saw the long line of riders and wagons start up the Platte in the night-time, so nobody could know, and go west, clear to the Wind River, finding only snow and coming back with the big American horses worn out because they would not follow Bridger's way. So the disappointed warriors did a little raiding before they went home, getting twenty-two horses but losing some good men. Still, it helped scare the whites from the trail, the wagons traveling only in big bunches again, with many soldiers around them.

Then Moonlight did a very bad thing, the stories of it coming thick and noisy as fall blackbirds gathering. The Oglala friendlies, Two Face and Blackfoot had taken a captured woman [1] to Laramie and now they were both hanging outside the fort. They had heard about her among the Cheyennes, traded guns for her, and brought her in as the soldiers always said, and then they were lifted up with chains around their necks. It seemed a strange way to do, although the Loafers admitted that the soldier chief was a bad man from the whisky of the traders and had already hanged a Cheyenne because some emigrants said he stole their horses. Now the Oglalas.

The Indians had been angry with Two Face because last summer the white man's newspapers said he told the soldiers they were carrying the pipe for a great war against them, carrying it even to the Utes and Snakes and Blackfeet. Probably the story was made up to get a big army of soldiers to drive the Indians farther back and to make money for those with the hauling wagons, but Two Face had visited the fort and got rations and a white paper to show any soldiers he met that he was a good Indian.

"Ahh-h, now he and his headmen are truly what the whites call good Indians," Crazy Horse said. He remembered the day at the lodge of Two Face when the little man of the talking wires came visiting in a soldier coat. The Oglala had saved a white man that day.

It seemed the trouble had started last summer, when the hauling wagons of Bordeaux and other traders were camped at the forks of the Platte. A few Indians drove off some of the stock and when the soldiers chased them, dropped a bundle with the good paper given to Two Face a few days before. So this spring, when he brought in the white woman, Big Mouth and his Indian police helped put him and the other men in the iron house with chains on their feet, for the captive told a story of many bad things done to her by the Cheyennes and by Two Face after he got her.

[1] Mrs. Eubanks.

"Who would be so foolish—bringing the woman to the soldiers if he had done very bad things to her!" the older men said.

"And what about the good paper?" others asked.

It was said he did not know about his young men raiding the Bordeaux cattle. He and two others had gone ahead scouting for buffalo because the people were hungry.

Maybe it was so. Anyway, nobody dared go near the place of the hanging to cut the men down because a soldier with a spear-gun was always walking there. All those on the Holy Road, and the friendly Indians too, could see the three men swinging a little in the wind, looking alike until the big iron ball on the Cheyenne's leg pulled it off, to lie on the ground there, the ball too heavy for the dogs to drag away.

Once more the northern Indians said: "Keep away from the whites," yet there was talk of peace even here on the Powder River, many of the southern people missing the whites and their goods. Knowing there was a new town of soldier tents at Laramie, come up like puffballs on the prairie after a thunderstorm, they still wanted to go back until a runner came to tell a story that scattered such talking as a wind rips the morning fog. All the Laramie Indians, both the woman's camp and the Loafers, must go far down the Platte to the place called Fort Kearny. Bordeaux and the other traders were to help move the lodges and the goods and their own families too, and those of the mountain men who had moved in to the posts in the two years of rising Indian troubles—about fifteen hundred people all together, with only a few horse soldiers along. Their little soldier chief was Fouts, the red-faced and loud-talking one not liked even when he was not stinking with the whisky cup. These men were to protect the people, the whites said, to hurry them along, the Indians knew, hurry them without guns or even bows and mostly afoot into the country of the enemy Pawnee.

The northern Indians sent some people down to mix with the moving camp while a big war party gathered, not only warriors like Crazy Horse, Hump, and He Dog but men like Spotted Tail and Red Cloud and Lone Horn of the North, for all had relations among those being herded away down the river like the white man's spotted buffalo.

By the time the war party reached the hills north of the Platte, the scouts reported that the people were very angry. They couldn't forget their relations left hanging at Laramie or the other men of Two Face's little band being driven along at the back of the moving people by the horse soldiers, the chains still on their feet, the big iron balls in their hands as they walked. The white woman who made the trouble was along too, her wagon flying past the Indians as they plodded through the wheel dust of the traders and the mountain men ahead, most of the women with packs or children on their backs, a few riding saddle-sore old mares with drags full of little ones, sick, and old.

There were other things to make the people angry. Any boys racing would be tied to the wheels and whipped, the man Fouts said, and when the road was near the river the soldiers threw the smaller children into the spring flood waters and laughed to see them swim out like puppies while their fathers wrapped their fury inside their blankets and the mothers hid their faces. Others called girls and young women away from the walking people or from the night lodges. This, too, the Lakotas had to stand.

"Let us kill these white soldiers—" the young men whispered to each other, speaking behind the hand, for even now some among them were for the whites, village men who hung around the soldiers or those who hoped for power. But the older men held them back. "Wait," they counseled. "Wait for the place where the crossing is bad, so nobody can follow us and ride down the women and children. Wait just a little."

Then came the camp on Horse Creek near the place where fourteen years ago a peace paper had been signed at a Big Council. Here the Indians made a dog feast, with much drumming and noise among the night lodges so the warriors could slip away across the river to plan with those from the north. Among them were the sons of the great friendlies who had stood much from the whites: Two Face, Blackfoot, and old Little Thunder, the Brule.

The next morning Crazy Horse and others with the far-seeing glasses crawled close to watch and to signal the waiting warriors. The wagons and the soldiers were started but the lodges on Horse Creek still stood, Fouts and some of his soldiers riding back to hurry the Indians. Before their dust the women and children began to slip away into the willows where the horses were hidden, while their men lined up to be counted, making a great confusion of it, the bows and revolvers from the northern people held under their blankets, as ready against any who might let out their plans as against the soldiers. The officer was as always, riding up and down before the Indians, calling out bad white-man words, and so once more the young men couldn't hold themselves. Two shots were fired from the line; Fouts fell, but all his men got away, spurring off towards the moving soldiers, calling for help.[1]

And now a bad thing happened among the Indians. A loud noise and fighting broke out, ending in revolver-shots and people falling. Then the men scattered, some to help the women and children through the marked waters of the Platte, others to kill the guards of the prisoners and get them and their iron balls on the horses, while the warriors with guns lined up under the sons of Little Thunder and Two Face to hold the soldiers back. And when the helpless ones were across the water, the marking sticks pulled up, they chased the soldiers back to where the wagons were corralled, the whites inside, hiding behind the Indian families. And because they would not shoot their relations, the warriors let the soldiers go and followed the trail of the people going fast over the hills northward, already so far away they seemed to be black ants moving.

Twice that morning the Indian women cried out, once when the troopers tried to cross the river and again as smoke rolled up over their camp on Horse Creek, their lodges and everything burning. Now a little wailing went up from the older people, but strong men like Hump and his young warriors rode behind them as protection, and just ahead waited the northern Indians with many horses packed with robes and lodges and a big herd of cattle the young

[1] June 14, 1865.

men had rounded up during the night. Soon they would be in the country where plenty buffalo grew for all.

Next morning a son from among the traders came in. He said that the soldiers ran away when Fouts fell because they had nothing in their guns. All they could do to get even for the soldier chief and the five guards killed was to shoot and scalp the poor crippled prisoner of Two Face's band who was in a wagon.

As soon as the Indians reached the deep sandhills they scattered to make the trails hard to follow, young Crazy Horse watching them from a high place, thinking of the four Lakotas who would never ride with their people again, the four who lay back there among the burnt lodges on Horse Creek. They were the old peace chiefs of the Oglalas and Brules, still for peace yesterday, and so they had to die, but even in this death they were men to be respected and their names never spoken. Now, with their relations keening a little, but softly, the people followed the sons of the dead men northward as though the shooting had never been.

At first it seemed no one would come after the Indians; then finally the soldier chief called Moonlight started with his riding soldiers, but very slowly. When he hit a widening trail up near the White Earth River, the Indians stampeded his horses while the men were resting. They did it without danger because the soldier chief had the few who saved their horses stand in a wall around him instead of chasing the raiders. Crazy Horse had never seen such a thing done before, nor had he ever seen a long row of soldiers walking out of the Indian country with the saddles on their own backs. For the first time since the Cheyennes died at Sand Creek he laughed aloud.

Now once more the whites left their ranches and drove hard into Laramie and the little posts of the Holy Road, while up on the Lodgepole fork of the Powder the chiefs drew in the warriors for the big attack to be made the same time that the Minneconjous and Hunkpapas were sending a party against Fort Rice, Sitting Bull to lead. It was a new planning the Lakotas were learning and it seemed very good to the sons of Worm as they talked it over in their sleeping robes.

When the Cheyennes had made their medicine-lodge ceremonial, and the Lakotas their sundance, they started. Slowly the great camp of over a thousand lodges moved up the Powder, the ponies fattening on the ripening short grass, the bullet-makers busy, particularly among the Cheyennes, where there were more guns, for they had been fighting the whites longer. All the war things, the lances, shields, and warbonnets, were made fine and holy for this old-time war party, the few men remembering the sacred ways receiving many ponies for their help. Even Crazy Horse got a new medicine from Chips of No Water's camp, one of his little stone-dreamer pebbles to tie into the tail of the fast bay horse that he had taken from the Crows and did not want to lose.

When everything was ready the warriors rode the circles of the great camp, singing their war songs, their shields bright and new-painted, the spears flashing, those with guns carrying them ready for war. At their head were Roman Nose and High Back Wolf with their Cheyennes, Red Cloud, Big Road, and Hump leading the Lakotas. So the thousand warriors and the two hundred Cheyenne women rode out of the camp and down towards the Platte, the pipe men guiding them in the old way.

Late in July, the Moon of the Cherries Reddening, they reached the place called Platte Bridge, where the Holy Road was pushed to the north side by the mountains coming down to the river. Here the trail crossed over a bridge that looked like a many-legged worm stretched from one bank to the other. Scouts reported rows of new soldier tents at the stockade on the south side, and herds of horses and mules not far away, so the Indians moved several miles off for a council, going very slowly, raising no dust that could be seen. Here twenty men were picked for the decoys, one of the Bents with the Cheyennes, Crazy Horse with the Lakotas. They were to draw the soldiers into the hills where the warriors waited in gullies and washouts, the *akicita* of both tribes to hold them back.

While some with the far-looking glasses crawled to the top of the ridge to signal what was happening, the rest got ready for battle, taking their war clothes from their cases, shaking them to the earth and the sky, making their medicine, singing their sacred songs. Crazy Horse had put a lightning streak from his thunder medicine on his cheek and scattered a little earth from a gopher pile over his bay horse to help fool the enemy, as the defenseless gopher must do to live. Then he rode out with the decoys, three men going with him, the rest scattering in gullies along the back trail to help if the fighting got too hot for so few.

Slowly the decoys moved down upon the river, looking over towards the herds, motioning that way. Now and then one of them would hang back, as of little heart, the others seeming to urge him on, or perhaps started off towards the stock, the stampeding blanket plainly ready. Soon some soldiers came riding out,[1] the iron feet of their horses clattering on the bridge, the wheels of the wagon guns rumbling behind. The Indians shot a few arrows towards them, shouted warnings to each other and then, as the bullets spurted sand near, began to withdraw, Crazy Horse and a young Cheyenne making little stands while the others whipped their held-back horses as if trying hard to get away, working carefully, for it was known that some of the horse soldiers had the many-shooting guns. When they got a mile or more from the bridge the soldiers stopped and fired a few charges from the wagon guns, throwing up clouds of loose earth, the echo rolling over the low hills.

It would have been good, for no one was hit, but the waiting warriors got afraid they might miss the fight, and breaking past the *akicita,* rushed to look over the hills until they were like a forest along the sky. It made Crazy Horse hot-angry, this foolish thing they did. Of course the soldiers went back, and the decoys were signaled in, but they hadn't come all this way for nothing and so they swung down towards the river and the herds beyond. Roman Nose, Red Cloud, and the others sent High Back Wolf,

[1] Battle of Platte Bridge, July 25–6, 1865.

the great Cheyenne fighter, down to bring them back. Today had been bad medicine; tomorrow they would try again.

But there was a lot of stock just across the river and a new party of horse soldiers coming up the Holy Road, a small one that could be given a good scare before they reached the stockade. So High Back Wolf plunged into the river with the decoys, through the scattering blue troopers and on towards the herd. Some walking soldiers came running out to help with their far-shooting, long-barreled rifles; and High Back Wolf, very strong today turned off and charged into the roaring of their guns almost to the walls, striking a little soldier chief with his horsewhip. Missing the Cheyenne, Crazy Horse looked back through the fighting and the powder smoke and saw this brave and foolish thing done among so many soldiers. He made the retreating call, but just then the circle of guns around High Back Wolf went off and he slid from his horse into the brush, the soldiers closing over him like water over a rock, so not even Crazy Horse with his strong medicine could get him away. The Oglala zigzagged his horse up close, hoping for a chance, but finally the bay was struck to his knees and the light-haired warrior knew he must follow the others and the little herd they had stampeded.

Up on the hill there was anger among the leaders for all the mistakes—the warriors breaking through the *akicita*, the decoys going after a few horses and mules like a little raiding party. Was this what they had come two hundred miles for, with a thousand warriors?

Crazy Horse was dark and angry within himself. He knew they must learn to work together or be lost; yet when their good decoying was spoiled and there was the promise of a little fighting just across the river, he had been weak too, and forgot, and now Blind Wolf, the father of High Back Wolf, was standing out there on the hillside crying with the women for his lost warrior son.

In the first gray of morning Crazy Horse and several Cheyennes sneaked down with the old man for the body. It had taken many wounds to drop High Back Wolf and from one deep hole in his breast stuck a bit of sinew as from a Snake arrow, perhaps that of Mitch Seminoe, the trader's son staying at the stockade, the one who had been honored at the Lakota camp when he came for the scalp of the son of Washakie.

Now it was remembered that Ice, the Cheyenne, had made the bullet-proofing medicine for his people before the fight, but they must touch no metal to their mouths, not even a spoon. High Back Wolf, reloading his pistol on his running horse, had put the bullet between his teeth while he poured the powder into the barrel.

Now it was another day, and as the sun came up, the camp divided into big parties, one hiding in the brush of the creek mouth below the bridge, others, many of them Cheyennes, behind the hills above it. Again the horse soldiers rode out, about twenty-five this time, with the little soldier chief on a tall, jumping gray that would not follow the bridle. Once more the decoys fell back, but instead of coming, the soldiers made the rows of four and broke into a gallop up the Holy Road towards the ridge that hid the waiting Cheyennes. At a signal the three or four hundred Lakotas from below charged out and up the right flank of the soldiers, some of the Cheyennes from behind the ridge ahead cutting along a low place to the left side. There was dust and shooting, and a great thundering of horses and the noise of warriors striking the enemy down, calling "Coup! Coup!" Then a lot of foot soldiers came running over the bridge, pulling a wagon gun behind them and scattering out like a spread eagle's tail from the river to the bench-land, firing fast and moving up, trying to help the surrounded troopers get back.

Still the little soldier chief on the gray horse charged straight on into the Lakotas that had reached the ridge, shouting something, and when he got close the warriors stopped their shooting and, pulling their horses aside, called out words to him. Then Crazy Horse and Young Man Afraid saw it was their friend Caspar Collins and that Red Cloud and the others were trying to stop him, crying out: "Go back, young man! Go back!" as he led his blue-coat soldiers through the path the Lakotas made for him.

But beyond them were the Cheyennes who did not know the young white man and were fierce in their anger at the loss of High Back Wolf. The officer called out his friendly greeting to them too, but it was lost in the noise as they charged upon his soldiers, too close for the guns that would only kill their own people, and so they used the spears, driving the sharp points bloody through the men, knocking them from their horses with the war clubs, trampling them, until half of the soldiers were gone. Then the officer ordered a retreat to the bridge, while he, with the wild gray horse and his revolver, tried to hold the Cheyennes back alone.

This was a brave thing to do and the warriors stopped to see it, not trying to fight the white man any more. But a wounded soldier who had been cut off began crying: "Don't leave me! Don't leave me!" and the little soldier chief tried to push through the Indians to get him. The excited, hard-mouthed gray was like a wild colt with its first rider. Bucking, rearing into the air, and then bolting off sideways and running hard along the ridge, it carried the officer out of sight beyond, into a swarm of waiting Cheyenne warriors.

Down along the slope of the river the Lakotas were charging the retreating horse soldiers, whooping hard after them, and pushing the foot men back towards the bridge too. But then the wagon guns began their hollow booming, the balls breaking along the north bank of the stream, tearing up earth and bushes, the shots climbing up the hillside as the Indians let the soldiers go and whipped back out of range.

Crazy Horse and some of the others went to see what had become of the little soldier chief. By the time they got to the ridge, the Cheyennes had the gray horse there, pulling it along with rawhide ropes, some behind whipping, many sitting on their horses watching. Good-aiming soldiers from the bridge began to shoot among them, but at each powder flash the warriors slipped down behind the horses and then came up again. Bent was with them and some others who knew the white man's words. They called out bad names and made insulting motions towards the soldiers, waving the fine scalps the Cheyennes had taken.

Crazy Horse watched this awhile and then rode down the river where some men were going out to repair the talking wires that the Indians had cut. He fought there awhile but it was mostly shooting at a few hidden whites and so he started back up the river where it was said the Cheyennes had a little wagon train surrounded on the Holy Road. Perhaps that was where their white-man friend and his soldiers were going, to try to help them. It was too bad that such a brave man had to die. The Indians had never seen him ride the gray horse before; they wondered who had given him this runaway present.

All through the hills north of the river Crazy Horse found warriors resting and smoking in little bunches, talking about the things that had happened. They had seen a rising cloud of smoke up the road awhile ago. Perhaps that was the Cheyennes. By the time Crazy Horse got up near enough to smell the burning, he met some of the warriors with their horses heavy loaded.

"Yes, we had a good fight," they said. The scouts had signaled soldiers coming down the Holy Road early in the morning, and a lot of the waiting Cheyennes went up there. The five wagons were already corralled as for a fight, some men hurrying towards the river with the mules. The warriors charged and the soldiers ran for the wagon corral, letting the stock go. A warrior caught the bell mare and led her off, all the mules following her like little ducks their mother, leaving the blue-coats afoot. When Roman Nose came he hurried up the fighting, sending those with guns to crawl in from all around while he got a charge ready. His medicine was strong and he led the warriors, the others trying hard not to have him beat them too much. Like the blizzard wind they swept through between the wagons, the horses jumping the tongues and the men, everything. All were killed except two or three soldiers who ran down a gully to the river and got away. So the Cheyennes took the rifles and scalps and what they wanted from the wagons and then set them afire.

That night there was a great dancing in the war camp, and much recounting of brave deeds done. Many had soldier uniforms, a Cheyenne dancing in the fine blue coat of the young Caspar. They had twenty-eight scalps, with horses, mules, wagon goods, saddle guns, and more coups than anybody could remember. But the next day the scouts reported long rows of soldiers coming, and so most of the party started towards the Powder. They were tired of fighting and would go to make the hunt. Some thought they had done very little for so many, and these went down the Holy Road for more raiding, the Cheyennes strong among them. They had all stood away from the Lakotas, saying that every one of the horse soldiers could have been killed if the Bad Faces and the Hunkpatilas hadn't let them go because the little soldier chief was their friend. This was no time for softness.

Crazy Horse didn't wait to hear much of this talking. He hurried back to No Water's camp to tell Chips of the good medicine he had made for the bay horse.

When the story of the bridge fight was told in the council lodges the eagle-wing fans of the head Oglalas swished angrily at what these wild young men had spoiled: Julesburg, Horse Creek, and now Platte Bridge, all within the time of a calf growing hair. Twice they had made the old-time war party and both times they had failed because the wild ones could not wait. Up at Fort Rice it had been the same for Sitting Bull. Their young men had forgotten the laws of all things of the earth about them—that the young must follow.

"But the old must lead!" Long Face said. "There are two sights to the gun—and both must be well used to make a hit!"

"Hou! hou!" Man Afraid agreed. Their brother had spoken well. The young warriors were wild but perhaps some of those who should be the leaders were soft from the days along the Holy Road, soft or lost to them, like those who were thrown away at Horse Creek.

"Those were lost long ago—" Sitting Bear growled in his chest that was like the whisky barrel, so round.

That was true, Man Afraid admitted, but their places must be filled. They needed new hearts among them. Perhaps it would be well to renew the chiefs' society, make the ceremony of the shirt-wearers.

When the people heard what was to be done they said it over and over to one another, the older ones remembering how it was when they had the society, before the bad whisky times, the younger ones wondering who among them would be given the honors of the shirt-wearers.

That could be well foretold, one who had long lived in the woman's camp said. Will not the father choose the son? Man Afraid, Brave Bear, Sitting Bear, and Bad Face each had one for the place.

Not the son of Bad Face! The others yes, but not the village man, Woman's Dress, a shirt-wearer.

But many things happened before the ceremonials of the chiefs' society could be made. First runners came with stories, some about the Platte Bridge fight, the whites saying that the Indians had burned the men of the little wagon train alive.

Alive? It was not the Cheyenne way, Crazy Horse knew. Besides, they brought back the scalps, and the soldiers probably had to be killed to get them. It was not like firing an Indian village full of wounded women and children.

Some of the whites were angry about another thing, about the killing of young Collins. He was just going through to his own soldiers on the Sweetwater and should not have been sent into the fight, particularly on a spoiled gray horse. To this the Oglalas made an agreement of sorrow. They had liked the young white man, liked to see him walk across the village space with Hump or Red Cloud or the younger Crazy Horse, talking together like brothers.

It seemed, too, that there had been little ammunition at the stockade that day, even for the wagon guns, and the Indians could have taken it easily. The warriors laughed. Use the place for an antelope trap, perhaps? What good to a sensible people were houses with a two-man high wall around them?

But it was the runner from Laramie that carried the story of trouble in his mouth. The soldier tents that had been gathering all spring like white clouds on a windy day were being loaded for the north country. Many soldiers wouldn't go, saying they had joined only for the war against the whites with black-man slaves, so the officers locked them up or turned the wagon guns in their direction. Now the great army was coming into the Indian country, the soldier chief called Connor saying that all male Indians over twelve would be killed.[1]

"Who is to catch us?" the young warriors asked.

The Pawnees in soldier coats, perhaps. Connor was bringing them along to scout, to pick off anybody they could, giving them all the horses they captured. They had already killed some Loafers sneaking back to the whites and got their horses. This angered Spotted Tail and his relations. The last Pawnee women they had captured had been sent home well mounted, their faces red-painted, their bundles full of presents. The next time they would be chopped up so small none would find what had become of them.

But the Lakota women saw only one thing. "A great army coming against us—" they told each other. Even the mother of Crazy Horse wondered if it would not be better to withdraw to a safer place.

"We are many," was all her men would say. But they were very busy counciling, planning, making ready the guns and arrows and knives, for now it was the whites or the Indians. One would be driven out.

When the great row of soldiers was only two sleeps away, the warriors hidden in ambushes, ready, they turned towards the Tongue and struck the friendly Blue Clouds, who had kept their sons at peace, the Pawnees sweeping off the pony herd. The warriors got most of them back in a running fight and then brought the people to the Powder River camps to complain. The Cheyennes,

[1] Powder River expedition.

who had been peaceful once too, looked up from their pipes.

"It is a dangerous thing to be peaceful when all around is war," Blind Wolf said.

But it seemed these whites wanted no war with the Lakotas; instead they went far up beyond the Wolf Mountains, and so the people started for buffalo. Then one day hunters hurried into the camp above Crazy Woman Creek.

"More soldiers coming! From another way!" they signaled. "Soldiers marching around in the Powder River Mountains, with many wagons and wagon guns!"

The criers ran through the villages, the pony herds were brought thundering in, the warriors grabbing any horse that looked good, as was customary in time of danger. Crazy Horse and his brother hurried home from the No Water camp. Long Face's little band had stayed behind at a spring known to help in the belly cramp because several of the people were sick. But the two sons of Worm heard about the fight later, when they drank the coffee with the sweet lumps the Cheyennes brought back. They had found a big corral of wagons with many soldiers but couldn't do much against the good rifles and wagon guns with their little powder. After many days two white men came to talk with Red Cloud and Dull Knife, who said they must get out of the Powder River country and not scare the buffalo. They left a wagonload of provisions, but no ammunition, not even for the pay-money. Later another party of Indians came along and kept the train corralled awhile longer, killing three men and getting some good horses and mules. Finally the whites left southward, going past Pumpkin Buttes, out of the country.

"Ahh-h, that is good!" Long Face told his brother Worm.

The time for the ceremonials of the chiefs' society had come, so the people gathered at the mouth of the Little Powder, with much feasting, dancing, and visiting, as always when the people are together, with plenty of food and the young men home. Then a Minneconjou came riding in from the north. They had been fighting still another bunch of soldiers near the mouth of the Powder, the whites acting like the gray arrowhead snake that has long teeth but lets even children tease it to dying.

The old Indian laughed. "Hou! Whites have been seen like that!"

"But if the soldiers will not fight, why do they come the long hard road?" the Minneconjou wondered.

There was no telling the foolish ways of the white man.

True, but they knew the soldiers must be driven from the Lakota country, so they had kept after them. And when a cold rain came up, changing to ice, many of the horses and mules never moved again. One among the Indians counted over two hundred dead, and the soldiers had to burn much equipment, saddles and bridles and loaded wagons that had no horses. Now they were coming up this way.

"Up this way? Are they everywhere?"

Yes, two thousand of them coming up the Powder under a soldier chief called Cole. So the ceremonial of the chiefs' society was put off and the warriors went down the river in small parties to meet the soldiers, Crazy Horse with some Cheyennes under Roman Nose. They got eighty saddled horses, found them standing tied in a brush patch, alone.

Hoye! It was indeed like the little arrowhead snake, the young Oglala thought as he helped drive the herd along. But they could do little against the soldiers because there was no ammunition. Roman Nose did ride boldly back and forth between the lines, bullets like summer hail around him until his horse fell dead. He was not hurt, for he wore the war bonnet made by Ice. The warrior had another medicine too that Crazy Horse knew about, the no-woman medicine that helped him guard all the people as a man does those of his own lodge, defend them as a husband and a father his helpless ones.

Several days later another cold rain took four hundred more of the American horses, and now there was a mountain of smoke from the burning wagons and goods. Although the bow-armed warriors dared not attack, they hung around the soldiers like wolves following a buffalo herd, Crazy Horse, He Dog, and Lone Bear charging in now and then, making them hurry, keeping the men from hunting, the horses from grass until the dead ones lay along the trail as from some white man's disease. The soldiers were killing some to eat now, carrying the meat along as they hurried southward, barefoot and hungry, out of the country. One day when the warriors were very bold the soldier chief laid most of his goods down on the ground for them and went away.

So they were gone, the great army of soldiers who came trampling the grass from three sides, scaring the game. They had killed a few Indians and left the camps full of American horses and mules, the warriors with many good guns, some they just picked up where the worn-out men let them fall. Crazy Horse got one like that, his first back-loading gun.

Hou! This was the big soldier chief who would kill all the Indian men and the boys over twelve. It was like the old joke the Frenchmen had with the emigrants who wanted to know how to make the big horn spoons the Indians used: "First you catch the big-horn!"

Now once more the travois moved together for the ceremonials of the chiefs' society—not the old, old society that the stories told about, but one started among those now called the northern Oglalas when the grandfathers of Crazy Horse, Black Rock, and He Dog were still strong men. It was found then that the ways fitting the life in settled corn-growing villages were not good for the new hunting people. They were like the old brown shell left behind when the worm becomes the beautiful flying thing. So, with the help of a great medicine man who had lived with the Blackfeet, some Oglala headmen built the new chiefs society to advise and govern the people when they camped or moved, hunted or made war—all the things of the new life.

The plan gave them seven older leaders, men over forty, sometimes called the Big Bellies, and four strong young men, the councilors or shirt-wearers, the owners of the people, with helpers chosen for shorter times, for a hunt, a war party, or for a winter.

In the years that they hung around the Holy Road they had let the whole society fall to the ground as they did other things that should have been saved. But now once more the people must be strong, with strong ones to go before them.

Hou, hou! the Hunkpatilas, Oyukhpes and True Oglalas agreed. Of all the northern Oglalas only the Bad Faces held back, not certain. Perhaps they would make their own society, as was their right.

"They want everything at their end of the circle or they will leave a hole," some complained. But anyway they came, still hoping, it was said, although even an enemy Crow was welcome to see this thing done.

So the ceremonial camp was set up, round as all sacred things are, with the opening to the east. A great council lodge was made and painted with the holy things of the people, a lodge big enough so all could see or hear what was done there when the sides were rolled up.

On the big day everybody was out standing around the lodges, watching as some horsemen, the helpers to the Big Bellies, circled the inside of the camp. Four times they did this, each time stopping to pick up a young man from among the people, and each time the women made the trilling and called out the name as Young Man Afraid of the Hunkpatilas was selected, and Sword, son of Brave Bear, the Oyukhpe chief, and American Horse, son of Sitting Bear of the True Oglalas. Then, passing by the son of Bad Face, grandson of Smoke, standing out in new buckskin as Woman's Dress would be, they went behind the warriors to Crazy Horse, watching like any other visitor. His father was no chief, only a holy man, and yet the trilling that followed his choosing ran through the camp ten times stronger than any other, for it was well known that this one never worked for himself. The warriors, too, made the noise. He had long been great among them and it seemed good that a man could be chosen for his deeds and not because his father was a Big Belly.

Now the young men were put on the best American horses and

carried to the council lodge, which was rolled up to look like a pointed mushroom, the people following in a great herd, first the warriors and boys, then the rest, to see the four taken inside and seated on the fine new robes spread in the center.

At one end were the old men and the leaders, Man Afraid in the middle of the half circle, the greatest among them. Across the lodge were the young warriors with their fathers behind them, and along the sides stood the women and children. Now there was smoking and feasting of buffalo and game and dog and all the sacred Indian foods. Then an old man known for his wisdom rose and talked to the young men on the robes, speaking of their duties in the village and in the wars. They would head the warriors in camp and on the march, see that order was preserved, no violence committed; see that every one among the people had his rights respected. For this they must be wise and kind and firm in all things, counciling, advising, and then commanding. If their words were not heard, they must use blows, and if still not obeyed, must kill. But never must they take up arms against their own without thought and council, always with caution and with justice. Man living alone can do as it pleases him; if he lives among others he must bow the head to the good of all. Without strong leaders to see this done, the people will fail, the nation break up into small, defenseless bands. Man is a selfish, passionate, and half-savage thing, and without discipline and restraint becomes lawless and dangerous.

"Hou, hou!" the people cried. "Hou!"

Now the shirts were taken, fine and new, from their cases. They had been made in the sacred way by the older men for these who were to wear them, each one of two big-horn skins, the dew claws left on, the skin from the forelegs making the sleeves, that from the hind legs hanging down at the sides. Across the shoulders and along the arms were quill-worked bands with pictures of men and horses and weapons, the sacred things of each man. The sleeves were fringed with hair, each lock for a deed done in war: for horses captured, a wound received, a prisoner taken or a scalp, a coup counted, the life of a friend saved or some other great thing done.

"It is said there are over two hundred forty on the Light-Haired One's shirt—" an old woman whispered, and was quieted by the angry looks.

Now the shirts were put upon the men and a single eagle feather fastened at the back of each head, flat, as where the earth meets the sky, and while these things were finished, an even older man stood up and spoke of the new duties to be undertaken, of even greater duties.

"Wear the shirts, my sons," he said, "and be big-hearted men, always helping others, never thinking of yourselves. Look out for the poor, the widows and orphans and all those of little power; help them. Think no ill of others, nor see the ill they would do to you. Many dogs may come to lift the leg at your lodge, but look the other way, and do not let your heart carry the remembering. Do not give way to anger, even if relatives lie in blood before you. I know these things are hard to do, my sons, but we have chosen you as great-hearted. Do all these duties gladly, and with a good face. Be generous and strong and brave in them, and if for all these things an enemy comes against you, go boldly forward, for it is better to lie a naked warrior in death than to be wrapped up well with a heart of water inside."

Now there was a great rising sound of joy from the people for the new strength that flowed through them from these brave young men. And as the people chanted their praisings, each of the four looked upon this place that was given him in the way that was his own. Young Man Afraid was as any day in his own lodge, for honors were taken simply by those of that great family. American Horse sat up straight, his shoulders and his head lifted almost from him as he looked all around to see that none missed his glory. Sword, with the face of respect and gratitude turned towards the seven chiefs, showed his acknowledgment of authority like no other among them. Only one was shrunken down, sitting motionless, with his eyes before him, embarrassed to be pushed forward in this way, even as he knew the joy it must be giving to those of his lodge and to Hump, his long-time warrior father and friend. Once the light-haired man of the Oglalas lifted his eyes and then he saw Black Buffalo Woman looking straight and open upon him. Not upon the four as the new councilors of the people but upon him alone. And seeing this, some were already speaking of it behind their palms, saying that certainly this time a woman of the Bad Faces had chosen wrong when she selected a big man to bring to her people.

But Crazy Horse saw only that Black Buffalo Woman had her youngest son on her back, with another one somewhere in the crowd, their father, No Water, there too, and that these were now of the people who must be protected, for a shirt-wearer shields all the people from anything that would harm them, every one.

The first to leave the ceremonial camp was the angry Woman's Dress, going with the Bad Faces, Red Cloud, their leader, stopping near Red Leaf and his Brules, the driven-out Conquering Bear people. He had many relations among them through his father, Lone Man, who was one of them before he married an Oglala. The next moon two more shirt-wearers were made and Red Cloud once more saw younger men, Big Road and his own nephew, He Dog, honored above him. Still, it was plain now that those people did not consider themselves Bad Faces but a new northern division of the Hunkpatilas. Besides, why should the heart of Red Cloud be troubled? some asked. The warriors followed him; very many left their own camps to live around him.

Truly it was so, others agreed.

Crazy Horse went to see his boyhood friend given the shirt. Listening to the heavy duties laid upon the wearer this second time, he wished once more that he could have had the strong heart of Man Afraid, who had said no to a much greater honor when it was placed before him.

The HUNDRED in the Hands

IT WAS fall of the year When Three Men Were Hanging at the Soldier Fort, the year called 1865. The first of the little snows had whitened the Tongue River country and melted away; the buffalo berries were frosted sweet on their gray bushes, falling easily under the beating sticks of the women into the skins spread underneath; the sun shone warm upon the drying meat.

In this good time a young Hunkpapa came riding from the north to visit his brother who had married a woman of Hump's people. Crazy Horse took him to the council lodge to tell the news. Mostly it seemed the same as down here, the soldiers shooting Indians.

"Ahh-h, all that they can catch!" Man Afraid admitted, the sound of concerned agreement going from one to the other around the fire. "But it is not so easy here now, with the people, even those from the fort and the Cheyennes and Blue Clouds, all together."

"Yes, but the soldiers came running through our country like rows of ants hurrying before the moccasins of winter," Worm complained.

Hou! They had found them so up around the Yellowstone too, and took some good horses, while at the same time the Great Father had a man going around the Missouri forts carrying another peace paper.

"Like the old woman trying to catch the dog with a piece of meat in one hand and the butcher knife in the other," Man Afraid laughed. They had heard that the Black Robe called De Smet, who laid his hand on the heads of the children at the Big Council, was

179

up on the Missouri. The Oglalas remembered him as a good holy man, but most of the children he touched died of the white man's sicknesses.

Yes, the Hunkpapa said, Black Robe worked hard to get the Indians in for another treaty-making, but even the old ones had heard enough peace talk. Only Missouri Loafers came to the council. At first it seemed like a thing for laughing, but now they knew the peace paper let the whites open roads through all the Indian country, with forts along them. Soon it would be carried around in the south too, at Laramie, to catch at least some Loafers with the rich presents.

So! This was bad news their friend from the north brought in his hand.

Before the moon had darkened, the Oglalas knew that the man from Sitting Bull had spoken true. The whites were offering much for one who would call the Indians in to another treaty-making, but even the traders' sons who liked the pay-money very much were afraid. At last, when the sparks flew upward from the smoke holes and the braids of returning hunters were frosted, Big Mouth and some of his Indian police, without the soldier coats, came bringing the tobacco.

Young Little Hawk stood at his father's door watching the herald take them to the council lodge. "Truly this Loafer chief who carries the white man's gun against his own people will do anything!" he called out loudly as they passed. Crazy Horse stood beside him and let it be done, for many much older were pushing forward with their bows, ready to whip these men away into the snow. But Man Afraid and Spotted Tail, even Red Cloud and Hump, said they must be feasted as visitors and heard as men of their own people.

So a great fire was built in the council lodge, until it glowed red as a sunset cloud through the skins for all the winter camp to see. And there the headmen gave their silence to the Loafer's talking, only Swift Bear taking the tobacco offered those who would go down to Laramie. Crazy Horse and the others were not surprised, for the Brule had always lived close to the whites until the Indians rose against Fouts. Having no wish to be left on the ground with the peace chiefs, he helped the fleeing people, but this snowshoe winter seemed very hard away from the log buildings and the hot coffee of his brother-in-law, Jim Bordeaux.

In January, the Moon of Frost on the Lodge, Swift Bear and his Brules signed the treaty giving the whites a road and forts through the Powder River country. It was said they told the soldier chief that the Oglalas were coming too, and that Red Cloud had driven out Big Ribs so he could be chief. The people wondered at this foolish talking; one did not become chief by a driving out. Nor would they go to the whites if twice as many of their horses starved and all the hunters came in snowblind. But there was no thawing, no wind from the Chinook country, until far past the time for the swans' returning to the Medicine Water—a long, hard winter for those among them sick with the white man's diseases, and as soon as the weather warmed a little, Spotted Tail sent word to the soldier chief at Laramie that his daughter was dying and he wished to lay her near the scaffold of old Smoke.

Crazy Horse felt bad to see his uncle go. He had less time for visiting away from the Hunkpatilas since he had been made a shirt-wearer, but he stopped at the Brule camp several times to leave fresh game, a grouse from some wooded valley or a little rabbit for the girl, yellow-pale now as the evening flower that fades so soon when the sun comes. He was there once after a bad night, when it had seemed the girl would die, and Spotted Tail was as one gone wild, the fierceness from this thing that had come upon his daughter driving him to his feet, making the tall man stand taller, as a tree seems to rise in the gathering wind.

"The white man steals our helpless ones with his coughing sickness!" he cried, his strong face lifted towards the sky where live the lightning and the thunder, the great powers that are brothers to the angry man. "It slips past the watchers of the villages, crawls upon them in the sleeping lodge, and we are without weapons against it!"

But soon the Brule chief was sitting in his place again, his winter robe drawn about him as though there were a chilliness in the fire. He had known the power of the whites that was even in their diseases. It had been a mistake to bring the girl with the coughing sickness out here into the wilderness, into this cold that tore the lungs, that brought the bright red blood, the breast blood, rushing from the mouth. The whites were indeed so many that one could not fight the things that were theirs.

And as he spoke the women of the lodge made the little moaning sound for this bad thing that had come upon them and upon their man. Crazy Horse heard them in silence, keeping back the few words he had brought for his uncle. He saw that one could not ask the sorrowing man to stay, and when some of Swift Bear's people came up from the agent, the chief went in and with him went the good Brule warriors they would be needing soon.

Later the Indians heard how it was with Spotted Tail at the soldier fort of the Holy Road. The girl had died on the way and the father carried her along with him on the backs of her two white horses, tied together. When they neared Laramie, the soldier chief and his men came to meet them with the colored flag flying ahead and an ambulance for the dead girl guarded by horse soldiers and two wagon guns. At the fort she was put into a big box that was soft as the down of a duck's breast inside and taken to the death scaffold beside old Smoke's, all the soldiers and the people of the fort following to honor her. Out in the north country Crazy Horse thought about this thing the whites did for the dead daughter of a Lakota. He remembered the girl before the sickness came, pretty as a snow stream leaping in the sun, and as dark and angry as its flood waters when she saw the white-man husband of her sister do as the emigrants along the Holy Road sometimes did to their women, hit her with his fists.

"What are you then, one of the weak-women of the pale faces?" she demanded of her sister.

Now she had been carried away to the Holy Road by her father, to the road that had brought her this dying as it brought so many bad things to them all; and as Crazy Horse thought of these things, his breast filled with a boiling as when hot stones are thrown into water, so he went out into the darkness where the sky was far and there was room for an angry man.

When the snow finally began to break from the south slopes, the horse-tenders fired the drying earth to bring the early grass. And as soon as the herds strengthened, Crazy Horse led his young men out for meat and then they went against the Crows, driving them back from the hunting grounds of the Tongue River, where they had followed the game drifting south with the winter storms. The grass lengthened, the yellow buffalo calves ran awkward among the feeding cows, and the snow swans were nested on the Medicine Water, and yet the heart of Crazy Horse was like the rock in a deep canyon where the sun never strikes, as it was from the day his uncle went from them. Now he heard that three hundred Lakota women and children from the woman's camp at Laramie had been loaded into wagons and hauled away to the Missouri because the soldiers would no longer feed them, the children mostly their own. Now who would do for those helpless ones so far from their people, with no one to bring them meat or a good word?

Then one day three young Brules came riding into the camp of Long Face with their guns, their dance clothes, and their war horses. They said they had come to stay with Crazy Horse and so they were given a lodge and an old woman to look after it. In a day or two they spoke their reasons. They had been willing to follow Spotted Tail to Laramie when his daughter was dying, but now he was signing the treaty of the roads and forts through the Indian country as any Loafer would. Roman Nose, the Minneconjou who had gone down with him, was angered by the Brule's peace talking. Face painted as for war, he rose up in the council and, letting his blanket fall from his scarred breast, he held out a pipe in one hand, arrows in the other. Which did the white men who came among them to steal wish?

But these peace men knew little about Indian ways, and the interpreter did not explain this defiance, and so they said they had come for peace and would take the pipe. It made Roman Nose very angry, but when a pipe is asked for, it can only be given. So the chiefs were letting themselves be fooled.

It seemed others down along the Holy Road were talking soft, promising to keep the peace until the new council in the summer, and now the whites were telling the emigrants that the Indians had sold the Powder River road and they could use it to get to the place of the gold much quicker.

"Just follow the Bozeman stakes from the Platte along the east slope of the Big Horns to the Yellowstone," they said. "Road fit for wagons all the way."

Some whites and two of the Richards and another trader's son brought their wagons of goods up as far as the Clear fork of the Powder and made trading houses by piling up sods cut from the earth. Once more the Cheyennes went to sit and watch as they had done six years before when some white men came to make a house and plant corn on the Crazy Woman. Those other people had been strange ones, kneeling on the ground together as the short-necked moose does when feeding on young grass. Putting their hands together, the whites had made the words of their language, all talking with their knees on the ground. It was very funny to see, but when the Indians found out that it was their medicine sayings, the praying, as they called it, they were ashamed of the laughing. But they drove the whites out just the same, for this was their good hunting country.

Now they drove out these new whites and the traders' sons too, although the Richards were relatives of Red Cloud. Even before they got their wagons ready the Indians started to set the sod of their houses back as it had grown in the earth, roots down, the grass looking up at the sky.

Now every few days messengers came north to tell of the fine presents being given away at Laramie, guns and ammunition and many other things, they said, particularly guns and ammunition, and just for touching the pen. So in the Moon of Making Fat, June,

Man Afraid went down and Red Cloud too. But not Hump, Worm, or Crazy Horse. These and many others stayed out on the Powder, some of them fasting and making the sweats, others going off into the hills alone with their medicine, hoping that the men at Laramie would be strong against the power and presents of the whites. A strange and unknown thing had happened at the council before the chiefs left. Twice a big, loud voice had been heard, calling out: "Remember Bear Ribs and Conquering Bear! No man who would be chief of all the Lakotas can live!"

Each time the guards who ran out into the darkness found nothing near. And in the lodge they all looked towards Red Cloud and Man Afraid, the two going down to talk to the peace men. One of these, their Brave Man, had said "No" to this thing long ago on the Running Water, the night that Bear chief died.

There must be another one among them wishing for power.

So the Oglalas sent some quiet men, with ears keen as the deer's, to sit among the people at the council. Others, like Little Big Man, rode back and forth carrying news in their mouths as the forked-tail bird carries mud. They said many wagonloads of presents had already come, and that some whisky was leaking into the Oglala camp, although none could tell the soldier chief how this happened. The night Worm and Crazy Horse heard this they sat up very late. Man Afraid, like Spotted Tail, was not one to warm his belly with the burning cup, but others were not so strong and it was hard to forget that Red Cloud's father had died of the whisky long ago. But the next day there was good news. Red Cloud would not sell the country, not for all the Great Father's sugar and coffee and the trader's hidden keg. The first thing the Oglalas had asked about was the ammunition. Then both Man Afraid and Red Cloud wanted everything in the treaty explained, so there would be no things coming up that they had not heard about, as happened to the Cheyennes down in the Smoky Hill country. And when they heard the peace paper talking of a Powder River road, they rose up, both Man Afraid and Red Cloud, and wrapping their blankets around them, started away. But the head white man of the council called them back with soft words. It was not a new road they were talking about, only an old one, already much tramped.

Ahh-h, and then they had come this long way to talk of an old road?

Yes, and to get their share of the wagonloads of the presents the Great Father wanted to give them, the whites said. Tobacco, coffee, sugar, blankets and calico, knives and hatchets, all were ready when they touched the pen.

But where was this old road, where did it go? the Indians asked. They knew of none except the Powder River trail made long ago by the feet of the buffalo and the poles of the Indian travois, the trail going through their hunting grounds.

In the middle of this counciling a long cloud of dust was seen coming up the Holy Road. In it were many, many soldiers, a band for music-making, some wagon guns, and several long trains of mule teams pulling heavy loads—all these soldiers and their goods coming here when there was to be peace. Whom did they want to fight?

Some of the Loafers went down to visit the new camp and asked the soldier chief called Carrington where he was going. Maybe he didn't know about the trouble at the council or maybe he was a little white man with a strong heart and a straight tongue; anyway, he told them right out he was going to the Powder River to build forts.

So that was it, the Loafers thought, but saying nothing, for they had lived in the middle of the soldiers and wagon guns a long time. Finishing their pans of molasses and crackers, they carried the news to the Oglala camp. Then there was really trouble in the council, with the northern chiefs telling the peace men they were like all the others, trying to fool them with the lying tongue.

"The Great Father sends us presents and talks about buying a new road while the soldier chief comes to steal it before the Indian can say yes or no!" Red Cloud roared.

And once more he wrapped his blanket around him, but in a

different way now, and Man Afraid too. With the others following at his heel fringe, Red Cloud marched out and started home to the north country. Any whites who came up past the Dry Fork of the Powder would have to fight.

"Hoye!" the warriors cried when they heard of this challenging. "Hoye! hoye!" They were not afraid. Last year the big soldier chief called Connor had come with his three thousand men, many of them on horses, and he couldn't do anything. Now another one was coming with only seven hundred walking soldiers, many of them music-makers, mule-drivers, and woodchoppers, and some of the weak white women along too. The Indians knew many good places for raids and standing fights between the Platte and the Yellowstone and there were no horse soldiers along to chase anybody.

"Hoppo! Let us go!" Crazy Horse said to the warriors. "Let us make a strong wall against the soldiers!"

But not even Red Cloud was ready to fight, with the cherries so close to darkening, the moon growing fat towards the time of the sundance that should be made before a big war was started. Crazy Horse, Lone Bear, and a few Bad Faces stayed south to watch the long rows of wagons and men coming into their country. At the Dry Fork, where the officer called Carrington stopped to build a little fort, they ran off the trader's herd and then helped some returning council Indians get their women away from the soldiers, losing a worn-out pack horse loaded with Laramie presents. When the soldiers started north again, the watchers picked off a horse now and then, or a mule or a man, just enough to keep the whites reminded.

In July, the Moon of Cherries Reddening, the walking soldiers reached the fork of the Piney under the dark wall of the Big Horn Mountains. Here Crazy Horse and Lone Bear sat on a ridge watching the whites camp and begin a stockade in the rolling foothills, far from wood for building and from good grass, but perhaps they had the white-man reasons that the Indians could not see. So a scouting camp was made, with somebody always on a hill, looking, while Red Cloud sent a pipe around for war.

Before the sundances were done, Crazy Horse saw some Cheyennes go to visit the soldiers, to ask if they wanted war or peace. Bridger showed Dull Knife and the other headmen around the fort, Carrington himself firing a wagon gun for them, the noise big enough to knock a good man down. They told him that Bordeaux and the other traders talked for peace, but that Red Cloud was strong as a rock, his camp circle twice as wide as the day he left the council in anger, even young men from the Loafers and Spotted Tail's Brules coming up now. Red Cloud made war talk and that was what the young men wanted.

Afterward the Cheyennes stopped at the camp of a trader called Gasseau who had followed the soldiers. While they smoked and warmed the mountain evening with a cup from the whisky wagon, a party of Lakotas was suddenly standing in a circle around them, demanding to know everything said and seen at the fort. Dull Knife and the others spoke it all freely, telling about the wagon gun and that the whites were staying, although some of their women seemed thin and afraid. Proudly they showed all their presents from the little white chief, saying there were many more at Laramie for those who went to touch the pen.

"Fools!" the Lakotas roared out. "Have the soldier guns shooting your relatives at Sand Creek taught you nothing of the lying ways of the whites?" With their bows they whipped the Cheyennes across their faces, crying "Coup, coup!" as though striking an enemy. And at daylight they came past and killed the trader and his six men, letting his Lakota wife and children run away into the brush. The next day the warriors counted more coups, this time on the whites of a wagon train, taking two scalps and a hundred and seventy-four mules that followed the bell mare.

These things were done almost in sight of the fort called Phil Kearny and no soldiers came out to chase the Indians, the little white chief seeming to notice them no more than a grizzly the ants running around his feet. When the fort was well started he sent some of his soldiers on to the mouth of the Big Horn River, near Crow country, to build another one. The Indians let them go as they had let the whites take a big herd of the spotted buffalo through to the gold diggings. They heard from the Platte that these people were not staying in the country and nobody up here wanted the stinking meat when there was plenty of fat buffalo.

As soon as the sundances were done, the warrior camp near the Piney swelled, split into several, until the soldiers only came out in big bunches, usually with a wagon gun among them, and yet many were killed, and many horses taken. Every wagon train coming up from the Platte was attacked, and men like Big Road, Hump, Young Man Afraid, and Crazy Horse led war parties as far down as Fort Reno on the Dry Fork, sometimes clear to Laramie, taking all the guns and ammunition they could. Sometimes they joined Red Cloud's warriors on the ridges overlooking the fort on the Piney, watching with the far-seeing glasses, sending mirror flashings and smoke signals, waving blankets or circling their horses to let the warrior camps know everything the whites were doing. And at night little fires burned on the hills, war whoops rose under the stockade, fire arrows were shot inside, or some carrying green scalps. Sometimes there was silence, with a hoot or a wolf howl made so foolish that anybody must know it was the warriors skulking around the little island of whites cut off by a great sea of Indians.

Any day Red Cloud might call the warriors for the attack.

But the Bad Faces organized no great party to go against the fort and so the others kept up their raiding. One afternoon Crazy Horse and his Hunkpatilas stopped with their captured American horses and soldier guns at No Water's camp in the bend of the Tongue. After the feasting and smoke they were asked to stay for the evening dancing. Once more Black Buffalo Woman and her friends teased the shirt-wearer about being an Old Lone One, already twenty-four and still standing off by himself while the others danced to the girls and back again, with great joking and fun as they sang an old Hidatsa courting song whose private things made the girls act shy and the old women laugh very hard. Soon Crazy Horse would be like an old buffalo bull that stands alone on a hillside, so cross even the blackbirds hungry for ticks and worms keep off his back. They really should try to find him a wife, but he must get himself some horses. They couldn't ask a woman to take one who seemed to value her so little that he gave nothing.

But the man made no words of defense to this old story, standing silent and waiting beside Black Buffalo Woman. Finally the others moved away, talking among themselves like cackling prairie chickens as they went to relieve themselves beyond the dusky plum thicket. Their blankets held out around them, as was customary, they went on as women do, about this Hunkpatila so often in their camp, with hair summer-bleached to the color of an elk's rump. Nor was he a big man, as a Lakota leader should be; instead he stood slender as a young warrior, almost a boy when riding beside the seven-foot Touch the Clouds. He did not sing or dance as a Lakota should, and never made the ordeals of the sundance to give himself fortitude and courage. It was true that he was strong in the fighting, but he brought in no scalps for the women to dance and no stories of coups counted or deeds done. He was indeed a Strange Man.

"He brings much honor and power to the people," old Makes the Lodge told them.

Yes, the others said, not contradicting this woman who was one of the few among the Oglalas who had made the sundance, but they wished Crazy Horse were more like the great Lakotas in other things, more like old Red Water, who had lain with a young wife when his grandsons had growing sons of their own. Or like his own Brule uncle, Spotted Tail. There was a man with a tongue to make the heart jump like an antelope! But their Strange One would never earn the name of Talks with Women, as Spot was often called.

They spoke, too, against Black Buffalo Woman staying behind with the young shirt-wearer. "No Water sees these things with a bad face. It will make trouble," Blue Bead warned.

"No Water is a strong man. He will not notice when a woman hangs back for a word with another, with one who chased flies from her cradleboard with the weed spears of his childhood," Makes the Lodge answered.

"It will bring trouble," Blue Bead repeated stubbornly, but she was only a weather woman, not one who looks before in other things, so the others laughed.

Crazy Horse saw the faces of No Water's camp, knew the talking of the women, but not these things nor even an annoyed husband could keep him from walking across the camp circle with Black Buffalo Woman now, making a few words of greeting for her ear— how good it was to see her, how well she looked, and saying all the silent things for which there were no words, things of the time past and of the time to come.

At his home lodge Crazy Horse found word of a big council called by the Hunkpatilas and Bad Faces to listen to more messengers from Laramie, this time with a brother-in-law of Bordeaux among them and Woman's Dress too, just visiting. He heard the messengers say the agent wanted Man Afraid, Red Cloud, and Red Leaf to bring the people in. Their Great Father wished them to live in peace and wanted to give them of the good things the whites had. He knew that winter would soon be upon them and felt pity for the women and children in the fighting.

"Pity as at the Blue Water!" Crazy Horse cried against the Brule messengers. But immediately he sat down, for some of their relations had died there, and one cannot speak of such things.

Many who had been Loafers before the fleeing at Horse Creek and were hungry for the whisky and the presents of the whites made the "Hou, hou!" But the others were silent, and when the messengers said that the soldiers would chase all who did not come in, there was anger among them and among the warriors sitting behind them, their dark faces lit up into fierceness by the blazing buffalo fat thrown on the coals.

The messengers stayed among the Tongue river camps for several days, eating fat rib roast and getting all the information they could. And later Crazy Horse and the others heard that they told many foolish things at Laramie, that he was in command of the *akicita* in Red Cloud's camp, when he was not even a Bad Face, that Man Afraid would have no warrior societies, when his son was a great leader among them, and that the Hunkpatila chief was kept out by the young men who wanted war, when plainly it was the whites who came looking for it up here where they had no right by their own peace paper. The messengers said, too, that Red Cloud had talked to them of peace, and this made Crazy Horse very uneasy, for it was well known that the Bad Face was stronger in words this summer than in fighting, and that he had a different wind out of each corner of the mouth.

But all except the Red Cloud story was little more than a coyote's howl in the night, the sort of things Woman's Dress might tell, for he was such a man. The summer had been a good one in the north country, with more of the white man's provisions in the camps than the people had ever had before, some from trading with the Loafers but mostly brought in by the raiders, even some that they could not use, like the wagonload of fat meat the whites called bacon that was yellow and stinking. Those who had been at the woman's camp said only soldiers could eat it, and the flour that was full of worms.

"Hoh!" Little Hawk made the sound of surprise when he heard about this. "Perhaps that was why the soldiers on the Crazy Woman were shaking the flour through the gray sack before they cooked it!"

"Perhaps that was why they were so weak you could take their scalps," Lone Bear teased.

There was a laughing among the warriors, Little Hawk helping too, for it was well known that he took more hair than any other young one among them. Only his brother Crazy Horse had fought better.

But truly these new soldiers did not try hard to live, Hump agreed, spitting on his whetstone, making a soft little song on it with his scalping knife. He heard the new ones coming were only lodge boys who had never seen an Indian, never fired a gun.

"It will be like shooting rabbits sitting," those who had not yet counted coups told one another, their teeth white in their hopeful faces.

But Worm thought it was making the young men too reckless. He said it over his smoking pipe, pressing a thumb into the red stone bowl as he told of a charge he had seen the last time he was near the fort on the Piney, not saying that he knew Little Hawk was in it. Two good men were lost close under the stockade, where no one could get to them until dark. It was foolish to go right up to the high walls guarded by men with rifles walking along them and by the wagon guns.

"Hou!" Man Afraid approved. He hated to lose even one of his people.

"Is it not better to die fighting than to sit and let the soldiers send down roots in our country like the willow stick at the river?" the young warriors asked one another, but not too loud, for they liked old Worm and the Hunkpatila was their Brave Man, not to be shamed by contradiction.

Although the Lakotas knew that Bridger and Beckwourth at the Piney fort were strong friends of the Crows, Man Afraid and Red Cloud had been up to visit the head chiefs and the Crows had come to receive the Lakota guest presents, as was common between the tribes even during the big wars. But this time there was more than friendly talk about the fights, about trading or even the release of captives. The Oglalas had brought their pipe for war to drive the whites from the Indian country. Together, with Cheyennes and Blue Clouds, they would make a great attack on the two forts, get guns and mules and scalps for everybody. The young Crows were hungry to go, but nothing was done, perhaps because the half-black Beckwourth had lived many years with the Crows and was still a big man among them.

In the middle of these plannings some of the Cheyennes sneaked away to Laramie, talking there like old women at the robe-washings. They told many things the soldiers must know—that all the stock had been driven from the Powder River road and that many war parties were out against the Platte. They said, too, that Man Afraid was a prisoner in the camp of Red Cloud because he had wanted to come in with the Cheyennes.

"For these words and for signing the peace paper giving up the Powder River road their presents have been many," a runner from Laramie told.

"For doing such foolish things they should have been very many," Crazy Horse replied.

There was other news, too: Red Leaf wanting to bring his people, the old Conquering Bear band, back to their relatives with Spotted Tail, the soldiers needing ammunition and guns and trying to get more messengers to coax those they called hostiles in. The northern people wondered how the whites could expect anybody to move down there, with the game all gone and nobody wanting to feed the hungry. Even Spotted Tail was saying if his people must live from the hunt they would have to go where the buffalo was, in the Powder River country. Besides, the young men of the friendlies were raiding almost as much below Laramie as the hostiles farther north.

It was a relation of Yellow Woman of the Cheyennes who came riding through a fall rain to No Water's camp with another story for Crazy Horse. The soldier chiefs had a new plan to stop the Powder River war. While talking about peace messengers they would send a big army against Red Cloud from Laramie, starting in the darkness so the Indians around there could not send out runners. The soldiers would strike the people on the Tongue as they did at the Blue Water and Sand Creek.

"So—" Crazy Horse said, "the soldiers plan to trap us as they did the friendlies? They will find those they call hostiles hard to catch."

"Hoye!" the warriors agreed. Let the soldiers come. Until then they would have a good time around the hated fort on the Piney, for the fall meat was made and the ponies many and strong.

By the time the snows were pushing down the flanks of Cloud Peak to the foothills around Phil Kearny, the Oglalas had drawn the scattered hunting people together, a thousand lodges of Lakotas, northern Cheyennes, and a few Blue Clouds. Once more they moved in a great camp against the whites, coming up along the Tongue and Prairie Dog Creek, stopping not far from the fort. Early in the Moon of Popping Trees, December, they tried the first attack. A few warriors were sent out to show themselves, the rest hidden back behind the ridges while Red Cloud and some others with the far-seeing glasses sat on a high place and made the signals. But nothing came of this. The decoys hurried back to be in a good place for the fighting, the soldiers were careful as a wolf who has lost a foot in a trap, seeming to smell danger on the wind, and once more the warriors could not wait. So a few coups were counted, a few scalps and horses and guns taken, but nothing that was part of a great war.

Crazy Horse had been among the Bad Faces as a warrior this day and came home to sit silent in the duskiness of his father's lodge, wondering how anything could be done when even the decoys were afraid another would get more scalps, the warriors still going off like a box of ammunition dropped into the fire, making a great popping and noise but doing little damage.

Two weeks later the Indians decided to try again, with Hump, the Oglala-Minneconjou, leading this time. Once more it would be a big party as at the Platte Bridge and the place called Julesburg, with the walking pipe-bearers going ahead, and Crazy Horse, He Dog, Young Man Afraid, and American Horse to hold the wild ones back. Now one would see if these shirt-wearers were strong enough with the young warriors to keep them from spoiling another ambush.

The last night in camp Hump talked strong to them, saying he was glad to have such a daring party but that they should remember they had little of guns or ammunition and so must work together and get the soldiers very close, surround them like buffaloes for the kill. Twice last year they had seen a good plan fail because somebody couldn't wait. Would they go on acting like small boys playing battle with stick spears? If that was true, then the buffalo ranges, their homes, and their helpless ones would all be lost.

The circle of young men stood silent, their heads hanging in shame, and so the warrior went on with the planning. The soldiers were not asleep, he said. They had been awakened by the long moons of fighting and knew that the warriors of the Powder were very many. The party must have a good leader for the decoys, one who was cunning and reckless, and careful too, very careful of the others, one who had long proved himself strong before the warriors so they would follow into any danger, and one who could make the soldiers hungry for his scalp. It would be Crazy Horse. With Crazy Horse to bring them in, and the warriors waiting for his signal, this would be a bloody moon for the soldiers on the Piney.

"It is known that the little soldier chief called Fetterman down there says with fifty men he can ride through the Lakota nation!"

Now the warriors made the great noise until it was like the roaring of the fighting bull moose. Hump and the others listened and saw that it was good. This time they would make the surround.

After the council the young warriors surrounded Crazy Horse, all wanting to go as decoys. Standing back and waiting to walk to the lodge with him were He Dog and the gay, joking Lone Bear, the one for whose horse badger holes were always waiting, the one who drew bullets as the smell of coffee cooking draws visitors to the lodge. Once he lost part of his scalp lock to a bullet and twice his breechcloth string had been cut, both times with many looking, so he had to run for shelter embarrassed as a maiden. But it was well known that his enemies had even worse luck. The arrows from his bow never stopped at the breechcloth string; his horses might step in holes and break their bones, but they increased until he had one of the best herds among the younger Oglalas.

Together the three friends walked across the frozen earth of the warrior camp. They felt good. This time they would make a big fight against the soldiers on the Piney, as Hump had said.

When only a few of the lodges still glowed red from the fires, most of them dark with the night-covered coals of sleeping, Crazy Horse went out to stand on the knoll behind the camp. The slim-horned moon had set, the stars low and cold-white, and the wolf's howling was loud, as for a storm or before a great meat-making. A long time the Oglala stood there, thinking of the white buffalo he had followed one winter day, of the snow thunder in a storm, and of the man who had ridden unhurt through the vision of his boyhood. With bullets all around him, the enemy dark ahead, and people grabbing at him from behind he rode on unhurt.

It was past the middle of the Moon of Popping Trees, the country patched with snow as a spotted horse, when the war party moved up the Prairie Dog Valley to Peno Creek. Here the Minneconjous decided to use one of their half-man dreamers to see what their luck would be. With a black blanket tied down over his head he was sent to ride the low hills, zigzagging his horse in the way known to him from his dream. After a while he came back, calling out that he had caught some soldiers. When he admitted that they were only a few, his horse was turned around and whipped out again, and three times more, until finally he came back making a loud shouting of victory. He had more enemies than he could hold in both hands, he cried. One hundred in the hands.

"Hoye! hoye!" the warriors answered him, feeling very good, even after the long waiting in the cold wind for this sign. They made presents to the dreamer and then sat in their robes for a smoking and the plans. Before daylight a party would start out against the wood camp beyond the fort. The whites there would make the quick-shooting signals for help; the soldiers would ride out that way. Here was where the decoys must be strong, for they were to coax the soldiers off in this direction, into the rough country and the waiting warriors. Very much depended upon the decoys in this plan, but they had a very strong leader, Hump said.

Hoye!

The next morning the warriors rode into the first gray light of

the winter day, their breaths in a cloud about them as they followed the ice that was Peno Creek to the brushy forks at the end
of Lodge Trail Ridge. Crazy Horse was leading a bald-faced,
white-footed bay that belonged to Little Hawk, a very fast horse
for a fight. He did not strip as he usually did for war, but went as
he was, his blanket belted around him against the cold. The red-
backed hawk was on his head, behind his ear hung the little stone,
and on his cheek sat the white lightning streak. He had made his
horse decoy medicine very carefully, sprinkling the bay with a
little earth from a pile made by the secret-working gopher, and
himself too. This day the soldiers must be fooled. Then with his
gun and his four shells ready, his bow on his back, his war club
in his belt, he led the decoy party of Oglalas and Cheyennes to
where the Powder River road crossed Piney Creek, not far from
the fort. Some left their horses in canyons back a way, for a soldier
will follow an Indian afoot very well. So, hidden in the string of
brush along the creek, squatting down, their backs turned to the
gray wind, they waited.

All the other warriors were ready too. The big party that was
to attack the wood train had started long ago and the plans for
the ambush in the forks of the Peno, at the end of Lodge Trail
Ridge, were done. The Cheyennes, as guests, were given the choice.
They took the southwest, the warmer side, the Oglalas and a few
Blue Clouds with them, the Minneconjous and the Hunkpapas
going to the winter slope of the ridge end with snow and ice all
through the brush.

From a high place Hump watched all these things with the far-
looking glasses to his eyes. There were the several shots, close
together, the soldier signal from the wood camp for help. The flag
on the signal hill above the fort moved and soldiers began to stream
out of the wide gate. First there were a lot on horses, riding four
abreast, and behind them very many walking soldiers. No one
took the time to count them but they seemed really the hundred the
Minneconjou dreamer had brought back in his hands.

As the soldiers left the fort [1] to help the wood train in the other direction, Crazy Horse led part of his decoy party out of the hiding and rode along behind the brush of the creek close to the fort, the bushes thin enough so they could be plainly seen. There was a shouting among the soldiers, much arm-pointing. As the little soldier chief stopped and looked towards the creek, a flash came from the wagon gun at the stockade and a ball burst over the decoys, knocking one of them from his horse, scattering the rest out into the open. Making loud scared howlings, they all ran for the hills and ravines, especially those afoot, jumping, zigzagging, as if afraid for their lives and scalps. And now the soldiers were coming hard after them, the walking men too, all of them running with their guns ready in their hands, the train they were to help forgotten.

While Hump signaled the party in from the wood camp Crazy Horse and Big Nose, the Cheyenne, and several others rode back and forth on the slope before the soldiers, the earth and rocks spurting up around them, the smoke making blue puffs in the cold air. First one, then another charged towards the whites, whooping, waving his blanket before their horses, as if trying to scare them, hold the soldiers off while the others got away.

Slowly Crazy Horse let his decoys be pushed up the travois trail running along the ridge, the horse soldiers stopping several times, perhaps to let the foot men catch up, perhaps because they were afraid. But the little soldier chief was Fetterman, the man who would ride through the Lakota nation, and so the decoys got them started again. Even the two other whites with the soldier, men who knew how to use their many-shooting guns and were probably hunters, kept coming. Several times Crazy Horse had to get off, once pretending to tie his war rope closer, once to lift up a foot of the bay horse, and then to lead it on a ways, jerking at the jaw bridle as he ran awkwardly from the soldiers. Once when it seemed that they had all stopped to turn back he sat down behind a bush

[1] Battle of Fort Phil Kearny or Fetterman Massacre, December 21, 1866.

as though hurt or worn out and built a little fire, the others going on, leaving him behind. Shots began to splatter close around him, one that glanced from the frozen ground crying over his head like a dying thing. Still he huddled over the few coals, pretending the smoke could not be seen, until the soldiers charged and he had to hurry to get out of their way. Whipping after the other decoys, he plunged down over the end of Lodge Trail Ridge towards the brushy forks of the Peno, the soldiers following fast.

Then, when even the walking men were past the mouth of the trap and not a warrior, not a horse of all those hidden had been seen or heard, Crazy Horse divided his decoys to ride across each other's trail. And at the signal the warriors charged out of the brush from both sides, crying: "Hoppo! Let us go!" whooping as they came.

The soldier chief halted his men, tried to turn them back, but it was too late. The Minneconjous were already across their flank, Thunder Hawk counting coup with his bow across the face of a soldier, the Cheyennes and Oglalas coming hard from the other side. Two horse soldiers went down and the rest stopped, trying to make a stand while those afoot ran for a rocky place up the slope, their long guns booming, the smoke puffing out blue and strong.

But the push of the warriors drove the troops back past them and higher up the ridge. Now the Indians charged the foot soldiers, He Dog and Lone Bear with the Oglalas and Cheyennes from their side, the Minneconjous coming from the other, the two parties like boiling flood waters meeting. Many soldiers went down under the war clubs and the trampling horses while those left were trying to reload and the two whites with the plenty-shooting guns kept firing. But the Indians were a great swarming and the air was thick with arrows. Several times somebody charged right through the rock-sheltered soldiers. Eats Meat, the Minneconjou, did it first and fell. By now the decoys had reached the fight, and Crazy Horse went through next. Then while the Cheyennes tried it he used up two of his shells on soldier heads showing. One of the men jumped up as he was hit and, falling forward, slid down the icy slope. A young Indian charged through the smoke afoot and, grabbing the man's gun, clubbed him over the head and came running back waving his capture, crying: "I have a gun! I have a gun!" like a crazy man.

And all the time some of the warriors were circling the smoke-darkened rocks of the soldiers, their horses jumping and dodging the ice on the slopes, and very hard to hit. Bowstrings twanged, rifles boomed. There were groans and cryings and the bad sound of horses in pain. Whenever a warrior fell, somebody behind dragged him away, the blood freezing as it dripped, the shooting going on until the guns in the rocks seemed still, the smoke lifting in the rising wind. Then just as Hump signaled a last charge, three men ran out and up the slope towards the horse soldiers, the Indians whooping after them, clubbing their war horses with their guns or bows. Here another man was hit but he managed to hang to the war rope looped into his belt and was dragged away. The rest charged on, firing arrows thick as a blizzard storm, picking them up from the earlier fighting and firing them again without slowing the running horses.

Now the troops began to back up the steep icy ridge, fighting as they withdrew, some riding and turning to shoot, some leading their horses and firing from a knee behind them. They kept in a close little bunch half lost in the smoke of their guns and the warriors couldn't get among them. Once when they pushed the whites too hard, one brave soldier dropped back to protect the rest, yelling names at the Indians, firing with pistol and gun as fast as he could reload until a Minneconjou rode up and shot an arrow through his breast. In the middle of that fighting the warrior stopped to take the scalp, for this white man had been very brave.

By now most of the American horses were wild from the noise and the arrows in them, squealing, plunging, jerking free, the warriors stopping to chase each one. At the top of the ridge the soldiers let the last of them go in a bunch, and with a whooping all the young Indians raced after them. It was a bad way to do, as Hump and Crazy Horse tried to show, shouting: "Hoka hey! Remember the helpless ones at home!" But none came back until the last horse was caught.

By then the soldiers had climbed to a rocky place near the top of the ridge, where it was just wide enough for them, and too steep and icy on three sides for the horses. So Hump called the warriors to fight on foot, get the battle over, for a storm was coming, the wind stinging.

"The walking soldiers took only a little while," he told them, "but now there is harder work ahead. Let us get it done!"

"Get it done!" the shirt-wearers agreed, the warriors shouting the words after them. So the horses were taken away and the Indians started crawling up the slope from all around, the cold pressing in on their hot bodies, their breath trailing over them as they kept their heads down, their guns and bows ready in their hands.

The soldiers had good back-loading rifles and could shoot very fast, but the Indians kept coming, jumping up, letting an arrow go at the top of the leap and then crawling again, those who had revolvers or ammunition for the guns they took from the soldiers using them only for the good shots. When they were close up around the whites, Hump and Crazy Horse shouted: "Hoppo! Up!" and with the warriors hard behind them they broke into the soldier circle, swinging the war clubs, striking with their knives, and making the hoarse fighting grunts of the grizzly in their throats.

Then the last white man was down and only a dog was left to run from among the rocks. He started away along the trail towards the fort, looking back several times and going on. Crazy Horse watched him, wondering that none among them had seen him until the whites were all scattered on the ground.

But the others had no time for such things. They were grabbing for the guns and revolvers of the soldiers and for the ammunition and the blue coats. They found very few shells but many other things, some of the round live iron stones that tell the white man's time, money, the paper called letters, a few small books, and a pretty picture of one of the sick-pale white women.

By now the scouts signaled that more soldiers were coming out of the fort. So when the last pair of pants had been jerked off, the last ring torn from the frozen fingers, the Indians went down into the valley, to make the travois for the badly wounded and for the dead—ten good men from the Lakotas, two Cheyennes lost, and a Blue Cloud. Not many for the hundred caught in the hands.

Crazy Horse spent no time on the hill when the fighting was done. A storm was coming, the gray wind biting the nose and freezing the hands out of the robe, and he could not find Lone Bear. No one, not He Dog nor Hump nor any other, had seen him. Somewhere, after that first charge on the walking soldiers when he had ridden in beside He Dog, Lone Bear had been lost. Even after the wounded had been collected and the Indians were hurrying to get to camp before the hurt ones froze, Crazy Horse was still searching every brush patch and gully for his friend. It couldn't be that he had left the fighting and gone home, for such a thing Lone Bear would not do. Besides, his horse was down at the frozen creek with a bullet through the shoulder. Poor Lone Bear, brave and strong-hearted, but so unlucky.

By now the new soldiers were coming along the ridge, almost as many of them as before, with a wagon along. maybe a wagon gun too. So most of the warriors stayed behind while the rest hurried away with the quick-made travois of the wounded, soldier coats and robes tied over them to shut out the cold wind.

At the top of the ridge the soldiers stopped, standing in bunches like uneasy animals, looking, probably wondering about the other whites. Below them the valley was full of taunting warriors, making the insulting motions of the Indian and some they had learned from the whites, calling out to them in Lakota and in English to come down and fight. But the soldiers made no move, and because it seemed they did have a wagon gun and the quivers of the Indians were so near empty, and their guns too, they had to let these other whites from the Piney go.

All this time Crazy Horse still hunted for his friend Lone Bear,

Hump staying behind to help him. The sky was darkening and the snow was on the wind when they found him in a little clump of brush, a clump so small it seemed none could hide there. The warrior was face down and when Crazy Horse turned him up, they saw that his hands and his face were already white-frozen, his bullet-torn breast a great lump of blood ice. As Crazy Horse lifted him, Lone Bear opened his eyes and even now there was a little shamed smiling for this bad luck. So he died in the arms of his friend, with Hump standing beside them, crying.

But Crazy Horse did not cry for this man killed by the whites so deep in their own country. His heart was cold and black with an anger that could not be made good until many more of the white men died like those scattered naked up there on the ridge.

So Long as GRASS SHALL GROW

THIS year it seemed that spring would never come to the Powder River country again, the new grass never be born. Then suddenly the sun was warm as dance fires along the south slopes. Snow water roared gray in the canyons, and the ice broke from the streams and piled itself high on the flooded banks. Geese came north on the wind, and at dusk the ducks quacked softly in the low places that were all lakes now, and in the buffalo wallows.

Early with the mornings the old men came out to sit beside the lodge doors in the sun, hurrying, their wrinkled faces glad, as though they had never hoped to feel this strength again. The women, too, stopped their complaining of the long hungry winter, and of the empty parfleches and the thin soup, and ran to hang out the sleeping robes and those from the floors. As they worked they looked towards the marshy grounds along the creeks where young shoots of the rushes would soon be starting, good to eat after a long winter of meat, mostly dried.

It was not that their men lay around the villages but that there could not be hunting enough for the great camp held together against the fort on the Piney, and since the day that the soldiers were killed the snow had been deep, the winter the coldest the Old Ones had ever known. Hunters came in with hands and feet swollen from the freezing, telling stories of the elk gone as from a dead country and the buffaloes too, the few who stayed behind standing frozen in the snow, hard as stone. There were three hundred in one gulch, it was said, the storms blowing over them so they would be lost even to the wolves until the thaws of spring.

The people had scattered, but even then it was hard to live. Some bands got lost from the others, the starving ponies floundering in the drifts, the people digging them out, helping them pull the travois. There was much snowblindness, and Creeping, the medicine man, cured so many that his women had trouble finding enough young cottonwood to feed his growing herd that was his pay. Creeping had a very strong medicine. He sprinkled snow in the eyes of the blind ones, sang his needle-fly song that he had got in a dream, and then blew snow from his mouth on the backs of their heads and they could see again. For this a horse was not too much.

The sons of Worm were out every day, it seemed. Their mother made bunches of buffalo-robe moccasins with the fur side in for the hunts and little sacks of soot grease for the cheek bones, so they were neither frozen or blinded. Still there was not always fresh meat, although they were good hunters, as was common in the men of their family. Crazy Horse had the heat of anger in his heart for the long, cold rides. The death of his friend was still unavenged and the whites on the Piney were very careful now. Then he heard that many more soldiers were to come and so he moved the Long Face camp down towards Fort Reno where he could watch the Powder River trail. There was not much cottonwood there for the ponies in that country, and game was hard to find, but there should be good hunting along this road for one who had lost a friend to the white man's guns.

When the meat in the camp was gone, Crazy Horse and his brother went up towards the Crazy Woman Creek together. Their horses played out, but they had some snowshoes taken from the Crows, so they went on afoot, carrying a robe apiece, a little *wasna*, and their knives and bows. The country was white and bare; even the little snowbirds that made the friendly winter sounds were gone. Then one morning Crazy Horse saw the tracks of a lone buffalo walking in what seemed a sacred way on the deep snow, the sharp hoofs not breaking through the crust at all. The brothers followed fast, their breath making clouds around their shoulders and frosting their woolen capotes, but they found nothing except a few hairs hanging over the tracks in a patch of plum brush. They were pale hairs, almost white,[1] and Crazy Horse looked at them a long time, his brother standing silent beside him. Then he put them away in the medicine sack hanging around his neck. Now they knew they would never find the buffalo they were following but that it would be good anyway. So Little Hawk pushed hard on the tails of his brother's snowshoes, laughing into the cold wind that was curling up feathers of snow from the edges of the drifts.

When the ice-pale sun had started downward they came to broken country. In a little bluff-circled canyon with a few bare trees Crazy Horse saw something dark that seemed to be moving. He dropped down and looked a long time, then turned his face to his brother.

"Elk!" he said.

It was true—a little herd of them surrounded by the windbreak of bluffs and the deep snow, probably a hundred elk. There was only one good side for crawling near and the wind was wrong, but the two Indians circled that way and managed to get pretty close before the animals caught the smell and scattered out into the deep drifts, the bulls plunging ahead, snow flying higher than their spreading horns. Bows and knives ready, the hunters ran hard to overtake the stragglers, the cows and yearlings, before they got to higher ground where the drifts were shallow; and when the last one got to the ridge, the two Oglalas looked back and saw eight dark spots in the torn drifts behind them, eight elk down in their blood in the snow.

By night they had the meat in a big pile covered with a foot of snow and surrounded by man smell to keep the wolves away. With the deadwood they build a good fire far back under the bluffs of the elk yard, out of the rising wind and hard for any roaming

[1] Some say a white steer escaped from a beef herd roamed the region in 1866-7.

Crows to find. When the air was sweet and rich from the roasting meat Crazy Horse cut off a piece with his knife and offered it to the sky and the earth and the four great directions. Then they ate until they could only lie back in their buffalo robes, feet to the hidden fire, and sleep.

After that there was fresh meat for the camp of Long Face until the herd of elk was gone. Crazy Horse didn't go out to hunt any more. He watched the little fort at the fork of the Powder, raided the soldier herds, picked off the mail riders, shot into the hunting parties and wood-haulers. He did not scalp those he killed nor count them, for the death of Lone Bear could not be rubbed out by any certain number.

Finally the streams ran free once more, so high from the snow that the people could hardly cross them. Before the Long Face camp started north some warriors came down from Red Cloud's village near the Yellowstone to see if they were missing anything. A few days later another party, this one from the Loafers and those down on the Republican, rode in, telling of many small raids on the Holy Road, and of the people in the south still having to run away from the soldiers although their chiefs had signed the white paper last summer. It was plain the peace talk was only made to fool them, and so they had come north to hear what was planned for the summer. It would surely be something big, even if it was only eighty-one soldiers that had been killed at Phil Kearny instead of a hundred.

"Do they say it was eighty-one?" Crazy Horse asked. "It was a hundred the Minneconjou dreamer brought in the hand, and one does no counting against the powers that give these things to us."

Eighty, ninety, or a hundred, it was good, and they had come to help, the southern warriors said. But they brought few guns and little ammunition. These things were very hard to get, they said. The soldiers came tramping through every trader's place and sometimes even carried away his own buffalo gun.

"Ahh-h!" Crazy Horse made the sound of concern over his pipe. It must be hard to live down there, with the game so scarce and wild for the bow. He heard, too, that soon the peace men were coming again, trying to coax the rest of the Indians in.

"Yes, with more presents than before," a Brule said. He spoke true, for in April, the Moon of New Grass, they were back, with long rows of wagons, and once more the Loafers made the good words and got the things meant for all.

Crazy Horse heard this when he got home from a fight with the Snakes. He found the Long Face camp full of young warriors from the south wanting to go along to the Powder, hoping for more fighting around the Piney this summer. Because Woman's Dress was among them, Crazy Horse went on ahead. He could not forget that it was this one who had hurried with the bad news of a marrying to his ears. Anyway, he must stop to talk with Chips about losing another good war horse, played out in a fight. And in his saddlebags were the teeth of the elk herd killed last winter. There were enough for several more rows on the dress of Black Buffalo Woman. It was already almost covered, the finest one among the Oglalas, probably as heavy as her second son, the shy one, so much as his mother used to be in the old village circle down around the Holy Road—shy and laughing too.

Nothing was done at the peace council of the spring and so the whites kept coming back like hungry dogs around the cooking pots or a wolf to a smelling stump on a hill. Man Afraid and Iron Shell, still hostile because the soldiers took his people, including his pretty young wife in the battle of the Blue Water, went down in June to talk to them. They felt strong from the big fight on the Piney and the many other things the warriors had done. It wasn't peace they wanted but the closing of the Powder River road, and guns and ammunition. The first questions they asked were about these things. Yes, their bands were coming behind them, they said, and when would the guns be given out?

Red Cloud was along but he made no words one way or another, as was good, for he was no chief, but when his warriors heard this, some remembered that he could talk loud enough when it suited him, even if he had no right, and that lately the Bad Face seemed to be working for the white man. Maybe he was just waiting to see how much they would give him. Soon the young men saying these things began to move over to the Hunkpatilas, mostly to the camp of the light-haired one who was surely making no tracks of peace in the direction of the whites. The newcomers were feasted and danced, but the mother of Crazy Horse looked upon them with uneasiness. "It will make for bad hearts where the lodges stand empty—" she said one night, speaking her words quietly from her place. And because there was no answer to this, her men gave her none. They were silent, too, when Little Wound of the Bear people, the southern Oglalas, came to say that they had decided to go back to their country. They had lived up here around the big-talking Bad Faces for two years, the chief told Worm and Long Face. It was enough.

And hearing this, the brothers made the whistling sound in their pipes and let it be, knowing that the killing of Bull Bear still lay like a bloody robe between those people. But some good warriors would be lost.

When the sundances of the year called 1867 were done, the ponies shining fat from the circling grass, the Lakotas and Cheyennes camped on the Rosebud River to plan attacks on the forts of the Piney and the Big Horn River. It was the first time the people were together since the many soldiers had been killed, and for days there was feasting and dancing, with all the warrior societies helping. The *heyokas*, the thunder dreamers, made their ceremonials too. They had let the things that protected them go too long and this spring, when the antelope were dropping their young, one of them was killed by lightning and several horses were struck. So they made the old, old ceremonials before the people, doing everything backwards and mixed up, as they must—wearing their clothes wrong side out or turned around, all singing together instead of one at a time, shivering in the heat of the sun, crawling through mudholes instead of jumping them, pointing their arrows at themselves and falling like dead when they missed, taking meat from the boiling kettles with their hands.

All these things brought much laughing to the people, made them feel new and strong, and yet among the leaders there was a splitting as when a great cloud is suddenly hit by many winds. They couldn't agree which of the forts should be struck first, talking this way and that until Crazy Horse went out against the Crows. When the headmen decided what they would do they could let him know.

Finally the warriors made the plans, part of them, mostly Cheyennes, riding against the north fort, while others, many from the Minneconjous, would strike Fort Phil Kearny, although there was not enough ammunition to be divided.

Late in July, the Moon of Cherries Reddening, the scouts reported that the wood trains were going out to the camp at the head of the Little Piney again, with about fifty soldiers along, four or five other whites, and the horse herds of the fort.

"Hoye! Scalps and horses!" the warriors cried, and moved out in a big party behind Hump, with Red Cloud and others of the older warriors going along to watch. Coming like shadows from the dusk into the rough country north of the Big Piney, they made a still camp not far from Lodge Trail Ridge and waited for the owl hoot of the returning scouts. In the darkness they came with good word: the woodcutters had their tents under the foothills along the Little Piney, with twelve soldiers guarding. On a little prairie about a mile this side, fourteen wagon boxes were set on the ground for a night corral to hold the horse herd, with tents there too, and about twenty-five, thirty soldiers. At the bank of the creek running between the two camps watchers, or pickets as the whites called them, walked up and down.

There was no planning for this attack except that Hump was to lead the decoys, everybody else doing what he wanted. It was the kind of fighting for young men going against Crows for scalps and horses, not against the whites come to take the country. But when Crazy Horse tried to say this, he saw there was trouble enough among them, and so he went along in silence.

Early the next morning Hump led his six decoys out, the warriors staying well hidden back in the broken hills until one of the soldier pickets shot at the decoys.[1] The younger Hunkpapas and Minneconjous charged down on the wagon-box corral and so the rest had to go too. Some swept the grazing herd off northward; others followed Crazy Horse across the creek to the woodcutters' tents and shot two of the men before they could get away into the timbered foothills. Crazy Horse chased the fleeing ones, but the warriors had stopped behind for the scalping, the plundering and burning of the camp, and when he came back he found them squatting in the shade eating molasses and hard bread, in the middle of a fight.

By now the older men, like Red Cloud, Flying By, the Minneconjous, and Ice, the Cheyenne, had settled in a row up on a hillside to watch, to smoke, and perhaps to signal a little advice. Hump had driven all the pickets into the wagon-box corral, getting one of his warriors wounded and hurting the whites too. Now there was only one place to fight, only the wooden boxes and the good shooting guns of the walking soldiers standing between the warriors and thirty or forty scalps for the victory dance. The young men were already circling the corral, firing arrows from behind their horses, charging up in the face of the cracking rifles. After several men fell and had to be dragged back out of the smoke, Crazy Horse and Hump stopped the rest. They must try something else to use up the ammunition, something safer. So leaving the horses out of range they got ready for a foot charge up a ravine from the Little Piney, some making their shield medicine, some their ground-fighting things to help them over the close-grazed little prairie.

Just as the soldiers tore down the tents so they could see, the Indians rose up in a wide running wave like wind sweeping over tall grass. Painted and dressed for war, with their spears and shields held high, they came, chanting war songs, zigzagging, sending arrows ahead, dropping into low places and rising to run

[1] Wagon-Box Fight, August 2, 1867.

closer, to fire again. But the soldiers' bullets came so fast and sharp that many were hit, some going down and being dragged away, even some of the shield men wounded through the bull-neck medicine shields before they got close enough to do anything. So the charge broke and scattered, leaving a brave, fast-running Oglala dead behind them, too close for anyone to get.

"We are butchered like the spotted buffalo without ammunition!" Crazy Horse cried out in anger at this failing.

"Ahh-h!" one with his shoulder red in blood agreed. "There seems no end to their shooting."

Just then a tall Lakota called Jipala, stripped to breechcloth and holding a big buffalo shield before him, rose up and went towards the soldiers, not jumping or dodging, just walking straight and slow, singing his war song. Everybody watched—even the guns still, for this brave thing. When he got close he drew his bow, jumped high into the air, and let an arrow go into the corral, then another and another, shooting faster than a good gun of the whites. The soldiers began to fire at him, the sudden echo like thunder in the foothills, the bullets striking closer and closer, so Crazy Horse led a fast charge from the other side, but it was too late. A fine, brave Lakota was dead, right under the wagon boxes.

Losing these good men made Crazy Horse and Hump angry, and calling the warriors together, they harangued them to be more careful. Strong fighters were getting killed foolishly. But the young warriors tried two more foot charges, losing another man and getting three wounded trying to drag a friend away. Crazy Horse watched this and saw again that the bow and war club were nothing against the guns of the whites; even with the heart of the grizzly and the arm of the north wind they would be nothing against the guns.

"Too many are getting hurt!" he warned.

So the warriors made another horse charge up close to the wagon boxes, which were splintered and torn by now, with arrows sticking thick as quills on a porcupine everywhere except along the middle, where the boards were spread for the gun barrels. But it seemed

there was no end to the ammunition. Besides, the scouts had signaled that more soldiers were coming from the fort with the wagon
guns along, already booming on the Little Piney, the advisers on
the hillside getting up and moving towards their horses. So the
fight was stopped, the warriors carrying the six wounded away
with them and one of the dead. Nobody could get to the five others.
They had killed some whites and got many American horses and
mules, but it was not a good day to count time by.

That evening Crazy Horse sat alone over his pipe, thinking about
the fighting of the last two years, wondering if the young warriors
were not right in their impatience with the old way of ambush,
of surround. The great war against the whites couldn't be won
by surrounds, even by good ones like the day on Lodge Trail Ridge.
They must have guns and ammunition, good guns for everybody
and powder enough to drive the bullets deep. Then they could
fight the whites wherever they found them, fight them and drive
them back.

But when he tried to talk of this to the others it seemed they
did not understand. It must be the poor words his tongue made,
not the truth he knew in his heart—that if the Indians followed the
old ways they were lost.

At camp they found out that the attack on the Big Horn fort
had been made in a hayfield, only a little fight, with a few hurt
on each side. When both parties were back the warriors made a
victory dance together, telling their deeds and dancing their scalps
and coups. But Jipala was not there to speak of his brave walking
into the burning guns of the whites, or the five others. To Crazy
Horse every man lost for nothing seemed one of his own lodge gone.

The pink flowers of the rattlesnake root were blooming on the
knolls to help the people through the days when the snakes were
angry, and the young antelope were running with the bunch before the Indians scattered to smaller camps. Once more some messengers, ten this time, came to coax the people to a peace council
in the round moon of September. They came fine to see, each with

a good new horse, a white-man saddle and the other things that belonged, a rifle too, and a new blanket, leggings, breechcloth, soldier coat, hat, and shirt—all given them by the whites. For those who would promise to come in each messenger carried eight squares of tobacco wrapped in scarlet cloth tied with ribbon, and in his pipe case was one of the white papers saying he was a good Indian.

"Like Two Face? His good paper got him hung up by the neck—" Crazy Horse said.

Not long after this a Loafer news rider came through from the northern camps of the Yellowstone, talking excitedly of the big things he had seen there, Sitting Bull's Hunkpapas so rich, with great herds of mules and horses, the parfleches bursting with meat, the lodges piled high with robes waiting for the trader. In the south they had only heat, dust, buffalo gnats, and more soldiers with guns marching up and down the hunting grounds. Below the Republican River Long Hair, the one called Custer, had been chasing the Indians until Little Wound's Oglalas and the southern Cheyennes got tired of trying to keep out of his way and had a fight with him. They got some scalps and carbines and left him standing.

"Hou!" the northern people said, pleased. But they knew that it would mean more trouble for their relatives, for the helpless ones in the south.

Then there was the iron road, the railroad of the whites, coming up along the emigrant trail. Some of the warriors had raided the workers, and when it was time for the peace council again, the southern Indians came, dark-faced, with knives under their blankets and strong words in their mouths. The whites were killing the buffalo, driving all the game away with their wagons and the new iron road, so the Indian must have guns and ammunition to help his people live. Remembering the roaring council with the soldier chief called Mitchell three years before and Red Cloud's defiance last year, they made a great and threatening noise too, and got all the things they wanted.

But Red Cloud, Black Twin, and Long Face sent word to Laramie they were too busy to come down; some other time, maybe next year. The treaty men talked big about sending a great army of soldiers against them, and still there was no sound of lodge poles falling for a running after peace.

It was true that the warriors of the Powder were busy, so busy that nobody could use the road in that country except the soldiers and then only when there were many together, fighting their way through. By the time the otter were making their winter slides and the beaver fur was thick a few traders slipped into the winter camps bringing only what their riding horses carried because the soldiers watched even their going for hunts. But there was a little powder and lead in the saddlebags and a few bright new things for the women. Black Buffalo Woman had her third baby bound in the cradleboard, and with vermilion for her cheeks and a new striped blanket she walked her village proudly, as is fitting in the handsome young Lakota wife of a man who has many ponies and a good place with his people. But the eyes of the women followed her more for another thing, for the many visitings in the village from the shirt-wearer of the Hunkpatilas, wondering if it was the dark looks of No Water's friends that kept him from emptying the lodge, or from lifting the flap when the man was away. The wife of Eagle Foot had just left him and everybody had wondered, for he was a violent man. But he sat smoking at his lodge as always, accepting the two young horses her new man tied there to show his good heart. And soon the Eagle was visiting the woman's mother and bringing her to care for his lodge, seeming glad that now he could speak to her again as he would to an aunt, not give her only respectful silence, as was customary with the mother of a wife.

But the woman of Eagle Foot had no important relatives, did not carry power in her hand, as did Black Buffalo Woman.

The traders brought news from the south country, including some funny white-man stories of the wagon-box fight. The soldiers at Laramie were saying that three thousand warriors were in it and that very many Indians died there, some claiming sixty, some as many as a thousand, ten times the circle that meant one hundred. The warriors laughed at this, but Crazy Horse wondered why these things were told.

"How can they say these foolish things? Do they not know that we are the same ones as last winter, when the hundred soldiers were left on the ground?"

It seemed that the whites thought the Indians were surprised by the back-loading guns which shoot fast.

"But they must know we have seen these a long time. I have one myself," Crazy Horse said. "And others among us got some from the soldiers who ran out of the country two years ago. Then there are the two many-shooting ones taken from the whites on the hill above the Piney."

Yes, the traders agreed, but the soldiers had to make up something to help themselves feel good.

As soon as the cold of winter broke, many of the northern Indians moved down for another council at Laramie, hearing this time that the peace men would bring good word from the Great Father and that the newspapers were saying the Powder River forts would be closed by sundance time. Even the Loafers were glad and talked so big around the trading houses where the soldiers could hear that the whites felt whipped and so one shot at an Indian, killing him. It stirred up the council camp like a spear thrust into a wasp nest. They would have the soldier turned over to them for punishment as the whites always demanded when the young Indians made trouble, even for a little thing like shooting a poor Mormon cow. When they did not get the soldier, the warriors went to raid the Holy Road, the depredations really by Indians now, not by the Gray Men that the whites called outlaws, dressed in paint and feathers and moccasins to fool people in their stealing.

Crazy Horse had come towards the Platte to watch the chiefs

at the counciling. When it was known about the Indian killed he got up a party of seventy, including Little Hawk and Little Big Man, to raid a little, mostly against the herds of the soldier towns. The American Horse warriors along were friends of the white men at the Horseshoe Ranch on the Holy Road and so he left most of the others behind a butte smoking and took the friendlies down to visit and trade, maybe get a little powder.

But the barking dogs of the whites ran back to the old station as the warriors came calling out "Hou, *cola!* Hou, *cola!*" their teeth shining in their dark unpainted faces. When the white men ran too, slamming their heavy door against the visitors, Crazy Horse pulled his pinto back, but Little Big Man and the American Horse Indians stayed near, laughing at this scare of the whites, calling out who they were until bullets began to come through the gunholes in the walls and two of them fell wounded from their horses.

So the warriors got ready for a fight and came whooping down upon the old stockade and station house. Splitting, they circled the place, Crazy Horse going around the sun's way, the short, squat Little Big Man the other. When two more warriors were hurt, they fired the stables and the stockade with the well, driving the whites who came running out with water buckets back to their log walls. But towards evening the Indians left the burning place and went to Twin Springs, three miles away, to visit with the old Frenchman, Mousseau. He was married into their people and might give them something to eat.

When they came back after dark the old log buildings still made a red light over the place. Little Big Man howled like a coyote and hooted like an owl, but no white men showed themselves nor did any dogs come out and after a while the Indians spread their robes and went to sleep. At daylight Crazy Horse saw that the whites were still there, but the scouts signaled quite a few horse soldiers and wagons coming up the Holy Road, so he led the Indians away into the bluffs.

"The whites down there will go away with them," the warriors said, sorry the fun was finished.

But they didn't, so there was another good fight that afternoon, with Little Hawk very reckless and Little Big Man making a great noise and showing off. By dark Crazy Horse had located all the gunholes of the house and Little Hawk and two others sneaked up and fired the building, the smell of the burning pine logs fine clear up to the ridge, while Little Big Man led the warriors in a dance, making songs about whites who shoot at people who come visiting.

In the morning the Indians found no bones in the smoking ashes of the house, only a hole in the ground showing that the white men had dug out to a little sod fort and got away in the darkness. The Indians followed their tracks toward Twin Springs, but the scouts signaled that the house there was burning, Mousseau and his family had gone, and the men had found horses and were riding down the river towards Laramie.

Little Big Man made a whooping and whipped out after them, the others stringing out behind him, remembering that the ponies were still weak from the dead, winter-washed grass. They surrounded the whites in some low hills, the Indians getting the horses and a lot of clothes from the saddle bundles. Young Little Hawk cut the seat from his first pair of white-man pants and put them on, feeling very good. In the pocket was a roll of paper. Crazy Horse knew it—pay-money.

"It may buy powder," he said.

By now the whites were running again, headed for a little pine-clumped hill. On the way one of them got shot in the eye, but he stopped and pulled the arrow out, the eyeball coming with it. The warriors saw him do this strong thing and did not shoot, nor did they shoot at the one who dropped behind to cover the retreat, Crazy Horse charging him to keep him up with the others. It was almost as if the Indians were driving a herd of wild young horses, not letting them scatter. Once when they got into a washout full of cedars, the warriors dropped big stones in on them, and shot fire arrows into the trees until the thick smoke of the burning cedar drove them out towards open ground. The first one the Indians got was the brave man who pulled his eye out, and because he had been so strong, many came to strike his body with their bows or knives or their hands. Soon an old man with a hairy face dropped behind, and when Crazy Horse came up he saw it was an old trader they used to know when he worked for the company called the Hudson's Bay. It made the Oglala feel bad. Perhaps they had killed enough today. But Little Big Man and his friends were still chasing the rest, only five now and three of them slow from wounds. Then one of these shot a bullet through his own head and the Indians turned their horses out around him and rode after the others, leaving his hair behind.

When the four men stopped again, in a bunch out on the flat country, Little Big Man and his followers circling them, Crazy Horse called out that it was enough. Laying down his gun and his knife and with his hands up in the sign of peace he walked towards the whites, his warriors, his brother too, calling out that he would be killed. He went out not like a fighting warrior but with his brown hair free of feather, his lean face unpainted carrying only his otterskin pipe case, like a man going to visit his friends. Before the tired, bloody whites with their guns held on him he sat down crosslegged and, filling his pipe, offered it to them.

"Enough good men have been killed today," he said, in the few white-man words he remembered and the Indian signs.

So they smoked and made peace. The whites offered to give him the goods they had cached at Twin Springs that morning if he let them go. He could bring up three more Indians to walk with their four, the others keeping back.

Thoughtfully Crazy Horse looked at the men, worn out, bad hurt, probably with few shells—four afoot to his many on horseback. Yet they faced him straight.

"Hou!" he agreed. "You are brave men."

So with Little Hawk back to help control the younger warriors and with the wild Little Big Man up where he could be watched, the four Indians and the four white men began their walk to Twin Springs. They went slowly, the whites tired and hurt. None of them had had a drink since morning and when they came near the water everybody ran for it, the warriors crowding up around the others, lying down to drink among them. One of the white men picked up the coffee pot of the Indians to dip his water, but when he saw there were scalps in it he drank from his belly, like the rest. This was a strong thing for a white man to do, Crazy Horse knew, and it made him glad.

At the burnt ashes of the buildings one of the whites stood off with his gun to see that all was done well. One Indian went to watch on the hill while the others stacked their weapons and sat in a half circle to smoke and wait while two of the whites handed out the goods from the cache hole. They brought up coffee and sugar and beans and other things, even tobacco. When one of the warriors smelled whisky they looked down into the hole and saw the burning water running out of a little barrel into the ground. The Indians grabbed old cans to catch some, but the whites would only give it to the headman.

"Take the keg to the camp for the dancing," they told Crazy Horse, making the white-man words and the few signs they knew.

When all the goods were divided the Indians left, Little Big Man and some of the younger warriors shooting into the air as they rode away, sorry to lose the four scalps. The scout who stayed back awhile blew his eagle-bone whistle when he saw the whites sneak out into the darkness, just to make them run a little. Then he rode after the others.

Now many people came swarming over the country of the hunting Lakotas with pack horses of presents like trapper bait to catch signers for the peace paper. Breeds, traders, and Loafers came, even Father De Smet, the Black Robe of the Big Council, a weak and sick old man now. They all talked of the good things in the new paper—the Powder River road closed forever, the Indians getting all the country from the Missouri to the White Mountains so long as grass shall grow and water flow.

"Hou!" the people said, even many in the hostile camps, not

listening to those who said this paper gave them nothing they did not always have—gave them only their own country. But it would give them peace, many hoped, and so early in May the southern Oglalas signed and took their presents, including guns and ammunition, the soldiers looking on with long faces. Man Afraid, who was with his old friend Little Wound that day, signed too, and then came back north. The rest of the hostiles said they would wait awhile, for the soldiers still had themselves locked inside the gates of the Powder River forts, were still riding up and down the hated road. But the stories the Man Afraid people told were so good that more went down and brought back axes, knives, kettles, blankets, and guns, new guns. Proudly they showed these things to Crazy Horse and he could only turn his face away and ride in anger against the Crows. Each time he came back more of the people had gone to the soldier town on the Laramie; only his own and those of Red Cloud and Red Dog stayed back. In the north Four Horns and Black Moon and Sitting Bull of the Hunkpapas would not touch the pen, but many others did.

Then one day the troops marched out of the fort on the Piney leaving the gate open behind them. Most of their goods were hauled away, but what was left had been given to Little Wolf and his Cheyennes. The women were very excited, going through the stockade, picking out their houses. But the chief said it was not good. They must follow the buffalo for meat; they could not live if they had to stay in one place. He burned the fort to the ground and Red Cloud did the same thing to the one on the Big Horn River; no soldiers would ever live there again.

Now, like the silence after thunder, peace had come to the Indian country. Everybody seemed very glad, all except the wild young men who had not yet counted enough coups for a wife, or taken scalps. But Crazy Horse and He Dog and many others sat over their pipes and wondered how long the soldiers could be kept away when there were so many whites along the Holy Road who wanted the army trade, so many with empty wagon trains that could only be used in an Indian war.

They could see how it was in the south country, where the people touched the pen to the peace paper last spring. The soldiers were still chasing the people, had even killed Roman Nose, the good friend of Crazy Horse. It seemed that in a Lakota lodge the warrior had eaten bread that had been handled with an iron fork and there was not time to purify himself before the fight. So a great Cheyenne died, one who had refused to be a chief when the people asked it, one who wished only to be a good warrior and a good man.

Nor was everything quiet among the northern Oglalas. The whites said the Indians had won a great victory in the peace paper, yet in every council there was a roaring between those who wanted to live from the hunt and those who wanted to go down and wait along the Holy Road for the white-man goods, even the women quarreling over it at the robe-making, two drawing the butcher knives from their belts over it, a shameful thing to be done, and when the man of one of them tried to quiet her, she went home and threw all his goods out before the lodge into the raining, his bow and spear and ceremonial shirt and even his war bonnet and medicine bundle. And on top of it all the high-backed bed from the man's place.

"So—!" she cried, "take your warrior stuff to the white man! It may be that you are still man enough for a Loafer woman, but not for my lodge!"

The headmen of the Oglalas had another trouble. The Great Father was still calling for Red Cloud to sign the peace paper and yet how could this be done, when he was not a chief at all? So the council was called for the fall at Bear Butte, the old gathering place of the Tetons, and here it was as if a great storm were blowing and shaking the council lodge. Not since Bull Bear was killed and they had to decide what to do with Red Cloud and his relations who helped spill the blood of the Lakota chief had there been such a bad time.

But today there would be no new break between the people. Today it was agreed to let the Bad Faces have another shirt-wearer,

Black Twin, a strong man with the warriors, and to make Red Cloud a treaty chief, a chief only for talking about this one thing with the whites, and only for his own people.

"It is a long time since there has been such a one among the Lakotas, not since the people crossed the Missouri," Worm told Crazy Horse. "And that one pleased only the enemy people, so he had to live with them."

Before long there was another ceremony—Man Afraid and Brave Bear stepping back from their places in the chiefs' society, giving them to their sons, Young Man Afraid and Sword. The day before this was done the Hunkpatila had come to smoke with his old friends, Worm and Long Face, to talk of what he planned to do. These were hard times, the road ahead dark as with the smoke of a great prairie fire. It was better to let the young men lead the way.

Worm sucked at his pipe. "Perhaps you were blinded by bad medicine that night on the Running Water—the night Conquering Bear died—" he said slowly.

Man Afraid sat silent in his blanket, his pipestem between his straight, strong lips, the lodge fire red over his face, and the quiet tip of the chief's feather in his hair. Crazy Horse saw him so, a strong man, a great man, one who had no need to defend himself. The next day Man Afraid laid his chief's blanket about the shoulders of his son.

Then in November, the Moon of the Falling Leaves, Red Cloud touched the pen of the peace paper, and the war, the one the whites called the Sioux War, was over.

◖◗ ◖◗ ◖◗ ◖◗ ◖◗ ◖◗

MANY THINGS *Thrown Away*

THE first blizzard of the winter came roaring into the stillness of a warm afternoon, scattering the buffalo, snow-caked and blinded, into any canyon or gully that stopped their feet, hurrying Crazy Horse home from the Hunkpapas, a big can of powder in his packs and enough blue beads for a fine woman's dress.

He found the people much disturbed. "The treaty men of the Great Father have once more spoken with the crooked tongue," Worm said, while the warriors used words of more heat. "The chiefs have sold themselves for another feast of crackers and molasses—" they were saying boldly for all to hear, and no one was laughing or calling them foolish now.

No open trade with the Indians had been allowed since the southern trouble of 1864, and by the time of the council this year the lodges were swelled with fine robes and furs, the women complaining loudly that they had no vermilion, no color for the quills and the parfleches, no beads, no cloth or awls or scissors and none of the other white-man goods to use or eat. Even the butcher knives were worn thin as grass blades.

So the chiefs touched the pen and told the people to get ready for a good winter with the high-loaded trader wagons once more in the villages. Then, as soon as the peace paper was signed, the soldier chief said that no goods must be taken to the camps and the Indians must keep from the trader houses. A band of Oglalas who did not believe this foolish talk went down to Platte Bridge and

225

came back fast with one of their headmen on a travois, deep hurt from the soldier guns that were turned on them when they came near the trading place.

"Ahh-h, it is a bad way to do!" Crazy Horse agreed, without surprise.

Yes, and now there was trouble about stolen horses too. The treaty chiefs said that all stock stolen after the peace was signed was to be returned, but now the whites would have everything, even that taken in the time when Julesburg was burned, and the Platte Bridge fight. Crazy Horse laughed at the chiefs' complaining. Why hadn't they asked for the things taken from the Indians at Blue Water and at Sand Creek? So far the whites owed the Oglalas very little and he would try to see that this remained true.

During the summer, when the soft sound of peace was still over the land, many traders' and soldiers' sons had come north to hunt, to visit, and to court the young women who grew up so slender and fine in the hostile camps. The Indians made them welcome, for it is good to lie down with the people of one's mother. But before long Crazy Horse discovered why these white-man sons came to them—all the Lakotas around the trails, even the Indian families of the traders, had to go to a new place called the Whetstone agency, up at the mouth of White Earth River, on the Missouri.

So many of the sons rode north, bringing their fiddles and their trader songs, making much new fun for the young people. And sometimes about the winter fires they told of the stories of the whites, showed some of their newspapers calling the Indian bloodthirsty savages and murdering hounds of hell. It was Deon, over from the Red Cloud camp, who tried to explain this hell to the Indians, although there were no Lakota words. It was as if the shades of the dead ones were captured and kept in a burning place forever. Worm nodded, meaning they had heard of the story and seen pictures of a hairy-faced man in a blue blanket with a yellow ring around his head. It seemed the shades of the whites who did not touch the crossed trees that he carried were sent to the burning place by the Great Power.

"It is indeed hard to understand—a great power doing a bad thing—"

But there was something else in the newspapers, a picture of naked, painted Indians with bloody scalps and war clubs dancing around three little girls tied to the door of a burning house. This was passed around the circle. When it reached Worm he held it to the firelight.

"It would seem that the Indians had gone into the white man's country and started to kill his women and children instead of the whites coming to kill ours," he finally said as he handed it to his son. But Crazy Horse would not be quiet about this thing. "Lies, more white-man lies!" he cried as he tore the paper through, his face pale as one of the sick women of the Holy Road in his anger.

Later he was told that the paper had belonged to the son of a soldier chief once at Laramie, one called Garnett. So he sent the camp crier to bring young Billy to his lodge and gave him a good spotted horse, one that the eyes of the girls would follow. Then he asked about the things along the trails.

It had been bad there for the traders for several years, as the Indians knew, with the iron road taking away the freighting, and trade with the Indians only possible in the night. Sometimes their sons joined the Gray Men in their stealing or made other trouble, fighting and killing.

Crazy Horse gave the sign of knowing. There was a trader's son like that living with the Hunkpapas, one called Grabber. It was said he got into trouble among the whites of the Missouri, killed somebody, and then ran away to the Indians. He was now in the lodge of Sitting Bull and shooting mail carriers between the upper Missouri forts. Crazy Horse had seen him the last moon—a big man, dark, and with the flat nose of the black man.

Yes, such things had been going on in the Platte country too, with no way to make a living, the quiet-talking Billy said. Some got a little work last summer, coaxing the Indians to the Missouri for pay and favor. Even old-timers like Bordeaux and Nick Janis took their sons up there and were glad to do it. But not all of the Indians followed well. Spotted Tail and other southern chiefs did not start until their agency at the forks of the Platte was closed and then they scattered in little bands up across the Running Water and were struck on the prairies by the winter blizzards. Finally one of the warriors drove his spear into the hard earth and said it was far enough, and Spotted Tail agreed. But there was no hunting in that bare country and the women and children must be very cold and hungry.

When young Billy was gone, Worm spoke out to Crazy Horse in his uneasiness about the grandmother of his sons, the mother of Spotted Tail. He had liked her so well he used to go to sit in her lodge, as was not considered respectful. He wished he knew how it was with the old woman today, in that bad land.

"We are fools to let the whites drive us around like their stinking cattle," the son said, remembering the day on a creek called the Blue Water, when Spotted Tail knocked thirteen soldiers from their horses with their own sword. But that was long ago, and since that the Brule had been in the iron house of the whites.

Soon there were other visitors in the villages, young men come from Whetstone to tell the bad things up there—the game gone, the goods from the Great Father not there, and the whisky traders thick across the river, their boats coming every night for the young men. Yet the whites were saying that the Indians could never come back.

The Powder River people heard these things in worried silence. The peace men had said that those in the north country could stay there and hunt and trade and live in the old way so long as the wild young men were kept from making depredations on the whites outside of the Indian country. Now the agents and soldiers were trying hard to push them all up there to that bare little island among the whites.

It was not only the younger men like Crazy Horse who showed no surprise at the news from the Missouri. "One does not go to a hilltop for water or to a white man for the truth," Worm spoke out, near anger himself now.

"But what will become of the starving people?" the visitors kept asking.

"It has long been known that it is better to die fighting—" Crazy Horse wanted to say, yet he did not, for it does not help to tell the keening woman that her son could have been saved. Instead, he wrapped himself in his blanket and went out to plan for arms and powder. Perhaps he should make a trip north with the Hunkpapas to see what could be done among the Slota, the Red River breeds—a thieving lot, but they always had powder.

There was news, too, from Red Cloud. His warriors were watching him close, remembering well how strong he was in the Powder road councils, touching no pen until every soldier was gone from there, and yet here they were, camped at the eastern edge of the Black Hills, Red Cloud looking towards the Missouri agency like a soldier mule for his corn. And after the long night of the winter had passed, and the game was very scarce, he still would not move back west although the scouts came galloping to report the breath clouds of buffalo herds hanging low over the morning hills.

Man Afraid, too, had left the meat country early and moved down to Lance Creek, towards the Holy Road. Now he was begging his friend, the soldier chief Dye, for a little trading to feed his people. When he was asked about some stolen mules he said all had been eaten this hungry time and still his women and children were dying with the lodges full of robes they had worked so hard to make.

The soldier chief offered them rations to get to the Missouri but Man Afraid set his face against this. "Some of the starving ones among my people are come from there, come back because there was nothing to eat," he said.

So the soldier chief let him trade a little with young John Richard, making all the other traders very angry. But it was not enough to feed the people and so they spoke of the time as the Hungry Winter, when they gladly gave Richard a mule or two horses for a sack of flour.

As the grass lengthened and the ponies grew strong even in that far Whetstone agency country, warriors came riding to the Powder camps from there. Even after hearing that Tall Bull's Cheyennes were being chased around south of the Platte by the soldiers they kept coming. If it was to be war, they wanted to be with the fighters, particularly after the bad thing that came into the sky. The sun darkened without clouds and while the old women huddled crying in their blankets, their men ran out and shot arrows at the shadow animal that was swallowing it until the enemy was driven off and the earth was bright again. But in the hostile country the time was a good one, with the cherry bushes bending black for the *wasna*, the young buffalo plentiful, and the *heyoka* making the people laugh and grow strong with the power of the thunders in the sky.

There was one among them looking into a tomorrow dark as when the sun was gone as he watched the Conquering Bear Brules and Lone Horn's Minneconjous go towards the Missouri agency. It was true that most of the people Crazy Horse still had around him were young and strong, and yet they were fewer, the camp circles smaller, the great hoop of the people scattered and broken.

Soon there was news that another trader's son had come to live among them. It was young John Richard, the one they called Lean Elk. He was with Red Cloud, his mother's relation, and it seemed that he, too, had run away from the whites because of a killing, not his first, but this time a killing that the officer at Fetterman did not like, a soldier shot right in the fort. It seemed the trouble was over one of the pay-women of the whites—a Bad Disease woman. So before anyone could arrest him he went north. Now the whites from along the Holy Road were saying he had threatened to lead the warriors against them, clean them out. The Lakotas found this very funny, even Crazy Horse laughing a little. It was strange, the foolish things the white man would believe. Only one who had proved himself in many good fights could get the warriors to follow him, and this Lean Elk was not a warrior at all, but a trader's son.

Still, he might be useful, Worm and Long Face thought. He had been to the white man's schools and, even better, he had lived with the Crows for several years. He might carry the tobacco of friendship to their camps.

But soon it was seen that it was not for the Crows that Lean Elk was carrying tobacco, but for Red Cloud. So Crazy Horse went to the Bad Face camp to visit his friend Yellow Bear, who had given his two sisters to young Richard when he first came north and was already sorry, for it seemed that this trader's son liked the whisky cup very much. He also had the peculiar belief of the white man that a husband has the right to knock his woman down as though she were an enemy warrior.

Yellow Bear had more than this to tell to a man whose mouth was as closed as that of the Hunkpatila shirt-wearer. Messengers were carrying secret letters from the Holy Road to Richard. The whites wanted Man Afraid, Brave Bear, and some others to go to visit the Great Father but they were having trouble with the Hunkpatila and so they hoped to work the Indians against each other, promising Lean Elk that if he got Red Cloud to go along the soldier killing would be forgotten. To get this done young Richard was offering many things, including hints that the whites might make Red Cloud head chief of all the Oglalas.

Hoh! Head chief of the Oglalas! He was not even a headman of the Bad Faces, only a warrior leader. But of these things the whites knew nothing.

One evening when Crazy Horse rode in through the night from a visit at the camp of No Water, he found his father still at the fire, the stem of his fine stone pipe in his hand, the fragrance of red willow mixed with a little tobacco in the air.

He offered the pouch to his son and then put new wood on the fire, and as it blazed up and he could see the face before him, he spoke of visitors he had had, a couple of quiet, sensible-talking men. They came on a friendly visit, it seemed at first, bringing warming gossip and news of the southern people and of the soldiers of the Holy Road.

They talked of things up here too, and when they went away they left the long flat stick of tobacco from which they had been smoking on Worm's cutting board. They knew he would accept it, for one cannot say no to a gift already used.

"Ahh-h!" Crazy Horse said, drawing at his filled pipe as he lit it with the fire stick.

Awhile the father smoked in silence too, not making the whistling sound of contentment in his pipe. Then he spoke again. The two men who came were Bad Faces, Standing Bear, the brother of Woman's Dress, from the camp of Red Cloud, and the other a relative of Black Twin.

The son was silent, the smoke from his pipe hanging about the lean, strong face that was like the unchanging stone of the high Black Hills. But Worm knew he understood why the men had come.

"They will not let you have Black Buffalo Woman," he said. "She is the niece of Red Cloud, the wife of the brother of Black Twin, and they say they will not let her go."

"Hoh! They will not let her go!" Crazy Horse cried out, his anger breaking his silence as a flood sweeps through a beaver dam. "Like the white man they come saying what others cannot do. Do they not know that the Lakota woman leaves her lodge whenever she wishes? They judged it so themselves the time the Bad Face stole the young relative of Bull Bear, and the chief's anger gave Red Cloud the chance to shoot him! And that one was not a woman grown, a wife free to choose, but a maiden—"

"True, but even the grown woman who carries power in her moccasin tracks cannot choose her own road lightly. They came to let me know it cannot be without a fight."

"A fight—within the Oglalas? They are fools; those who would break a people because a woman leaves her husband's lodge are fools!"

"It is not the woman but the power that is in her tracks," Worm said quietly. "The fight would be for that, as all fights among the people are, and always the helpless ones suffer."

Ahh-h, the helpless ones! And thinking of them the son looked straight before him, into the darkening fire. Yes, the women, like his mother lying there in her sleeping robes, holding herself to silence in this thing that she knew weighed so heavy with this one she called son. The women and the children, the old and the crippled and the blind among them would suffer.

When the lodge skins turned light with the coming of morning Crazy Horse still sat in his blanket before the ashes of the fire. All this night he had sent his heart back over the years of his life. From childhood he had known that his people were as a stone broken in two never to become whole again, always turning the broken side, as in blame, towards each other. But with this trouble his family, such men as Long Face and Worm, had little to do. They were Hunkpatilas and remained so. They had never liked the trader chiefs even at the start, not Bull Tail or Bull Bear or Smoke, but were friendly with all their people for they were friendly men. They believed that anyone who killed among his own should be destroyed, but in this, too, the people must decide.

At first it had seemed to Crazy Horse that perhaps his family was less torn by the troubles because they were of other bloods besides Oglala: a little Minneconjou, even a little Cheyenne, and his mother a Brule. But so were the troublemakers. Red Cloud was no Oglala at all, with his father a Brule and his mother the sister of Smoke, one of the old Saones. Perhaps that was why that family worked so hard for power among them. And now it was Standing Bear, of those people, the brother of Woman's Dress, who came here to tell Worm what his son must not do or they would break the Oglalas again.

Break them again—when those here in the north had already been divided by the white man's presents, even Red Cloud signing the peace paper and still working hard to reach more power through the Great Father. It was true that his warriors had begun to drop away from him, moving not only to Black Twin and No Water but coming to Big Road and Long Face of the Hunkpatilas too, many living among them here in poor little wickiups, but glad to be away from the foolish talk of the little islands called agencies. And now the Bad Faces came to talk of breaking this scattered people once more.

He could not let this thing be done; even if he had not been a shirt-wearer and vowed to protect the people he could not have let it happen, and this Crazy Horse told his father, but he said the reason of the Bad Faces for fighting was not a strong one.

Worm had agreed, yet there were so many against this, the relatives of Black Twin, who did not wish to lose the following of a woman of the Red Cloud people, and those of the Bad Faces too, although they would be much stronger with a Hunkpatila shirt-wearer among them. For some unspoken reason Red Cloud himself was very hard against it.

Yes, Crazy Horse knew these things, and knew that they seemed very big in the eyes of the men seeking power and ponies, power in the councils and ponies for the gifts in the secret meetings of the night to buy a following. Yet all he had wanted was the good of his people and the woman of his long waiting.

It had not seemed that these things could never be the same.

Some said that Lean Elk was truly making a very strong story to Red Cloud, telling him that the whites saw his importance and considered him the head of the northern Oglalas. There was another thing he did not say, but it was in the lodge between them—that in the councils Red Cloud had no more standing than any other warrior, less than some, for even among the northern Oglalas many saw him still as a chief-killer.

"There are whites who know that you are a very big man—the biggest living Lakota—" Lean Elk was saying in the ear of Red Cloud. "The Great Father will start to make this plain to all. He is waiting for you to come to Washington. Perhaps he is looking for a head chief for all the Oglalas. It would be good to go to him."

"Ahh-h, a Bad Face the head chief of the Oglalas!" some said when they heard the story. Yes, that would warm the heart of Red Cloud, would help still the tongues of those who kept remembering that he was the one who fired the killing shot when Bull Bear lay on the ground, wounded in the leg from another Bad Face gun.

So on a warm day in the Moon of Shedding Ponies, Red Cloud and Man Afraid packed their regalia to go with Lean Elk to the Holy Road and then far away to the town in the center of the white man's country where the Great Father lived. From almost every family somebody loaded a travois and moved out behind the two men while the others stood watching, here and there a woman keening softly into her blanket, for it seemed this going away to the south was something like a dying.

Later they heard how it was at Fort Fetterman the day the whites welcomed the chiefs and the trader's son who brought them into the place where he had killed the soldier. It seemed that the storms had gathered dark for this day when Man Afraid, Red Cloud, Brave Bear, and four hundred men, women, and children reached the Platte River. While the travois and pack horses spread out along the second bottom, word was sent across to the post that John Richard and those going to the Great Father were ready for the road. The soldier chief who had come up from Laramie to meet them sent the ferry boat over for the headmen. It was a small one and had to make many trips, bobbing and jerking at its rope on the gray, swollen river. Lean Elk stayed back to the last. By then a slow drizzling of rain was falling, and the thunders rumbled. When he got into the boat the women sent up a great keening for the brave young man going back to the soldiers crowding in a thick row along the bank. The trader's son looked very small and dark standing up in the boat, looking back towards the people of his mother. Near the other side he turned to face those so hungry to avenge the one he had killed.

As the boat touched the shore the soldiers pushed forward and the keening across the river dropped into stillness. But the officer motioned his men back and with the chiefs and Lean Elk beside him he started to the fort, the Indians singing strong-heart songs as they went through the door and were lost to the watching ones.

Inside, Man Afraid sat calmly in his blanket and said he wanted nothing of the whites except what was promised them in the white paper signed for so long as grass was growing. Red Cloud, it seemed made a good talk. He tried to find words easy enough for the whites to understand. So he spoke a name the Black Robe had told the Indians once, a little white-man name used by them as though it could mean all the sacred powers for which there were no words. This Great Spirit, as the whites called it, had put the Indian down on these prairies before all other men, had given him the clouds to look at and the game to live on. It had made the four winds to blow—the east wind too, the one that brought in the whites to overrun the Indian lands. It was to talk with the Great Father about this that the chiefs wanted to go to Washington, Red Cloud said. They had sent him many words but it seemed they fell into bad ears on the way and were held. Now they would go to see his face, and they wanted to take this young man called Lean Elk along and open a door of the Great Father's house and put him inside where he would not be hurt.

Crazy Horse left his camp so he need not see Man Afraid, their Brave Man, go from his people to the Great Father as a dog might run after the smell of fresher meat. Nothing good could come of this, for nothing the Indians wanted was in a place called Washington. What they wanted was here, and here was the place to keep it. And yet their Brave Man had gone with the others, carrying the people in their hands like robes taken to a very rich trader, with the finest goods. Only a few weeks ago Crazy Horse had stopped from a thing that was very big in his heart because it might split the people and now it seemed there would be nobody left. Perhaps he had given up too soon.

With these thoughts to ride beside him Crazy Horse went against the Crows. He wished Hump were around to join the party, but he had gone north to his Minneconjou relations in anger at the things he saw happening here this winter. He was against the peace papers and Red Cloud's two-faced way of looking towards both the Indians and the whites. When he saw the work of young

Richard he left, telling Crazy Horse that he was going where the people were still Lakotas.

"It is in my heart to ask you to come along, but I know no words strong enough to win against the woman," he said.

"You never thought our sister was a good thing—" the Oglala replied, slowly, making the first words for this old sorrow between them.

In a short time the Oglala party was back, bringing in some good Crow horses and word of many more waiting to be taken. By then there was news from the south. Worm said that Man Afraid had not gone to the Great Father. At the last he had refused, and so no Hunkpatilas went, only Red Cloud, Brave Bear, Sword, Red Dog, Yellow Bear, and Sitting Bull, the Oglala, and their men, twenty Indians including the four women. It was said that about as many started from Whetstone under Spotted Tail, and that the Brule chief had looked with anger upon Red Cloud when he saw him, saying: "Have the Oglalas lost all their chiefs?"

But where was Man Afraid? Crazy Horse asked.

It was said he and the others were camped near Rawhide Buttes waiting to hear what was done in the talks with the Great Father about an agency and other things.

Their Brave Man sitting around waiting on what those others would do! It was enough to drive even a tired man to the warpath and so Crazy Horse talked up another party against the Crows. This time He Dog and many others asked him to lead a big one, with lodges along and some women for the cooking—an old-time hunting and war party. So it was done, and just before they left, the people put a great honor upon Crazy Horse and his friend, He Dog, one not given to anyone for many years—they were not only made lance-bearers of the Crow-Owners society, which was good, but were given the care of the two lances of the Oglalas, the two lances that had been with the people longer than any man could remember. Surely it was far back beyond the Missouri, Worm and old Bad Heart Bull thought. No one remembered, either, how they came except that they were given to the people as a sign that their strength and power should live again as the grass in the spring when brave warriors carried the lances into battle in enemy country.

And as the party rode away, Crazy Horse and He Dog holding the lances high, the people followed them out a ways, making the great cheering chants of the Oglalas, heard only once or twice in a man's lifetime.

The party started off feeling very strong. They found a big camp between the Little and Big Horn Rivers, on land that the Crows claimed as part of their reservation. With the Lakota women sitting on a hill to taunt the enemy, the warriors attacked. They got some scalps, some good war horses, and a few of the very fine ones that the Crow women used in the ceremonials. Then the Lakota women really made the cheering songs, to shame the Crows.

Both Crazy Horse and He Dog carried the lances all through the fighting, always first and closest to the enemy, always last to retreat from the charges, showing the people had chosen well. And when they started home the Crows gathered up their scattered warriors and came on in a running fight, getting some of the horses back, and losing thirteen more scalps. The Lakotas lost a few too, and were ready to stop, but the Crows turned and hurried away so fast towards their little soldier chief, their agent, that Crazy Horse and He Dog decided to follow them awhile. Leading the warriors with the lances, the scalps and feathers on them fluttering fine in the wind, they chased the Crows right up to the soldier guns at their agency. And after the fighting there, the Lakotas camped not far away for several days of hunting and raiding, even sending spies out to hear the Crows tell their agent that there were a thousand Lakota warriors in the attack and that they had the flour and ammunition of the white man, the warriors making angry signs at this, as if the white-man goods were for Crows only. It was good to laugh over those things, and after the lances had been unchallenged in enemy country for many days, the party went home with a good parading through the village and a long victory dance. Many from the other camps were there and all the evening Crazy Horse was surrounded by warriors.

"Let the peace chiefs go to the Great Father. The real Lakotas are still here," young Black Fox said.

"Hoye!"

Coming so soon after his heart dropped to the ground, it made Crazy Horse feel good enough to remember another day, ten years ago, when he was seventeen and his father gave him the honored name of Crazy Horse, with a Bad Face maiden looking him full in the face in her pride.

No Water's camp had been moved to a little creek not far from that of Long Face. The headmen were all gone to the Holy Road, to get news of the traveling chiefs and welcome their return. They were with the rest of the waiting people down near Rawhide Buttes, over a thousand lodges, wanting to trade their robes, Black Buffalo Woman said. It seemed strange, having so many of the big men gone, and dangerous too, with the Crows probably hot for revenge raids now, so she had asked that they be brought closer to the Long Face people for protection.

Hou! For this wise thing Crazy Horse would see that his sisters in the camp had the woman's feast.

A few days later a friend of his mother's among the No Water people made a big cooking. She had been a white man's wife and was a very good bread-maker, so there was the pan-fried bread, coffee, and a big kettle of dried apples cooked with the sweet lumps for the head women whose men were away. And afterward they had a noisy time with the plum-stone game, playing for the beads and ring gifts that were part of the feast, with a fine yellow-spotted Crow woman's horse as the best gift of all. Many people walked down that way to see the lighted lodge so gay with laughing that evening. Some were even saying that they knew it was Crazy Horse who brought the things of the feast across the back of his horse when he came to the village. But nobody seemed to notice that one rode out into the darkness that night heading for the Bad Faces camped at Rawhide Buttes, yet Standing Bear, the brother of Woman's Dress, was suddenly gone.

The next day someone was missing from the lodge circle. Black Buffalo Woman had put her three children out among relatives and was gone. There was much soft padding of moccasined feet from lodge to lodge with talk of the news. Most of the women were excited and happy in the thought of what had been done, but a few were uneasy about No Water and the Red Cloud people, and one or two were saying that Black Buffalo Woman had picked the one she thought the biggest man and, finding herself fooled, had picked again—saying it angrily, with mouths sour as from the green gooseberries, their tongues sharp as the thorns.

Everybody knew that Black Buffalo Woman had gone with Crazy Horse. It wasn't that he had taken her as a Snake come to steal a horse in the night, but openly, with others of the village along, making a small war party to go into the Yellowstone country against the Crows. The two had ridden out in the bright sun of morning in the middle of the party, Crazy Horse as always in white buckskin shirt and dark blue leggings, the one feather of his vision at the back of his head, his long braids wrapped in beaver fur almost the color of his hair. Today his lean, unpainted face was less serious than usual, and even with the others around, his eyes turned often to the woman beside him. She was still slender and tall-sitting on her horse, dressed in plain buckskin as was customary for a woman going in a war party, but her hair had been braided by the man riding beside her and her cheek carried the vermilion circle of one greatly beloved.

There was none of the shyness about her that young Curly saw the time he threw stones at her when she was picking plums with the women on the Running Water, or when she stood in his blanket outside her mother's lodge and drew away from his hand. Now she went with him as a grown Lakota woman goes with the man she chooses, openly, untroubled, as was her right. To be sure she could never again join in the dance of the Only Ones, those who had had only one man. But many honored women of the Lakotas were barred from that. Nor was this that happened between them a sudden meeting of the eye but one of long years of looking from far apart. Now she was a woman, warm and good as the May earth.

On the second night the little party came to several small bands camped at a timber-lined creek. They were invited to a double lodge of friends and sat together at the coals with Little Shield, who was a brother of He Dog, and Little Big Man and several others for a feasting. Suddenly there was a shouting and noise in the camp and without a scratch at the skins or any signal at all, the lodge flap was torn back and No Water stood before them, his eyes red as an angry grizzly's as he looked over the feasting circle about the fire.

"My friend, I have come!" he cried, aiming his revolver at Crazy Horse. The Hunkpatila sprang up, reaching for his knife, but Little Big Man caught his arm from behind and held it as No Water fired. The flash stung the eyes of Crazy Horse, the bullet crashed through his upper jaw, and he fell forward across the fire. And before any could put a hand upon him No Water was gone.

Little Shield and the others lifted the wounded man from the coals, laid him back on the robes like dead, and sent for the medicine man. Black Buffalo Woman was already gone. She had slipped out under the back of the lodge and run to some relatives for protection from her angry man. But No Water was not looking for more people to shoot. At the other side of the lodge circle he was telling those he brought along from his camp that he would have to get away quick for he had killed Crazy Horse.

At this even his friends stood back from him, and their women began the wailing and keening for a good man gone. "Crazy Horse dead!" they cried. "Our Strange Man killed in an Oglala camp!"

Yes, yes, No Water told them, but now he must get away before the friends of the shirt-wearer came for him. The revolver he gave to Yellow Bear to return to Bad Heart Bull, from whom he had borrowed it a few minutes before.

"Crazy Horse is dead," Yellow Bear told the tribal historian. 'Shot with your gun—for the woman."

Bad Heart Bull sat silent with the warm revolver on his palms.

Their great warrior, their Strange Man dead, not from the bullet
of an enemy but from one sent by an Oglala as his vision foretold,
and with the revolver borrowed from him, from his friend. It had
been a foolish thing to do, giving No Water the gun today, but he
had seemed to feel good, saying he wanted to start on a hunt early
in the morning. Who could know that a man like No Water would
have so little strength over a woman going to another? There
would surely be troubled times now: No Water never a big man
among the Lakotas again, Crazy Horse dead, and the northern
Oglalas broken with who could say how much blood on the village
earth between them. This was indeed a bad day for the people.

By now the hum of anger at the far end of the camp was rising
to a roar loud as a hailstorm, the women keening, or singing the
strong-heart songs to encourage their men, the men singing too,
of war and of death, getting ready to take No Water. But they were
too late. Grabbing the first horse he could find, he left the fast mule
that had brought him into camp, and when the friends of Crazy
Horse could not reach the owner, they killed his mule instead,
hacking, stabbing him with their knives, one finally cutting his
throat in a gushing of hot blood. But it brought no color to the
face of Crazy Horse, still pale as buffalo tallow. The medicine man
stirred his bowl, shook his rattle over him, and made his song, but
the eyes of the wounded man remained closed.

Down at No Water's camp there was trouble too. Chips was
being accused of making love medicine so Black Buffalo Woman
would run away with Crazy Horse—something that was put into
her bowl at the woman's feast, they said. When the warriors
gathered to kill Chips, Black Twin had him brought to his lodge.
The medicine man said he knew nothing of the woman troubles
or a love medicine. It was protection for the war horses that he had
made for the Hunkpatila that day, and a little medicine bundle
some time ago to keep away the white-man bullets.

"What was in it?" Black Twin would know.

Only a little black pebble from his stone dream, no bigger than one of the painted beads, and one of the center feathers of the spotted eagle's tail to be worn into battle. From the same eagle Chips had made a wing-bone flute to carry on a string for signaling.

Black Twin grunted. He had seen Crazy Horse have these things along when he was a lance-bearer in the fight already called When They Drove the Crows Back into Camp. So they had to let Chips go, but he would never live in that lodge circle again.

It was not known to the friends of Crazy Horse where No Water was hidden, but some said that his people had made a sweat lodge to purify him of the killing and then took him to Black Twin. His brother welcomed him, saying: "Come and stay with me and if they want to fight us, we will fight."

And now, all over the Oglala country, people were saying it was not to be wondered at, this killing, for the Bad Faces had long been jealous of Crazy Horse and the following the warriors gave him, jealous of his daring and courage, and of his silence when they were bragging, blowing their deeds up into greatness as the women blow up buffalo bladders. Some remembered, too, that Red Cloud had indeed made an angry face the day he saw the much younger Crazy Horse carried to the place of shirt-wearer of the chiefs' society, and many said that was why Red Cloud went to the whites, because there he could be a great Oglala.

The Crazy Horse friends in the camp were very angry; the warriors painting for war. They would have No Water turned over to them for punishment or else drive his people out. For a while it looked as if much blood would be spilled on the Lakota earth. But in the meantime Crazy Horse had begun to live again and was saying there must be no trouble, saying it with signs because the bullet had torn into his face below the corner of his nose, taking speech away. Neither must Black Buffalo Woman be punished. As a Lakota she had done no wrong. She must not be blamed for what foolish men do.

So the warriors made a watching wall around the lodge of the wounded man, and before the day came again it seemed very bad with him, his face swollen as the *wasna* sacks, his eyes burning with the fire of sickness. Many times he tried to sit up, making a growling in his throat like a trapped grizzly, mumbling: "Let go! Let go my arm—!" through his broken face. The first time those about him heard this they looked to each other. They had forgotten his medicine. Only with his arm held by one of his own people could Crazy Horse be killed.

Seeing how bad it was, his friends did not take him back to the Long Face camp. It was far, they said, meaning it would make very bad hearts if the Crazy Horse warriors saw him now, or if he died there. So they took him to the few lodges of Spotted Crow, another uncle, camped away from the rest. And when Worm and Long Face came riding to the place of the shooting, none would say what had been done, except that the son lived.

It was good that the reckless young Little Hawk and his friends were away towards Snake country. The peace men had enough trouble without his hot anger, his bad heart to excite the warriors, but it was known that a runner had gone to find him, so they must work fast before the brother came charging back, his horse as ready to ride down the enemies here as on the warpath.

By the time of the first sun's going it was clear there were three sides in the troubles: those hungry to avenge the shooting of Crazy Horse, those who followed No Water and then the three peace uncles of the wounded man, Bull Head, Ashes, and Spotted Crow. These three and Worm and Long Face, too, were strong in their concern for the people. They were very angry over what had been done against their son, yet they could not blame No Water without blaming those who had pushed him a long time against this thing when it should happen. Although it was once more the Red Cloud people who made the trouble, they still worked for peace, Bad Heart Bull and He Dog, known as the good friends of Crazy Horse, helping. These two had to move carefully, for they were related to both sides, and it was known that Bull's revolver had been used for the shooting.

As Crazy Horse lived through the third, the bad, day, the camps seemed to quiet down a little. No Water owned two very fine horses, a roan and a bay. He sent these and another good one to Worm to help heal the wound he had made. Then old Spotted Crow and some others brought the woman to Bad Heart Bull's lodge and left her there, telling him Crazy Horse said whatever else was done, she must not be punished. Bull, known as a calm and just man, arranged for her to go back to No Water in peace, and so she was brought to a silent camp, not a head showing anywhere to make her feel eye-followed or shamed for the trouble. Quietly she gathered up her children and went about her work, but there was no more vermilion on her cheeks, and her fine elk-tooth dress, with the rows added from the herd Crazy Horse had found through the tracks of the white buffalo, was put aside.

As soon as Crazy Horse seemed better his people moved him away so the others could get together for the sundance, already much too late. But now the traveling chiefs were back again and those who had been waiting down at Rawhide for the trading too, and so the ceremonials were begun.

Once more in his home lodge, the one Crazy Horse called mother cooked the things to make him grow strong again, take the white-woman paleness from him. In a few days the runner that had been sent to Little Hawk returned, saying he had found nothing of the party. No one believed that he had tried, for it seemed he was very much afraid. Worm and Long Face called him to the lodge and talked to him of the things he had seen, and finally it was discovered that he truly was scared by the whites down there, not the soldiers, but the miners calling themselves Big Horners because they wanted to go to those mountains to look for gold. Helped by the freighters, bullwhackers, and Gray Men, they organized a secret society to kill Indians, to keep them stirred up and prevent peace and the loss of the good pay-money for their wagon-hauling and to open the country to miners. Several old Loafers from around the forts had been shot, one of them while he was carrying a message for the soldiers. He was found face down at the edge of the little spring where he had lain to drink, a bullet through his back. They were even killing the moccasin women, those who mended the leather things of the soldiers, and so these were told to move their lodges inside the stockades at the places that had the walls.

"All Gray Men—all outlaws!" Worm said, in unusual anger.

Hou! the runner agreed. The country down there was indeed bad medicine. So Worm and Long Face let him go. It is difficult to learn much from a man who is afraid.

When Crazy Horse and He Dog chased the Crows back to their agency the time they carried the lances, they saw many buffalo north of the Yellowstone. So after the woman trouble seemed settled and the sundance was done, many of the people went up there for a good hunt, knowing that a busy hand helps the angry heart forget.

As soon as Crazy Horse could ride a saddle, the Long Face camp followed the others to the meat-making, leaving the buffalo-head signs behind to guide Little Hawk and his party to them. They found their people across the river from the mouth of the Big Horn, in country that the Crows claimed, but there were many Lakota camps close together, with over a thousand good fighting men ready, so nobody was afraid. The meat was fat and Crazy Horse was strong enough to ride for a little slow shooting.

Then one night Little Hawk's party slipped into the camp in the darkness, two of the warriors coming straight to the lodge of Worm, their blankets torn, earth streaks on their faces. Ahh-h! their luck had been very bad. Little Hawk was lying on the ground in that south country, killed by some of the Indian-hunting whites, shot on the way home from the Snakes. Suddenly many bullets came flying past and because they were few they whipped up and got away, but Little Hawk was not among them and so at night one slipped back to see and found where he had charged into the whites alone.

As this was told, the two women of the lodge began to make the keening, doing it softly under their blankets, for they knew the Strange Man among them did not like this way of his people. And when the story was done the father arose and went silently into the night. But Crazy Horse sat still, the new scar at the corner of his nose paling in the firelight.

So Little Hawk was gone, the gay, brave younger brother, lost to the bullets of the whites while he had stayed behind with his woman plans. This thing had happened because a man thought of himself instead of the good of his people and so misery fell on all those around him, upon all those who loved the laughing young Lakota. And as Crazy Horse realized what had been done a dust-gray bitterness settled in his heart, a bitterness that would take a long, long time to be gone.

The next day he saw No Water. Towards evening, coming in loaded with meat, Crazy Horse noticed the fast buckskin of Moccasin Top ahead of him, golden as sunshine on a fall hillside. When he found the Top still at his skinning he spoke in surprise. "It seemed I saw you go on the buckskin—"

Without looking up from his work Moccasin Top answered that it was No Water, who had seen Crazy Horse coming.

"No Water!" the Hunkpatila cried out, all the misery of the past weeks and the anger for his brother killed coming out in his voice. "I wish I had known it! I would have sent him a bullet in return for the one he gave me!"

Stripping off the load of buffalo meat, he jumped on his barebacked horse and started after No Water, chasing him clear to the Yellowstone. He would have caught him there but the man plunged the sweating buckskin straight into the river and swam it across, Crazy Horse standing on the bank, looking after the one who ran away, his hand on his gun.

The next day No Water's lodge and several others were gone from camp. It was said they went to live in the south and were never coming back. Many were glad. Now the trouble was done among them.

But in a few days the Big Bellies called a meeting of the chiefs' society to consider what one of their shirt-wearers had done. The oath they had all taken was repeated, and Crazy Horse was found to have broken it by acts endangering the peace of the people and by chasing a man away with a gun after the gift horses had been accepted from him. And in the circle of old men not one spoke for the Hunkpatila, for none was his father and all of them had either become white-man peace chiefs or were related to Black Twin or Red Cloud or both. Only the Big Bellies were allowed to hear what was said, but all the camp knew what was being done, and everywhere people stood behind their lodge flaps watching to see what would happen when they went for Crazy Horse. Finally four men came from the council lodge as on the day of choosing, but now they were afoot and carrying their guns, with ten others behind them, also armed, including Standing Bear, the brother of Woman's Dress, and two brothers of No Water, the rest all from the Bad Faces except Young Man Afraid, who pushed in and walked along.

"It is not only the whites who shoot the prisoners they say tried to escape," he told them, and the others kept quiet and let him come.

In the lodge of Worm they found Crazy Horse, and when they told him the work of the Big Bellies, he motioned to his mother for the hair shirt of the big-horn sheep. She brought the case, crying upon it as she gave it into the hands of the son.

But there was no sorrow over this thing in Crazy Horse, or anger, for it was nothing to the black load of blame he had laid upon his own heart. Straight, slighter than any of them, he walked free and alone as a mourning man upon a hill among them, and Young Man Afraid saw he need not have come, for there was not one here who would dare touch him except in secret or from the night.

So Crazy Horse returned the shirt to the Big Bellies and then, before he was allowed to go, someone started to speak of putting it upon Red Cloud. The Bad Face had done a great thing in Washington, he said, healing the bad trouble with the Bear people by making Little Wound a chief, as if he had not been made one long ago by his people, not by the foolish talking of the Bad Face or any other. Red Cloud was a big chief now, the man told them all, called so by the Great Father, and the chiefs' society should see it was time to honor him.

At last Man Afraid leapt to his feet.

"My eyes have looked upon enough bad work this night!" he cried, and so the council of the Big Bellies closed, never to open again.

BOOK THREE

The Man of the People

MARRIAGE *and the* DEATH
of a Friend

NOW more than ever the Oglalas spoke of Crazy Horse as their Strange Man. He was getting well from the No Water shooting but the powder-blackened scar at the corner of his nose made his skin look even lighter, and his hair seemed to have grown longer in his sickness, the brown, fur-wrapped braids hanging far below his belt. It seemed that he went about the village a little oftener to see that there was meat in the kettles, a horse for every travois. His dress was plain as ever and his passing more silent than the summer wind. Women still stopped their work to look after him, but instead of cheering him as a bold young warrior they looked after him with warming faces.

There was another difference. This evening of the young moon when Crazy Horse came in from hunting he turned not to the lodge of his mother but to a new one set close by. Stooping, he went into the duskiness where a woman worked alone. As he entered she rose to take his bow and quiver and hung them beside his place at the back of the fire and then went on with her bread-making in silence.

Crazy Horse settled himself, lit the short pipe the man who has lost a high standing must smoke, and watched the neat head of the woman in thankfulness. She was indeed one of strong heart to take him. It was not, he knew, just because He Dog and Spotted Crow and other good men had gone to her people and asked for her, nor the coaxing of her young brother, Red Feather, of whom she was very fond. She was not a child any more, nearing the twenty-eight winters of Crazy Horse, and had a woman's way of setting the wishes of men aside if she did not want them done. He Dog and the others had gone to her, saying she must know how alone this man was, reminding her that he had not only lost the woman of his long waiting to save a fight among the people, but been unshirted for it, not by those who lived with him in his way, in the Lakota way, but by those who were for the whites, and against them all out here. She was of Big Road's band and knew the jealousies they did not name, and these things she saw were not to be remedied by a woman in the lodge, but by anger and strong fighting. Then there was the beloved brother lost, and this, too, could only be healed in vengeance. It seemed indeed that their man did not need a woman at all but a strong gun and plenty of ammunition.

Ahh-h, the fighting he could do, they said, but a man does not live well from this alone.

That she knew, but what was to show her that the Strange Man wished this thing they were planning, or were they taking her there as they would tie a horse outside the lodge of a man who has made trouble, a horse he must take or seem to be of a bad heart, wanting a fight?

Crazy Horse heard all this talk and had no patience for it. So he spoke to his mother. It was true that he had given his friends enough trouble and wished to ease their hearts. Now he wanted her to go to Black Shawl, telling her he wished this thing very much but that she must know how he was, not only now, but always, never speaking much or singing and dancing as other Lakotas do.

"You must say there will be little joy in a life with me—"

"The Black Shawl knows these things. She is also a quiet-mouth one," the mother said.

But there was something more that he had not given to words before. "Tell her she will choose a man who is as a dead one, for I have now no wish to live—" speaking as the warrior whose heart can only be made good by seeking death, some day, in battle.

Covering her woman's tears with the old blanket of mourning for the other one dead, the wife of Worm went to carry the message to Black Shawl. After a while she came back with a fine pair of moccasins beaded in the lightning marks of his vision and set them before Crazy Horse.

So it was settled.

Now Crazy Horse leaned against the back rest of his place and looked around the lodge with the strange feeling that comes to a man who has lived through his wild years and well into his quieter time in the lodge of his parents—with the strange and good feeling of a man for a lodge because the woman moving calm and easy about it is his own.

A long time the Oglala sat so, until there was the smell of the bread frying in the iron pan. Then finally he spoke. "Tomorrow I go to the Platte."

Black Shawl bowed her head in hearing as she pounded the coffee for the pot, shaking up the little buckskin bag and pounding it again with the *wasna* hammer of stone.

"My sister, will you come with me?" the man asked, and the woman looked quickly across the fire, her dark eyes shining with tears that he had asked this good thing of her.

So in the morning they started away together, Crazy Horse with his brown hair hanging loose as always when going out to a fight, the little stone half-hidden at his ear, his rifle across his horse before him, a bow and quiver at his back, for the arrow has many good places with its silent song of death. Behind him rode Black Shawl on her spotted pony, her buckskin dress deep-yoked in beads, her saddle hangings long-fringed and beaded too, in the design of her family. It was true that she was not Black Buffalo Woman, but it was better to be second with such a man than first with another, and so she rode with her vermilioned face woman-strong and proud.

They took along a pack mule and one of Little Hawk's fine war horses carrying a new red blanket and a big rawhide sack to bring the bones of the warrior back to a safe place. Together they started away towards the western end of the Holy Road, all the village watching them go, the warriors standing off silent, most of the women keening for the lost one, but many more singing strong-heart songs and calling out the name of Crazy Horse going alone to avenge his brother. The unshirting they pushed aside as man-foolishness—a lot of Big Bellies sitting around trying to take honor from a man by words spoken in a smoky lodge. One might lose honor, but it could not be taken from him.

So they sang:

> *"Ey-hee! A warrior rides out from among us.*
> *He is a strong man, and many sitting*
> *In the lodges*
> *Are jealous of him!*
> *Ey-hee!"*

When the moon had grown fat and died again the two came riding back, dusty and worn out, saying nothing except that the bones of Little Hawk had been found, wrapped in the red blanket and put on a scaffold in a place safe from the enemy. Soon the Indians heard white-man talk of war parties loose in the upper Platte country again, of many men found killed, men of the Big Horners, those who had started in the spring with a big train and a wagon gun to search the White Mountains of the Indian country for gold. The soldiers had driven them back but the miners had sneaked out again in small parties. Now one was found dead here and another there, until no one could tell how many, not scalped or cut up, but always with a Lakota arrow sticking through into the earth, even when shot by a gun.

At the camp of Crazy Horse there was no victory dancing, no counting of coups over these, only the strengthening man going his silent way through the lodge circle, without torn blanket or gashed arms or any other of the mourning signs. A give-away dance was made and the whole herd of Little Hawk, with some fine American horses and mules among them, was distributed among those who had need, for it was well known that only things not made less by division, like an honorable name and respect of the people for a great family, are to be inherited. And after this there was the name-taking ceremony in which Long Face put aside his name for that of his daring nephew killed by the guns of the whites. From now on he would be known as Little Hawk again. And so well did this old name fit the uncle that the other one was lost as a stone that is thrown over the shoulder.

Although there was no victory dance the warriors knew what had been done against the whites and so they once more looked upon Crazy Horse with friendly eyes, certain that the taking of the woman, the bullet in the face, and the unshirting had not weakened his very strong medicine.

"Hoppo! Let us go!" they told each other, and gathered at the new lodge to talk of war. Even Hump was back now.

When Red Cloud had rested from his visit to the Great Father he went around from one camp to another in the north country, sitting in the council lodges, talking big of the great things he had seen among the whites and the fine presents he had got for all who would come down to Laramie. But when he talked of what was in the treaty they had signed, the people really listened and heard him. They could keep roaming where they were, the Bad Face said, but the whites did not like it and would not give them either goods or traders until they went to a reservation.

"And what is this reservation?" Worm asked.

It reached from the Missouri River west to the top of the Black Hills and not even as far south as the Running Water, with all this country here, between the Black Hills and the White Mountains, left out.

"Who says these things?" the younger men in the Hunkpatila council demanded, barely waiting for the Bad Face to finish.

"The paper your chiefs signed, for as long as grass shall grow—"

Now the listening warriors flew into an uproar like a great storm striking. "Nothing of these things was told us at Laramie!" those who had touched the pen said, even Man Afraid agreeing.

Red Cloud sat quiet in the middle of the noise, letting smoke come out of his thin nose, admitting that he, too, had not known these things were in the peace paper until he was told at Washington.

"And what did our white-man chief say then?" Little Big Man called from his place far back. "Did he talk against these things? No, we know that he said there could be an agency somewhere on the headwaters of the Cheyenne, on our Good River, letting the whites get right into the middle of our country!"

"That was to make them give me more presents for you, foolish one!" Red Cloud said in his haranguer's voice. "I told the whites I could not say about the agency alone, but must council with my people. That is why they are sending you the fine presents that are coming—to make you feel good!"

Hou, hou! That was a good trick, some of those who had grown up around the trader chiefs thought. But not the younger men. "We will listen to no more white-man lies!" they cried. "Red Cloud has become an Indian with a white man's tongue!"

Now it was the hostile warriors in the back shouting their "Hou, hou!" and from among them Black Fox, too young and too little a man to speak in council, pushed forward to stand over Red Cloud before any could stop him.

"Does the Bad Face chief-killer think we do not know that he went around among the whites saying that he was the head man of the Lakota nation? Let him go to the whites again and tell them this!" and with one motion the young warrior jerked his breech-cloth free in the face of Red Cloud. Then he was gone out into the night, leaving only the silence of the great insult behind.

Crazy Horse did not go to these councilings, although someone there always asked that the crier be sent for him and then spoke for the things it was known the Oglala wanted for his people when he did not come. But against him stood the promise of the great presents Red Cloud seemed to hold in his hand, promises working strong against those who wished the free life of the hunt and the open country.

Then, while the talks were still going on, Lean Elk, the young Richard, came north once more, calling all the Oglalas to Laramie to meet two peace men bringing the fine goods.

"We will not let the chiefs go to be fooled with the sweet lumps and the sweet talking of the whites!" some from the *akicita* said.

"What do they want to take from us this time?" others asked.

But many had another question: would there be the white-man weapons? The buffalo was getting scarce and wild; good rifles were needed to feed the people, to drive back the Snakes and the Crows pushing in upon the hunting grounds, and for that other war of which there was no open talk in the councils. When the time came for the meeting at Laramie, Man Afraid went straight down from the Powder, taking the Minneconjous and the Cheyennes with him. He had come quickly, he told the peace commissioners, because he was so glad to see his pale-face friends. And where were the firearms?

The white men too, were glad to see their friend, and had brought many fine things in the wagons that he could have.

"There must be guns and ammunition or my warriors will be dissatisfied and say the old man has been fooled again," the chief insisted.

Red Cloud waited until he heard that there was no new paper to be signed and then he came in too, on a bad, windy day, the beaded trappings of the women's saddles flying, the bundles and blankets flapping, the pony manes and tails tangled and dusty. It was good to see this, the old people said, much like those long-ago times when the Holy Road was first started, the road that had let all these whites come in.

Up in the Tongue River country Crazy Horse smoked over the news brought from the counciling on the Laramie. It seemed there was much trouble about an agency, or at least about a trading place near the fort.

"At Rawhide Buttes, as Red Cloud agreed in Washington—" the

peace men kept saying, proving that the Indians had heard right about this.

But now the Bad Face pulled back. Once they had a house there to give out their goods and it was struck by lightning, showing the place was not a good one. Besides, the warriors would kill the chief who agreed to an agency away from the soldier town of Laramie. They wanted their own traders too, like Janis and the Richards and others—men they had known a long time. These and their agency they wanted at the old houses three miles above Laramie, on the south side of the river.

"Is Red Cloud then not a man of his word?" the whites asked.

At last Man Afraid stopped the council. "There is too much talking," he cried. "Give us the presents and let this other matter sleep!"

To this the peace commissioners quickly said: "Yes, yes, talk this over through the winter and come back in the spring."

The warriors still kept saying they would not change, but their voices were lost in the noise of the wagon train of presents brought into the great camp circle of five thousand Indians, with Red Cloud selected by the whites to divide them. It was Red Cloud who had the goods put into four big piles, one each for himself, American Horse, Red Dog, and Man Afraid. So even the old Hunkpatila who was once chosen by the dying Conquering Bear to be chief of all the Lakotas had to take his goods from the hand of a Bad Face.

There was some trouble about the dividing, and a great deal of riding up and down in war paint and noise, one angry headman even shooting a horse or two, but all this seemed forgotten in the full bellies of the feast. "No matter what is done here, we must remember that we are Lakotas," Man Afraid had told his son, and because they were still strong with the people far outside of the Hunkpatila circle, the whites could write to the Great Father that there was only good feeling among the chiefs.

All these things were talked over in the warrior lodges and councils, many wondering how Red Cloud had become such a big man down there. He was a great warrior, but one does not give the care of the people into the hands of a man just because he is strong in fighting.

Soon pack horses began to come into the northern camps loaded with the new goods that made a great laughing among the hostiles —blankets that were too small to cover a man, tin kettles that mashed flat in falling or turned red and rusty when they wanted strong iron ones like those they took from the soldiers, butcher knives dull as a bone. Some of the returning Indians had white-man hats with the tops already cut out for the head feather sticking up. Some were on the ponies, with two holes for the ears.

Now once more the man that Hump was could not stand to see these things being done, so he went to Crazy Horse saying he would lead a little party against the Snakes if his friend felt strong enough and thought he should go so soon after the things that had happened. Seeing how it was with the restless old warrior, Crazy Horse agreed. But at the Wind River they rode into a long raining, not hard, or with fall thunder to speak to Crazy Horse, but just a slow dripping that turned to half snow on the muddy earth, wet the bowstrings to stretching, spoiled the powder. And when the scouts came in they reported a great camp of Snakes in a clay country, the ground very soft from the raining and as slick as bear grease.

But Hump was impatient; he would go on and so Crazy Horse started with the rest, doing this uneasily, feeling that they should turn back before some good men were thrown away. He was leading one side of the warriors, Hump the other, and so he sent a messenger to his friend. It seemed that the horses couldn't stand a fight in this slush. They were sinking to their ankles, slipping and falling. Hump came riding over in anger. "You called off a fight here once before and when we got back to camp they laughed at us. We have our good name to think about. If you do not care about this any more, you can go back but I shall stay and fight."

"Hoye, my friend!" Crazy Horse replied. "We will fight, but I think we will get a whipping. You have a good gun and I have one, but look at our men—only wet bows and the enemy twelve to our one, with the far-shooting rifles."

They fought hard but soon the Snakes had the Oglalas using their wrist whips to get away, with the three men who had guns, Good Weasel, Hump, and Crazy Horse, guarding the retreat, first one charging back, then another—very dangerous, with their horses slipping, falling in the path of the oncoming Snakes.

Then Hump's horse began to limp and to stumble. "We are up against it now!" he called out. "My horse is wounded in the leg."

Ahh-h, they had been up against it from the start, Crazy Horse knew, but the Snakes were coming very fast and so he jumped off to shoot at the leaders, trying to hold them back a little longer, and when he could look again, Hump was surrounded, fighting off warriors all around. Crazy Horse gave the challenging cry and charged in, but it was too late. There was a wound in the breast of the old fighter, and blood in the mouth. Holding out his revolver to his friend, he slid from his crippled horse to the ground, dead in the middle of his enemies.

Several more times Crazy Horse charged in, trying to get the body, to sweep it up from his running horse, but the ground was so heavy and the Snakes so hot for him that at last Good Weasel grabbed his war rope and led him away, scolding like an old woman. Wasn't it enough for today, one good warrior lost? Besides, their shells were almost gone and if they stayed back longer others must come for them and be lost too. So Crazy Horse went with the warriors, keeping them moving most of the night until the way of their going was silent under the snow.

When they finally halted for sleep Crazy Horse sat hunched over a few coals, the revolver in his hand, thinking of Hump and his ending. The great warrior had been his father-friend all the days since the boy Curly had first clung to the string of his breechcloth on the back of his running horse. Now he was gone, killed this day when their hearts had not been good towards each other. It was another thing that had never happened before a foolish man rode out of a camp with the wife of No Water beside him.

A few days later Crazy Horse and his young brother-in-law, Red Feather, went to get the body of Hump. They found only the skull and a few bones where the coyotes had been, and no Snakes anywhere in the country. When they saw the man they had killed they moved their village far out of the way of the Lakotas.

The muskrats had finished their winter houses and the buffalo were beginning to move southward, sometimes long, dark rows of them following the leader, looking like great black horsehair ropes dropped along the ridges and across the flatlands. So the Oglalas scattered to the late hunting and then to the winter camps at the mouth of the Rosebud, near the Minneconjous and No Bows on the south bank of the Yellowstone. In the time of thawing the Hunkpapas came to move westward with the other Lakotas for grass and game. Here Crazy Horse and He Dog got to know more about the trader's son called Grabber living with Sitting Bull. It seemed the Hunkpapas had found him near the forks of the Missouri several years ago, little more than a boy, standing waiting for the warriors with his hands raised high over his head. So he was named the Grabber, one who raises his hands as if grabbing for something.

They saw he was probably half Indian, with a grayness to his skin, his lips thick and his nose flat as from a blow. Because he spoke Lakota, if it was a bad kind, and knew some sign-talking, they took him to Sitting Bull. There he told that his father was a trader's son called Brazeau.

"Hoh!" some of the old Hunkpapas said in surprise. They remembered such a one who was part black man. He had come up the river on a fire boat long ago and sometimes did the whipping the whites used on those working for them at the Missouri trader forts.

"Hou!" others agreed. They had heard of this Brazeau.

Well, the Grabber was his son. He had been to the white man's school until he killed a man and had to run away. Since he had been with Sitting Bull he had brought in many newspapers from the mail carriers he shot on the Missouri roads, and soldier letters too, saying what was planned. Sometimes he brought whole packs of these into camp when they lived up there.

The Oglalas looked a little sourly upon this Grabber. They had sheltered one trader's son who had killed a white man, and for the promise that he would not be hurt he had taken Red Cloud and his warriors away.

"Hah! Red Cloud!" the Hunkpapas laughed. Sitting Bull was no power-hunting Bad Face.

In the spring those coming back from the Laramie country had a story of Black Buffalo Woman to tell. She had given birth to a daughter, light-haired as a little prairie chicken, almost like a white man's young one.

"It was so with Curly when he was small," the old women told each other. "The whites often called him a captive."

Most of them already knew that No Water had taken a second wife soon after Black Buffalo Woman returned to him. Some said it was she who got the new woman for his lodge so she could live alone in another one set back from the camp circle.

Anyway, it was good about the little one, the women thought, good that she had something of that unhappy time. For their Strange Man there was only the scar he must carry. One could not even tell if he knew about the young one born.

Crazy Horse knew, and it seemed that the child must be given to him, that he must go down to claim it. But then he remembered that up here they needed to stand together like buffaloes holding the wolves away from the weak ones. If the circle of horns was broken, some, perhaps all, would surely be lost. Trying to take the little one would uncover the old trouble with Black Twin and the other relatives of No Water, even with his good friend He Dog and his family.

And what was there for the children of the Lakotas? Crazy Horse and his brother warriors could die fighting on the plains but it seemed that their sons must surely rot on the white man's islands that they called reservations, their daughters become the pay-women without pay of the whites. And as he thought of these things he looked over the fire towards Black Shawl moving heavily about her work. They had taken an old woman relation of hers into the lodge. Even though he was no longer a shirt-wearer there were many guests to be fed and now there would soon be a young one here too. Perhaps it would be a warrior to take the place of his lost brother, and as Crazy Horse thought of this, he forgot about the white man's islands for the Indians and planned to teach this son as Hump had taught Curly—show him the Lakota way to save himself from the blizzard, to heal wounds with marsh earth, to cook soup in a buffalo paunch filled with meat and hot stones for the boiling. He would lead this son to know the nature of all things, the sky and the air and the earth, and the ways of every animal, the buffalo, the bear, the wolf, even his little brothers the fox, the beaver, and the mink. Perhaps some time when he helped the boy twist one of these smaller ones from his hole with a split-ended stick it would be a skunk and the women would drive them from the lodge together, as they had done Hump and young Curly, long ago.

Yes, he would try to teach his son to fight, to hunt, and to live as a good Lakota. And often now he sent the crier to bring in the young Black Elk or some other boy who might some day become a man to help the people. He told them stories while they ate from the wooden bowls the women filled, and teased them a little as one would a puppy or a colt to make it gentle and yet give it fire. The boys all seemed a little shy, acting almost afraid of this friendly man who was called strange by their people. They did feel a strangeness about him, as the thunders are strange, or the bull elk walking. But they always came back for more stories, their eyes shining as the buffalo fat that was thrown on the coals blazed up, making dark people-shadows against the painted lodge lining that showed the sacred things of the vision of Crazy Horse, lighting up, too, the friendly faces of the women. It reminded the man of his father's fire, where he and young Little Hawk used to tease their sister, particularly when Black Shawl put sweet-grass and cherry bark upon the coals as his mother did, making a fragrance inside

and all over the village, letting the people know that everything
was good in the lodge of Crazy Horse.

By spring Red Cloud was asking that all trade with the Indians
be stopped at Fetterman on the Platte and from there down to
Laramie—getting even, some said, for the bad words he had to
stand in the Hunkpatila camp and the insult of the breechcloth
jerked off before him, trying to starve them so they must come to
sit under him on an agency. But others wondered if he wouldn't
be afraid to have the famous hostile warriors live among his people,
drawing his young men to follow at their heel fringes.

Summer brought more news of him, waiting for his agent, with
Red Leaf and Little Wound and the others long back from the
Missouri, all camped around Laramie eating the beef and flour of
the soldier chief. And when the agent finally came he was not the
one Red Cloud had been promised and so the Bad Face made an
angry counciling. He had been shamed before the people, he said,
and so would accept no agency north of the river. Besides, the
traders warned him that as soon as the whites got into the Indian
country they would keep pushing until they had the Black Hills.

"Hou!" Crazy Horse agreed when he heard this story.

Yes, but the agent and the peace men listened to Red Cloud with
cold hearts, keeping their gifts in their pockets, reminding him that
he had already been given power and presents for this thing and
now his tongue spoke from the other side.

At last Red Cloud said that he could not decide alone for the
Bad Faces but must go to the north to council with Black Twin.
The whites looked surprised. Who was this Black Twin that the
man who claimed to be the big chief of the Lakota nation must ask
him about anything? However, he could go, but there would be no
rations for the people until the Indians agreed on an agency.

So as soon as the headmen got hungry they came, walking one
behind the other, to speak to their new father, agreeing to a place
near the mouth of Horse Creek, the same Horse Creek on which the
Big Council was held almost a warrior's life ago and where Fouts

and the four chiefs were later killed. Near there, north of the river, the agency was made.

When this was known among the hostiles some of the Crazy Horse warriors went whooping down to count coups on the peace chiefs, even on Red Cloud, sparing only old Man Afraid. And when the friendlies were all moved to the new place and their goods did not come, their own young men, painted for war, stirred up a great dust through the new tent town, shooting into the air, laughing as the whites scattered out of sight like mice running under leaves. And when the goods finally came they would not let the wagon train for Spotted Tail go north to his new agency beyond the Running Water.

"No whites are allowed in the Indian country! Hoppo!" the warriors cried, Little Big Man and others who always appeared with trouble as the split-tail bird comes with the storm hurrying down for the fun.

So Spotted Tail got his goods at Red Cloud and then went south to hunt on the forbidden Republican, his people well supplied with new canvas lodge covers, new blankets and kettles, and many white-man clothes—coats, pants, and hats, that could be traded back to the whites for ammunition and whisky.

When a pack horse of the new annuities reached the northern camps family parties started to slip away to get the good things of the agency before the snow winds came. Crazy Horse and the others had to see this happen, see their camps shrink like sandbars in a flood. But some thought it was just as well, for every year the meat-making was harder.

"The buffalo is going—" some of the older men said, starting once more the old, old story of how it used to be, with so many buffalo that every year thousands were driven over the bluffs into the Chugwater below the Platte. Men still alive had camped for days along the Holy Road waiting for the herds to pass, the ground rumbling under the great dark blanket that swept by night and day, night and day. Who could have killed so many? They must have been driven away by the bad living of the people.

"Too many of our women have become the village property of the soldiers!" some said angrily, as they had many times before. And one or two remembered that to deny a woman the right to leave her man when she wished made the cows barren, the calves few. But the younger men said it was not these things but the skin hunters working north and south, and went to melt lead in the kettles, cast more shiny bullets. Now let the whites with the buffalo guns come into their country.

Early one morning towards fall the flap of the Crazy Horse lodge was lifted and Black Shawl came in, walking slowly, a little bent, carrying something that she laid gently before her sleeping man. He sat up and looked at the doeskin bundle a long time, then to the weary woman squatting on her robes, her face pale, dust and grass in her tangled hair.

"It is a daughter—" she said, making the words sadly, for every man wishes a warrior son.

Crazy Horse lifted the little bundle. "Hou!" he said softly, "then it is a daughter, a new daughter for the Oglalas, and she shall grow up a great mother of the people, and everybody shall stand in wonder before her sacred ways and she shall be called They Are Afraid of Her."

It was a bad-weather winter, so cold that some Indians froze themselves just walking from one camp to another. The mothers scolded. One couldn't get these young men out for a little fresh meat, but for waiting on a girl—

Yet it was a good winter too, for by the time the trees were popping with the cold the hostile camps seemed almost as large as in the days of the fighting against the fort on the Piney. Even Red Cloud and Red Dog had come north just ahead of the ground's freezing. It seemed that their father, the agent, must be very lonesome down on the Platte, with everybody running away as soon as the annuities were given out. Only the traders' sons and a few old Loafers were with him. Some claimed he stole their goods but others said that the Loafers were trading their issue for whisky and then complaining of the hungry belly.

During the winter all the shells were reloaded, most of them with powder enough to make good shooting, for Crazy Horse had learned that no medicine was strong when the powder was divided so the bullets of the Indians barely rolled out of the gun barrels and those of the soldiers knocked the warriors to the ground. With so little powder for the practice shooting, many of the Indians were poor shots—not as poor as most of the soldiers, but not good as the mountain men were, or some of the traders' sons. Crazy Horse had hunted with Little Bat, the son of Garnier, and it made the heart warm to see the shooting of that one. Not Bridger or any other was like this son of the Lakotas.

Yes, powder the Indians must have or else get their travois ready for the move to the agencies. So Sitting Bull made a treaty with the Slota, the Red River breeds. These people used to come from the north with their two-wheeled carts to the old rendezvous on the Green River, going even as far as the Spanish place called Santa Fe. Now they were often on the Yellowstone for buffalo, moving in the same way, their families along and a Black Robe with his holy cross, fighting Indians from earth forts like the whites, with the newest rifles and plenty of powder. After the treaty they came to the Hunkpapa camp. Crazy Horse had gone up to get guns and ammunition, but it was time thrown on the wind, for the five sleighs they brought held mostly whisky. When he came back he stopped at his lodge for a bowl of soup and a little playing with the big-eyed They Are Afraid of Her, watching her breaking into a little laughing when he touched her nose with a rabbit's tail hanging on a string, Black Shawl looking up from work, her calm face happy as earth in spring. But he had seen something up there in the north country that made him uneasy. The whites were trying to get Grabber, the trader's son, to do as young Richard had, bring Sitting Bull in and get a white-man killing forgotten, so he hurried to tell it to Worm and old Little Hawk.

"Ahh-h!" the uncle said, making it the sound of anger. Worm

smoked in silence, thinking about this, and finally he told that Lean Elk had been chopped to pieces down near the agency on the Platte. He went to get the two wives he had left behind the time he took Red Cloud in, and when Yellow Bear, their brother, said they were gone to a dance, the drunken Richard shot him. So the Indians cut him up with their hunting knives and threw him outside into the camp circle.

"Lean Elk was the son of a Lakota woman but he was a bad man—" Crazy Horse admitted, "and there may be others."

But there was more news from the Platte. The old agent was already worn out, a new one coming, and more talk about moving the agency up into the hunting lands of the Lakotas. Red Cloud, it seemed, was going to see the Great Father again.

"Wonder what he will sell this time," Crazy Horse said. Perhaps somebody had better go down to see what was happening. But Little Big Man and his followers were already there. And by the time Red Cloud got back from Washington the Loafers had agreed to move the agency, the Bad Face talking very loud and angry against it. Then they heard that he was not against the moving but angry because he had not been paid to allow it done.

Hoh!

Early in the new summer the Oglalas drove the meat-hungry Crows from their northern buffalo ranges and then joined Minneconjous and Hunkpapas below the big bend of the Yellowstone for a great sundance, one to make the people strong again and of good heart, for there was uneasy talk of white men measuring off the earth east of them, and coming this way. Towards the middle of the Cherries Blackening, August, some Hunkpapas came riding fast to say four hundred soldiers were up the river although nobody could say how they got there.[1] Almost half of them were horse soldiers, with a lot of other whites along. So while the older men helped move the people back from the soldier path, a big party of warriors went out, Crazy Horse coming behind, for his little

[1] Troop-protected Northern Pacific Railway survey, summer 1872.

daughter had the white man's summer cramp sickness, and it was hard to leave his lodge.

They found the camp near the mouth of Arrow Creek and got behind a ridge near the beef herd and the horses, ready to stampede the stock as soon as it was light enough to follow them. But some of Sitting Bull's young warriors sneaked out before the daybreak star and then came galloping back with a few horses, the herders chasing them hard, guns booming, the soldiers all awake and hurrying the stock inside the camp.

Crazy Horse was angry. "It is spoiled now," he told his Oglalas, "so be careful! The soldiers have far-shooting guns and plenty of shells. No use losing good men when there is nothing left to get."

By this time it was day, so the Indians gathered on a little ridge to attack the soldiers hidden behind a cut bank near the river. It was a hard place and Plenty Lice, the first one to charge out, went too close and fell into the tall grass. Two more rode out and had to be dragged back, wounded.

"Be careful!" Crazy Horse warned again. "Somebody besides soldiers are there; hunters or mountain men!"

When the sun came up hot on their backs, Long Holy, the Minneconjou with a strong vision, made the bullet-proofing ceremony for six men. These were to ride out with him, circle the whites the sacred four times, and then charge, all those from the ridge charging with them. So it was done, the warriors on their fast horses circling towards the smoke-hazed, fast-shooting soldier line, singing the vision song of Long Holy. One was hit, then another but they were strong and kept riding until two more were hurt, then the leaders ordered them back. Four wounded out of seven was enough.

After that there was some more charging and once Sitting Bull and a few of his warriors went out to smoke before the Indian line, the northern soldiers seeming to know the limping Hunkpapa and firing thick upon him. But no lead touched him that day. Once Crazy Horse made the ride along the soldier line himself, hoping to draw some whites out for the others to shoot, riding slowly, as if out looking at the country. When bullets clipped hair from the tail of his horse and knocked a splinter from his lance stick, the young warriors made a loud cheering. But the Hunkpatila knew these things were foolish. The whites would not be kept out of the country with this kind of fighting. They understood only the bullet that brought the man down.

When the warriors were leaving, Crazy Horse helped search the tall grass for the wounded. He tried to get to Plenty Lice but his horse caught a bullet in the breast and he had to run to save himself, dodging in the zigzag pattern of the sacred lightning. And after the Indians were gone the scouts saw the soldiers throw Plenty Lice into one of their cooking fires, smelled his burning far over the hills.

Crazy Horse rode home alone, saying he would get some small game for Black Shawl and the little daughter sick, young prairie chicken or sage hen or the long-billed brown bird that cries on the hill. He wanted to think of the raid spoiled too, and one more bullet-proofing that failed. On the way, the scouts found him to say that the soldiers had gone back, but Crazy Horse knew they would not always run away so easily. By the time he got home many of the Indians were already making ready to visit their relations on the agency, to taste the white man's food again and to brag about the good fights they were having in the north, of the coups counted and the horses taken.

Then when the leaves were gone and the boys were chewing the fall-sweetened hackberries, soldiers moved from Laramie to the agency of Red Cloud. The whisky-selling whites had killed two Indians down there and so the warriors charged the stockade, trying to find somebody to shoot to make their hearts good. But when the soldiers came, they found no warriors hungry for fighting, only Indians riding off into the hills, letting them take an Oglaia place without a shot, come where no soldiers were ever to be. It happened that Red Cloud was away north, making strong words against pushing the agency deeper into Indian country. But his talking did not fool anybody now, not even the whites, as

Crazy Horse told those who came to speak about these things. They found the Hunkpatila trotting around the lodge with his daughter riding his shoulders, one bare brown foot on each side of the father's strong neck, holding with both hands to his scalp lock.

"Pony, pony!" she cried to her mother, "pony!" her eyes dark in the pale, delicate face, the soft brown hair around it fluffing out of the stubby braids. But she was soon tired and went to sleep in her father's arms while he talked with his visitors. He often held her so, for she was not strong, and a fear for this one more being he loved lay deep in his heart.

It was a spring of yellow flowers and many spotted colts in the herds, a good sign for the summer, the weather women said. There were quite a few buffalo too, but people closed in like wolves from all sides upon them, even the Slota from the north, Sitting Bull going out to fight them away. Up the river in the west it was the Crows and their friends pushing in, and when the sundance on the Rosebud was done the Oglalas and some of the Cheyennes left the big camp and moved up towards Arrow Creek, where the scouts had found four hundred lodges of Crows, with some Bannocks and Nez Perce along. Leaving the people safe between the Little and Big Horn Rivers, a few Oglalas went out to drive the hunters back but found too many. So they retreated and the Crows went back to their hunting camp feeling very safe.

Here Crazy Horse and the others struck them, this time coming with enough warriors to fill the big valley with riding, whooping Indians, some brave enough to push right up to the village. But the Crow and Nez Perce women had dug rifle pits around the lodges, and the horses had been taken to an island in the Yellowstone, so all the Lakotas could do was ride up and down, showing off. There were several whites in the camp, painted and wearing the Crow roach of hair. One of these, with a red feather on his head, came riding out like a warrior to sing a song, but Crazy Horse, seeing with the far-looking glasses, signaled that the man had a

long rifle and nobody must go near. It was good that they didn't
for they found out afterward that it shot seven times.

Both sides had their women along and many were up close to
the fighting, calling out bad names, making insulting motions, and
singing strong-heart songs every time a warrior rode out. In the
quiet times between there were visiting questions back and forth
about people they knew—Bridger, Beckwourth, Big Bat—and a
wondering why so many horses were dead along the Crow trails.

"It's the epizootic," one of the whites called back. "Dying like
flies, or like the antelope up north this year."

Some of the Lakotas understood this. They knew about the
prairies full of rotting antelope, dying as the buffalo did once not
so long ago. Another bad white man's disease.

While this was happening Crazy Horse saw Mitch Bouyer, a
trader's son he knew from the Platte country, come riding into the
Crow line. What was he doing up here?

Mitch answered for himself. He had just come from the Missouri
with the peace men who had been at Laramie. He was here to
call the Crows to their agency for a council.

"You will lose your scalp among those people!" a big Lakota
called out. He was one of the war-bonnet men of his *akicita* and
sat on his horse far ahead of the rest, not moving or shooting, just
shaking his coup stick at the enemy and laughing so his white
teeth gleamed. It seemed he could not be hit, although many young
warriors from the enemy crawled out to try.

"Come closer," some of the Oglalas called to them. "Come get
some Lakota women! They are much better than the Crows!"
everybody laughing very loud at this old joke.

But the sun was getting low, time the women started back to
camp and so the warriors made one more charge and left too. A
party of Crows and whites following behind them found some Lakotas sitting around smoking in the darkness and made them drop
their bundles to get away. Some horses were lost in this and two
men didn't come in. Afterward they were found scalped and with
parts cut off, showing that the Crow women were still angry over

their men killed near there twenty-five years ago, in a big fight with arrows and war clubs.

There was keening in the Lakota camp that night, but there would be dancing later, for they had some good scalps, including that of a brother of Long Horse, a chief. Afterward there was complaining about the fight down at Fort Laramie. It was said that the Crows and Bouyer told the peace men that the Lakotas had good rifles, Winchesters and Henrys and Spencers, with plenty of shells and powder. They must have very good friends among the whites to get these things.

The Crazy Horse people were in another fight this summer. Several times the scouts had brought news of soldiers coming up the Yellowstone with the whites who were measuring the ground for another iron road, right through the Lakota hunting grounds.[1] One of the soldier chiefs was Long Hair, the one who had driven the Cheyennes around in the Republican River country not long ago and struck Black Kettle's friendlies down on the Washita where they had gone to keep out of trouble. He left the women and children butchered in the snow there the way the whites liked to do.

Some of the Black Kettle Cheyennes were with Crazy Horse. They knew the soldier chief by his yellow hair and went out to meet him, riding like wild men, so hot to fight him that they couldn't wait and helped spoil the ambush the Hunkpapas and No Bows had planned. So it wasn't much of a fight, but the Indians spread it out over many campings, picking off some horses and a few whites. One of these was a trader and another had a box of the knives and bottles the white medicine men carried.

For several days those of the sundance village at the mouth of the Rosebud watched the soldiers and the long string of white-topped wagons come winding up along the river. When they were close the people moved away, but Long Hair with some horse soldiers and Indian scouts hurried ahead and chased them all night and so they crossed the Yellowstone on rafts and the skin

[1] Expedition under Colonel Stanley, summer 1873.

bundles made of their lodges, the women sitting on them, the men pulling them across with their horses. Long Hair and his blue-coats came galloping close behind, but his American horses wouldn't swim the deep, swift stream to the Indians waiting for him back in the hills, ready to wipe him out before he could get away.

The soldier chief called Custer camped there at the Yellowstone and so at dawn the next day the Indians attacked him from across the river, with some warriors gathering on the bluffs behind him too. Before they could do much the long line of men and wagons came hurrying up. They shot the wagon guns into the people watching on the hill, scattering them like antelope before lightning striking in dry grass. But even when the soldier train moved on, some of the warriors kept after them, like wolves following the buffalo herds, picking off those who dragged behind.

Now there was more bad news from the agency—the Loafers had let it be moved north into the Indian country. Many of the friendlies had cried no! no! but the whites gave out a lot of secret presents and the next thing the hostiles knew, the agency was up beyond the Running Water on the White Earth River, close to Crow Butte. After a while Red Cloud folded his chief's blanket around him and went to the agent with Red Dog to make the words and some others walking behind. Now they were moved, the Bad Face wanted the things he had been promised, the guns and ammunition. It would please the northern Indians so much they would all come in. There were eleven bands and he wanted ten guns for each band, four kinds of guns: needle, Winchester, rifles, and revolvers, and shells for all.

"They were not given?" the northern people asked.

"No—no."

The *akicita* were talking loud down there now. They would run the agency. No white man must come north of the White Earth River; the beef herd must eat the grass south of the Running Water, and they would say where the woodchoppers could cut the timber. They would say about other things, too, it seemed, for when the trader wouldn't pay five dollars each for beef hides, they locked him up.

"Looks like trouble," some of the hostiles thought.

"Looks like they will get more crackers and molasses," Crazy Horse said. He sat as in a lodge of darkness all this winter for it seemed that Black Shawl was shrinking within her buckskin dress, and when the weather was wet there was coughing as from the white man's disease under her blanket.

DEATH, *and the Thieves' Road*

THROUGHOUT the memory of many generations the Teton Lakotas sent their hunting parties westward across the Missouri to
bring hides and meat and the other things of the buffalo back to
their cornland villages. Then one summer a big party with the
shoulder packs and dog travois did not return and each year more
stayed out until the Tetons were a wild, free, hunting people.
And in all the time since they turned their backs upon the bone
hoe they had come together only a few times.

One of these Crazy Horse could remember. It was at Bear Butte
after the council with White Beard, the one called Squaw-Killer
Harney. Crazy Horse was only a slim boy of fifteen then and when
he saw the great camp filling all the plain below him, from one
sacred direction to the other, it seemed that his Lakotas were surely
the greatest people on earth, and the most in number.

Now, sixteen years later, in 1873, the Tetons were together again,
not just in answer to the great council pipe but living near, often
in one camp for the sundance or other ceremonials. But now their
number was no longer like the shadow of a great storm over the
land. Now many of each band were on the white-man agencies,
only a few of the Bear Oglalas and the Brules left free, or the Blackfoot and Two Kettle and No Bows.

It was not only because the whites were pushing in across the
Missouri that Sitting Bull and the others had left their old country

around the Grand River and the Cannonball and come up the Yellowstone. A worse thing had happened back there—the buffalo was gone, even the chips lost in the grass, and only the piles of white bones waiting for the iron road showing that any had ever lived.

Many long evenings the headmen talked of this around the council fires. Crazy Horse always had a place at these now, the crier calling him as he did the others, even if it was for all the hostile Tetons together, for the old chiefs' society was done, its members gone to the agency, its foolish things forgotten.

Usually some medicine man arose in these councils to say he could bring the buffalo back, sometimes by his secret medicine, sometimes with the sundance or a buffalo dance. One of them even went to live with the Blackfeet awhile to learn their very strong buffalo medicine. He came back with the whole story, the steps, the bull headdresses, the painting, the songs, and the drumming. But when they asked him about the hunts of the Blackfeet, he had to say that there was almost no buffalo meat in the villages.

In these days Crazy Horse was often away from the camp. Sometimes a hunter or a trapper told of seeing the lone Oglala in the timber or at a cave in the hills somewhere, and once when the scouts came upon a buffalo herd they found him on a knoll downwind, only a little way from the feeding animals, his gun silent across his knees, as if he were herding his cattle. At the next council he arose and said that the Crows and Snakes must be driven far from the hunting grounds of the Lakotas, for there were already not enough young cows left, not nearly as many as there were old ones and bulls. That meant fewer calves each year—always fewer calves.

Ahh-h! some of the old men agreed, mostly those who would not believe that the buffalo had turned his back on the Indian. It was the people who were lost, running after the whites whenever they were hungry instead of doing the old sacred things long used to bring their brother the buffalo back to them.

"Hou!" Worm spoke from his place. He remembered a very bad

time in the years the whites called 1842 and 1843, when the skies
held their rains, the rivers forgot their ways, and the clouds were
only grasshoppers. There were almost no buffalo in those years,
the hungry wolves coming right among the lodges and finding
nothing. The Oglalas had to eat their horses then too, or go far
out on the Laramie plains for a little poor meat. But the people
danced and made the buffalo ceremonies and the herds came back.

"Hou, hou!" the old ones said, Crazy Horse sitting silent among
them, looking into the coals, ashamed to remind his father and the
others of the things they all knew—that there was probably not
one buffalo to be found on all the Laramie plains today, perhaps
only scattered bulls within two hundred miles of there. And the
southern Oglalas up visiting said the great herds of the Republican
and Smoky Hill Rivers were gone too, only small bunches left
hiding in the breaks, so wild it took plenty of powder to get them.

Always plenty of powder.

Towards fall and the big annuity day many of the coffee-coolers
came up from the agencies of Spotted Tail and Red Cloud with
stories of the fine things down there. Every five days, holding up
the fingers of one hand, every *so* often the people all moved in close
for the goods. Then at the pole corrals the name of one headman
after another was called out, his cattle turned loose, the warriors
chasing them and killing them like buffalo, only these bellowed
loud when they ran and did not hit the ground so hard when they
fell. But the women came out in the same way with their big knives
for the butchering, the children running behind them for bits of
fresh liver or a piece of the small entrails with a touch of gall from
the knife point on it. Then there was the fighting of the dogs over
the bones at night, the dogs and the wolves and coyotes, and in
the villages everybody rich enough to feast his friends.

"What do you get for carrying these stories up here?" young
Black Fox demanded. But the headmen reminded him that one
did not talk so to guests.

Some of the northern Indians went down to see about these wonderful things and it was truly as the friendlies had said, rations every five days, but some of the food was fit only for whites to eat, like the salt pork, so yellow and moldy that the Indians and even the dogs left it on the ground. The flour was dark and full of worms, the tobacco black and sticky, the sugar like sand to the teeth. The clothes were bad, too, small, thin blankets, the pants coming to pieces in water like black paper, and the beef herd not American cattle at all but the Spanish long-horns, so tough from the walk north that even the wolves sat on the knolls and looked at them.

Then the agent called the headmen in to say the Indians must be counted. To this the northern warriors made a great noise, scolding their father in the councils, riding around stripped to breech-cloth and paint. But he kept talking about it as more and more people showed up for ration day. Touch the Cloud's Minneconjous had slipped into the camps and were making big complaints on these days, not only against the agency things but against the iron road coming through the north country. First it was the Platte they lost, with the fire wagons so noisy and stinking that they scared even the stupid cattle of the whites. Now there was talk of the same thing at the Yellowstone.

Nor were the young hostiles satisfied to sit around like the agency Indians, feasting on the rations of one issue day and waiting with thin bellies for the next. Red Cloud and Spotted Tail were only a good pony's travel apart and many managed to draw allowances at both places, sending pack-loaded ponies up the worn trails to the north. And when there wasn't plenty of everything, the warriors kept the friendlies stirred up like a stick shaking a wasps' nest. After a while Man Afraid and Little Wound tried to help the agent, but it was hard because by then there was snow and no goods were coming up from the Platte and some of the Indians were butchering their horses.

"It is strange that the freighters cannot get through down there, when the gold-hungry whites are bringing their wagons into the Yellowstone country all winter," Crazy Horse told the visitors with these stories.

There was news of Red Cloud too, and his anger at the hard life on the agency this winter. Perhaps he was turning hostile, for he said that when the grass came in the spring it would be time for another Indian war to throw the white man from the Indian country.

After the agent called Saville came back with the Cheyenne and Blue Cloud chiefs from Washington, he made a feast for the Lakotas and talked very strong about the counting. Red Cloud said he wouldn't allow it, not until he got the guns that had been promised him for the moving to White Earth River. Red Dog and High Wolf and many others cried: "Hou! hou!" while the Loafer chiefs sat silent.

There was the trouble over this and so much quarreling among the *akicita* that Lone Horn's Minneconjous decided to go back north. But they didn't, after all. Instead they made up war parties right on the agency, for it was good to have the helpless ones safe and fed while the warriors raided, and good, too, this living so close to the trails and the ranches. With the tails of their horses tied up for war they shot out all the windows of the agency before they started away and all that the whites could do was lie in corners and on the floor so they wouldn't get hit. Nobody fired back.

Soon there was news of depredations all along the trails, soldiers picked off around Laramie and mail carriers ambushed on the way to Red Cloud—all blamed on the warriors of Crazy Horse. Then one night he was awakened by a scratching at his lodge flap. It was a runner from Red Cloud, saying a white man had been killed inside the stockade while his uncle, the agent, was away at Spotted Tail. One of the Minneconjous, bad-hearted because somebody was dead, climbed over in the darkness. Young Billy Garnett ran through the night to Red Cloud's camp and from there others were sent to Little Wound and Man Afraid. All three came to sit beside the dying man, silent and dark, for he had been the little agent and there was sure to be bad trouble.

And now the soldiers were going up there from Laramie.

Ahh-h, that was bad, Crazy Horse thought. Soldiers on White Earth River, right under the edge of the Black Hills, with already so much talking about gold in there—the soldiers of the Great Father coming into the middle of the Lakota country because one white man was shot by a bad-hearted Minneconjou when so many Indians had died from their guns.

All the night Crazy Horse sat in his blanket, not moving even when Black Shawl arose to heat a little soup for him. Then, when the sun came over the snow, he rode out and two days later he reached the frozen lake called the Medicine Water,[1] where, in troubled times, many dreams had come to the headmen of his people. On a wind-bared ridge of red earth he built a sweat lodge spread with the sacred gray sage weed, but through all the days and nights of his fasting not even a wolf came near to howl. There was no vision and in the nights no dreaming, only the steady knowledge that the Indians down around the agency would not work together. Standing solid as a rock they could hold back all the soldiers at Laramie, but in this, too, they would fall apart like winter-frozen sandstone.

In three days word was brought him by a man worn out from the cold and the hard riding. It had happened as they feared. The soldiers had come right through all the Lakota country from Laramie to White Earth, and instead of fighting them the Indians fought each other, the Loafers against the hostiles, Bear people against the Smokes. When the soldiers set up their white tents at the agency, the hostiles went north, burning some of the agency haystacks and the barer slopes of the prairie behind them. But the soldiers were there, with flag and bugle and the far-shooting guns, and when had the soldiers ever left after they came like that?

Living was hard in the north that winter, with the game driven out by the snow and no powder in the camps. A party had gone down to try to get some at the agencies, but they took long in returning, and so some of the young men started out to meet them.

[1] Lake De Smet.

Grabber, who had had trouble with Sitting Bull and was now living with He Dog, usually in the Crazy Horse camp, went along. He had two shells but he used them up on game too far to hit, and so they almost starved before they got back, for there was no ammunition on the agencies either, and no food to bring away.

Towards spring the Chinook came, bringing visiting traders' sóns with the white man's newspapers and their stories. From these Crazy Horse and his camp knew that it was not only the Indians at the agency who had starved this winter, but many, many people in the great white-man towns that Red Cloud had seen. With times so hard, many more whites would push westward this summer, following the smell of gold as the hungry Indian follows the buffalo. The papers said, too, that Custer, the long-haired soldier chief they had fought on the Yellowstone, was getting soldiers and wagons ready to go into the Black Hills this summer.

"To *Pa Sapa*?" Crazy Horse said in anger.

Yes, to *Pa Sapa*. It was something about helping get money for the railroad coming up the Yellowstone. There would be more than a hundred white-topped wagons, a thousand soldiers and miners, sixty Indian scouts, and wagon guns at both ends of the long train.

Ahh-h! Let anyone believe in the white man's true-talking now. "So long as grass shall grow and water flow," the peace paper said, and even Red Cloud had spoken for it.

Red Cloud, *pagh!* He most of all angered the warriors, for he had fooled them, made them believe he was working hard for their good.

Once more the hostiles counciled. They would send word to the agencies for help. They were of strong heart, but there were not two good shells apiece for the warriors in the northern camps, and even the oldest man among them knew that they could not fight these whites with the arrows and war clubs of another day.

This council did not break up in a great talking that was like an old scatter-gun shooting into the snow but in a silent going away, each man to his own lodge. Crazy Horse led a little party against the Crows among the buffalo herds and to try a sacred smoking for a way to save the people. But nothing came and so they scattered the Crow hunting camp, got a few horses, and started home. They had left the people on the Little Big Horn where the Rosebud comes close, but the camp had moved, the signs on the buffalo heads and the sticks laid along the lodge trail pointing towards the Tongue. And when they neared the blue smoke hanging along the bluffs, no one came out to meet them, and when they reached the village all the Crazy Horse people were in ragged blankets, their hair loose and cut off, the women with dried blood on their gashed arms and legs. Worm, with Little Hawk, in torn clothes, came to take the rope of his son's horse and the sage hens he had shot, his bow too, and would have taken his rifle but Crazy Horse was not the one to give up his gun easily, not even to his father in sorrow.

"Son, be strong now," the two men said as they followed him to the lodge door. Inside there was only the cold duskiness of a dead fire. Then he saw Black Shawl, but in torn dress and earth-streaked face, her body swaying in soft moaning, and so he knew that it was They Are Afraid of Her, his daughter.

"Be strong, my son!" Worm said again. But Crazy Horse could do nothing wild. A long time he stood silent there, not moving, tasting the full bitterness of this new thing laid upon his heart.

"How was it?" he finally asked, and Worm answered him, saying that it was the choking cough brought by the traders' sons.

Ahh-h, another of the white man's diseases. Was there no end to the bad things he sent against the people, not only in the noise and heat of battle but in the quiet darkness of the lodge, striking straight as an arrow through the heart.

Later they told him where she was, and he went out alone through a country known to be close-watched by the Crows for scattered Lakotas. It was in a little flat place at the edge of a few trees, they said, a small red bundle on a scaffold.

At last Crazy Horse came in sight of such a little prairie. In the sky over it a few small clouds floated white as swans on water and at the far edge were the trees and the scaffold with its little bundle. He knew it was the one, for on the posts hung the playthings his daughter had loved: a rattle of antelope hoofs strung on rawhide, a bouncing bladder with little stones inside, a painted willow hoop. And on the scaffold, tied on top of the red blanket, was a deerskin doll, the beaded design of her cradleboard the same as on the dresses the little girl always wore, a design that came from far back in the family of Black Shawl.

When he saw this the father could hold himself no longer. Face down beside the body of his daughter he let the sorrow locked in his heart sweep over him, the rickety scaffold creaking a little under his weight.

The wind died in the sunset of that day and rose again with the sun's returning. An eagle with his buzzards following circled in the far sky, and over a low rise a bunch of antelope came grazing. Seeing the scaffold before them, they lifted their heads and ran down that way, circling a little, but coming close in their curiosity, until they caught the man smell. Then they bounded away, their rumps showing white. After a while a wolf came along a little ridge, tail high, his nose in the air. He, too, got the scent of man and with a leap was off over the prairie. And when it was night again a little mouse came creeping up a post to sniff at the bundle of cloth, stopping, listening to a slow sound that came and died, came again. Suddenly the little animal leapt down and fled away into the grass, frightened that in the smell of death there was the thing of life, the breathing.

The next daylight brought nothing of the sun, only gray clouds and a drizzling of fog closing in around the scaffold. When even the earth below the posts was lost, there was one pale flash of lightning and a fog-softened rumble of thunder. This the man heard, and knew that it was time to go. So at the first lifting of the clouds he went to find his hobbled horse, eat a little from the *wasna* bladder. Then he rode down to the soldier town of Fetterman to watch for whites, and when he had brought three from their horses and chased another clear into the parade ground of the fort, he went away, for in this sorrow it did not ease his heart to kill.

When Crazy Horse returned to his camp there was bad word waiting from the Missouri forts. Long Hair, Custer, had really gone into the Black Hills, into that sacred place where so many of their fathers were buried, so many warriors had gone to make their dreaming. Now there was a wide trail into it right past Bear Butte, the old, old place of the Teton councils. The Thieves' road, the Indians called it, even those of the agencies, and many young men came hurrying north because Long Hair was saying there was gold all over that country from the grass roots down.

Ahh-h, gold! The older men still living among the hostiles, like Worm and Little Hawk, had long known about it. Some of the yellow stones had been brought to the Black Robe, to Father De Smet, almost thirty years ago. He said to bury them deep in the earth and in forgetting, for even a sight of one of these stones would bring a burning to the brain of the white man, a craziness. And it was indeed true. Already the shooting had begun. Custer had found a few friendlies in the Hills, and while he talked peace to them, his Mandan scouts killed old Stabber and wounded Slow Bull, the son-in-law of Red Cloud, before they could get away. It seemed Black Elk and his little camp barely escaped the whites, too. They were hunting along one of the lodge trails near the hills and decided to come north. That day Chips, the medicine man, made a sweat and heard a voice saying that the band must flee at once because something bad was to happen there. So, although it was near evening, they started back towards the agency, traveling all night. At daylight they met some scouts who said that many soldiers had gone into the Black Hills and that Oglala blood had been spilled there.

"Perhaps finding out that Black Elk was coming to us helped the medicine man hear the voices," some said, for there were still many in the north who looked upon him as a trouble-maker, and Chips knew it.

But the big thing was that Long Hair had come into their Black Hills and was going back without anybody shooting at him. It was true that the fires they set made the sky of the night shine as from northern lights, the sun of day blood-red from the smoke, the soldier horses hungry, the game scared away. It would have been better to attack him but they had so little powder and the Long Hair's wagons were full of ammunition, with many soldier guns to guard them. So they could only burn the prairie.

By September the wild Lakotas started to come into the agencies, making a great noise about *Pa Sapa*, the Black Hills, many talking big of cleaning out all the whites who were digging their earth with the shovels. Then near the end of October, the Moon of Changing Seasons, the agent had a long tree brought in from the hills. Some of the headmen came to ask about this and were told it was for a flag. They rose in anger. They would have no flag on their agency, or anything else of the soldiers, and so the warriors charged the stockade and chopped up the pole with their axes, the whites running to hide in the corner towers of the stockade and anywhere they could from the whooping Indians. When a few soldiers came from the little fort set up above the agency, the warriors charged out to meet them, shooting, circling them as in war, knocking their horses out of the way. But Sitting Bull, the nephew of Little Wound, and Young Man Afraid had gathered up a lot of the friendlies and, driving the warriors back with clubs and Indian whips, they took the soldiers into the stockade and slammed the heavy door.

In a few days Crazy Horse knew that the flagpole fighting had brought the old troubles between the people boiling up like sand in the flooded Platte. Young Conquering Bear, the Brule, was clubbed from his horse and two Bad Faces laid a bow across his throat and stood on the ends until he was like a black man. Then they whipped him, and Bear Brains, the brother-in-law of Red Cloud, waved a revolver in his face telling him he ought to die, all his band ought to die because they were trouble-makers. If his father, old Conquering Bear, had given up the Minneconjou who killed the lame cow, there would have been no fighting with the whites, there would never have been a Lakota war with the soldiers at all.

Once more Sitting Bull, the Oglala, came riding up. With his three-bladed knife on a curved handle he knocked men and horses aside, scattered the quarreling Indians, driving through them like a great wind.

"Hou!" the older warriors said, remembering how this Oglala used to scatter the Crow warriors. It was too bad to waste a good man like that on an agency.

And what was Red Cloud doing during the fighting, somebody asked.

Red Cloud? He sat smoking on a lumber pile inside the stockade, helping neither side, watching.

The warriors who had once followed every step of his moccasin tracks made the wondering sound. Those like Little Wound and Man Afraid they could understand—peace men for a long time, believing that the buffalo would soon be gone and that they must get the best trade they could from the whites and then work hard to make them keep it. But it seemed Red Cloud was always sitting up on something, waiting to see what would be offered him to come down.

Crazy Horse wasn't home to hear the messengers tell this story. He was out with a party against the Black Hills miners and seemed long in returning. Ever since the days away in the country where his little daughter lay on a scaffold, the family of Crazy Horse was uneasy whenever he was on a raid, Black Shawl trying to keep her eyes from the direction he had gone. She walked thinner in her dress these days and worked harder than ever, drying the meat, dressing the robes, making moccasins, cooking for the many guests that came wanting to see the Strange Man of the Oglalas, some from the far peoples who lived many days north of the Milk

River or from west of the Shining Mountains, waiting with serious faces to talk of what might be done in these bad times to save the Indian. And often Worm or his wife came to ask if there was news of the son, knowing that Black Shawl would run to them with it as soon as anything was heard, yet having to ask.

Others saw the recklessness growing in Crazy Horse, a bad thing in a man soon to be thirty-three years old, with the weight of the people upon him. Even his warriors spoke of it with uneasiness. He still jumped off to take aim, making every bullet find its place, but there was a new fierceness in him, a new daring that seemed as young and foolish as that of the brother whose name was never spoken now except when it meant the uncle. The enemy seemed even more afraid of him than before, a Crow captive saying it was well known among them that Crazy Horse had a medicine gun that hit whatever it looked at and that he was bullet-proof. These things must be so, for he was always closest, striking and killing more than any other, yet they could never hit him.

By the time Crazy Horse was back from the Black Hills with some pack mules of white-man goods there was more news from Red Cloud. The agent down there was cutting off the rations until the Indians let themselves be counted. It seemed that the Bad Face got up in council and scolded the little man, saying the warriors would not let it be done, but Young Man Afraid and Sword, the nephew of Red Cloud, moved their people in for the agent, the other camps coming behind. When this was done the last of the northern Indians hurried away as from the stinking disease. This counting of the whites must be a very powerful medicine or why should they want it done so much? Later they heard that there were more than ten thousand Lakotas getting rations at the agency, almost as many as there were days in thirty years, the Grabber said, in the lifetime of a warrior.

So many, and all counted, when Red Cloud had said it should not be done—surely enough to wipe out all the whites if they had followed his words. It seemed that the Bad Face had really lost his power.

The winter the whites called 1874 and 1875 was a very bad one. It was cold, the snow deep, and many snowblind from the hunting —truly a Hungry Time. But it was much worse at the agencies, with no game at all, no beef coming and no wagons. And those goods already there were poor and too little, the sacks of flour small and moldy, the pork as stinking as bloated buffalo carcasses on the prairie. Even the agent said it could not be eaten. There was only one thin blanket for every three Indians, and if it hadn't been for the robes brought in from the north the people would have been naked. Even some of the cloth that reddened the bluffs where the dead of this bad winter were laid came from the north.

At last the Indians moved up around the soldier fort, setting their lodges close to the buildings, hoping that the little soldier chief would pity their hungry women and children. They butchered their old ponies before his eyes, letting the bones, stripped of every redness, stay where he saw them all the time. They complained against the agent. He was not a little father to them. He must be stealing their goods for there was nothing to eat, not even the moldy flour or the shelled corn that the soldier chief had said was not fit for his horses.

In the north country the Indians were still fighting miners, not only the many pouring into the Black Hills like spring floods from all sides but a big party along the Yellowstone and the scattered ones in soldier coats that the Grabber called deserters. He was much at Red Cloud now, and much around the officers, who told him they wanted the runaway soldiers back, dead or alive, and would give the Indians pay-money for them. There was word, too, that Red Cloud was asking to go to Washington again, this time to get another agent. The hostiles looked upon this with cold eyes, knowing how hungry the whites were for the gold in the Black Hills. So Crazy Horse went down that way, his young men riding on to make a threatening noise around the agency and the Bad Face camp, burning some haystacks and talking loud about white-man chiefs. But it didn't help, for the Red Cloud party was ready to go, with Lone Horn, Little Wound, American Horse, Sit-

ting Bull the Good and many others along, and young Billy Garnett
to help interpret.

So the hostile warriors stood along the bluffs overlooking the
agency, motionless as the scattered pines around them, watching
the wagons go south towards the iron road. Then they whirled their
horses and rode off north. Later Crazy Horse heard how it was
with the traveling chiefs. At the iron road they found many whites
starting to the Black Hills, not miners sneaking in, but a big party
going openly, with soldiers along.[1] The Indians were very angry.
The Great Father got them out of the way so he could send his
soldiers through their country. Perhaps Young Man Afraid had
been right in refusing to come along, as his father had refused five
years before, the day that Lean Elk brought Red Cloud in.

And when the chiefs got to Washington they were surprised to
find that there were so many of them together, not only from Red
Cloud and Spotted Tail but from all the northern agencies of the
Teton Lakotas. And when the Indians were asked to sell the Black
Hills they acted surprised again, saying they must council with
their people. No one had told them anything about this when they
were brought here.

Out on the Powder the hostiles laughed, not in joy but as one
laughs at fools who are bringing the people to bad danger. So the
chiefs hadn't known they would be asked to sell the Hills? Maybe
they should come out to visit the northern camps and hear some
of the news.

It seemed there were many fine presents from the Great Father
for the Indians, including a silver-trimmed rifle for Red Cloud
and one with gold for Sitting Bull, called the Good because he
helped scatter the warriors in the flagpole trouble, making Red
Cloud and his followers angry at this gift to one of Little Wound's
Bear people.

But Red Cloud showed himself strong in complaining about the
agent and the Indian goods stolen and so some men were coming
out from the Great Father to look at the sugar and coffee counted

[1] Jenney Expedition, summer 1875.

twice, the sacks getting smaller and smaller; at the long-horn cattle driven around a hill and counted twice too, or stolen in the night by the cowboys and sold to the agent again. Everybody knew these ways, the whites all laughing over them out here as at a great joke.

But there was one thing the Indians hoped the men coming would not find out—that sometimes a few guns and boxes of ammunition were hidden under the wagonloads and that Boucher, the one married to Spotted Tail's daughter, was selling the guns to anybody who had enough of the money.

When the hostile warriors who went to Red Cloud before the chiefs left returned to the Cheyenne River, they found Crazy Horse still there, with Young Man Afraid beside him. The two friends had talked a long time but there was no joy in their faces, and with the crossed handshake of respect they parted, each to go on walking the old path of his moccasins.

Before starting home Crazy Horse led the warriors against the Black Hills roads. They got some fine goods from a wagon train and some white-man shirts that they tied to their guns to blow in the wind until the sweat stink of the whites was gone before wearing them. From a far hill they watched the big expedition the traveling chiefs had seen going out—many wagons with soldiers and the colored flag ahead, moving into *Pa Sapa*, to find out more about the gold.

The warriors were too few to make a fight, so they hurried home to another story sweeping the north country like a fall prairie fire. The whites were sending peace men to the agencies with great loads of presents to get the chiefs to sell the Black Hills.

"Yes, to sell *Pa Sapa*," Worm said. Now everyone must be a warrior again.

So the people hurried out to make a little meat and then moved out of easy reach of the Crows, for the warriors had something besides coups and scalps and horses to think about, even something more than defending the helpless ones.

Awhile before the time of the treaty council Touch the Clouds rode into the Crazy Horse camp with his people behind him, come

to live with the hostiles, to fight beside them to the last. The Minneconjou's blanket was old and faded, the feather gone from his
hair, for his father had died. Old Lone Horn of the North had
come back from Washington full of sorrow. He had tried to talk
strong against selling the Black Hills, using the words that had
made him known as a great orator among the Lakotas, saying that
one cannot sell the earth any more than the sky, or the four great
directions. But in this time of need his tongue had failed, for it
seemed that the Hills were surely lost. Since he had come back he
sat out behind the lodge on an old blanket, not eating or sleeping,
as one already dead. It seemed that after his talking the whites had
made the good noise, but when they spoke again they asked: "What
do you want? What do you want the Great Father to give you?" It
was then he seemed to die, shamed by their words before his own
heart.

And perhaps it was true, for after he returned he rose no more
from the old blanket and now he was on the scaffold.

"Ahh-h!" Crazy Horse said, making it the sound of sorrow as he
passed the visitor's pipe of welcome to his tall cousin.

The next day a large party came to call the Indians to Red Cloud
for the Black Hill council in September. Although many people
were always going back and forth over the trails, the agency Indians made the whites believe that it was very dangerous and so
they sent a hundred Loafers with the Richards to carry the message, giving the traders' sons good pay-money and the Indians
travois-loads of presents to make a great showing, make all the
northern people feel good and want to come in. The Loafers came
hungry to taste fresh buffalo roast once more and to see if these
wild relations were really as rich in ponies and fine things as was
said. Some of the mourning Minneconjous wanted to charge them,
count coups on them as on an enemy, but they saw Crazy Horse
and Big Road lead the visitors to the council lodge.

Yet none were too friendly to the Loafers, even the women
holding away from the presents. Only a few of the headmen ac-

cepted the bundles of tobacco, and at the first word about selling the Black Hills the council lodge shook as with a great windstorm. What was this foolish talk of going to meet those who wanted to steal their land? When thieves come one goes to meet them with bow and gun, not soft words of the mouth!

Ahh-h, that country was already lost, some of the Loafers said, run over with whites. But if the northern chiefs would come down and help touch the pen they would all get good pay for it.

"One does not sell the earth upon which the people walk," Crazy Horse told the agency messengers. He spoke quietly, as always, his voice so low it was barely to be heard around the large circle, but everyone knew the messengers had failed. Crazy Horse would not go to the council.

As soon as the visiting Loafers were gone the warriors moved down towards Red Cloud to raid the miners and to watch that the agency chiefs did not sell the Hills. One of the camps of friendlies made a sundance to give the people strength, but not many came. Someone told Crazy Horse a funny thing about that—two men dancing together, one who had lost a leg and one an eye in the battles around the fort on the Piney, making a three-eyed, three-legged dance.

Ahh-h, he remembered those men; they had been good warriors.

And while the people were trying to dance the agency chiefs were quarreling over the price they wanted for the Hills country, and even about the place for the council. Not on the Missouri, said Spotted Tail, or at Red Cloud either, but between his agency and that of the Oglalas, and now those who had always thought that the Bad Face had great power with the whites saw the Brule win over him.

When the treaty whites came, there were many that the traders' sons recognized as contractors of goods and beef or those who had other ways to make money from the peace paper. There were a few white women too, and several of the men who write down everything for the newspapers and some who catch the shadows

of the people in black boxes called cameras, another strong medicine to make the Indian helpless. This was done to Red Cloud, it
was said, when he went to the Great Father in 1870, and see what
happened to his power with the warriors and the whites.

When the treaty people found the country full of Indians, the
higher prairies of fall dark with pony herds, they talked big, certain that three fourths of the Indians, as the peace paper of 1868
required, would be at the Lone Tree council place to sell the Lakota lands. Crazy Horse heard this from the messengers who came
riding north through the breaks to him every evening, so it was
as if he watched the valley of the White Earth River with a very
far-seeing glass for his plannings with Big Road and Touch the
Clouds, hoping that Little Big Man could be held back until the
right time.

When the council day came the white men settled in the shade
of their open-front tent, their soldiers in rows behind them. As
the other Indians moved up into a thick, dark circle to see, the
warriors came charging down from the hills, turning aside only as
they reached the treaty grounds, separating, making a great corral
around everybody, the tent and all the soldiers too. Next the chiefs
came in, walking one behind the other, to sit in a half circle before
the commissioners, and when the smoking was finished one of the
whites arose to talk to their Great Spirit, asking that the hearts of
the Indians be made good for what was to be done here. Then
another got up and asked not only for the Black Hills but for the
Powder River country and the Big Horns too.

Even before this was interpreted a silence thick as a winter
robe fell upon the Indians, spreading out over the knolls and along
the ridges. Two messengers slipped away and rode northward, and
that night Crazy Horse and the others sat at their council fire a
long time. Some of the warriors wanted to ride down and kill all
these whites, others to kill the peace chiefs before the bad thing
could be done, for where would the people live if the Powder
River country was gone?

That night there was late talking among the council Indians

too, many wanting to sell, saying the country was lost anyway, and these would have very much money. Some would not sell at all, and these were the warriors.

The next day and for three days there was no counciling. The whites were·there, waiting, but first Red Cloud did not come and then Spotted Tail, so finally it was arranged that both would start to the council ground at the same time. They came together, yet in their hearts they were still divided, their people armed, the horses in close, the women ready to strike the lodges and flee.

But the treaty men did not seem to know this. They sat under their tent, their soldiers behind them, the valley full of riding, whooping Indians, the hills dark with those waiting. Then, towards noon, there was a great dust on a ridge and over it came two hundred painted and feathered warriors with rifles in their hands. They charged the tent, turning aside only at the last jump and then circled the council place, singing war songs, firing their guns. At last they stopped in a solid line before the commissioners and at a signal a second party charged from the hills and then a third, until thousands of armed warriors were there, many from the hostile camps, many who had not seen this country since the whites set their tracks upon it.

Now Spotted Tail led his men to their places, then Red Cloud came and finally the chiefs of the Missouri agencies—Minneconjou, No Bows, Hunkpapa, Blackfoot, Two Kettle, and some Yanktonais. They smoked and counciled among themselves, trying to decide who should begin the talk-making, none wanting to do this, for it was said that the hostiles would kill the first man up to speak for selling the Black Hills. An hour the chiefs counciled while the whites had to see the Indians ride around in what seemed a wild and foolish way, not noticing that they were making a double circle behind the soldiers, each with a gun in his hand.

Suddenly the mounted warriors parted and Little Big Man came charging through on a fine gray American horse. He was stripped to breechcloth, his bare, scarred breast fierce in paint and fresh running blood. Holding his Winchester in one hand and in the other a belt of shells, he spurred down upon the council, roaring out that he had come to kill the whites who would steal his land.

So now the Indians saw the treaty men of the Great Father turn pale, pale as their sickliest women when they noticed the wall of warrior guns around the soldiers, around all the whites. The breath stood still; even the traders' sons were afraid to move, afraid it might bring the shot that would start a killing, a massacre of these few whites lost in the great cloud of angry warriors.

Then a man rose from the circle of counciling chiefs. It was Young Man Afraid, without paint or beads, only the feather of his chieftainship standing in his hair. With his arms folded upon the blue blanket about him, he stood tall and straight and silent before them all.

At last he spoke. "Go to your lodges, my foolish young friends!" he said in a quiet, strong voice. "Go to your lodges and do not return until your heads have cooled!"

For a while, the time it takes to lift a gun, there was not a sound, not a motion, all waiting for the shot from a warrior gun that would bring the Hunkpatila down. But it did not come. Instead there was a movement among the Indians. One group of warriors behind the soldiers backed from the circle and, turning, rode away; then another and another, and finally the wild ones from the knolls, all silent and orderly, and even Little Big Man with his gun and his scarred and bleeding breast.

Then the peace men went too, hurrying away like a lot of old women with their heads down, the soldiers all around them. From the high places along the road dark gatherings of warriors watched them go. And everywhere one thing was said over and over. This day Young Man Afraid had surely looked upon death.

The peace men did not ride to the council ground again. Instead they called the agency chiefs to the stockade. But it was the same there. Red Cloud would sell the Black Hills, wanting six million dollars and rations for seven generations after him—speaking the traders' words the commissioners knew. Spotted Tail had his own price and the other men theirs. And each day there were fewer Indians left, those from the Missouri saying the storm powers were already spreading snow up in their country and they must go.

The warriors saw the peace men leave and then they started north too, riding heavily, with dark faces, for they knew the miners were running thicker than ever into the Black Hills country and that the men from the Great Father went away looking back over their shoulders towards that place of gold.

Crazy Horse had started home the night after Young Man Afraid stood up before the guns of the warriors. He knew that this brave thing would break the council. As he rode along feeling good about his old friend he saw what looked like an Indian sitting alone on a hillside, so he crept up a gully to see. It was a man, a very old one, leaning against a sandbank, his head lifted to the sun that he could never see again, for his eyes seemed blind, but on his face was a glowing bright as the fire in the lodge of a new wife. And when Crazy Horse walked up to him he saw that the man had only one leg, and that his eyes were truly white as the flint arrowstone.

"Hou, my uncle!" he said. "You are Lakota?"

"Ah, yes," the old man answered, speaking very low. He was a Lakota, come from the Missouri to Red Cloud when some of the Little Wound's people returned to their home country. But there was no more peace at the agencies down there than up where he had lived, and so he begged some good people coming north to take him along. When they got to where the grass was tall enough to scratch the bottom of the swing and to hide an old man, he rolled himself from the travois. It was better to die here, with the sun on him, than to live in the darkness of the agencies.

So Crazy Horse rode away to the breaks for poles to make a drag. It was far, and when he returned the sun was setting and there was only the tall yellow grass of fall around the sandbank. But the old man was still there, stretched flat to the earth, his blind eyes looking up, dead. Crazy Horse stood over him and in his

heart was joy for this strength of his people. Many old Lakotas
died like this, just crawled off into the bushes or rolled from a
travois and in some strange, sacred way died very soon.

After the council to steal the Black Hills many small parties,
like Black Elk's band, left the agencies to go north in the warm
days of the second summer, stopping at one creek after another
to hunt a little, make meat and robes if there were buffalo. When
they found the hostile camp on the Powder they settled at the
lower end of the village, as was customary for newcomers, and
took their place in the life and the councils. But when young Black
Elk went to the lodge of his warrior friend there was a pile of
crossed brush before the door, showing that it was empty. Perhaps Crazy Horse had gone against the Crows, although nobody
seemed to know anything except that Black Shawl was visiting
with her relations up in the Big Road circle. The people looked
uneasily to each other when they talked about it. Their Strange
Man was often away alone.

After a while there was smoke from the Crazy Horse lodge and
this time the son of Black Elk was asked in. But there was almost
no talking any more, no teasing over the bowl of meat Black Shawl
had ready. It was as if the man were thinking of trouble coming,
and the boy, who had a very big medicine vision, went away to tell
his father that there was something sacred around the lodge of
Crazy Horse.

When it was plain that the winter would be long and cold, the
big camp scattered for grass and game. The Crazy Horse people,
as the old Little Hawk band was now called, about a hundred
lodges, with Black Elk's few along, settled on the Tongue, with a
corral of poles to protect the horses at night, for the Crows had
been pushing south across the Yellowstone after game this hard
winter. But there was plenty of young cottonwood here to be
stripped for the night corral and so the horses lived.

This winter Crazy Horse left much of the hunting to the others,
staying close to the lodge to keep Black Shawl from running out

into the cold. Each night the coughing seemed worse, and when the January thaw did not come, he made a little house of robes on the travois and hauled her over the snow to the Medicine Water because it was said that a sweat made of that ice thrown on the hot stones had cured some of this white man's disease. They were gone two weeks and when they came back Black Shawl did seem better, riding her horse almost as a well woman rides, leading a pack mule loaded with fresh meat.

But already there was bad news waiting: those who went out to meet their returning man said messengers sat in the council lodge. There Crazy Horse heard Lakotas speak the words that meant their brothers must come to the agency by the end of January, the Moon of Frost in the Lodge, or be considered hostile, with a great army coming out against them.

More soldiers marching through their country!

Yes, and although the messengers, strong young men on good horses, had a hard time getting through in a whole moon of days, the whites would give the northern people only half as long to get down to Red Cloud with their families, and the old and the weak and the sick.

While Crazy Horse sucked at his little pipe, Black Twin made the words they had to say to the messengers. The snow was too deep and the ponies poor. Anyway, this was their country and no one could tell them where to go or when. So the council was ended. Two days later they moved up the Powder to talk to Sitting Bull and his northern people about guns and ammunition from the Missouri country. The soldiers would surely come with the grass and this time it would be a fighting to the end.

The GREAT ENCAMPMENT

IN FEBRUARY, the Moon of the Dark Red Calves, there was a big thaw, the ice of the rivers cracking with the noise like the guns of soldiers already in the villages. The snow went so fast it left the earth dark and soft as marshland to the foot. In this warm time Black Elk's little party started for the agency, as the messengers had ordered, although late. But the hostiles stayed out and to those going it was like leaving one's relations behind on the scaffold to separate from them now. It would be very hard for the women and children when the soldiers came to chase them, and many would fall to the ground.

So Black Elk's people went, looking back with uneasiness, and with uneasiness ahead too, for it was known that this had been a starving winter at the agency, with often only horse meat to eat and the soldiers always there, the sound of their wagon guns shooting the sun into the sky every morning.

In the council lodges there was much questioning of the runners, much talk of the soldiers getting ready at the Platte for the march to the north. No matter how many of them there were, the Indians could make a long fight if they had guns and ammunition and the buffalo lasted. But without these things they must all go in to the agencies. Perhaps it would be good to go now, before the soldiers came.

"Hou!" many agreed, while others asked what they could expect from the Great Father when there were no more hostiles to coax in, no more troublesome warriors fighting. Who could say that he would not let them all starve then?

So the talk went around the circle of broad, strong faces reddened by the firelight. Only one man was silent—Crazy Horse, a little leaner now, his nose seeming thin as an eagle's over its scar, his eyes down. Finally they looked to him. What was their brother thinking? So he had to rise, straight and slight as a young warrior, his braids hanging far below his belt, his blanket over one arm.

Yes, it was the guns and the buffalo that were the life of the helpless ones now, he admitted. But even if they failed, he could not go to the agencies.

"It is not that I have always hated the whites like some others here. You know that Black Fox drew bitterness against them from his mother's breast, poisoned by the white man's stinking disease that scattered her relations like bundles dropped along the fleeing trail. Or Iron Man, who saw his brother kill their own father when he was crazy with the whisky of the whites. It was not so with me. I played with the children of the Holy Road when I was small, not like Woman's Dress and other lovers of the whites but like boys together. We were friends. I showed them how to make good bows to shoot the rabbit and quail, even brought them meat from my mother's drying racks when they were hungry. But that was before I saw Conquering Bear fall from their guns, or all their bad deeds of the long time since."

Against those who wished to take the white man's trail today he had no words. Many had little children who could not run in the snow from the horse soldiers, or perhaps their women had fled from their guns before and were afraid of the coming time. He wanted to tell them all to stay, but he knew that each one must do what seemed good for him.

"No man can fight when the hearts of his women have fallen down. But for me there is no country that can hold the tracks of the moccasin and the boots of the white-man side by side.

"Hou, hou!" the dark circle about him agreed, for these were very fitting words. Only one among them was silent, and Crazy Horse could not look his way and shame his oldest friend.

So the next morning when He Dog and his eight lodges started away, Crazy Horse was already gone to the hills. This day he had many things to remember of those who once stood with him as trees stand together: Lone Bear dying in his arms that day on the Piney; Hump, his warrior father, going down in the fight against the Snakes; Little Hawk killed on the Platte alone; Young Man Afraid at the agency this long time; and now this last one, He Dog, going from him too.

Sitting on a hill he watched the small band of Oglalas crawl along a slope towards Two Moon's Cheyennes near the mouth of the Little Powder. When the ponies got stronger they would all move out upon the long road that led to the agency, a road that now had no returning.

But today there was little time for sitting in regret. Already a scout was signaling from a ridge towards the Platte. Soldiers coming, far away but coming. So Crazy Horse choked the fire from his pipe and went back to his people.

Early in the Moon of Snowblindness, March, Crawler went around all the camps with a message from Red Cloud: "It is spring; we are waiting for you."

In the councils the men listened to this and wondered what it meant. Did the agency chief really want the warriors to come in, and the men they would follow, or did he mean he was waiting for something else, for some trouble they would start? And there was no knowing how he had sent this. He might even be a prisoner of the soldiers and having to say it.

When Crawler had told his message to everyone he went around by way of the Cheyenne camp to take He Dog in with him, to show that his work was good and get more pay. But as suddenly as the snow had left a month before, winter was again upon the camps of the north. The Crazy Horse people were well protected on a creek east of the Little Powder, but their relatives with He Dog might be on their way south and caught out on the bare plains. Then a runner came from a camp near Fort Fetterman, saying that it was told there that the whole Crazy Horse village had been destroyed, the people scattered in the snow. At first this was funny to those gathering around the crier, but soon they saw that it was really very bad. The Crazy Horse village was not destroyed, so it must be another. And now a scout was signaling from a hill that many people were seen coming up the creek, coming with only a few horses and travois, walking wtih the heavy feet of many days' travel.

"Something bad has happened!" Crazy Horse cried, and sent the old herald around the camp asking the women to fill the kettles. Then he and many others rode out leading horses with packs of meat and robes, and with travois for the sick and old, and perhaps the wounded.

They met the people on a little slope, He Dog and Two Moons, the Cheyenne, walking ahead, the men and women and children trailing far down the little creek behind them, many with their feet tied in ragged water-soaked pieces of blanket, their backs stooped under bundles. Warriors on the few good horses were guarding the sides and the rear of the line, helping the boys with the poor stock that could not be ridden, mostly old mares and colts, weak now, but good when the grass once started, and bringing up the beef herd taken from the soldiers, the cattle so poor they fell down all along the way.

While Crazy Horse smoked with the headmen, *wasna* was given out to the tired, hungry people. Then the weak and the old were loaded up and once more everybody started ahead. When they got to the village, the Oglalas went to their relatives, while everywhere there was calling: "Cheyennes, come here! Come and eat here."

When the people were full and warm and dry, they were given shelter and robes for sleeping, and that night there was a council of the headmen to hear the story told.

It seemed that Last Bull and his family had come from the agency to say the soldiers would be out to fight everybody found in the north country. But he stayed, so they thought it was only white-man talk that he did not believe himself. When others came, with new canvas lodges and a little ammunition, saying the same thing, they counciled, He Dog and Crawler with the rest. Old Bear got up to say it was only some whites trying to get them down to sell their goods and whisky. Under the snow the grass roots were strong, the buffalo would be fat, and there were many new colts in the herds—a good summer coming. They were fifty lodges and safe from the soldiers so far north, beyond the flooded Powder. Anyway, they could stay out a little longer, for it was well known the Cheyennes were not making war on anybody.

Hunters did see the soldiers and watched them go off towards the Tongue. After that the camp was moved away, into the canyon at the mouth of the Little Powder, where the people felt safe, for it was a hard place to find and to attack, with their scouts out all around. But there was snow and cold enough to freeze a man, too cold for anybody to be away from the robes, so perhaps the scouts sat too close to their fires. And early the next morning there was a loud crying through the camp.

"The soldiers are right here! The soldiers are right here!" [1]

It was true; some were already between the good horse herd and the camp. The women and children ran crying before the sound of the guns, the old people hobbling away from the bullets that sang among the lodges. The warriors, many naked from the sleeping robes, tried to defend the people, but they were afoot and most of them had only bows against the horse soldiers carrying repeating rifles. First a lot on white horses charged them, then more on bays from another direction, while the women scattered up the steep bluffs with a few bundles and the crying children. The soldiers kept shooting at them, and the traders' sons and Indian scouts who were with them did too. Some of these called out Lakota words to the fleeing people, and now He Dog saw something that made the calm man as hot for killing as a young warrior—Grabber was with the soldiers, the Grabber who had found refuge with them after his trouble with Sitting Bull. He was the one who had guided the soldiers to this hidden camp, brought them charging into the women and children. A long time the Oglala waited behind

[1] Reynolds's attack, March 17, 1876, from Crook's Big Horn Expedition.

a rock but the Grabber stayed far back from the Indian guns.

The boys had rounded up some horses too old and poor to stampede and helped the people get away with them, while He Dog, Two Moons, and Ice and the others with guns tried to hold the soldiers back. There were four, five of the whites for every warrior, but the Indians seemed strong that day and some of the soldiers fell, while they lost only one man killed, one woman wounded. A blind woman who got left behind was found safe in her lodge afterward. The soldiers had saved her when the village was burned, showing somebody had a good heart under a white-man skin. So the people got away, but they had to see their village destroyed—the lodges, meat, robes, parfleches, even the beadwork and the shields and medicine things.

When this was done they started towards the village of Crazy Horse as fast as they could, wading the melting snow, crossing the flooded Powder, and pushing on. All that day the young men stayed back to watch the trail and at night they got many of their horses again, but lost some when they ran into more soldiers coming. These all belonged to Three Stars, the big soldier chief the whites called Crook. Some of the warriors stayed behind to watch them, shooting into their night camps and taking the beef herd that was mostly starving cattle with worms in their backs big as a woman's finger. But the people were glad to have them in this bad time, with no meat and so few robes and clothing and no large fires allowed because they might taunt the soldiers to follow. In the day their feet were in mud and in the night so cold some would surely lose them. But now, after four days, they were here.

The Oglalas were very angry over what had been done. They had seen Brules and the Cheyennes chased by soldiers but never their own people. Now it was really time for a war council. There was no more talk of going to the agency, not even among the Cheyennes, who had only come north for meat and a little visiting. To He Dog it was as though the agency had never been, or anything of his going to the whites. Crazy Horse saw this and was glad that Three Stars had not come later, or these people would have been lost to them. If the soldier chief had waited until the ponies could travel the long trail to Spotted Tail and Red Cloud, perhaps most of the Indians would have been lost. Now they could send runners to the young men down there, saying: "Come—there will be good fighting this year, plenty coups and enough American horses for everybody! Come and bring the guns."

But there were the many hundred soldiers, with traders' sons and Indian scouts loose in the country, and so the next forenoon Crazy Horse and Two Moons led their people up towards the camp of the Hunkpapas at Chalk Buttes. There were horses enough so nobody had to walk, and travois for the old, the wounded, and the frost-bitten.

When they reached the Sitting Bull camp, bigger than that of the Oglalas and the Cheyennes together, the people set up two double lodges, one for the Cheyenne men and the other for the women. Then the girls came in twos, carrying kettles of meat between them, and kept coming until there was enough left over for all the next day. While this was done the herald rode through the great camp crying: "The Cheyennes have been made very poor by the soldiers! All who have blankets or robes or lodges to spare should give to them!"

Once more Lakota women and girls came with presents for these Cheyennes. Robes, clothes, even tobacco and medicine pipes were laid on the ground before them. Then horses with pack saddles and travois were led out, and with these and the backs of the women heavy-loaded the Cheyennes moved to the place set aside for them. Every household had a lodge; some were small, but very good against the cold until they could make a hunt.

There was a little ammunition too. The Gros Ventres who came visiting in Sitting Bull's camp awhile ago traded off all their powder and arms there. They would go home to their agent and say they couldn't hunt because the Lakotas had robbed them, and then they would be given more, for it was well known that the Lakotas were a bad people and took what they wanted.

The plans made to trade for arms at Fort Berthold on the

Missouri would be spoiled now by the news of the soldier fight over the talking wires, but the Slota had some they would let go if they were paid enough.

Ahh-h, the thieving Slota! But guns and powder the hostiles must have; with enough of these things they would chase all the whites from the Black Hills, the young warriors said. Even the older men seemed strong against the soldiers' coming. They would make a good fight. So the talk went, and the road to the white man's islands seemed indeed forgotten.

But if it was to be war, everybody must work together and so the Oglala council made a new kind of chief for themselves, one who would be both a strong, bold leader of the warriers and a gentle, firm, and wise father of the people. It would be a hard place to fill, but there was one who would never fail it—their Strange Man. So now the council laid this new duty upon Crazy Horse, saying it was one in which no foolishness about the little jealousies of the lodge or about bringing power in the hand from one family to another could make any difference. It was a long duty, they warned him, a chieftainship for life, and it could not be put away this side of the red blanket upon the scaffold.

And when people outside of the council lodge were told of the new place given to Crazy Horse, they made a great cheering, for their hearts that had been on the ground were lifted. The next morning more runners were sent to the Spotted Tail and Red Cloud agencies. "Come!" they would say. "Crazy Horse leads us all!"

This news brought the warriors riding fast, for they remembered how strong was the medicine of Crazy Horse. In two weeks they began to come in through the dusk, bringing much news. They said that the scouts with Three Stars were back and that his soldiers had gone in to Fort Fetterman with their fingers frozen to wait for more help to come, and the warmth of summer. The whites were still saying that it was the Crazy Horse village they struck because the Grabber recognized some of the horses as from the Oglala camp.

"Ah, yes, the He Dog horses—"

That is what the Indians knew. Now Three Stars, Crook, was trying to get more scouts from the friendly Oglalas and Brules who were led by Sitting Bull, the Oglala, but Red Cloud, Red Leaf and the others were against it. It was not good to set the young men hunting their relatives, they said. Not even the wolf stalks his own kind. With this their new agent agreed, but it seemed that the soldier chief was very angry, calling the Indians bad names which he thought they did not understand.

Ahh-h, bad names they all understood! Those were the words they heard so often from the whites.

But it was said, too, that the Three Stars spoke very angry about the rations given the Indians at Red Cloud. Could the hostiles be expected to come in when the Indians at the agency were starving, he asked. There was talk among the traders' sons of another big party of soldiers coming against the hostiles, this one from the Missouri forts. The Indians must make meat and get ready for a summer of fighting.

The scouts reported buffalo in the Rosebud country and so the camps began to move slowly that way, giving the horses time to strengthen. Almost every day the great river of people got longer, Lame Deer and his northern Minneconjous joining first, then the No Bows and many little parties from the far agencies. When the grass was good the Blackfoot Lakotas came too, and a few Santees who had been chased ever since the big fighting in Minnesota, over ten years ago. These were now called the No Clothes people because they were so poor, their few small lodges and bundles moved by dog travois. They had met some soldiers on their way from the northeast, many more were already coming along the Yellowstone, and Long Hair, the one the whites called Custer, had started from Fort Lincoln on the Missouri.

Ahh-h! Long Hair! The warriors knew him, the Cheyennes from the people he had killed in the south country, the Lakotas from the fighting along the Yellowstone and from the Thieves' Road he opened into the Black Hills. But the Indians had a soldier chief from the south to watch too, the one who had already struck the Cheyennes and He Dog this year. He was coming again, past the old fort on the Piney and the Medicine Water and nearing Goose Creek, where Cloud Peak of the Big Horn Mountains stood tall as a white-haired old warrior.

By the time the great encampment reached the valley of the Rosebud the horses were strong and the lodges had been made. At every council the younger men talked about attacking the Three Stars' soldiers camped in the middle of their country. But even Crazy Horse was against this. The soldiers were too strong in their own camp; until they came against the people the Indians were at peace.

One evening crippled old Black Elk came in from Red Cloud with quite a few lodges. He had returned to his cousin Crazy Horse to fight to the end, for it seemed the agency chiefs would sell the Black Hills. With him were some Cheyennes and many of the friendlies come to fight too, even Red Cloud's son, carrying the silver-mounted rifle his father was given in Washington. When they reached the ridge of the Rosebud what they saw almost stopped the heart—a valley so full of lodge circles and ponies that no one could have believed still existed, an encampment so long it couldn't be seen from one end to the other.

Yes, it was indeed good to see their number, the people agreed, and good to go past the big council lodge and see the great men gathered there: Crazy Horse and Big Road of the Oglalas; Sitting Bull and Gall, Black Moon and Crow King of the Hunkpapas; Spotted Eagle of the No Bows; Fast Bull and Touch the Clouds of the Minneconjous; Two Moons and Old Bear of the Cheyennes, even the famous old warrior Inkpaduta, now sitting among the few Santees and Yanktonais here.

Soon the great camp moved farther up the river, going in the old way, with the walking councilors. In the evenings there was feasting and dancing, visiting and courting, and not since the days when the Oglalas first moved away from Laramie did so many young

people walk through the village under the blanket held over them
by their warrior friends in the old marrying custom. Only a few
of the older Indians seemed to think of their relatives on the
agencies, or to remember that scouts were out to watch for soldiers
from two sides. White-man soldiers had marched all through their
country before, back in the year the whites called 1865, and gone
away.

Sometimes it was days before visiting warriors saw the man
they had come to follow, for often Crazy Horse kept far from the
noise and the drumming, perhaps making a fast, hoping for a vision
or a dream to tell him what must be done. It seemed if he could
make himself more a part of the earth and the sky and the things
between that a way would come to save the people. He even tried
the medicine things of the Old Ones, and for two days he looked
unmoving towards the far Black Hills, overrun as by ants digging
up the rocks and the cool green valleys and the slopes red with the
grass berries so sweet to the tongue. But it was no more than a
wind in a gully and on his way back to camp he saw that the buffalo
chips were indeed becoming few, the trees no longer rubbed
smooth by the backs of the shedding herds.

Once he went down to look upon the camp of Three Stars, the
rows of soldier tents a great patch of white, like left-over snow.
There, below him, were many fast-shooting guns and he wished he
could go to the place of his first vision, where the horseman who
was himself rode unharmed through the bullets of many enemies.
But that was on the far Running Water, near the place where
Conquering Bear had died, and now the boots of the white man
cut deep into that earth too.

He brought home only one thing, the skin of a calf from the
soldier herd, and the next time he rode against the whites he would
have a new war cape flying from his shoulders, a red skin with
many small white spots on it, like the hailstone painting of his
thunder dream.

In the bright time of the Moon of Making Fat, the Hunkpapas
held their great sundance. It was near the sacred Deer Medicine

rocks where hunters sometimes went for help. Here Sitting Bull gave one hundred pieces of flesh, fifty bits of skin large as a grass seed lifted from each arm with an awl point and cut off, the Hunkpapa singing while the blood ran. Then he made the sun-gazing dance, not moving his eyes from the sun until its setting and facing it again at the rising until he fell as dead, and when he lived again, he told of a vision: Many Soldiers Falling into the Camp.

The people heard and made a great chanting of joy.

When the game and the grazing on the Rosebud were worn out, the camp moved over the backbone of country to Ash Creek, emptying into the river called Little Horn or Little Big Horn by the whites. There in the middle of June the Cheyenne scouts came hurrying back through the evening, making the wolf howls of danger.

"Many soldiers have been seen coming! Indians are with them!"

Runners were sent to the lower camp circles, and the chiefs came to sit in the great council lodge, the sides lifted all around so everyone could see and hear, even far out in the darkness. Then the Cheyennes told their story.

"The Rosebud is black with the Three Star soldiers from Goose Creek, many Crows and Snakes along, and some traders' sons we knew through the glasses—Big Bat and the Grabber—"

The Grabber again—the one Sitting Bull had taken into his heart as a brother when the whites were after him, the Grabber that He Dog and Crazy Horse had protected when the Hunkpapa found he was scheming to sell him to the whites. Now that one was bringing the soldiers against them, already less than one sleep from the great camp.

"Hoppo! Let us hurry; let us send the new kind of chief, Crazy Horse, with the warriors to drive them off," some said.

"But do not forget the helpless ones here!" the more cautious cried, those of the little fears. "If the warriors go out to attack the soldiers, who will protect the camp and keep the women and children from being killed? We must not divide our great power!"

"Would you have the soldiers charge upon us here—scattering the helpless ones to run before their American horses across the open prairie?" someone asked.

"Let the warriors stand around them like a wall!" the cautious ones advised.

But at this there was a roaring from the warriors. "We hear old men speaking!" they cried, and would not be quiet. "Hoka hey!" others called out, starting to push towards the far edge of the crowd of people, making much work for the *akicita* to keep them from running off into the hills to fight the soldiers in foolish little bunches.

At first the inner circle of chiefs sat motionless around the council fire through this as though there were no trouble at all. Once one of them did get up to speak and was lost in the noise of the warriors and the sharp whacking sound of the bows and whips of the *akicita*. But with the young men stirred to move against them, the chiefs' circle looked to one man, those near reaching out for him, and finally Crazy Horse arose, looking slighter than ever in the open, fire-lit center of the great dark crowd.

"Wait, my friends," he said to the warriors. "There will be fighting pretty quick—"

"Hoppo! Let us go!" one called from far out, hearing only the repeated words, not knowing who had spoken them first.

But the quiet voice of Crazy Horse went on and slowly a silence came over the people, starting around him and spreading outward like the branches of a great tree, reaching far into the night, until every woman and child could hear or was told what he was saying.

First of all, the people must be well protected. Let the older chiefs and their followers stay to guard the helpless ones as was customary, remembering that there might be plenty of fighting right here, for had not the great vision of Sitting Bull foretold many soldiers falling into camp? Then a strong party must be sent to the Rosebud to drive the whites away there. Such a party he would lead if the warriors wished to follow.

"Hoye!" they answered him in a roaring. "Hoye!" the sound of approval sweeping out over the people, where anger had been only a little before.

Ahh-h, it made his heart strong to hear them, he said, but let every man think carefully before shouting the Hoye! This was a new kind of war that had come to the country of the Lakotas, not the old one of driving off a few raiding Snakes or Crows who made a little fighting between the time of the hunts and the other things of their lives. With the white warriors it was killing every day, killing all the time.

"These soldiers of the Great Father do not seem to be men like you," Crazy Horse told the warriors. "They have no homes anywhere, no wives but the pay-women, no sons that they can know. Now, my friends, they are here in our country looking for us to kill. In this war we must fight them in a different way from any the Lakotas have ever seen, not with the counting of many coups or doing great deeds to be told in the victory dance. We must make this a war of killing, a war of finishing, so we can live in peace in our own country."

In an hour a thousand warriors were ready to go with Crazy Horse, two parties of Cheyennes and three or four of Lakotas, to ride awhile apart, each under its own leaders. Some of the warriors had guns, some only bows and war clubs, but many strong men were among them, and many, too, who were only boys or who had never fought except with an agent for rations, like the young son of Red Cloud, proudly carrying the silver-trimmed rifle of his father.

At the lodge Black Shawl had everything ready for her man when he hurried there from the getting started. As he took the ropes of his war horses from her hand, he swung his blanket about her and for a moment held her in its folds as if she were a maiden he was courting. He pressed her face against him, feeling the wetness of her cheek. Then she was gone, for the warriors must see no softness in their leader this night.

In all their regalia and paint, with their guns and spear points gleaming the warriors rode around the great fires of the camp circles as the drums rumbled and the women cried their greatness. Among the leaders rode Crazy Horse, the spotted calfskin flying from his shoulders, but in his breast lay a heaviness as of something dying. Who could say if another Lakota war party would ever circle the camps like this?

MANY SOLDIERS *Falling into Camp*

THE night was thinning in the east when Crazy Horse stopped his Oglalas for a little resting. They were not far from the Rosebud now, and once a little wind brought a smell of water that stirred the tired horses and once the sweetness of the roses blooming so thick in that valley. But soon there was the soft owl hoot of another war party coming, so they rode in closer, for the soldiers must not escape them now.

Daylight came upon the warriors behind the ridge north and west of the bend of the Rosebud. Stopping there, they ate of their *wasna* and made ready for the fight. Crazy Horse loosened his long hair, tied on the calfskin cape, and threw dust over his spotted war horse while not far away the eighteen-year-old son of Red Cloud shook out a long-tailed war bonnet and put it on as though he were really a bonnet man of the *akicita,* the other young men standing away from him, even the older ones silent, for this son of the agency could be told nothing at all.

While the horses rested, the scouts were sent out to locate the soldiers, bring back word of them; but as they crossed the ridge they rode into the Crows coming up from the other side. There was shooting, a Lakota fell, two Crows were wounded, and all the warriors, forgetting about the resting horses, whipped them to the ridge and stopped there in dark rows against the sky.

Below him Crazy Horse saw the Crow scouts fleeing down the

slope into the valley of the Rosebud, full of soldiers and Indians,[1] so many they looked like a resting, cud-chewing herd of buffalo, the horses grazing, the men in dark little bunches. Beyond them was the willow-lined creek, with more soldiers on the other side, and then the bluffs and the far ridge, so far that a horseman would look like one of the scattering of little trees. And between him and that place, as in the palm of a browning hand, were the soldiers, and once more Crazy Horse wished for guns, plenty of good rifles and warriors who would strike together in waves like flying hail.

As the Crows fled howling back to the soldiers, they stirred into moving, running to catch their horses or lining up and then going off every way in little bunches, many horse and walking soldiers hurrying up towards the hostiles, coming in rows, a flag waving, a bugle sounding clear in the warm air. Behind them the Indian scouts were riding hard up and down, raising a great dust, making ready to fight too, now that the soldiers had gone ahead, shooting into the hostiles.

Crazy Horse held his warriors together for a long time but there were so many soldiers and their rifle-fire was so close among them that finally they fell back to the rocks of the second ridge, hoping to draw the whites along. And they came, off their horses now, crawling from rock to rock, and when they were well scattered, Crazy Horse led a charge. It was a hot little fight, many men going down, some even from arrows. Then more soldiers, followed by the Snakes, came galloping up from the side. In the smoke and dust the Lakotas couldn't tell their friends from the scouts, so they withdrew awhile to rest their horses and to see how the fighting was going in other places.

The Crows had been getting bolder too, and when young Red Cloud lost his horse and ran away without stopping to take off the war bridle to show that he was unafraid, they rode upon him and whipped him hard, grabbing his father's rifle from him and jerking off the war bonnet, saying he was a boy, with no right to wear it. Crazy Horse and two others charged the Crows and got the young

[1] Battle of the Rosebud, June 17, 1876.

Bad Face back, not looking at him, shamed that they had seen one of their young men crying to his enemies for pity.

By now the sun was high and the fighting had spread off to the opposite ridge, the charges going back and forth over miles of rough ground, with many brave things done, many afoot and wounded ones being carried off the field by warriors whose horses were so tired they could barely be whipped out of a walk. The Hunkpapas were helping strong now. They came late, their horses were fresher and their guns still loaded. Crazy Horse was with them awhile, shooting from the ground as always. When his spotted horse was played out, he got his bay and went to the bluffs where the Cheyennes seemed to be making a very good fight. Once, when the smoke and dust lifted, Crazy Horse saw the sister of Chief Comes in Sight charge forward to where he was afoot and surrounded. With him on behind her she zigzagged back through the soldiers, bullets flying, the warriors making a great chanting for this brave thing done.

Ahh-h, the Cheyennes were indeed a strong people, Crazy Horse thought, but not the strongest heart and the longest arm, Lakota or Cheyenne, with only a bow was enough against these rifles. The warriors fought hard but always they were driven back. It was happening right now to his own Lakotas, his bravest men breaking into retreat before the bullets whistling hot around them, whipping hard to get away.

Then suddenly they found Crazy Horse before them, his horse turned into their faces, crying out to them: "Hold on, my friends! Be strong! Remember the helpless ones at home!" And with his Winchester held high as a lance he charged through them towards the coming soldiers. "This is a good day to die!" he called back over his shoulder, the calfskin flying out like bat wings behind him. "Hoka hey!"

"Hoka hey!" the strong voice of Good Weasel answered him as he turned to follow, and then Bad Heart Bull, Black Bear, and Kicking Bear. "Hoka hey!" the warriors roared out together, thundering close behind them, charging back into the soldiers among the rocks, lifting their arrows to fall among the horses. When the frightened animals began to break from the holders the soldiers jumped back on and now even the youngest Loafer could see that the whites were afraid and so pressed them harder, charging through them, shooting under the necks of the puffing horses, or from flat on their backs, until the Crows and Snakes fled from this wild charging, whipping, crying, towards the little bunch of soldier chiefs and traders' sons down around Three Stars.

Soon the whites were breaking as their scouts had, the Lakotas right among them, knocking the men from the saddles with their empty guns and the swinging war clubs, riding them down, never stopping except to pick up the dropped carbines, Crazy Horse ramming the stuck shells from them. So they drove the whole party like scattering antelope back into the valley, the warriors chasing after them. Here Crazy Horse saw many hurt ones, and many brave ones, too, particularly a little soldier chief sitting against a tree, his face all blood, still shooting with his revolver.

Now there was a loud bawling of bugles and the soldiers fell back together and made a thick new line that would be hard to break. Besides, the sun was moving away and so Crazy Horse decided it was time to try something else. Turning, he led his warriors around over the creek and down the other side, letting their tired horses walk, making it seem they were giving up. As he hoped, a bunch of soldiers and some Crow scouts saw them go and followed down the other side, and once more Crazy Horse became the old thing he was so often—a decoy, making little stands behind the others, little charges towards the soldiers across the creek, as if to hold them back. So they came faster.

As the Oglalas neared the bend of the Rosebud, signals were sent back, calling the others to come down to the narrow place in the valley, where it would be easier to fight with bows and tired horses. More and more hostiles began to string out down the creek behind the whites, who did not seem to notice these Lakota warriors coming.

But before the soldiers got to the place for fighting, the Crows with them stopped, making the wild Crow howling, pointing ahead, refusing to go to where the ridge came towards the creek, with rocks and brush for the enemy to hide. And when a messenger from Three Stars came galloping after them, the soldiers swung far out around the Indians following them and hurried back in time to strike the rear of the warriors still fighting.

So the Indians scattered. The shells were gone, even those they had got with the new guns, and the horses worn out. It had been a hard fight.

The daybreak star was in the sky when the warriors got back to the camp on the creek that flowed into the Little Big Horn. The news had been sent ahead from where they stopped to make travois for the wounded and so they were brought home in the good way, two of the older chiefs from each circle leading them in. The great encampment was fine to see, with cooking fires burning everywhere, the women moving dark about them, ready to feed the hungry warriors. There were some bad things to tell—eight men who would never charge the soldiers again, two from the Oglalas, and more wounded. It was bad, too, about young Red Cloud sneaking away to the agency like a shamed little boy, without the borrowed war bonnet or his father's fine gun. It must be hard to have a son come home like that. But that was only the act of one foolish young man, and the Indians killed were very few for so many in the fight, and the soldiers had been hurt too.

By the time the warriors had rested, scouts came riding with good news. Three Stars had fifty-seven men to haul away, dead and bad-wounded to need hauling, and it seemed that his ammunition was almost gone too. Anyway, he was turning his dust around and going back to Goose Creek, not so hungry to chase more Indians now. When the heralds rode through the camps with this word, even the mourning people stopped to make a little sound of joy.

After the news was talked over, Crazy Horse went out to sit on a ridge above the great camp, to think about the fight. There had indeed been something new among the warriors, as he had asked. The old Lakota way of fighting for coups and scalps and horses, of a man riding out alone and doing foolish things to show how strong he was, seemed gone. Yesterday most of them had charged in bunches, straight into the soldiers, breaking their lines, almost nobody stopping for coups or scalps until the fighting in that place was done. And they had driven Three Stars back. It was the biggest thing the Lakotas had ever done against soldiers who really came fighting, not just sneaking like coyotes through the canyons, trying to keep from being seen. Perhaps it was really bigger than the fight on the Piney, for the soldier chief there was no warrior like Three Stars.

And there was still the vision of Sitting Bull: Many Soldiers Falling into Camp.

The next day the whole camp moved down to the Little Big Horn, leaving the death lodges of the Lakotas behind, the women keening as they looked back from the first rise. That night the victory dances began, only the scalps of the Indian scouts hanging from the women's staffs, those of the short-haired soldiers thrown away as no better than so much horse skin. They danced the things taken too, the guns, including many of the short saddle ones, some thrown away by the soldiers when they jammed in the heat of the fighting. But one called Good Hand, who had helped the black-smith at the agency, knew how to make them work very well, even those the soldiers had broken whipping their horses.

The drumming and dancing and singing lasted all night, the people going from one camp to the next to hear all the great things done on the Rosebud. But the best of all was down among the Cheyennes, where the story of Buffalo Calf Road, the woman who carried her brother from the battle, was told and retold. Their dancing lasted four days; the sacred buffalo hat was brought out, a new scalp tied to it, and the ceremonial of its renewal made before all the people.

Crazy Horse never helped with the dances, but there was work and planning to be done. Scouts were sent to follow Three Stars, to shoot into his night camps and keep the soldiers watching and afraid. Runners went to the young men of the agencies, north and south, carrying the good news of the fighting in their mouths and the pay-money taken from the soldiers in their pipe cases for powder from Boucher and others who traded in the night. One morning he took a little party of Oglala boys over to the Rosebud to pick up the scattered ammunition, for it was well known that the soldiers often take handfuls from their belts, lay it down handy, and then move on with the fighting. The boys filled several unborn buffalo calf skin sacks and got very many empty shells to reload, some lead too, from bullets flattened against the rocks, and many arrow points and the shoes from the dead American horses.

"Nothing must be forgotten when iron is so scarce," he said, and told the boys some stories of the stone arrow makers, a people so long gone they seemed forgotten, the Crows claiming they were a small people like eight-year-olds that lived in the cave rocks near the Yellowstone.

"Guns are better—" a Loafer son said impatiently.

"Guns are as the eyes and the hearts behind them," the Hunkpatila said, and then spoke no more.

In the great camp were many kettles to be filled and so hunters packed in fresh meat from the buffalo herds west of the river and some went clear beyond the Big Horn to where the antelope were like a great cloud shadow running over the grass. And every day more people came from the agencies, those from the north telling of soldiers marching up the Yellowstone like the black singing cricket, so many. Ahh-h? Then the women and children must be taken to a good place, with the river between them and these new guns. There seemed no danger now from Three Stars. He was headed into the mountains to hunt the big-horn, and his Crow scouts had gone home in anger right after the Rosebud fight, and the Snakes too. So his soldiers hunted, fished, and pulled arrows from the rumps of their horses, reminders that the hostiles were watching.

On the sixth day after the Rosebud fight the great encampment moved across the Little Big Horn, the old herald on the far bank calling out where the people were to go—the Cheyennes, leading, going farthest down the stream, the Hunkpapas at the back stopping near the mouth of Ash Creek, all the others between. It was an old-time moving camp, the councilors ahead, the women fine with their bright saddle trappings, the warriors singing, the young men playing tricks and showing off before the girls, the boys racing up and down, the great horse herds a thunder on the ground as they came. By evening the five great circles and several small ones were spread along three miles of river as orderly as after weeks of living.

That night there was dancing everywhere, not of ceremonies but for the young people. Groups moved from camp to camp, singing, joining around the drums in the light of the great fires, and then going on, the prettiest girls choosing their partners from among the young warriors who had done big things on the Rosebud. It was a night of fun lasting until the stars faded into dawn.

The next morning the camps slept late, many going straight to the river for bathing when they awoke, men and women and children splashing and laughing in little parties all up and down the swift, cool water of the Little Big Horn. As the climbing sun burned hotter, they scattered, some to move the grazing camp horses, many to the shade of the trees along the stream, most of the women going to the lodges to some easy, visiting work like rubbing the buckskin or waving the fly brush over the sleeping children, some of the younger ones taking the turnip-diggers to the hills north of the river. Many of the warriors loafed in the shade of the rolled-up lodges, talking lazily about the fighting the other day. Even the few boys around the camps were quiet, the whole great encampment like a dog lying in the sun.

It was true that the Cheyenne prophet, Box Elder, had sent out a crier a few days ago to warn the people to keep enough horses up, that he saw soldiers coming in a dream, and yesterday a No Bow went around saying the soldiers would be here the next day. Then there was Sitting Bull's vision of soldiers falling into camp. But the people were not uneasy. The scouts said Three Stars was going farther away and that the soldiers from the north were still far down the Rosebud. Even Crazy Horse had left his lodge, to visit in the Cheyenne camp.

But an Oglala crossing the ridge on his way to Red Cloud happened to see a dust hanging like smoke on the breaks up beyond Ash Creek, with many men moving under it. He whipped his horse back across the river and to his lodge, crying out: "Soldiers coming here! Soldiers coming here!"

It was like the shot of a wagon gun over the quiet valley of the Little Big Horn, setting the Indians into a swarming. Runners started to the other camps, warriors hurried out for the herds, or got their fighting things together, and the turnip-diggers were signaled in, for already the women were crying of danger close. There was dust to be seen from here, a great pile of it just up the river, on this side, with many fast-riding horse soldiers in it.

That was true, for already they were near the upper, the Hunkpapa circle, stretching themselves into a line of blue riders from the river to the hills, their Ree Indian scouts on the higher end. A row of smoke puffs came from the soldier guns, bullets tore through the lodges, the echoes roaring all over the great camp as they moved slowly ahead, shooting. And before the soldiers' coming the women grabbed up their little ones and fled down the river, the old men and the camp dogs following. The Big Bellies hurried out too, some going along to quiet the afraid ones, others staying to help make a wall between the people and the soldier guns until the warriors could come up with their arms and horses to stand off the whites. And as the herds came flying in from the hills, the young men caught up the first good horses they reached, jumped on, and with a whooping charged off into the fight.

With many Hunkpapas facing them and more Lakotas and

Cheyennes coming hard, the soldiers got off to fight on foot, and when the warriors saw this done they felt very strong. First they struck the Rees, driving them from the fight, making them drop some Hunkpapa horses they had cut off, and leaving the whole end of the soldier line open. Only one, a half-Lakota that the northern people knew as Bloody Knife, stayed with the whites, and him they cut down like a sneaking Crow found in the woman's lodge.

By the time Crazy Horse and Big Road with some Oglala warriors reached the Hunkpapa camp there was already much damage done, the lodges torn by the bullets, many knocked down, some burning. And just beyond where the fighting was several hundred warriors stood against the soldiers, with Sitting Bull, Black Moon, and Gall leading them. Crazy Horse was on his yellow pinto, stripped to breechcloth, a splattering of hailstone marks on his body, the lightning streak down his face, and the red-backed hawk on his head. And when the warriors saw him coming they made a roaring and lined up for a charge. But he remembered their need to save ammunition, and all the jammed guns they got from the horse soldiers on the Rosebud.

"Be strong, my friends!" he called out. "Make them shoot three times fast, so their guns will stick and you can knock them down with your clubs!"

He said this over and over, as another would sing a song, holding the warriors back while he rode up and down before the soldiers, drawing their fire to him as the man in his vision had, bullets like hail around him, and not touching. And when the shooting slowed down, the men beginning to jerk at their guns, making loud words, the Indians charged and the scared soldiers broke and ran like crazy men for a patch of brush and trees near the river, the warriors getting many on the way. But now they had a little hiding-place and the Indians had to crawl up over flat ground, so the fighting slowed.

But it seemed the soldiers couldn't stay still. They kept coming out and looking back up the trail and finally they jumped on their horses and retreated through the warriors between them and the river. There was no crossing, but they spurred their horses to jump the high bank into the water, with the Indians after them as after buffalo caught in shifting quicksand, knocking them from their horses with war clubs as they tried to get out on the other side, their horses slipping and falling back, the Indians making the "Yi-hoo!" the game-killing cry, each time they struck. But many got away, and with the little soldier chief in the lead they headed towards a hill, some of the warriors after them, others going back to finish the scattered soldiers and to pick up the guns and shells and round up the horses.

While they were stripping the whites one of the Cheyennes from the south country stopped to look carefully at the markings on a soldier coat. It was the same as on the one he had got in the Washita fight, where Long Hair had killed his mother and his wife. So these must be the same soldiers, these who were laying on the ground here, and who died like buffalo in the river. With the blue coat held out in his hands he ran from one to another, showing it, crying for all the valley of the Little Big Horn to hear: "My heart is good! This day my heart is good!" the water running as with a raining down his dusty face.

But now a messenger came riding, his arm pointing off across the river. More soldiers! Many more soldiers going down along the ridge on the other side, just across the river from the lower camps, where the helpless ones were. There was a fork-tailed flag ahead, and behind it a long double row of soldiers and dust, so much dust that one could hardly see the bunch of gray horses that were among them.

Hoh! It was indeed as in Sitting Bull's vision—soldiers come falling into camp. Crazy Horse saw that the big fight would be made down there. Good, let it come. He felt very strong today because the warriors were as they had been on the Rosebud, not after coups and showing off, but striking hard, striking to kill. That was what had scared the many soldiers of Three Stars away, and broke those who came here. So Crazy Horse and Gall and Knife Chief called their warriors together with their bone whistles and spoke a few words for a charge on those soldiers going against the lower camps, already so close to the fleeing people.

"A few stay here to watch those on the hill, the rest go against the new ones," Gall told his Hunkpapas, and started off down the soldier side of the river.

"Remember the helpless ones down there! This is a good day to die!" Crazy Horse said to his Oglalas. But they needed no heating words now. "Hoka hey!" they cried, lifting the new soldier guns high as they swept off down the river behind the Hunkpapas while Crazy Horse hurried to gather up the warriors still scattered over the fighting ground and to bring up as many as he could from below. By the time they got to the half-struck lodges of the lower camps he saw four men ride out of the river and up towards the soldiers. They were half a mile away but they looked like Cheyennes, four Cheyennes, going out alone to hold hundreds of soldiers back from the river crossing until the Lakotas coming hard along the bottoms got there. They rode in a brave little row, their horses moving together as in a dance, their guns blooming into smoke together and making a stir among the soldiers as if some were hit. Then there was a long row of smoke puffs from their guns, but the Cheyennes kept riding, shooting together again, four guns against almost three hundred. It was a great thing and Crazy Horse whipped his tiring pinto faster to where Black Shawl, indeed a warrior's wife, had another horse waiting.

He stopped for a word of counciling with Sitting Bull and the other Big Bellies holding the people together, making plans for a stand or flight and a scattering if more soldiers came, too many more soldiers. He saw Worm and Little Hawk and limping Black Elk among the women and children, speaking calm and quieting to them, showing them all the guns and bows and war clubs ready among them if the soldiers came near.

"Hoka hey!" a small boy tied to his anxious mother's back cried when he saw Crazy Horse. The women heard and made the trilling to see that even a little one on the back knew this man.

"Hoka hey!" answered Crazy Horse as he threw a handful of

fooling gopher dust over his fresh war horse and put some little grass spears through his braids because they were like the driving snow of the winter storm. Then he led his warriors off across the river. By now many Indians too late for the fight at the Hunkpapa camp were over the crossing and charging up the ridge towards the front of the soldiers as Gall and the others came sweeping along the slope, driving some of the back ones before them. Soon the two streams of warriors would have come together among the enemy as they did in the battle on the Piney. But the soldiers were stopping along the ridge in little bunches, many off their horses, the warriors already charging the horse-holders and getting a hard-shooting defense, the guns of the whites making a roar like a hailstorm before a wind, a great cloud of smoke and dust rising to hang along the ridge.

With his heart singing the war song of the drums back among the helpless ones, his Winchester ready in his hand, the Oglala led his warriors through the river, around the end of the soldier ridge, and up a ravine behind it to cut off their retreat. And as he rode, more and more Indians fell in behind him, until the fresh war horse was the point of a great arrow, growing wider and longer, the dust of its moving standing in the air.

They reached the head of the ravine just as the Indians from the river side pushed the soldiers to the crest of the ridge, and with a great whooping the fresh warriors charged the back of the retreating blue line, using mostly arrows, spears, and clubs. They were hot for this fight today, and the soldier guns seemed little more than grease popping on the winter fire, their horses jumping a Lakota that fell among them like so much sagebrush or stone. The first charge by the Crazy Horse warriors broke the line, cut down horses and men on that hill before the soldiers could make a circle. At the next charge a few Indian horses were hit, another man or two—nothing at all in the fight of this summer day on the Little Big Horn. As the hundreds of warriors circled and charged and circled again, many brave deeds were probably being done everywhere, but nobody had time to see them in this great roar of fighting that deafened the ear, the dust and powder smoke that made a darkness as of evening.

There were some good men on that hill, some still trying to shoot carefully from the knee even as the Indians closed in, but the circle was getting smaller, the dead horses and men piling up around the soldiers as their guns stuck, the breath of their revolvers died in their hands. One bold warrior rode through them, followed by a whole charge, and so the whites went down under the hoofs and spears until it seemed nobody could be alive in that bloody pile. But there were a few, and jumping up together, they headed towards the brush of the river, so very far away, the whooping warriors running them down like new-born buffalo calves, striking them to the ground, looking for more, until suddenly there were no more.

While the warriors were still sitting around on their horses, almost not believing this easy thing, two young Lakotas came back from the breaks disappointed to miss the finish. They had been chasing a soldier who got away on horseback and were feeling cheated because he put the revolver against his head and fired. Now all the others were rubbed out and they only got the killed-himself one between them, and so no plunder at all.

Yes, it was truly a strange thing that only a little while ago there had been several hundred soldiers and now suddenly there were no more to kill. Even the horses were gone, rounded up down along the river by boys from the camps. They had been so worn out that they were not afraid of Indians as American horses usually are, just stood to be caught.

When every brush patch had been whipped through for any hiding ones, Crazy Horse went back to the ridge of the dead. By now they were all stripped, lying naked and white as buffalo fat where the clothes had kept off the sun, looking so pitiful, so helpless. It made him feel bad for them, so many and dying so foolishly. Why did they have to come shooting the people?

Slowly he went among them to see if there were any more he knew besides the one who had died fighting so hard down at the river, the small white man called Reynolds, who used to be a boy living with his family in the upper Platte country. Crazy Horse had been told that the Cheyennes liked his little-girl sister and stole her. California Joe, the old mountain man with the red hair on his face, had helped get her back, it was said.

There was a trader's son among the dead too, Mitch Bouyer, the one they had seen in the fight with the Crows. Crazy Horse was sorry about killing him, but if the Cheyennes were right, these soldiers were the ones who had struck their people in the winter camp on the Washita, who came to the Yellowstone three years ago, and later made the Thieves' Road into the Black Hills. He found nothing of their long-haired chief called Custer, the man with the yellow hair falling loose over his shoulder, yet they were bad people and the trader's son should not have been with them.

Stopping his horse at the end of the ridge, Crazy Horse looked down upon the scattered camp circles of his people, the women back among them, hurrying like dark ants to gather up their possessions, a few of them crossing the river and stringing up towards the battleground to seek their own dead, to strike the soldiers who had made it so. Crazy Horse felt almost dead too, so tired. Finally he started towards the crossing and home, the warriors who had been held away by his standing coming up beside him from this side and that, all talking of the great things done this day, especially of the four Cheyennes who rode out alone against the hundreds of soldiers, holding them until the others got there, four against so many—a truly great thing.

Yes, Crazy Horse had seen it.

Then there was Moving Robe, the Cheyenne woman who carried the staff of her brother killed on the Rosebud into the fight today, and Yellow Nose, the Ute captive among them who had been brave, and the strong Lakotas, too many to count. But the greatest deed of all was cutting off the retreat of the soldiers.

That was not a thing done by one man but by many, following the plannings as they were made, Crazy Horse told them.

Hou! and the plannings of the surround were good ones, and came from one man—

But Crazy Horse had not stayed to listen. Remembering now the other bunches of soldiers he had seen along the ridge, he went back to look at them, particularly those where a very brave little soldier chief had held the warriors off a long time. Most of these whites, too, had been struck down close together. Truly it seemed that almost nothing was done for glory or personal power today, but all for the protection of the people. It was a great battle, and it should make any man feel good.

But there were Indians lost too, their people coming to haul them away with the travois now. Then there would be keening in the villages, and angry relatives riding for revenge against those other soldiers still waiting on the hill above the Hunkpapa circle. Crazy Horse was surprised to remember them now; they had been so forgotten.

At the river crossing he saw an American horse standing alone with many bloody wounds. He thought of shooting it but he had no bow along and a bullet might be worth very much after today. So he rode away to his camp. Black Shawl was back, if she had ever fled very far, and came running out to meet her man, to see that the blood mixed with the dust and sweat and paint was not his own; that he was not scratched.

She brought him hot water and a piece of soapweed root for washing, fed him, and had another fresh horse ready so he could go to the hill where the live soldiers were. On the way Crazy Horse saw some young warriors dressed in soldier clothes, with flags and bugles, riding around in twos like the soldiers. It seemed some whites left hidden in the brush from the morning had come out when they saw the blue coats and then ran back into the bushes when the warriors began shooting with the captured guns that were good after they knocked the stuck shells loose. They had shot at some of the soldiers from the hill who tried to come down for water, too. Maybe they had hurt them but they hadn't tried very hard. After the big fight they felt too good for much more killing.

When Crazy Horse got up on the hill, he saw it was true that more whites had come there, bringing pack mules, as the watching warriors said, and that they had really been digging themselves down into the stony hill as a turtle digs into sand. But it seemed they were not satisfied with that place either, and while Crazy Horse signaled for more warriors, some of the soldiers came out and started off along the ridge towards the ground of the big fight, several miles away. They stopped on a high point where they could see very many Indians sitting on their horses down there, the smoke and dust like a wind cloud high above them. There were warriors coming across the river too, and the ones the soldiers had been fighting on the hill were trying to cut them off, so the little soldier chief led his men in a gallop back to their hole. The Indians attacked there, trying to scare them as they had done in the morning, to get at the horses. They made a few good hits but the whites seemed different now, much stronger, and they had a good place to defend. After going against them several times, afoot too, the tired Indians gave it up for that day. When the sun stood red on the hills west of the Little Big Horn, a night guard was set around the soldiers, and most of the warriors went back to the mourning camps across the river, where the death lodges had been put up for the twenty warriors killed, the medicine men working over the many wounded.

As soon as he could, Crazy Horse went to cover his head in his sleeping robe so he need not hear the keening; he tried to sleep so he need not think about the fight today and why it did not seem as good as the one on the Piney ten years ago. Many, many more were killed here, and he had lost no one like Lone Bear, and yet it seemed almost that he wished this hadn't happened. Could it be that his warrior days were over?

The next morning some of the headmen went up to look at the soldiers dug in on the hill. There was talk of making a great charge to finish the fight right away, but some were against it, saying good men would be lost, and their little ammunition used up.

"Wait," these advised. "The whites will soon come out for water."

Crazy Horse was there too, planning a few charges to try the hearts of the soldiers today, but the scouts signaled that another great army was coming up the river, many more than they had been fighting, with wagon guns. Short Bull and some of the others had stayed behind to shoot into their camps, to charge the horse herds, to make them move slower so the people would have time to get away, for they were already very close.

Once more the great encampment set out upon the trail, going up the river this time, and fast, with no beaded saddle hanging on the women's horses, no gay singing, no jokes and showing off. When the last travois pulled away past the Hunkpapa camp ground the grass of the valley began to burn, the pale smoke rolling up like midsummer thunder clouds behind them. So the long line of people hurried away towards the shelter of the White Mountains, leaving the places of the soldier fights behind—the ridge with the dead ones bloated fat in the hot sun, and the hole with the live ones, too, the last of the watching warriors from there falling in with those who guarded the rear of the people as the camp disappeared into the breaks along the river.

The battle of the Little Big Horn was done.

The SMOKE OF VICTORY
Hangs Low

BY the time the Moon of the Black Calf, September, was growing in the evening sky Crazy Horse knew that the fighting at the Little Big Horn would never be done. At every campfire, at every smoking on a hillside, the deeds of that day were told, and not as of a time close past or of people still living among them, but already as part of the great hero stories of the Lakotas. Sucking at the marrow from the roasted bones of the hunt that thinned the buffalo very much, the men talked of that one big day, saying nothing of the tomorrow or of the day after that.

By now the hostiles had heard many things carried to them from the agencies: that it was really Long Hair with his hair cut off that they had killed on the ridge the day Crazy Horse came up the ravine behind him, and that the soldier chief died because he went against the plans made by the others. He was told to find the Indians and watch them until all the soldiers got there to help. But he could not wait, not even when his Crow scouts showed him the great sundance place on the Rosebud, and the biggest lodge trail they had ever seen.

"Very many Sioux—too many Sioux!" they had said, making the Crow howlings of being afraid. And when Long Hair went on without even resting his horses or his men, they ran away.

Then there was the story one of the Ree scouts had been told by Bloody Knife: that Long Hair would whip the Indians quick and be made the Great Father.

"Be made the Great Father—!" The Lakotas could not believe it. One who went around killing the helpless ones could not be a Great Father. But Bloody Knife, the scout they chopped up at the big fight, had said it, claiming Long Hair had made many talkings to him in the three years of his scouting, many promises of what he would do for this Indian friend when he was the biggest man on the earth—the Great Father of the whites.

As Crazy Horse looked back over the summer he saw that it was as some of them had feared—that the victory on the ridge was a black one. It was not only that their ammunition was used up and that the whites were angry and shamed, but that somehow the people were afraid, unable to scatter as they must before the soldiers came, wanting instead to sit together in some hidden canyon, more like rabbits that have been long hunted by dogs than a conquering grizzly that has just destroyed a powerful enemy. True, there were strong ones among the young warriors who chased all the scattered white men that came through the country, bringing in scalps and soldier coats, keeping the prairie fired between the rains, filling every clear day with great rolling clouds of smoke, reddening the night sky from the grass that the soldier horses needed to live.

To most of the people, tired of fighting, the Black Hills seemed very far away now, but as soon as his yellow pinto was rested Crazy Horse had gone against the whites of that country. Usually He Dog, Short Bull, Black Fox, and some younger warriors were along, perhaps a few Cheyennes and their women too. They brought in pack mules of wagon goods, once two big skin sacks full of raisins, the dried berries of the white man that Crazy Horse had not tasted since the old days around Laramie. He sent the crier for the children and held the sacks open while they filled their hands and watched them cram the strange sweet things into their mouths. Another time there was a big roll of white cloth for summer leggings, very fine with beaded bands down the sides, or blue strips with bells. There was cloth for woman dresses too, and even a shining red sunshade on a handle for old One Moccasin, who had been bad hurt by a grizzly and sometimes fell like dead from the heat. Only ammunition was hard to get, seldom more than the shells the dead men carried.

On one trip deep into the Hills Crazy Horse slipped away from the camp alone, and by daylight he was looking down upon the big town of tents and shacks the whites had made, seeing how very many of them there were, with women and the young ones along, like people come to stay. Against so many he could do nothing, but all over the Hills scattered men were digging into the earth like the prairie dogs and these he hunted out, using not the Winchester that would send its war whooping loud among the rocks, but the silent arrow and war club.

It was He Dog who found him, and spoke in anger against this secret work, against this going out alone into a country so full of enemies. "My friend, you are past the foolish years of the wild young warrior; you belong to the people now and must think of them, nor give them such uneasiness!"

Crazy Horse heard the blaming of his friend in silence. He had killed many in these few days, more than after the whites shot his brother, young Little Hawk, but here it was less than one palmful dipped from a flooding stream.

There were other things done this summer. Some friendly Cheyennes had started up the lodge trail from Red Cloud and were driven back, with Yellow Hand killed in a volley from the soldier guns and scalped before the eyes of the frightened women and children.[1] This was done on Warbonnet Creek, only one sleep from the agency, in the country of the friendlies. They had been making no fighting, just going out for meat because there was so little to eat at the agency, and the winter coming cold and long. So now Yellow Hand, the friendly, lay on the ground without firing a shot.

And while Three Stars was waiting for the Crows and Snakes to come back, the hostile Cheyennes and a few Oglalas found some of his soldier and traders' son scouts in the Big Horns and tried to

[1] Colonel Merritt's interception of the Cheyennes, July 17, 1876.

talk to them as friends.[1] When they got only shooting they chased them into a patch of trees. Here White Antelope, the Cheyenne, was killed and the scouts left their horses and ammunition and ran clear back to Three Stars, several sleeps away over very rough country, and with nothing to eat. The Grabber was along, sitting sideways on his horse, and when he got on the ground the Indians made a loud laughing, for it seemed he had the bad-disease walk the soldiers get from the white man's pay-women. It must have been a long, hard trail to the camp on Goose Creek, the warriors after them, with no resting and no food, and the Grabber coming along behind, walking with his legs far apart, Big Bat trying to make him keep up.

He Dog and Crazy Horse laughed a little over this too. The Grabber had traded his breechcloth and the things his mother's people had taught him for the pants of the white man and the soldier's pay, but he had got no bad-disease walk while he lived in the hostile lodges and courted the Lakota maidens of their camps.

Finally the scouts had reported that the soldiers were starting against the Indians and now the great camp had to break up. There were a few good-by dances, the people telling one another that some day the whites would be gone again, as they had gone from the country before, and then they could be together in peace.

But there was a sadness even among the strong-talking ones when the first camp, the Cheyennes, started away. Dull Knife's people, who left Red Cloud too late for the Custer fighting, were along. They wanted to get far from all who would be called hostile, planning to winter over in the Big Horns somewhere, so now, as they moved out along the Powder into the morning sun, many women stopped their work to look after their friends with an uneasiness upon them. Here and there a man watched too, and a few of the young ones hurried to their horses and rode after the Cheyennes, some of the best warriors of the Oglalas. It was hard for Crazy Horse to see them go, but the Cheyenne women were very

[1] Sibley Scouts, July 7, 1876.

good—not so beautiful as some of the Oglalas, but they stood strong beside a man, very strong beside a man.

The next few days many little parties slipped away towards the agencies, Crazy Horse and Big Road letting them go in peace, for they were agency Indians. Then the rest of the Lakotas separated into bands and started towards the Bear Butte country as was usual in late summer, to fatten the ponies on the good grass and to make a little trading with the eastern people, perhaps for ammunition.

As the hostiles scattered, the great army of soldiers, those from the Little Big Horn and those from Goose Creek, broke into two parts, one going along the Yellowstone, where no Indians were; the other under Three Stars with some traders' sons to guide them followed the fresh trails, so the Lakotas fired the prairie behind their travois here too to make the soldiers and their horses hungry. But the rains came and kept falling until the drag poles plowed up the soft earth as the whites do for planting.

There was bad news from the agencies too—more soldiers there, with little soldier chiefs for agents and more treaty men coming to buy the Black Hills, making a strong talk of starving the Indians into going to the Missouri or the south place called Indian Territory.

One night a visitor from Standing Rock agency on the Missouri came to the Crazy Horse camp. He told that Grass, a friendly, had risen in the council there to say that the Indian country could yet be saved if the men at the agencies were strong enough to grab all the arms, ammunition, and provisions and joined the hostiles.

"Hou, hou!" a few had answered him, but most of the agency chiefs had kept quiet, their faces turned down.

"See their noses point to the ground, like played-out ponies!" Grass had taunted them. "Can we hope to win this fight with such men?"

And then some of Three Stars's soldiers struck Iron Plume [1] and his forty lodges near Slim Buttes. Many of the people belonged to Spotted Tail agency and were working their way around the Black

[1] Called American Horse by the whites. The Roman Nose along was of Lone Horn's friendly Minneconjous. September 9, 1876.

Hills, hoping to keep away from the soldiers and to reach the agency before winter filled the canyons. Most of the men were away, some out to get a little ammunition for the hunt, others to see the agent about coming in. Then the soldiers came out of the foggy rain, their guns shooting. Women and children were killed and Iron Plume was shot so he had to hold his belly together and couldn't shake hands with the soldier chief when he came. As soon as the whites chased the people from the lodges they took everything, many of the soldiers sitting down in the middle of the fighting to gnaw at the dried meat, so starved were they. The Grabber was among the scouts, but he stayed far back, with the wagons.

"Afraid somebody would kill him," Little Big Man said. There were enough who would have liked to see him laid on the ground like Bloody Knife, half Lakota too, but chopped up just the same for bringing the soldiers against the people. The Indians knew the Grabber was the only one among the scouts who had been in this country. Maybe he was afraid because Iron Plume had seen him around the northern agencies when he was a boy and knew the things he had done before he ran away to the Indians. Or maybe the trader's son still had trouble walking from the disease.

But Big Bat helped the people all he could. He went to tell the soldier chief of the women and children hiding in a deep gully with the soldiers shooting into it, trying to set it afire. So they were stopped and Bat jumped down to get the wounded Iron Plume out and the other helpless ones, although he might have been killed, with so many bad hearts over the hurt and the dead.

"Bat is a good man," Crazy Horse agreed when he was told the story on the way to Slim Buttes. He had hurried over with He Dog and Kicking Bear and the warriors as soon as the runner came with the news of the attack. But a thousand more soldiers under Three Stars had come up and all the Oglalas could do with their few shells was to make the whites go so fast that many of their starved horses died in the mud and some of those they took from the Indians played out. Most of the captured people were turned loose. Perhaps the soldiers would have been much harder on the helpless ones if they hadn't been so weak themselves from the starvation march, for they lost some whites there and had found the things the visiting Little Big Man warriors had brought to Iron Plume's camp—a fork-tailed flag from the Custer fight and some soldier coats with blood on them.

Iron Plume had been left behind. "It is always the friendly ones who are struck—" he said before he died. At first he would not let the white medicine man look at him. He had no wish to live. Finally, with a blanket tied close to hold himself together and the white man's medicine to cover the pain with sleep, he lay down.

In November, the Moon of Falling Leaves, came the news that the Black Hills had been sold and all the country west to the Big Horn Mountains, the home of the Lakotas. The people heard this and came to Crazy Horse like children new wakened from sleep. It could not be true; who would be so foolish? Then they thought that the chiefs must have been given the white man's whisky. But later it was known that they had been put inside the stockade and the paper read to them, a paper taking everything from the Indians and making them go to the Missouri or that south country so hated by the Cheyennes, the Indian Territory. This was too hard a thing for even a great friendly like Sitting Bull the Good. Angrily he rose up.

"We know nothing of these far places!" he cried. "We want to stay in our own country. Talk of signing this paper is all foolishness, with most of the people north and not nearly enough here to do anything!"

But the whites and the Indians gave him no listening, so he drove the chiefs from the stockade, whipping them, even Red Cloud, with the flat side of his three-bladed knife, calling them weak, cheap men who would sell the homes of their children for money.

Nothing was done that day, or the next, until they knew the Oglala had gone to the Crazy Horse camp in anger and defeat. Then the paper was brought out again, Hinman, the white-man interpreter, saying: "Yes, yes," to every change the chiefs wanted, making everything very friendly, with much feasting and drink. And when the Indians still would not sell, the doors of the stockade were shut and the chiefs told that the children would not eat until they touched the pen.

So they signed, Spotted Tail too, when he heard that Red Cloud had already done this. There were thirty or forty men all together, and yet the treaty of 1868 said that nothing could be sold from the Lakota country without three out of every four Indians agreeing.

"They see that we are truly very few," old Worm said, tears running down the furrows of his brown cheeks when he heard how it was done.

Before the next moon there was more news. Even while the treaty men were coming to ask for the Black Hills, Three Stars had sent an order that all the horses and guns were to be taken from Red Cloud and his band, but not until he had signed the paper. Now it was over, the soldier chief made the excuse that the Indians had moved away from the agency after the treaty-signing. But some around the soldiers knew about the order long before the Black Hills council.[1]

Red Dog and Red Leaf, the brother of the long-dead Conquering Bear, were with the Bad Faces that cold morning. Standing helpless from the sleeping robes, with the soldier guns held against them, they had to see their horses taken by the hated Pawnee scouts, their bundles searched for guns and ammunition, some of the lodges burned, and everybody, Red Cloud with the rest, marched to the agency stockade, with Pawnees in soldier coats making insults to the Lakota warriors now that their hands were empty. Even the white chickens of Red Cloud's wife were lost.

At the agency they found some of the commissioners of the Great Father back again, this time to take the chiefs to the Indian Territory, the same good-talking men who not a moon ago had promised that if the Black Hills were sold the people would be cared for

[1] Confidential letter, Crook to Merritt, September 25, 1876, Letter Book #28, Dept. of Platte.

and protected, and already they were walking prisoners.

Three Stars was at the agency too, asking for young Oglalas, even Bad Faces, to help him against their relatives in the north. And in a counciling he told Red Cloud that Spotted Tail had been made head of both agencies, head of the Oglalas too.

"Ahh-h, it must be hard, after so many years helping the whites—" the hostiles said.

Yes, after so many years the once great warrior of the Oglalas was no more than any other who had no pony for his travois, and this was done by the people who had given him great power in that white man's town called Washington, power over the friend-lies, their agency and annuities, even over the kettle of old Man Afraid; and power enough in the north country to break up the chiefs' society, strip the hair shirt from Crazy Horse and take Black Buffalo Woman from him, power that somehow reached into every Oglala lodge as the dampness of long rain creeps in, or blizzard cold. Now, in one word from the officer's hairy mouth, it was all gone.

But Worm and Big Road and even Black Twin, those who had known Red Cloud a long time, told many stories of his scheming and cunning. Against this Bad Face might not the soldier chief called Three Stars find he was only a child in the cradleboard?

There was news from the north for the Crazy Horse people too. Miles, the officer the Indians called Bear Coat, made a fort on the Yellowstone, right at the mouth of the Tongue River, like a wagon gun aimed against the heart of the people. The Hunkpapas found him first and struck his wagon train, getting many mules but letting the people go as soon as their wheels were turned back down the river. In a few days Sitting Bull had more shooting with the soldiers; so he had Big Leggins, another trader's son in trouble with the whites, write a letter to be left on a stick in the prairie asking Bear Coat why he came to the Indian country and scared the buffalo.

Crazy Horse looked with uneasiness upon this thing. He did not like these writing sons of the traders. First it had been Lean Elk coaxing Red Cloud in, then the Grabber after Sitting Bull, and now this Big Leggins, Johnny Brughier. But Bear Coat acted like the other soldier chiefs. He read the letter and made a council with Sitting Bull, and while the smoking and the talk went on his soldiers moved up to attack the people. The Hunkpapas got away but they had to run and they lost much of the winter meat, many lodges and ponies.

"Truly one cannot trust these soldier chiefs near the helpless ones," Crazy Horse said to those around his fire.

"Hou! But they push in hard from every side, and the buffalo are very scarce," a man with little children in his lodge complained.

"Soon there will be no buffalo any place, only soldiers—and the Bear Coat promises good treatment if we let him catch us——" another said, with many agreeing.

Ahh-h, the people were like sick ponies this winter, their heads hanging down, Crazy Horse thought. But one spoke up loud against this giving up, someone sitting back in the woman's line. "It is better to die fighting!" she cried, saying it loud and in such anger that the heart of Crazy Horse swelled to hear. They were not whipped while there was still such strength in the women.

The next day he went and swept off the beef herd of the soldiers on the Tongue—stinking meat, but it kept the belly from falling in.

Late in the Moon of Falling Leaves the Crazy Horse scouts rode in from their watching along the old Holy Road. The soldiers had started north from Fetterman for a winter campaign, coming afoot and on horses. They had buffalo coats and fur caps, and while Three Stars did not get the hundreds of Indian scouts from the southern agencies that he wanted, he got some—traders' sons, Lakotas, Cheyennes, and Blue Clouds, sixty all together.

"Sixty of our relations and friends helping the soldiers!"

And many more from among their old enemies, the Snakes and Pawnees, over three hundred Indian scouts.

Barely had this been told through the center camps of the

Lakotas when once more a Cheyenne village came walking through the snow, the men ahead breaking the path for the freezing feet of the helpless ones.[1] This time it was Dull Knife's people, the ones who had gone to the Big Horns to keep out of trouble. They had even sent word to the agency that they would go back if they would be well treated.

Ahh-h, if the Cheyennes could only watch for the soldiers as they could fight them, Crazy Horse thought as he went out the second time in one year to meet these people fleeing to his camp. Today it was indeed bad, many almost naked except for a few green skins of horses killed, many with their hands and feet frozen, women carrying young children dead at their breasts. He found the heart of old Dull Knife on the ground in self-blaming. They had known that the soldiers were around, going past their hiding-place in a canyon of the upper Powder, on towards the Crazy Horse camp, the scouts said. He and many others wanted to move back out of the way, but Last Bull, chief of the Fox society, was stubborn. They must make the victory dance over the thirty Snake scalps just taken, and so it was done, nobody knowing that young Beaver Dam had been caught by the Indian scouts and had told where the camp was before he knew they were of the soldiers. The dancing had lasted all night, the young women tied together, as the Cheyennes sometimes did. At daybreak they heard four or five shots. Then a lot of Snakes were seen on a ridge, with Pawnees and soldiers already in the valley, driving the horse-herders before them. The dancers tried to run away, but they were still tied together and fell into piles as the scouts and soldiers charged. The first to die was the young son of Dull Knife. He rose up before the soldiers alone and was shot.

By then all the camp was awake, the women and children scattering towards the steep canyon walls, many half-dressed and without moccasins, most of the men fighting naked from the sleeping robes, trying to hold back the attackers. There was dying here, and much wounding, Little Wolf getting hit four times. They

[1] Dull Knife battle, November 25, 1876.

fought most of the day, a long time behind breastworks they threw up, but the horses and the camp were lost, all the meat and robes and the fine beadwork of the Cheyenne women.

When everything was destroyed they started north, coming up along the slope of the Big Horns, past the Medicine Water to the Tongue and down it to Beaver Creek, eleven sleeps of hard travel, the wounded, the very young, and the weak dying on the way.

"Eey-ee!" the women cried when they heard of this bad thing done, and while there were many Cheyennes to be helped, and the Oglalas were not rich any more, nobody went to sleep hungry or cold that night.

In the council lodge Crazy Horse puffed at his little pipe while he listened to this story of soldiers and their scouts who came like shadows over the frozen snow, so quiet that the Cheyennes out watching saw and heard nothing. There was an uneasiness among the Lakotas around him, an uneasiness like that in a new-foaled mare at the smell of a mountain lion. And as Crazy Horse saw this he rubbed the short stem of his pipe thoughtfully to his face without remembering the scar it touched, for there was much here to trouble the heart.

When the council was done at last, he went out to walk among the lodges thrown together for the far-chased people. The new camp was dark under the shrinking rib of moon, and silent too, except for the moaning of a wounded woman whose feet were so frozen they would be lost like a wolf's paw caught in the iron of a winter trap. But when a child cried out in his sleep: "The soldiers, mother, the soldiers!" there was a stirring all around, dark woman-heads pushing out between the lodge flaps, and then the quiet voice of the mother singing:

> *Sleep, my little owl, no soldiers come shooting.*
> *This is a good place.*
> *The medicine of the Strange Man*
> *Covers all the people.*
> *Sleep, my little owl—*

making a song of it in a little wickiup so poor that it seemed no more than an old pony resting in the shadows of·the camp circle.

Quickly Crazy Horse slipped away, going towards the hills as he did so often, even when some were saying he should stay with his people now that their hearts were like the frozen stones.

It was so that he happened to see some Oglala lodges fall through the dying moonlight, the women working fast and quiet, rolling them, the men helping to drag them off to the travois waiting below the camp—people running away because of what had happened to the Cheyennes, Oglalas running like scared dogs with the tails between their legs towards the white man's islands, where they would not even have their ponies left them when there was nothing except ponies to eat.

But then he saw that it would be like a few buffalo breaking from a surrounded herd, with more and more trying to follow. So he called loudly for the *akicita,* sent them after the runaways. The people were brought back, their lodge poles and their bows broken, their horses shot. It was no more than would happen to them on the agencies, and here so long as anybody ate they would have food.

After a resting for the Cheyennes all the people started up the Tongue, hunting as they went. The ice was strong and several times the big camp crossed back and forth on sanded trails to reach a few buffaloes—to make a little meat and some lodges for the robbed ones. The snow was deep and the little herd of beef cattle Crazy Horse had taken from the soldiers at the Tongue River fort were getting so full of bones they had to be butchered, and every morning more of the good American horses captured in the summer fighting had died, for they could not paw grass from the snow or eat cottonwood bark, but they all made skins.

By the time the moon was growing again, some men came from the Red Cloud agency with news. The Indians and the traders' sons scouting for Three Stars had gone to him after the Dull Knife fight saying that if he would go away, stop chasing the Indians around in the snow, they would try to get the chiefs to come in. But before they would do this he must promise they would be given agencies in their own country, not be sent to the Missouri or to the Indian Territory but be allowed to come back up here.

They talked very hard for this and so General Crook made the promise.

"A white-man promise—!" Crazy Horse said, emptying his pipe.

Hou, hou! others agreed, even Sitting Bull, the Oglala.

Yes, a white-man promise, the messengers admitted, but he had taken his soldiers away, out of the Indian country, and surely there were other good whites besides their old father, Major Twiss. They believed that Three Stars was such a man. He never talked of wiping out the Indians as Long Hair did, and Grattan and Fetterman on the Piney. Three Stars loved peace.

The hostiles counciled a long time over this and decided that even if they could believe the promise of their own agencies, it might be better to stay here in the north country so the whites wouldn't forget about them. They could go to Bear Coat and keep away from the land down around Red Cloud where the smell of the whites was on every wind, where there were the old troubles among the Oglalas and now the newer jealousies between Red Cloud and Spotted Tail. The four hundred lodges of Missouri Indians and Hunkpapas who went to the Tongue fort were well fed, with nobody punished for the fighting of last summer. So Crazy Horse, Big Road, He Dog, and Lame Deer decided to send men in to see what the soldier chief would do for them: some Oglalas led by Sitting Bull, without his gold-trimmed rifle, and some Minneconjous under Bull Eagle, who had already taken his people there and had been told by Bear Coat to come in to talk any time, always carrying a white flag, so there could be no mistake.

Late in the Moon of Popping Trees, December, the men rode down towards the fort at the mouth of the Tongue, with Sitting Bull the Good at the head, carrying a lance with a big white cloth on it. Behind him came the others in a row, all unarmed, leading some American horses stolen from the fort by the young warriors—eight good men come in peace. And back a ways on a hillside waited the twenty-five headmen of the Minneconjous and Oglalas, including Crazy Horse with Bad Heart Bull beside him to make the picture story of this great day for his people.

As the Lakotas got near the fort some Crow scouts camped outside of the stockade came running, crying: "Hou, hou!" shaking hands, and then firing into the visiting Indians from behind the big woodpiles of the soldiers. At the shooting those who could whipped their horses away, but five of the peace men had to be left there on the ground, among them Sitting Bull the Good.

The soldiers came charging out, their rifles turned against the Crows, calling: "Hou! Hou, *cola!*" to the Lakotas. But Crazy Horse and the others retreated to the bluffs, out of range of the wagon guns they knew were at the fort. While one little soldier chief tried to coax them back, another chased the Crows already running away towards their agency, took their goods, and sent twelve of their horses to the Lakotas, but Crazy Horse would not let anybody else go down there now. Five good men had been lost under the white man's own sign of peace. It was enough.

So they rode back to their people, waiting not far away for the good words of peace. And when Black Shawl saw the face of her man she went silently to strike her lodge for more wandering through the snow, chopping cottonwood for the horses, the men hunting buffalo for the kettle, everybody ready night or day to run from the horse soldiers brought against them by their own people.

It was the worst winter that the Old Ones could remember since the people crossed the Missouri, back in the hero-story days. The snow had come hard on the fall whistle of the mating elk, and as the cold deepened, the hostiles moved to the warmest place they knew, on the Tongue below Hanging Woman Creek, where the bluffs stood behind them against the north wind. The people were so uneasy that the medicine men got many horses. One who called himself Long Hair since the fight on the Little Big Horn, claiming he worked with the spirit of Custer, made particularly strong medicine. To show that he was bullet-proof he let some of the warriors shoot at him and then picked flattened pieces of lead from under the belt of his breechcloth, holding them up for everyone to see. But what the warriors liked the most was his power to make ammunition. All one night he made medicine in his lodge, the smoke rising from its top in strange, unknown smells, his songs and the drummings to be heard all over the camp. In the morning he showed them eight big boxes of shells, new ones, fitting the guns taken in the fight with Long Hair. When the young men saw this they tied good horses outside of his lodge and, filling their guns and their belts, went away very strong in their new hope.

When this was done Crazy Horse rode out into the hills again. He had seen those shells before, had helped get them in a council with the Slota, the Red River breeds, earlier in the fall. Perhaps it was good to have Long Hair giving strength to the people, lifting their hearts this way, but Crazy Horse knew he had to look in another place. So he went through the snow to the ridge where he had seen the white buffalo long ago. Today there was no track except those of the rabbit and the wolf, no sign of buffalo anywhere, nothing speaking to him.

Towards night a gray cloud did come fast from the north, with wind and snow in its heart. Crazy Horse felt the strength of it, the strength of all the earth and the sky close around him, if he could only reach it. Nothing less could save his people now. Quickly he made a little sweat lodge and rubbed himself with the silver sage plant he had brought along, and afterward he lay on the hilltop wrapped in his robe, hoping to dream out of the storm. But it went as swiftly as it came, and then there was nothing except the stars, the howling of the wolves and coyotes, and a clear cold sunrise.

Before the mourning over the peace men killed was done two messengers came from the northern agencies saying the whites wanted the Indians to come in, would give them food and clothing, even canvas for lodges. This the messengers swore by the knife point, knowing they would die of it if they lied. But another thing they must tell—all the weapons of the people would be taken from them, and their horses.

"Hoppo!" some of the younger warriors cried, springing up to count coup on the messengers. The older men spoke more quietly, saying they would never submit to this, not so long as there was life in their breasts, and when a No Bow talked for going in, Red Bear, another of that people, spoke against him in anger. They had sent good men to see how it was on the agencies. Now they were kept locked up and a brother, one of the messengers sitting here before them, had come to bring the rest of the people in.

"Can the whites think we do not know that there is still room in their iron houses for more people and that their chains are strong and very many, enough to hold us all?" he cried.

So it went, until very late. When the council was over, the messengers tried to get the families of the hostages to go in. But Crazy Horse said anybody who left the camp would be followed and punished. Yet even after this, thirteen lodges moved out into the white darkness of the snow, getting far away by daylight. Then Crazy Horse was suddenly before them on his yellow pinto, with many warriors behind him. As he had promised, the horses of the fleeing people were shot, their guns, bows, and knives taken. Now they could go to the whites if they wished.

But the snow was very deep, the road to the northern agencies too long for the moccasins, and so they returned to the camp, trying again the next morning, openly, before all the people. This time the *akicita* came up and made a silent wall about them, and so the messengers went away alone, sneaking back for the four lodges that belonged to the hostages. Crazy Horse saw them go into the darkness and he let them, for now he saw that at least a hundred and fifty lodges of the Minneconjous and No Bows would have gone if they dared. It seemed that the people were truly broken.

Then, in the middle of this peace-talking, Bear Coat's soldiers started up the Tongue, many men, with two wagon guns along. The camps were right in the way but they did not move. Where would they go? the people asked, and even Crazy Horse walking among them no longer gave them the heart for more fleeing.

By the first of January the soldiers reached the lower camps. The warriors went out to hold them back until the people moved up the river. Two days later it had to be done again, the soldiers after them like magpies after a sore-backed horse, and there was no black oil from the Poison Springs to keep them off as one does the long-tailed birds. Finally they decided to scatter, leaving the warm canyons of the Tongue country as reluctantly as moose or elk leave their winter yards.

But once more there was a crying in the night: "Soldiers are coming!" the people hurrying back through the foggy darkness, back to the Tongue, up to Crazy Horse on Hanging Woman Creek as fast as they could, the warriors putting themselves between the soldiers and the helpless ones, ready to fight with the little ammunition they had and the bows and war clubs.[1] When they were together Crazy Horse led the men to a high bluff overlooking the river, hoping to hold the place, for the women would not go on without the warriors, too much afraid in the winter fog that had frosted every tree and grass stem and hid so well what was just before the eye.

From the high ridge Crazy Horse and his warriors watched the walking soldiers come out of the early winter morning as from a cloud and stop in the valley below them. They seemed to be making camp, and built great fires for warming and to cook, the smell of their coffee coming strong to the watching warriors and the people behind them, cold and hungry and needing to keep their bundles packed for flight. Then the wagon guns began shooting, their booming low and deep in the fog, but they didn't seem to scare the Indians any more. Women with little ones tied on their backs came to watch the round balls burst and scatter the hairy frost from the grass like flour blown into the air. Boys ran after those that stopped half-buried in the frozen earth and rock without flying to pieces. Young Black Elk and another boy brought Crazy

[1] Miles's attack on Crazy Horse, January 8, 1877.

Horse one, carrying it between them. He looked at it with them, remembering how he and the other boys had talked of these things on the summer night after the Mormon cow was killed, with the wagon guns coming to the camp of Conquering Bear the next day. He remembered that Young Man Afraid, already seeing far ahead of the others, had said that a wagon gun would be no good to the Indians because they could never make the ammunition. It seemed a lifetime since that one went to the whites.

After a while, when the fog lifted a little and a gray snow began to fall, the soldiers started across the slippery river ice, the Indians shooting at them, mostly arrows lifted high to fall among them; but their buffalo coats were very thick and their guns shot far, the bullets keeping the warriors down among the rocks.

Of them all there was only one warrior angry to foolishness this day—Big Crow, a Cheyenne. He had lost relations in the Dull Knife attack and among some women just captured. Boldly he walked up and down along the ridge between the Indians and the soldiers, the feathered ends of his war bonnet trailing to the snow, a gun from the Little Big Horn fight in his hand, the soldier bullets glancing on the rocks around him until he fell and somebody dragged him back, through lead thick as the driving snow around them.

With spears and arrows, and swinging the empty guns like clubs on any soldiers that pushed out of the storm, the warriors held the whites back until the women were gone up the Tongue and over towards the Little Big Horn, with Crazy Horse, He Dog, and two Cheyennes guarding the rear. Several soldiers fell in the close fighting, but there was no time for coups and scalps and no heart for taking anything but ammunition. Finally they, too, dropped back into the blizzard, leaving no trail and keeping the soldiers from knowing for a long time that the Indians had gone from the Hanging Woman.

All night the people traveled in the cold north wind, and the next day too, the tails of the ponies pulled tight between their legs, the sun pale as frozen mare's milk and making himself great fires on each side. Big Crow died on the way. With the two Lakotas already lost, that made three men gone to many more soldiers dead but nobody talked of a victory dance. And when the scouts came to say that Bear Coat had started back to his fort the Indians kept going, without the heart to stop. If a Crazy Horse camp could be struck by the soldiers, where would the people be safe?

So they pushed on, into the country that was black earth under the snow from the fires set last summer, with no wood, no grass for the ponies or for game. Even the rabbit tracks were lost. There had been a few buffalo on the Tongue, but very wild, and with so many empty bellies among the people, no meat was left. They were poor in other things too, now, the lodges blackened and patched, the moccasins worn. Most of the dresses and leggings of the white-man stuff were gone, the men wearing buckskin breechcloths as they had before the traders came to the upper Platte country, sixty years before. Even the vermilion was all used up, and the red-earth paint too.

But meat the people must have, so Crazy Horse led them clear over the burnt country to the upper Little Big Horn. Here they heard that the soldiers were marching through the country north of the Yellowstone, chasing Sitting Bull's Hunkpapas, the women speaking of it among themselves with hushed, pitying words. But there was little rest for them here either. Every few days, it seemed, they were feeding messengers from the agencies, north and south, hoping to coax the Indians to come sit beside some soldier fort.

Then one day the scouts signaled many people coming, riding like Indians, with pack horses and women along. It was Sword of Red Cloud, brother of the one who had been a shirt-wearer with Crazy Horse, bringing thirty visitors. And as they came towards the camp the women ran out to meet them, crying: "Relatives, relatives!" and Crazy Horse heard a joy in their voices that had seemed dead a long time. And when he went out, almost the first one he saw was Woman's Dress, riding big in his beaded blanket, his leggings trimmed with silver up the sides, as for some great ceremonial.

That night there was a big feast with the goods sent by the agent: coffee, sugar, and flour for the fried bread to add to the buffalo Crazy Horse had luckily found so they need not be shamed before their guests. And at the council Sword told them that they had not come as spies but as volunteers from White Hat, the little soldier chief of scouts that the whites called Clark. They had heard that their relatives were suffering out here, so the agent sent them to tell Crazy Horse to come in. If he would do this, he would be given rations, blankets, and clothing, and then he could come back here, for it was indeed true that the northern people would be given agencies in their own country if they came in.

Hoh! This was better than the Missouri whites were offering, and better than what Bear Coat said. Besides, some of the headmen were afraid to trust him near the people after all the shooting his soldiers and Crow scouts had done this winter.

But Crazy Horse still would not take the red-wrapped present of tobacco. He told Sword and the others that it was good to see the people had friends who would come so far through the snow to help them, but he could not say what anyone must do.

"Go to He Dog and Big Road, see what they want," he said and sat down, his face unmoving as the pale brown stone of the northern bluffs, his otter-wrapped braids quiet on his breast.

Not long before this, Crazy Horse had been to a council at the camp of the Hunkpapas. He had a long talk with Sitting Bull, going over all the things since the fights of last summer. It was indeed as they had seen it then, not a summer of great victory, but one that closed the corral around the Indians like the gate of an antelope trap, leaving nothing before them but the pit—the agencies where the young people became loafers and drunkards and bad women, where the children starved and shriveled under the shadow of the wagon guns, where even the peace men of the Great Father were thieves, stealing the Indian country.

Ahh-h, but the gate was closed, the free life finished, some of the men, even here, were saying.

"Finished, finished!" roared out the stocky Sitting Bull, making a noise like the falls of the Yellowstone in flood water. Nothing was finished for those who were still Lakotas! Let them come north with him, to the Grandmother's country. She spoke with the straight tongue of a good mother, and her soldiers killed no women and children.

"Hou! Hou!" cried the circle about the council fire of the Hunkpapas.

But the Oglala among them was silent. The long traveling of this winter through the deep snow, through cold that stung the nose and burned the breast, had brought the coughing back to his lodge, and this time a sweat at the Medicine Water brought no help. Up in that north country that the whites called Canada the snow moons were much longer, even the summer nights cold and wet.

So Crazy Horse sat silent as the others talked of the move into the place they called the Grandmother's Land, and when he got back to his people he was even more silent than before.

Many were uneasy about this thing growing so strong in their man this winter, this staying out in the hills of snow alone. They talked it over, those who were afraid they might lose him in some strange way. They even went to Worm, but the father could not help.

"Perhaps my son must prepare himself for some hard thing—" he said sadly. "The Lakotas seem very few today."

So the men made their own plannings for Crazy Horse. Perhaps a pretty young wife might help keep him among them. To be sure, he had nothing to pay for her because so many had needed help this winter, but that could be managed. After looking around they decided upon a relative of Buffalo Calf Road, the young Cheyenne woman who had saved her brother in the Rosebud fight. The girl was pretty and already proud and free-walking in her fifteenth year. But one must speak to Black Shawl first, the Oglalas among them said, for she had done a brave thing when she made a lodge for the unshirted man.

So they came and the woman listened, choking the coughing under her blanket. Before they were done she made the sign of consent, and when they brought the girl, Black Shawl set food before her and gave her the welcome. Then she went out for wood, so she could not be there when Crazy Horse returned. Seeing what was planned, the girl sat very quiet, shaking a little in her blanket, as though afraid to be alone in the lodge with the Strange Man. Black Shawl knew this, but there was nothing she could do, so she took her ax and led the old wood mare far down the river.

When she returned across the reddening snow of evening, Crazy Horse came to take the load and sent her ahead to warm herself in the empty lodge.

"You were long away," he said as he came in and hung the ax in its place. "We had a little visitor from the Cheyennes, but she could not stay. There will be dancing and singing with her people tonight over the Crow fight we had, and she is to carry a staff with a scalp taken by a young Cheyenne—"

"Oh, she did not return alone!" Black Shawl cried, ashamed that a bad face might have been brought upon the girl.

"I did not send her away," the man said. "She ran between the lodges when she saw me coming—" laughing a little as he told it, the first little laughing this long time.

But in a moment it was done and forgotten as he sat at the fire, barely touching the horn spoon of soup before him. That night there was more coughing from the long hours in the cold, and so the next day another woman came to the lodge of Crazy Horse, one who had lost both her man and her young warrior son in the fighting last year. She was silent as a shadow, for it seemed she had no words at all left, but soon it was as if she had always been the old woman of the lodge, bringing wood and water, walking proud with her burdens to the honored fire of her people.

Now another messenger came, from Bear Coat again, and it seemed that the two big soldier chiefs, Miles and Crook, were really fighting over the hostiles. This time it was Big Leggins, the trader's son, now interpreter at the Tongue River fort, bringing two pack horses of goods and some captured Cheyenne women. But neither Big Road nor He Dog would touch the presents. Crazy Horse was out in the hills and they must wait until he came to say what should be done. Anyway, if all the horses and guns, even the knives, must be given up at the fort, how could they live?

Next there were more people from Three Stars—a little soldier chief with two hundred and fifty Indians and traders' sons under Spotted Tail, bringing good word and many loaded travois. They scattered out all the way to the north country, Spotted Tail stopping for a little hunting west of the Black Hills, the others heading for the different camps. The largest party came to Crazy Horse— many good men he had known as friends long ago. They made strong talks, saying that the wild, free days were over, the hunting lands and the Black Hills gone, the buffalo only white bones lying on the prairie, the skulls looking towards the setting sun. So they had come through this bad cold, sent by the agent and by Three Stars, who had truly promised the agencies. If they went in they would be given rations and clothing and then they could come back.

Ahh-h, this was a good thing, the people thought, and looked towards their Strange Man. Could he deny that they were ragged and cold and hungry, or that the soldier chief must be speaking with a straight tongue, for behind him stood Spotted Tail, the brother of Crazy Horse's own mother?

But while those around him thought of these things, the Hunkpatila remembered all the people who had died because they were near the soldiers, from Conquering Bear, who fell at his lodge door over twenty years ago, to the peace men who were shot down at the Tongue fort such a little time past. So the messengers visited in the camp and Crazy Horse went out into the hills again as he had so often, where hunters and scouts found him far from his lodge fire and asked him home with them. He never came but sometimes he told them where to find the trail of a buffalo, or perhaps of an enemy Crow.

This time it was crippled old Black Elk who found him out like that, alone on a little hill, with the snow and the wind around him. Crazy Horse saw the sorrow and uneasiness in the wrinkled face of his friend.

"Uncle," he said, "you notice the way I act, but do not worry. There are caves and holes for me to live in, and perhaps out here the powers will help me. The time is short, and I must plan for the good of my people."

And Black Elk, who was a holy man, went away in silence.

Sitting on the WHITE MAN'S ISLAND

MAY, the Moon of Shedding Ponies, lay spring-warm over the plains of the upper White Earth River and the bluffs that rose here and there like walls against the wind. On a bank above the timbered little path of the stream was the stockade of Red Cloud agency, where the father of the Oglalas lived and kept their goods locked inside the high walls that nobody could climb. A mile westward was the soldier town called Fort Robinson; to the east, rising alone beyond the greening slopes of the broad river valley, stood Crow Butte; and across the north stretched a row of the whitish bluffs with a straggling of pines along the top, the Indian horsemen among them dark and motionless as the trees. Scattered over the rolling ground about the agency and the fort were more Indians, thousands of them, sitting together in little bunches like chewing buffaloes or slouching on their horses, waiting, watching the bluffs for the circling signal of many people coming.

When the sun had passed over the head awhile there was a movement on the bluffs, and a stirring among the people below, not much, for the Indian police in the blue soldier coats were among them, to hold them back. Then, far up where the lodge trail dipped into the valley, riders came into sight against the sky. As they wound down towards the fort, the watching ones saw that the little soldier chief, Clark, called White Hat, was in front. With him were Red Cloud and his headmen and some horse soldiers too.

Then there was a long empty place with only dust in it, and behind that came the one the Oglalas called their Strange Man, and to see him the people pushed forward.

When he came closer those who had not known him made surprised words to one another. He was a small man for a fighter, less than six of the white man's feet, and slim as a young warrior. But they knew it was Crazy Horse, for he wore no paint and nothing to show his greatness. One feather stood alone at the back of his head, and his brown, fur-wrapped braids hung long over a plain buckskin shirt, his Winchester in a scabbard at his knee. Beside him, making a straight row, in paint, war bonnets, and fringed buckskin, rode his headmen, Little Hawk, Big Road, He Dog, and Little Big Man strong among them. Behind these came the warriors and then the people, reaching clear back to the bluffs and out upon the highland, men and women and children, with travois and bundles and horses and dogs.

At the little army post everybody was out to see this wild war leader who had scared the whites so many years, who whipped two of their big soldier chiefs, Crook and Custer, in eight days—to see him give up his gun and his horse and become a coffee-cooler like the rest. But there was one among the watching soldier chiefs who was not pleased with what the far-seeing glasses he held to his face told him. "By God!" he said to those around him, "This is a triumphal march, not a surrender!"

And as the warriors neared the little fort, with all its blue-coated soldiers out, they began to sing, the women and children behind them taking it up, carrying it back through the line, until all the broad valley of the White Earth and the bluffs that stood against the northern sky were filled with the chanting of the peace song of the Lakotas.

Slowly the Indians moved down past the fort, the painted warriors with their weapons, the women with the beaded saddle hangings, the travois baskets of children, the lodge drags, and the horse herds. So the people followed their man past the fort, around the agency, and out upon a wide, flat place that had been kept clear of watchers, all the Indian scouts who had gone north to see the hostiles in standing rows on their horses along the side, as if waiting. Here White Hat stopped, and while many of the friendlies pushed up close, No Water and Woman's Dress and his brothers in the front, the bad thing began to happen, the horses and arms were taken.

First it was the horses. They were counted, seventeen hundred of them, and turned over to the waiting Indian scouts, and now Crazy Horse and all his people saw why they had so many good friends on the agency willing to come north through the snows of the winter to bring them in. Even men like Young Man Afraid and Sword led away the war horses of their friends and the pack mares of the women when the soldiers gave them.

And while this was done those watching Red Cloud saw that his face was motionless, his eyes looking straight before him, but they knew he must be remembering the day only a few months ago when he, a long time agency chief, was so dismounted, his chieftainship taken from him, and his heart made dark for a long, long time.

When the horses were gone the lodges were pitched in the usual circle camp, round as all the sacred things are round, with the opening towards the rising sun. Then there was the counting of the people, one hundred and forty-five lodges, two hundred and seventeen grown men, eight hundred and eighty-nine people all together, not counting those with stronger ponies who had come in ahead, or those who had preferred to live under Spotted Tail, as did Touch the Clouds and even Worm, the father of Crazy Horse.

When the counting was finished, White Hat made a little talking through Billy Garnett and the Grabber, saying he would now take the arms, all the arms. First he went to Crazy Horse and his uncle Little Hawk. When the others saw this done so quietly, they laid their guns down too. A few of the men did try to hold something back, but the friendlies who were with them from the headwaters of the Powder had been watching and spoke out. So one hundred and seventeen pieces were taken, revolvers, muzzle-loaders, rifles, cavalry carbines, and a few Winchesters. Some laid sticks on the ground, saying: "Friend, this is my gun and this short one my pistol. Send to my lodge to get them."

It was hard, but the people let it be done with good face, the two interpreters making the words, and when they didn't please White Hat, who understood a little Lakota, he made it good with the sign-talking he knew.

As soon as he could get away, Crazy Horse went to his lodge. While the women bent over the cooking fires in the warm evening outside and visited with their relatives who came with presents for the kettle, the bowl, and the pan, he sat alone in his place, the little pipe cold in his palm. Now it was done he had to look back as a man who is still wet from crossing a dangerous river looks back to his own country left behind forever for a new one that seems cold and bare and strange.

He did much thinking the next few days as he began to see that although many good words were made here, with plenty of giving, there were other things too, things that caused him uneasiness. Once he thought of walking over to the Running Water, to the hill where he lay in that confusing time after Conquering Bear was shot. But it was very late to look for help now, he knew, with the guns and the horses gone, the soldiers all around them. Besides, he felt that he would be followed if he tried to go, not by the soldiers, but by the Oglalas, by agency Oglalas. There seemed no telling why. Did they think he was a man with a heart like the spring winds, blowing one way today and another tomorrow?

But his uneasiness remained in him, a thing that he must go over and over as a woman works a piece of stubborn doeskin between her palms. It was after Spotted Tail came north with the messengers to them, putting his word behind Three Stars's promise of an agency in their own country, that they decided to come south instead of going to Bear Coat. Dull Knife's Cheyennes had started in right away, their poor ponies dragging the travois through the deep snow. The others waited, but as soon as the earth could be seen again all the Oglalas and Touch the Cloud's Minneconjous moved southward too, scattering for game and grass but all turning their backs hard upon that north country.

At the headwaters of the Powder, they had found Red Cloud waiting with pack horses of presents and a large party along, including old traders like the Janises, and many friends and relations of the hostiles, even Young Man Afraid. Here the people camped together for the night, and the smell of boiling coffee was fine on the south wind.

After the presents were divided and the smoking made, Red Cloud rose before them to speak. He looked very much older, far too much older for the six years he had lived on the island of the white man. Some who had seen him last year said it was the anger in him over the things the whites had done to him last fall, turning their backs upon the chief they had made and giving his power, even his agency, into the strong hand of Spotted Tail.

But the words the bitter-faced Red Cloud made for them were good ones. "All is well," he said. "Have no fear. Come on in."

It made the headmen feel good, Crazy Horse alone sitting silent, wondering about this sudden welcoming from Red Cloud. The Bad Face had not been anxious to have them come in before—pretending to be working for it on top, but underneath burrowing like a mole to make the path rough. Perhaps it was because Red Cloud had nothing to lose now that he came to call them in.

Nothing to lose or very much to find.

Crazy Horse puffed at his little pipe and let it go. Had he been like his Brule uncle, Spotted Tail, or like Red Cloud and the other Bad Faces, he would not have rested until he knew more about this puzzling change, found out about the secret council between the little soldier chief, White Hat, and Red Cloud, with only Billy Garnett, the interpreter, hearing. Billy was young and it would have been very easy for a sly Lakota wanting to know what had been done.

It had happened when Sword and the others came back from the hostile camp. White Hat sent for Red Cloud to come to the fort, to his own little place instead of the open council room.

Through Billy he said he felt sorry that the agency chief had been thrown away by Three Stars and everything given to Spotted Tail, for when they came to enlist scouts they got only one man from the Brules and many from Red Cloud's people.

It was true that the Great Father was angry because Red Cloud's son had been in the Rosebud fight and lost his gift rifle there. But White Hat knew how a father feels when his son goes looking for danger. His own father had wanted him married and settled near home instead of living among the Indians, spending his money on them. But the father cannot control the son, only grieve his heart for him. So White Hat wished to help Red Cloud out of the troubles his son brought upon him. Now that it seemed Crazy Horse was agreeing to come in, Spotted Tail had run out through the snow to get him. White Hat wanted Red Cloud to hurry up there and take him away from the Brule, bring him here, and get him to go to Washington to show his good heart when they went to ask for an agency that was not on the Missouri or down in the Indian Territory. Then White Hat would go to his friend Three Stars and help lift Red Cloud to his place as chief of all the Oglalas.

"Chief of all the Oglalas—" the Bad Face said over his pipe.

Yes. White Hat would help this be done if Red Cloud would go out and bring Crazy Horse here. He would make him the highest of all the chiefs enlisted in the scout service, let him pick his men, give him all the rations he needed, and then would send out beef and provisions to meet the people coming in to Red Cloud, while those going to Spotted Tail would get nothing.

Red Cloud sat in his blanket and considered this. Three Stars was a powerful soldier chief who could do great things for those who pleased him. It was true, too, that this one walking up and down in the restless white man's way before him was only a little soldier chief and would like very much to make himself bigger. Perhaps something could still be done.

"Hou! It is good," Red Cloud had said, making it sound well satisfied. So they smoked on this talk and made some presents to young Billy to help him forget all that had been said there. In three days Red Cloud and almost a hundred men with pack horses and travois had started north, going fast, to catch the Oglalas at the headwaters of Powder River.

Everything happened as White Hat said, and when the Indians reached the place where the lodge trail crossed the Laramie-Black Hills road and there was still talk of taking the fork to Spotted Tail, they were met by some soldiers and American Horse with his Indian police guarding ten wagons of rations and one hundred head of cattle.

American Horse, always working for himself, brought his fifty men to sit with the little soldier chief across the path of the hostiles, and as the northern Indians came up they gave him and each of the others a horse and one to the surprised officer, who did not know of this old-time custom. Then Crazy Horse shook hands with the white man, the first time since the killing of Conquering Bear that he had touched the hand of a soldier chief except as an enemy. But now the fighting was done.

The people camped here three days, resting, feasting, and dancing; then they moved on towards Fort Robinson. Two miles out White Hat with more scouts and soldiers came to meet the hostiles, to bring them in. Here again the chiefs sat in a row, and because Crazy Horse had no war bonnet to put on White Hat as should be done in a surrender, He Dog gave his to the little soldier chief, and his war shirt and pipe and beaded tobacco sack, too. It was a thing to be remembered.

Then they talked, and Crazy Horse said there was a place over there behind them called Beaver Creek. On the big flat west of its headwaters he wanted his agency. The grass was good for horses and for game, and when the agency was put there he would go to Washington and talk to the Great Father. There was another place he had picked, one near the Big Horns, in the Goose Creek country. But if he couldn't have that one the Beaver Creek place would be all right. First the agency, then the going to Washington.

"Hou! It is good!" his chiefs agreed.

Now they were here, with all the old free days behind them, and at night Crazy Horse lay down to sleep with the soldier guns over his people. And in the morning, when the sun came up red behind Crow Butte, he was already out, walking through the circle of his camp, watching the women at their cooking fires to see what they had to eat, to see that none had been overlooked, angry that they were now carrying the wood from the far bluffs on their backs, as poor in horses as the No Clothes people were.

By noon of the second day the newcomers had more in their lodges than since the day they had fled from Hanging Woman Creek before the soldiers of Bear Coat. Their little father, the agent, had issued a week's rations and sent a man out to show them how to make the frying bread of the flour. They were also given some blankets and pants and shirts for the men and boys, a few rolls of bright cloth for the women's dresses. It was mostly poor stuff, that no trader would have dared offer them, and much less than they had been promised, but the many presents from their relatives made them feel a little better, and the agent was saying more goods would come soon. When it came to signing for what they got, none of the northern Indians would touch the pen. Why need they do this? Did not these things belong to them—pay for all their country that had been taken away? Besides, who could tell what unknown words were in these papers?

Soon they heard that while the soldier chief from the fort was complaining to the Great Father that there were not enough annuity goods, blankets, lodge canvas, or kettles for the northern Indians, the agent was writing to him too, saying that the Crazy Horse people were dissatisfied and uncooperative, meaning wanting to know why they should do this or that, old Provost explained. And up on the Yellowstone Bear Coat was complaining that Three Stars had stolen his Indians by promises he had no right to make and that the hostiles just came in to fatten up and get supplies and ammunition and then would run away to fight again.

"What good would the ammunition be with no guns—and how

far can our people run afoot?" Little Hawk asked.

All these things and many more were told around the Indian camps. But Crazy Horse was busy with other work. Every day, at first, he tried to find someone to council with him about the agency promised his people. Always there was something not ready, the agent not ready, Three Stars not ready, or the Great Father. Even Red Cloud had no time. But the soldier chief at the fort encouraged the hostile chief to come often. There might be news for him, and in the meantime they talked as friends.

Then there was the coughing-sickness of Black Shawl. The day after they came Crazy Horse went to ask that the medicine man of the soldiers be sent to look at his woman. He was known to the Indians as a good man for he had tried to help those hurt at Slim Buttes.

"Ahh-h, your medicine is strong—" the wounded Iron Plume had said to the white doctor as the pain in his torn belly eased towards the sleeping.

So the white man with the little leather sack came and talked to Black Shawl. He came horseback, with his wife along, sitting on her horse in a way very funny to the northern Indians. Some thought she had only one leg, others saying it was only the sideways riding.

So—? Then this must be the way the Grabber rode when he had the bad disease.

But those who remembered the Holy Road said it was not disease that made the wives of the whites ride like this, but the shame of having legs.

"Hoh!" the Indian women cried in astonishment, and ran to see the white woman so very fine on her horse, with the black cloth thin as smoke tied over her face and the green feather blowing on her hat. Inside the lodge they saw her man working with Black Shawl, a trader's daughter along to interpret, explaining that the thumping on the breast, the laying of the ear against the back was part of the white man's medicine way. And as she talked, the pretty girl turned her big black eyes upon the hostile leader even though he had no notice for her beyond the hope of help for his woman.

So Black Shawl let the things that were to make her well be done, and Crazy Horse had another friend among the whites. There were some among the Indians who thought he should keep to the medicine men of his own people, and soon there were some, too, saying that he was beginning to see the bold-eyed traders' daughters around the agency, particularly those of Long Joe Larrabee, the scout for the soldiers.

The first time Crazy Horse went to the agency he saw something else there—the angry, burning hate in the face of a boy that he suddenly knew was the son of No Water. And then one noon as he came around the back way from a smoking on Crow Butte he found Black Buffalo Woman in the shade of a tree, sitting alone, as she usually did, working with awl and sinew. She arose and pulled her blanket over her face, as one who wishes not to be seen, and so Crazy Horse passed her in respectful silence, remembering all that had been between them. Playing down the slope was a girl, six or seven years old, and upon her Crazy Horse looked openly. It was true she was lighter than the others—about like young Little Hawk as a boy. But she did not seem a daughter, not like They Are Afraid of Her, whose bones lay alone in that far north country.

Almost before the grass was worn from the camp of Crazy Horse, two Oglalas slipped in from the north. They searched out his lodge, brought bad news. Lame Deer of the little band of Minneconjous who had stayed out was dead. Not killed in open fighting but in a council with Bear Coat, under a white flag.

Ahh-h, once more it was done! And when the messengers were fed and resting on the visitors' side of his lodge Crazy Horse went away to a little hill to sit alone, thinking of this thing. Another good man killed by the soldier chief who had very many Lakotas and Cheyennes in the shadow of his guns at the Tongue River fort. And here, too, there were many thousands of people and all had to sleep within three miles of the fort. Even if the soldiers could be trusted, it was bad to live so close together, not only for the smelling of the camps that were not moved but here, with nothing for the people to do, there was too much talking, scheming, and quarreling—not quarreling loud and before the lodge as the whites did, but in silence, behind the blanket and in the darkness of the breast.

When Crazy Horse got back to the lodge the northern men were gone and White Hat and some others sat in their places. They were on the way to a medicine dance at a camp of the Loafers and wanted him to ride along, had brought an extra horse. Many would be there.

Crazy Horse knew about it—a show put on for some visitors of the soldier chiefs, the medicine man painted up to look bad, singing the howling songs, throwing his voice around, making things come out of the air for their astonishment, and pay. When it wasn't something like this it was the dances of the traders' sons, with the whisky and the fighting, or, in the daytime, the racing by the horses of the scouts.

But Crazy Horse knew he must keep the soldier chiefs of good heart—and so he went with White Hat.

All the first week there was much of this visiting from the soldier chiefs and the agent, beginning with friendly talk and ending with questions about the Custer fight—who was in it, were any soldiers captured, did the Indians have white men to direct the battle, and who killed Long Hair—and never one word of their agency or when they could go home, as had been promised. It was making others besides Crazy Horse uneasy.

Soon the soldier chiefs were speaking well of the hostile Crazy Horse, calling him a fine, quiet, and modest man, one much concerned with the welfare of his people. Even his anger at the picture men, those with the black box who would catch his shadow as that of Red Cloud and others had been caught seemed good to them. Soon they no longer came to ask questions but sat at his fire as they did at no other Indian's, talking about hunting and about war as one soldier chief to another.

The first to show concern about this friendliness, turning his thick lip down as he spoke of it, was the Grabber, Grouard as he now called himself, claiming he was born somewhere in the salt sea and not Indian or black man. He had seen White Hat in the lodge of Crazy Horse the first evening after the hostiles came in, when he was hot with anger at the laughing of the northern women as he came through the camp circle.

"Hoh! See the Grabber!" they had cried out to one another from fire to fire. "He is walking well again!" Perhaps it had not been the bad disease after all but the rubbing of the white man's pants that made him walk like that the time the Cheyennes chased the scouts back to the soldiers.

But when they saw that it was the flap of the Crazy Horse lodge that the Grabber lifted, they were silenced. While he was there White Hat and another officer had come in, Crazy Horse already treating them as friends. And so when they left, the Grabber made them a talking, saying to White Hat not to go to the hostile's lodge unless he was along to protect him. It was dangerous.

The little soldier chief laughed. "Oh, come off," he said.

Soon others around the agency noticed this good face that the officers were turning upon Crazy Horse, noticing too that the young friendlies who followed him with their eyes that first day were now following him with their moccasins. Once more Woman's Dress had to see the people gather around the light-haired one, even Young Man Afraid and others who had never given him the notice he felt a grandson of Smoke should have. But he was a scout and some of the little soldier chiefs liked him. Perhaps he could use the hostile leader to get even closer to them, particularly now that the agency had no chief of its own.

Nor was Red Cloud blind to these things, with even White Hat, who had promised to help him, going to the hostile in friendliness. Wrapping his blanket about him, the Bad Face went angrily to his lodge, where the new white chickens of his wife roosted on the top of his bedstand and on the case that held his war bonnet. Here he sat a long time, his pipe cold. Finally he called his relations to him, special ones, Woman's Dress and his brothers, and No Water.

Like the smell of a dead dog spreading through the village on a warm afternoon, and as hard to find and to drag away, came a whispering of plans to make a big chief of Crazy Horse over everybody. And before anyone seemed to know where this talking started, came the news that White Hat was letting most of his winter scouts go and was enlisting two hundred and fifty new ones, many from the hostiles. Once more the Grabber made warning words against Crazy Horse, but the soldier chief was having other troubles with the hostile leader. Crazy Horse did not want to put on the soldier coat; he wanted his agency.

Still, there was nothing here for a man to do in the waiting and as scouts they would get a horse and a Sharps carbine each, and could at least chase the whistle of the fleeing antelope once more. So Crazy Horse and twenty-five of his followers finally joined. They were to work like the *akicita* of an Indian village, help keep order around the agency, chase troublemakers and any young warriors who might sneak off to a little raiding.

Now more scouts and traders' sons went running to the fort, saying it was dangerous to arm the hostiles. Besides, Three Stars had promised them last winter that they would have the good places around the agency, be set up over those they brought in from the north. When the soldier chief said he wanted to show confidence in the hostiles, treat all the Indians alike, there was much grumbling and anger and jealousy, even Billy Garnett in it, some saying it was to please his sister. She was beading a flower-design vest for the Grabber and it was well known that he wanted the northern Indians kept sitting around their lodges, prisoners in all but the irons, saying they might make trouble.

"Make trouble for the Grabber," those who knew about the white-man killing in the Missouri country told each other. He had been living with the whites so long that he thought the Indians would tell this thing against a son of their own people. It seemed that was why he had gone to Spotted Tail agency until the time came to take some scouts to the north country, although he was having trouble with the traders' sons there too, the Bordeaux family and their friends.

Some from the Indians were going to the soldier chiefs, too—Woman's Dress and No Water and even Red Cloud himself, with Red Dog close behind, going up there with long faces, speaking of Crazy Horse as a dangerous man. It seemed the officers only laughed, and soon there were more stories about the Hunkpatila being made chief of all, of the Brules too. What would Spotted Tail say when he heard his nephew would sit over him? And how about the son of the one who had been made head of all the Lakotas by Conquering Bear, the Red Cloud people asked, suddenly remembering the bigness of Young Man Afraid.

But Crazy Horse was busy working for a home for his people, disappointed that not even the soldier coats they put on to please White Hat worked, not knowing about his promise to help put Red Cloud over all the Oglalas. One story Crazy Horse did hear from the traders' sons and daughters around the fort. It seemed that the big soldier chief called Sheridan was talking strong for locking up the hostile leaders, taking them away, or even killing them as was done with the Santees that were caught after the Minnesota troubles.

"But Three Stars has promised that nobody will be hurt," some said.

"A white-man promise—"

Yes, that might be true, Crazy Horse agreed, and did anybody say when Three Stars was coming?

Towards the end of May there was news of short rations at Spotted Tail, and of many buffalo seen in the north country where the scouts had gone, making the people look that way with hungry eyes, for the beef was bad at Red Cloud too, and very little. Never before had the northern people been hungry when the grass was tall.

But now Three Stars was coming after almost a whole moon wasted. Spotted Tail was one of the first to reach the council ground and Crazy Horse went over for a visit. The Brule was heavier, almost like the day he had come back from the white man's iron house, twenty years ago, and sitting in a robe of coldness towards everything to be done here. He, the head of two agencies, had to get permission from the Great Father to come just this little ways, he said. So the Three Stars who had lifted him high was just another soldier chief to him, just one of many soldier chiefs.

Finally the day had come, with the visiting officers settled on a prairie hill south of the agency, the Indians gathered thick on both sides, leaving the place before the whites empty. Here the scouts with the soldier coats over their breechcloths made the drillings that White Hat had showed them. On their many-colored horses, Crazy Horse riding his yellow pinto again, they rode up in fine, straight lines, turned, charged, and turned again, swinging around like wheels running inside wheels. When it was done the warriors fell back and the headmen rode up in a slow line to the whites and, dismounting, marched past to greet the one called Three Stars.

A long time the soldier chief held to the hand of Crazy Horse, looking at the straight, boy-slender warrior, the brown hair, the long, light-brown eyes, the soldier chief's hairy face seeming hard as a rock above a winter-brown thicket. While they stood so, their hands together, the Lakota thought of the two attacks on the peaceful Cheyenne camps, and on Iron Plume at Slim Buttes. And finally he thought of the good day on the Rosebud. Perhaps the white man remembered this too, for a little laughing seemed to move his bearded mouth.

"Hou, *cola!*" he said a second time, and then letting his old enemy go, turned to the impatient friendlies pushing up.

The big council was held on a flat place, two miles southeast of the agency, with Crow Butte looking down upon them. It was true there were the white tents of many soldiers standing near, but there were no walls around anybody as when the Black Hills were taken away.

The chiefs came up in a walking line to their places in the circle —Oglalas, Brules, Minneconjous, Cheyennes, and Blue Clouds— with the bearded, gray-eyed Three Stars, the other soldier chiefs, and Billy Garnett, the interpreter, on folding chairs before them.

When the smoke was done, Young Man Afraid arose to welcome their white brother. Many had been here to make the crooked talk to the Indians, he said, trying to fool them into leaving this country. But the chiefs who had been to the Indian Territory saw that even the trees grow hollow in that country, and many among them knew about the Missouri from living there, and they would not go there either.

"When the scouts were with you last winter they told you what we wanted and you promised strong to help us. So we sent word to the Crazy Horse Indians that when they came in we would have an agency in our country. We are shamed before them that this has not been made true, but now you are here and we remind you so you will not forget."

Next Three Stars turned to the hostiles, to Crazy Horse, but he was silent and Little Hawk rose to speak for him, his fine voice making these soldier chiefs look at each other in surprise.

Yes, he was a hostile, the old Oglala said, and glad of the name. They had been living out in their own country in the good way that was given them by the great ones of their people, long ago, eating fruit and the game that grew there and looking for no trouble. But the soldiers kept coming into their lands with the shooting guns, so what could they do? It was not the Indians who went out making wars in the white man's country, but always the whites pushing in, killing the helpless ones, burning their homes, taking everything.

Then, in the Moon of Frost in the Lodge, the scouts rode up to ask them to stop fighting, saying if they came in the great soldier chief Three Stars would help them get an agency in their own country.

"But now—" Little Hawk stopped to look all around the circle of Indians, "now," he said, "that we are here, we are told a very bad thing—that the whites want to put us into another, an unknown country!"

With his arms folded over his breast he looked sternly into the face of Three Stars until the white man's cheeks turned redder under the beard and the windburn of the plains, and the interpreter was told to hurry the Oglala up.

"Yes, I will finish," Little Hawk said quietly. "There is only one thing more. We wish to know if you are the same man the scouts represented to us as Three Stars, the white man who speaks with the straight tongue?"

There was silence over the people, the hostiles and the friendlies too, many afraid at such strong talking. Then, before any more words could be made, Red Dog, speaking for Red Cloud, was on his feet, facing the Indians, holding up his hand for waiting. "One of the agency Indians has spoken, and one of the Crazy Horse people. Now we want the soldier chief to give an answer before anything more is said. Too much talk confuses the white man."

So Crook arose, his gray eyes hard and angry, but the words of his tongue soft enough. He was glad to see the northern Indians doing so well on the agencies. It was not he or the other soldiers who wanted to fight the Indians but the orders of the Great Father, who must be obeyed. And the Indians always shot at them when they went there.

"It was the Indian's country!" some cried out, others giving the anxious signs for silence, seeing that the soldier chief's bearded face looked like a dog's with a squirrel in his mouth when another comes to steal it.

But soon he was talking again, admitting that he had told the scouts he would help them. "When the stragglers are all in from the north country we will go to Washington and I will ask help from the President. There is a new Great Father there, not the one some of you saw. He is very busy but we will go when he has more time. And in the moon for the late summer hunt I shall let you go to the north country as I promised some of you. Go, and return here without making trouble for anyone, with time enough up there for drying the winter meat."

"Hou, hou!" the Indians cried, some of the northern people among them. Only a few with Crazy Horse seemed to see that this was throwing away the promise of the agency, and giving them a smaller one of a hunt to be made and a traveling to a new Great Father, when he had time. Now the heart of Crazy Horse was truly fallen down.

After the council there was a feast, with Iron Hawk, a man noted for his knowledge of the history of his people, making the ceremonial. Silently he offered the first piece of meat to the sky and the earth and the four directions. Then he spoke of the great ones of the Lakotas in the buffalo days, and of the time now and to come, when they would all be walking in peace beside the white man on the good new road.

Then the *akicita* carried the food around, the soldier chiefs, as honored guests, receiving the ceremonial kettle of dog. Three Stars cleaned his wooden bowl but White Hat passed his to the Indian behind him with a dollar. There was great laughing over this, that the one always with the Indians had not learned to eat their meat as well as his chief, who seldom sat at their fire.

When the feasting was done Three Stars went to the railroad to meet the great soldier chief Sheridan, who was going up through the Indian country. Some said he was planning to make more soldier forts around the Powder River. The Crazy Horse Indians heard this in silence.

Then almost at once another bad thing was done; the Cheyennes were driven south. They had tried hard to please the hurry-up whites, coming in through the deep snow, eating their worn-out horses on the way, instead of waiting for the grass as the others did. Now, almost before they could fill their lean bellies, they had to go to the Indian Territory that many knew as a country where the earth was iron, the streams long dead, and only the gullies that were the memory of their paths cutting across the land. There was mourning in their camp over this but they went. Truly the soldiers have ways of making the people do what they want.

Crazy Horse watched them go, with soldiers on all sides so no one could turn back, and he thought of the few still out in the north country. It was good that Buffalo Calf Road, the brave young woman of the Rosebud fight, was there. It was indeed true that a people is never whipped until the hearts of its women are dust.

But what can they do when there is nothing for the children to eat?

Since the big council Crazy Horse seemed like one with the no-motion disease, like old White Wolf, who was only a load of meat on a blanket. All he could do was make a talk with his father and Touch the Clouds before they returned to Spotted Tail agency, wondering if it might not be better for his people there, with everything done through one man and no rows of moccasin tracks to the agent or the soldier chiefs every day or so, making complaints, working for power. Besides, there were so many bad whites around Red Cloud, thieves and killers and robbers—the Gray Men. It was not only that they stole the Indian horses but they had much whisky around and were bad for the young people, both the traders' children and the Indians. He would try to speak of the Brule agency to his friend the officer of Fort Robinson.

But they were very busy, White Hat drilling his scouts, going to the races, dances, feasts, and the beef issues—anywhere the Indians gathered. He was always with some of the younger Oglalas —getting to know the Indian, he called it, asking questions about the camps and councils and wars. Only later did they find out that he was sending the stories straight to the Great Father.

"Like a young village-man, trying to get ahead by laying his ears to the lodge skins and carrying the stories to the old chiefs!" Little Hawk said.

Barely had the travois of Worm scratched up the dust towards Spotted Tail before White Hat knew of the talk Crazy Horse had had with his father, his impatience with Three Stars and the things done here, and his looking towards the peace of the Brule agency. So the little soldier chief talked to some of his favorites and then called in Joe Larrabee, asking the old French-breed scout about the pretty daughter who interpreted for the doctor and Black Shawl.

"But she is a wearer of the flowers, the flower patterns in the beadwork, a trader's daughter, as we say," Long Joe complained.

"Crazy Horse is lighter-skinned than she. Anyway, what difference does it make? You married a full blood."

"But my daughter is the woman, and the one she marries must come to her people—"

"Doesn't she belong to her mother's people, as her brother would?"

"It is not the same," the scout insisted. "Besides, this Indian, he has nothing to pay—"

White Hat went away looking pleased. Perhaps a few American horses could help keep Crazy Horse satisfied here at Red Cloud.

But in the lodge of the Oglala there was something else of trouble. Men came to sit at his dark fire late at night, bringing news from the white man's telegraph and his papers. The soldiers were fighting the Nez Perce, chasing them with guns, the warriors fighting back.

Ahh-h, a tribe of friendlies, always at peace with the whites. If there was no safety for the women and children of the Nez Perce, others better look out.

Crazy Horse lived as far as he could from the whites, the whole three miles from the agency, with the other northern Oglalas around him and some from the other camps, too. As the moon began to fatten towards sundance time, almost everybody else, including the breeds and whites, moved down with their tents and covered wagons to watch this ceremonial done in the old-time way by the northern people.

Crazy Horse knew why they came but he made them welcome, the *akicita* showing the people where to camp for water, wood, and grass. When the time came all the Indian lodges were moved into a great circle, set very close together, and yet making a camp over two miles long. In the center stood the holy pole with its smooth dance place and the sun shelter of new-cut pines all around the outside. White Hat was there to see everything, watching the pole selected and carried in, and the warriors from all the camp charge the man-monument that was made as nearly like a man as could be in all its parts, the one striking it first to be the strongest against the enemy all the year. They made a great running for it, even though there was no enemy left that they might fight.

Next there was the play battle, this time the fight on the Little Big Horn, with the Crazy Horse warriors taking the part of the Indians, the friendlies and some of the traders' sons being Long Hair's soldiers. But when the fighting started the blood of the warriors ran too hot and instead of using the bows just for touching, they cried "Hoka hey!" and struck hard or even grabbed up the war clubs from their belts. So the scouts and traders' sons fired with their revolvers and drove the unarmed Indians from the dancing camp. But they got some guns and came charging back, and now there was real shooting, the women crying out as the sides pushed together. If one man was hit to fall, it would be a bloody fight. White Hat saw this and galloped in to stop his scouts, but the fighting was done before he got there. Crazy Horse had ridden into the place of smoke and bullets between the two sides and, holding his hand up in the peace sign, cried: "Friends! You are shooting your own people!"

Everything stopped, the air still as before lightning, the people not seeming to breathe, afraid a bullet might find the man of the Oglalas, for there were surely some who would shoot if they thought no one could say who it was, afraid only that the Crazy Horse people would tear them to pieces as the angry grizzly does the rabbit that gets in his way.

The rest of the dance went on as always, some making the sungazing, some dancing with the tongs from the top of the holy pole tied through the bloody breast, others dragging the buffalo skulls from rawhide ropes fastened through the back muscles until they tore loose. The whites watched these things, their faces excited or pale according to their nature, but seeing everything, White Hat speaking often of the following the warriors gave Crazy Horse and his power not only over the hostiles, but over the young men of the friendlies when they were war-heated. It beat anything the soldier chief had ever seen, he said, some noticing that his mouth was sour as from green plums as he spoke, for it seemed he would like to call the young men his own.

Crazy Horse never was much to watch the dancing, besides, there was a new woman in his lodge, the eighteen-year-old daughter of Joe Larrabee. She was pretty, one of the prettiest of the traders' daughters, and Long Joe had hoped to make a better marriage for her, not just a few ponies.

"Wait, if things come out right, you will be well paid," White Hat had promised him.

And as soon as Long Joe had the ponies, Crazy Horse carried the girl off on his pinto. It was said the wives of the soldier chiefs liked this way very much, and came riding towards the northern camps more than ever, hoping to see the great war chief and his young second wife.

It caused much talking over the beadwork and the plum-pit games, or in the line waiting for the weekly issue of rations—wherever the women gathered. Some of the northern Oglalas thought Crazy Horse should have taken a wife from his own people, at least an Indian. But the friendlies said not many of the flower-pattern women, the traders' daughters, married full bloods until they were old and thrown away. They thought Crazy Horse had been honored.

"Hoh!" the northern women cried in astonishment at this foolish talking. There were many traders' daughters, but only one Crazy Horse on all the earth.

Some of the Indians looked at this thing done as the bait of a dead-fall swallowed, thinking there must be something secret to this, with the agents and other whites always talking against the second wives, wanting them thrown away, a thing the older people had found hard to understand. And now a soldier chief himself planned it for Crazy Horse to take another wife into his lodge. It was the girl who told these things. She liked to visit and talk. Long Joe, too, had the busy and complaining tongue.

"Another woman to take his heart from the people, when they

are needing him—" Little Hawk said to Worm in the lodge carefully darkened so none could know that he had left Red Cloud
agency without permission.

"Ahh-h, it is a little thing, and if it gives him even a short time of
joy—there may not be much more for the Strange One," the father
said, speaking slowly. And Little Hawk, remembering the holy
medicine of his brother, made no more words of his uneasiness.

But nothing of this seemed to touch the lodge of Crazy Horse.
With more resting for Black Shawl, no meat to make here, no skins
and robes to tan, no lodges to strike for fleeing over the snow, and
with the good white man's medicine, her face, bent over the beadwork with her friends, was rounding once more, as a Lakota
woman's should be. Under the pine-branch shelter beside the
lodge Crazy Horse listened to his new wife talk of the white-man
things she knew and the news she brought back from her visits with
her people, from the trading store or the dances, for as a Lakota
wife she was free to go where she liked.

Sometimes she brought back the white-man newspapers, with
stories of the iron road, the railroad, wanting to give the people
running it less pay-money, and when they would not have this
done, the soldiers shooting the strikers. Truly the whites were
hungry for killing to be making war on their own people all the
time, Crazy Horse thought.

It seemed there was some complaining that the soldiers were not
anxious enough to shoot, but were mixing with the workers like
friends and helping them in some places.

It was still hard to understand.

It was also hard to understand that there was no flour at Red
Cloud for the issue. The new agent, who had just come to them,
could not have stolen it already. Yet there was no flour, and the
agent, who had been the father of the Snakes a long time, with no
liking for the Lakotas, might be planning to starve the people. It
would be easy, with no parfleches of dried meat, no smoky bladders of *wasna,* and almost no hunting. The soup was indeed very
thin.

So, before the rations came, Crazy Horse was talking for his own agency again, and it seemed that the White Hat's little plans were failing, and that Long Joe would get no more horses. But there was another thing that might make the northern leader forget the agency—the hunt; and so late in the Moon of the Cherries Reddening a council was called at Red Cloud to hear the message from Three Stars about it. Seventy headmen of the Oglalas gathered, both friendlies and leaders from the northern camps. Clark, the White Hat of the agency scouts, read the paper. All who wished to go for buffalo might start as soon as the arrangements were finished. They could be gone forty sleeps, but they must go straight to the hunting country, be peaceful all the way, and return the right time.

"Hou! Hou!" the Indians cried, so loud that it was hardly noticed that some of the older men sat with silence in their mouths.

Three Stars wrote other things too. The Great Father had agreed that eighteen Indians could visit him in Washington to tell their complaints against the agency on the Missouri. They should select their best and strongest men, those who would work hard for the interests of the people. These should be ready to start the middle of September, the Moon of the Black Calf, and for the feast after today's talk. Dr. Irwin, the new agent-father, promised to issue three cattle and some coffee and sugar as soon as they decided where it was to be held.

Now Young Man Afraid arose. He said their friends and relations from the north had been with them several moons and had never been given the things to make a big feast for the others, so he thought it would be good that Crazy Horse and his cousin, Little Big Man, be given this honor.

There was a stilling at the Hunkpatila's words, as at something unexpected. Many made signs of agreement, but some of the older men sat silent within themselves, and finally Red Cloud and his shadow, Red Dog, pulled up their blankets and went away through the door. No one made talk for another place, so it was settled that the feast would be at the lodge of Crazy Horse.

When the camps were dark that night two Indians with blankets over their faces came pounding at the gate of the stockade to see the agent and would not go away. And when he went out more men came from the darkness behind the two, big men among the friendlies, and so the agent sent for the interpreter. In his office, by the light of the stinking-oil lamp, he listened to a long complaint about the things done in the council that afternoon. There was much dissatisfaction among Red Cloud's people and other bands over holding the feast with Crazy Horse. Their father, the agent, had been among them only a few days and did not know how things were here. Crazy Horse was nothing but a wild warrior who had been thrown away by the chiefs' society because he made trouble among the people, and the headmen would not go to him. They looked upon him as bad for the young men, as hostile and unfriendly to the whites.

When they said this the white-haired agent of the Oglalas looked surprised. He had been told the officers liked the northern chief, even Three Stars.

The Indians grunted at this and made the sign for children, but to the interpreter they said that Crazy Horse was no chief, that the chieftainship given him was a new kind, one in which they had no voice, and so was nothing. He did not talk to people or laugh and sing and dance as the Lakota of good heart does and they were certain that if he and his band of two hundred and forty warriors were armed for the hunt they would go on the warpath and destroy many whites. True, he did not speak of this, for he was a secret man, of whom one could know nothing, silent, going around alone, with no respect for the older men of the agency.

And as they told this story, the Indians saw that the white-haired agent of the Snakes heard it with interest, so they said they would only tell their new father what was true, for they were pleased with the years he had upon his head and respected him. Should the hostiles break out they would help him all they could.

So there was no feast at the lodge of Crazy Horse and the next day when the order came from Three Stars to let the Indians trade for ammunition for the hunt, the agent sent messages over the telegraph against this, first talking as if Crazy Horse were starting an uprising, with a warrior giving four horses for an ordinary rifle, and then saying that all the Indians were against him, even his uncle Spotted Tail.

Now there was talk thick as the sand of a windstorm sifting through the Indian camps, talk that the men pounding on the night door of the agency were friends of Red Cloud and some who hated Crazy Horse or were afraid of him.

"Ahh-h, Red Dog perhaps, and No Water and the Grabber, or some of his friends—"

"Some are saying that a brother of Woman's Dress was along."

Yes, Red Cloud and his nest of coffee-coolers, and all making strong complaints against Crazy Horse and the hunt and saying they would not go to the feast there.

"Even when Young Man Afraid was for Crazy Horse? The Young Man makes no bad plannings."

No, but he sometimes stood in the light of the jealous old men, and now it did seem that Crazy Horse might get the hunt for the people and then go to Washington, perhaps really get an agency for them in the north country.

But if the others think he is a bad man, why not let it be done? Why not let him go away from the agency here?

There is no telling. Everything is mixed up like a moving village hit by a windstorm, or the smell of a panther.

Many came to Crazy Horse to tell him these things, Little Big Man loud among them. Then the new wife came home from a visiting to say it was really mostly Red Cloud who would not come to the feast, and that Spotted Tail was strong against the hunt, as was his shadow, Swift Bear. They talked a whole day and night against it, saying the hostiles would never come back.

"Ahh-h, my Brule relative has indeed lived long among the

whites if he has forgotten that a Lakota promise is kept, even to the life of the man who makes it," Crazy Horse said over his short-stemmed pipe.

In a week it was plain that the old agency Indians had won the fight, had reached everybody with their bad talking, White Hat, the agents, the soldier chiefs at the fort, Three Stars, even the Great Father, for the trade in arms and ammunition was stopped.

"Can a man go hunting without a gun?" those who came to buy asked angrily. The traders shook their heads and showed their orders. They showed them the newspapers too, with many stories of Indian uprising, hungry Indians raiding from the country of the southern Apaches clear up to where Sitting Bull's warriors were reported coming back across the Canadian border to join the fighting Nez Perces in the Yellowstone valley by now. There were more stories of the soldiers shooting the whites called railroad strikers, some big officers wanting the Indians made helpless so the soldiers could be taken away to fight these whites.

"They say it is a revolution," old John Provost, son-in-law of Black Elk told Crazy Horse. It was as if the Indians tried to throw away all their chiefs and *akicita* and it made trouble, which it couldn't, because Indians followed anybody they liked.

It was said, too, that the whites in the Black Hills were offering a hundred and fifty dollars apiece for Indian scalps, and calling for the soldiers to come save them.

"There is nobody up there, almost nobody out anywhere, only enough to count on the fingers," Crazy Horse said.

Yes, but the contractors were missing the big money from the expedition of the last two years. They would make a noise like an Indian war, keep the soldiers from being taken away and getting many more brought in.

Truly, there was no understanding these pay-money white people, or the Lakotas either after they lived among them.

A RED BLANKET *from His Own*

THE news that the hunt was to be stopped was like a slap of the rawhide whip across the face to the northern warriors who had hoped for something to do, for a little while away from their island in the great sea of whites. The women were uneasy about it too, both those who had spent the cold, hungry time in the agency before and those who had never faced a winter, even the hard one last year in the north country, without some meat in the parfleches. To Crazy Horse and his headmen it would be one more white-man promise broken, this time by Three Stars himself, along with the other whites under whose guns their people must live. Next they would be told they could not have the agency promised them, that they must all go to the Missouri, and then there was no telling what would happen, for their faces were set very dark against this. From her friends around the soldier fort the Larrabee woman brought the story that the whites were afraid to try to move the Indians so long as Crazy Horse was around.

"They talk like old women at the robe-washings up there—" Crazy Horse said, and went out, leaving the young wife to look after him.

"What do they mean by that talking?" Black Shawl asked as soon as he was gone.

The girl lifted her black eyes from the mirror in her hand. "They mean they will put him out of the way—" she said, turning to admire the new silver hoops in her ears that Crazy Horse had not even noticed. "Perhaps when he goes to Washington—"

"Ey-ee!" Black Shawl made the woman's cry softly, covering it under her blanket.

There was little dancing or racing in the camps the week after the ammunition trade was stopped, even among the friendlies, the warriors mostly standing around silent, their dark eyes under the plucked brows following the backs of the whites as they passed. So when Billy Garnett came back with the scouts from the north he was given provisions to make a little feast for the old hostile leaders, Crazy Horse, Little Big Man, and several others, to see how they felt.

They came, Crazy Horse too, because he liked this young man who had lived some of his boyhood with them up in the Belle Fourche country. That Billy had been scouting for the soldiers up north Crazy Horse decided to forget. There were no robes to make among the whites and one had to get the pay-money somehow, it seemed. There was much that needed thinking out in this strange way of selling a man instead of the things he made, and when he had the agency, he must look to the great powers for wisdom to walk on this new road.

At Billy's they were given tin plates full of beef cooked with rice and wild onions from the hills, plenty of strong coffee with sugar, and bread fried brown. It was good and the talk among them easy, Little Big Man as usual making the bragging words, about the hunt this time, with Crazy Horse speaking quietly. They had not yet been told they could not go. It might be just more agency stories, too many old women, some wearing the breechcloths but old women just the same, sitting around with their mouths full of talk because their hands were empty.

He asked Billy about the white-man things that the soldier's son knew. It seemed he should learn the way of eating with a fork before he went to Washington. So Billy brought him one and he used it, the others laughing at this foolishness when the point of the hunting knife was as good as the fork to catch the meat and always handy at a man's belt.

But Crazy Horse spoke seriously of these things, wanting to know how it was for the Indians on the way to Washington, how a man could relieve himself and how he slept. Billy, who had been there two years ago, told it all, and the Oglala listened and seemed content. When they went he would take young Billy along, for he knew both the Lakota and the white-man ways and spoke with the straight tongue. It was good.

But it did not seem good with the whites, for messengers came riding to the Crazy Horse camp on Little Cottonwood, saying that he must move in near Red Cloud's band for a big council. The Oglala listened and made the sign of hearing without approval or agreement. He knew now that the promised hunt would be taken away, but that seemed too weak a reason for moving in with the bad-faced one who had refused to come feasting at his lodge, or for making a big council. It must be news about the agency in the north country the whites were bringing. With one promise of Three Stars lying broken on the ground, who could say what else might be done?

The new order was considered during the evening smoke the headmen always made in the center of the camp while the women worked at their cooking fires. Those who were going should move across the creek for the time of starting, Crazy Horse said. Those who had heard enough talking could stay here with him.

"You are not going?" He Dog spoke out in concern. "Ahh-h, this is no time to stand against the soldiers. Let all who love their women and children cross the creek with me. All who want their helpless ones killed by the guns stay where they are!"

To the listening people this was like the lightning come to strike among them. They had known nothing of such danger, of soldier guns aimed against them right here, and no place and no horses for fleeing, most of the warriors unarmed. But Crazy Horse spoke to quiet them. "If our friend knows of such bad trouble coming, he has kept it hidden from the others," he said.

But He Dog did not retreat. "Bad trouble is very close," he insisted.

A few days later Crazy Horse sent for him and old Iron Hawk, to show them the two cigars and a new knife in a leather sheath brought him by some big soldier chiefs called Bradley and Randall. It seemed to him that they shook hands in a bad way, and he did not like the talk they made, or the presents. The knife might mean trouble coming. When they asked him to go to Washington he told them he wanted to do what was right but had to think about going before the promised agency was made for his people.

And when Crazy Horse asked about the hunt, they looked at each other and once more he felt the bad thing around them. "Nothing has been done about that," they said.

A long time He Dog studied his old friend, sitting in a peculiar way with the knife in his hand. "My brother, you are strange to-day," he said. "Something has happened, and I wonder if it means that you will be my enemy if I move across the creek?"

Crazy Horse laughed, a sound they had seldom heard this last while. "I am no white man," he said. "They are the only people who make rules for others and say: 'If you stay on one side of this line it is peace but if you go on the other side I will kill you all.' There is still plenty of room, my friend. Camp where you wish."

So He Dog went away, his thoughts like a dark blanket about him. A few days later White Hat had him make a feast so the two soldier chiefs who had been to Crazy Horse could talk to him again. But the Oglala did not come. "Tell my brother that I am grateful," he told the messenger, "but some people over around the agency have said too many bad things about me and the soldier chiefs. I don't want to talk to them any more. No good would come of it now." He Dog told this to the officers, saying he felt very sorry but that Crazy Horse had a very strong medicine. Perhaps it was warning him.

How about the stories that he planned to break out? they asked. He Dog said he did not believe such talk. As many times as he had fingers he had heard his brother-friend say: "I came here for peace. I will not change that word." Crazy Horse was a brave man who had no need for a crooked tongue.

"Yes, he's all right. He's just had too much talking to. Don't buzz him so much," the one called Colonel Randall told White Hat. "Let him alone."

But nobody was left alone. For two weeks more stories flew back and forth, some saying now that the soldier chiefs who brought him the knife had really offered to put Crazy Horse on top of everybody. The people called Congress in Washington had said there should be no money to feed the Oglalas or the Brules unless they moved to the Missouri. Crazy Horse would be made head chief of them all if he led the Indians quietly there.

"Our Strange Man will not sell his people for power!" was the answer made. But nobody could find out how much of this story was true from Crazy Horse. "The soldier chiefs came making bad words—" was all he would say. Even Long Joe went away complaining against close-mouthed Indian sons-in-law.

The big council was not made, but a little one came together in White Hat's place with Crazy Horse and Touch the Clouds and their headmen sitting on the floor on one side, the agency Indians across the room. Grouard and Louie Bordeaux son of old Jim, were the interpreters—two men with already much trouble between them, even fighting at the agency dances. With the Grabber making the Lakota words, White Hat began to speak much of the Nez Perces. It seemed they had really come from their own country clear into the Yellowstone region and he wanted Crazy Horse and some of his followers to go up there as scouts.

The Indians gave no sign of their surprise, Crazy Horse speaking as quietly as ever against it. His people had untied their horses' tails before they came in and were done with fighting, wanting to live in the peace that had been promised them. But it seemed that the whites could not let them alone. First they were asked to give up their guns and horses and they did it, then to enlist as scouts

and they did that too, and finally to throw away the promised buffalo hunt. When, like a horse with the white man's bit in his mouth,
his own head was turned towards Washington, he had looked in
that direction. Now the Great Father and Three Stars and White
Hat were trying to put the blood of war on the faces of his people.
But they were tired of fighting. They wanted to go to the north
country, but to hunt.

Crazy Horse had spoken quietly to the end, but many around
him made the sound of approval, so many that the face of White
Hat got very red.

"You can't go on the hunt! The trouble is on up there!" he
shouted. "That is the reason I am trying to get scouts, to chase
those on the warpath out of that country!" scolding the headmen
before him in the loud, rough, white-man way that the soldier chiefs
had, as Harney had done more than twenty years before, when
he had just killed the Brule women and children. But that man
was at least a big soldier chief, not a little one like this White Hat,
and without the Grabber's bad Lakota to make the scolding words
seem worse.

Finally Crazy Horse lifted his head. "We came in for peace," he
said. "We are tired of war and talking of war. From back when
Conquering Bear was still with us we have been lied to and fooled
by the whites, and here it is the same, but still we want to do what
is asked of us and if the Great Father wants us to fight we will go
north and fight until not a Nez Perce is left."

The Grabber turned this into the language of White Hat, telling
it very fast and at the end he made it a little different, saying: "We
will go north and fight until not a *white man* is left," changing the
one name, watching the chiefs with his round black eyes. But none
of them understood what he had done, only Bordeaux, who started
up. But White Hat was too angry to hear. Waving him down, he
shouted many bad-sounding things over the head of Crazy Horse
in his unknown tongue.

The Indians wondered at this strange anger over the good words
that had been made, but before any interpretation could be given

them Three Bears jumped up from among the Red Cloud Indians, saying if the light-haired one was hungry for killing, to kill him.

Crazy Horse looked over to him in surprise. "Your hot blood must be making a great noise in your ears. Nobody is talking about killing."

By this time there was a low, angry quarreling between the two interpreters. "You speak with the crooked tongue!" Bordeaux was saying, but in Lakota, so White Hat would not understand, for he wanted to keep his pay job with the soldier chief.

"You Indian bastard!— You're one of those always trying to get me in trouble!" the Grabber answered, and slamming out through the door, left White Hat and the Indians looking after him. By now Bordeaux the trader's son had dropped into the Indian silence about quarrels, particularly before a white man. It was all around the little soldier chief, like an iron ring, so he sent for Garnett.

In a little while young Billy came in to finish the council. White Hat began again, asking Crazy Horse to change his mind and go out with the scouts and some soldiers.

"I have already said that we will go to fight. We will take some lodges and women along and make a little hunt at the same time."

"No, we are going to war. You can't fight with lodges and women along."

"We have made some good warring with all the people along—" Crazy Horse reminded the officer.

"I don't want them! You cannot take them along!" White Hat said, talking loud again.

So Crazy Horse pulled his blanket up about him. "These people don't know anything about fighting," he told his men. "Let us go home. There has been too much talking here already."

So with the Indians following him in a row, Crazy Horse left the room, the seven-foot Touch the Clouds the last of all, stooping as he went through the door.

By the time the Minneconjous got back to Spotted Tail it was spread all over the agency there that they were going north with

Crazy Horse to fight until every white man was killed. Close behind them came White Hat to tell the same story to their agent. A
council was made there, with Bordeaux and the Grabber interpreting again. Here Touch the Clouds and the others told the soldier chiefs that they did not understand this story White Hat had
carried, that Crazy Horse had said nothing about fighting the
whites, and with Clark saying he did, they could only think that
he was the man who had spread the bad untruth.

But here, with many relations around him, Bordeaux was stronger
than at Red Cloud and so he told Grouard before them all that it
was his lying words that caused the mistake, changing what Crazy
Horse said about fighting the Nez Perce until not one was left to
mean they would fight the whites until none were left.

"So it is your crooked tongue again!" Touch the Clouds said to
the Grabber. "It was not enough to lie about yourself to the whites,
but you must lie about those who have helped you."

Turning his back upon that trader's son as a worthless thing
thrown away, the Minneconjou told the soldier chiefs everything
that was done at the council, the other Indians and Bordeaux making the signs of agreement. The soldier chiefs said they believed
the word of Touch the Clouds, for they had learned to like and
respect him. But White Hat was still talking as strong as ever
against this, until it seemed that he was really a little man trying
to play big before them, perhaps planning to play big before Three
Stars too. Not even when the Grabber admitted that he must have
been wrong would White Hat change.

That night the Minneconjou rode over to talk to his cousin about
this thing that was done. Yes, Crazy Horse had heard the story and
thought it just another of the many lies that come out of the white-
man places as rattlesnakes crawl out of a rotten sandstone bluff
with the spring.

"It was the Grabber who changed your words, saying you would
fight the whites instead of the Nez Perce."

"The Grabber! And the White Hat believed him—" Crazy Horse
said slowly. "It seems that the little soldier chief has truly let the

dust stirred up by the troublemakers fill his ears." But Three Stars was coming in a few days. They would make a straight talk with him, ask about a little hunting.

Touch the Clouds heard this and filled his pipe thoughtfully, wondering at his cousin-friend. Crazy Horse must know the bad things laid out before his moccasin and yet he sat there and talked quietly about a little thing like a hunt for the people.

When the Minneconjou was gone, Crazy Horse started out for the dark bluff. As he came around the lodge a man with a blanket over his head slipped away to the other side. The Oglala looked after him. Always there was somebody smelling around his tracks these days, like wolves following a wounded bull. There seemed to be many people who wanted to make trouble, maybe get him killed, but they were all too weak to shoot him, even from the dark. It was said that No Water offered to bring his scalp to the soldier chiefs for a hundred white-man dollars—No Water, who once jumped on the handiest horse and whipped away southward to live on the agency when he saw Crazy Horse coming.

Yes, if the whites wanted him killed they would have to find somebody besides No Water to earn their money dollars.

That night Crazy Horse had another dream, one of many this last moon. Always it seemed that a spotted eagle flew high over the bluffs north of Red Cloud, but this time he plunged to earth at the dreamer's feet. And under his wing an iron knife was stuck deep, its blood filling the eagle's moccasins, strange things for a bird to be wearing—Indian moccasins beaded with the sacred zigzag of the lightning.

The story of Crazy Horse saying he was going on the warpath had traveled far over the talking wires and already the orders were coming back from the Great Father and his soldier chiefs, orders that were folded against the eyes of the people around the fort. And this made new talk. At the very least it meant more soldiers coming here, and who could say what other bad things this new secrecy covered?

When Three Stars arrived for the council, Lee, the chief of the soldiers at Spotted Tail, was there to meet him, to explain the story of the Crazy Horse trouble to him and to General Bradley of Fort Robinson. Three Stars listened and then had them tell it all to White Hat again, but still the little soldier chief said he was certain that the Grabber had talked straight. Loud words were made over this for the interpreters to hear and to carry away to the Indian camps. Surely the White Hat was letting some very bad people walk across his shadow, the northern Indians said, and some of the friendlies thought so too, and the traders' sons who knew the crooked tongue of the Grabber and what he had done that day at the council.

It seemed Three Stars said he was very glad to know what had happened. "To make a mistake in this matter would be the basest treachery to the Indians," he said. But many new horse soldiers came riding in from Laramie just the same.

Finally the day of the big council was here, and when it was long past the time for the people to be gathered, Red Feather, the young brother of Black Shawl, came riding hard to the camp of Crazy Horse, and sliding from his horse, scratched at the lodge flap, crying: "Brother, brother! Are you still there? Something very bad has been done!"

Crazy Horse was at home. "Sit and smoke and cool off, my son," he said. But the young man could not wait. Looking around the darkness of the lodge, he saw no outsider was there, no one but his sister. The Larrabee woman? She was gone, Crazy Horse said, making no more words about it.

So Red Feather told his story to the one who was still the Strange Man of the Oglalas to him. Because he had heard a bad thing at the agency store today, he went to ask Garnett about it. Yes, Billy said, the story was true, and so Red Feather had hurried here to carry the warning.

It seemed that today Big Bat and Garnett had started to the council ahead, with Three Stars and White Hat coming behind them in the ambulance, their soldiers riding around them. Out a ways they met Woman's Dress, who said that Crazy Horse and sixty of his Indians would be at the council and when he shook hands with Crook he would kill the soldier chief and then his warriors would finish the other whites. Little Wolf, the Oglala scout, had listened outside of the Crazy Horse lodge and heard this plan and told it to his brother, Lone Bear, who told it to Woman's Dress.

"The Lakota Little Wolf, who fought with us on the Little Big Horn, and who has lain so many nights beside my fire, making such bad words!" Crazy Horse said in surprise.

Yes, that was the Little Wolf. White Hat wanted to turn around as soon as he heard the story, but Three Stars asked to know if Woman's Dress was a reliable man, a man straight-talking. Young Billy thought it was too heavy a thing upon him in this bad time and said he would let Big Bat make the answer. And Bat named Woman's Dress as a truthful man, not saying that he was his cousin, nor did anyone among them seem to distrust a thing that was heard from so far away, passing through the mouths of three men, Little Wolf to Lone Bear to Woman's Dress.

At first the one called Crook still wanted to go on, saying he never started any place that he didn't get there. But White Hat talked strong against it, saying they had lost one good man to Crazy Horse when Long Hair was killed and they did not want to lose another. So Billy was sent to the council to say that Three Stars was called to the railroad. They gave him a list of Indians to bring to Fort Robinson right away, doing it secretly, so Crazy Horse would not know. But that was easy, for the chief was not there.

No, Crazy Horse said. Old Little Hawk had watched on a hill for the soldier wagon coming from Fort Robinson, and when there was none, they did not go. One does not go to sit with his enemies for nothing.

But Red Feather had more to tell. At the council Garnett took

American Horse aside, told him the message from the soldier chiefs, picked the headmen and scouts, and in half an hour they were all at the fort.

"Ahh-h, the old coffee-coolers are hot as young warriors today," Crazy Horse said.

Yes, and there, before Three Stars and Clark and the friendlies, Woman's Dress told his story again and then plans were made to take the Crazy Horse village.

"Ey—ee!" Black Shawl cried her woman's fear and slipped out, going for the horses, the men knew, for the horses to flee.

"Coming against our people!—" Crazy Horse looked around the lodge as though it were all the camp with the darkness of long night coming upon it. "They have done nothing—"

No, but the friendlies were coming against them anyway, and with guns. Crook had given orders to issue extra ammunition to the Indians. Red Feather did not know just how many there would be, but each chief had picked some followers and White Hat was offering one hundred of the dollars and a sorrel horse to the one who killed Crazy Horse. Once more No Water had stepped forward, and the soldier chief called it a brave thing to do for the Great Father.

"For the Great Father!" Red Feather repeated angrily, "—that one who has already left the track of his bullet on your face when you were not looking."

"But who are these people who are to come for us?" Crazy Horse wondered.

Red Cloud, Red Dog, Little Wound, American Horse, Three Bears, and others.

"All my old friends—"

Yes, but there were more, the Grabber too, and Young Man Afraid.

Now the face of the Oglala grew very sorrowful. Even the friend of his boyhood in this, and because of a story told by a man who got it from one who got it from a lodge-listening brother. Three tongues away, and the man they heard only the Pretty One. It would indeed have been better, Crazy Horse saw, if he had dropped his robe out in that north country than to bring an old friend into such a shameful plan.

But now there seemed only two things left to do. Slowly Crazy Horse reached above his head and lifted down his gun, the one given him as a scout by White Hat. A moment he held it across his knee, touching his fingers to the buckskin case as to a woman's hair. Then he held it out to Red Feather and the young brother-in-law took it and, blinded with tears, stumbled out into the open.

And when he was gone Crazy Horse slipped the new knife that the soldier chief Bradley had given him inside his clothes and went out to bring Black Shawl back.

But the Indians and the soldiers did not come that day, nor any of the usual string of visitors riding back and forth. Only one, a friend, slipped down from the bluffs to say that Three Stars had ordered the Indians and soldiers to capture Crazy Horse that night and then the big soldier chief had hurried away to the railroad.

Ahh-h, so Black Elk and Provost and even the Larrabee woman —all those who said that Three Stars was like all the other whites— had spoken straight!

Yes, but even more had been done at Fort Robinson. Spotted Tail was called from his agency and Bradley, the commanding officer, sent for Garnett to ask about an attack the Indians said was planned on Crazy Horse. It seemed he had not been told of the thing to be done this night, with the scouts under a man of his own fort, and his soldiers having to fight if it made trouble.

The agent came too, and He Dog. Perhaps he was the one who had carried the word to the soldier chief. Anyway, when Bradley heard the plan from Garnett, his face was red with the white man's anger.

"I will not countenance such an attack on a man like Crazy Horse, not that way, in the night!" he said. "His life is as sweet to him as ours are to us, and much sweeter to his people—"

So White Hat was told to have Garnett stop the Indians, ask

them to come to the fort early in the morning. When he started to
say that it was Crook's order, the soldier chief said he knew nothing
of that, and with the general away he was in command here. So
Billy went out and when that was done He Dog took the hand of
the soldier chief in both of his and then, turning quickly, threw the
blanket over his head and left the council.

Towards noon the next day the watchers on the bluffs saw a big
dust raised by many hundred men riding along the White Earth
River. There were agency leaders and their following, from Red
Cloud to Young Man Afraid, and many northern Indians too, even
Big Road and his warriors, with several companies of horse sol-
diers and some wagon guns along, all moving fast down the White
Earth trail, while across the river rode Clark with Little Wound's
Bear Oglalas and some Blue Clouds and Cheyennes.

So they came towards the Crazy Horse camp, the Indians in two
parts, only a few of those from the northern people with guns,
the friendlies and traders' sons all on good horses and armed like
soldiers. At first they were mixed up, but after a while the Crazy
Horse Indians noticed the others drawing together and hurrying
ahead. And in the meantime Little Big Man was riding back and
forth from one group to the other, then over to the soldiers, and
finally off to the Crazy Horse camp. When he came back he reported that the Oglala was gone.

By now sixty or seventy warriors with shields and bows and
spears, many stripped and painted for war, had collected on a
high place overlooking the river and the trail to the northern camp.
As the command approached, Black Fox, in beaded buckskin, the
tails of his war bonnet trailing below his stirrups, rode in a gallop
down upon them, singing as he came:

> *"I have been looking all my life to die.*
> *Today I see only the clouds and the ground;*
> *I am all scarred up!"*

As the warriors behind him took up the song, Black Fox stopped and folding his arms on his breast, waited for a bullet from the hundreds of rifles ready in the hands of the scouts. Everyone saw it was a brave thing to do on this day dark with weak and cowardly deeds, and even some of the friendly scouts began to sing the warrior songs, swelling the sound into a wild chanting, seeming ready to join the northern people.

But before anything could happen, American Horse rode out with the pipe, holding it up before Black Fox. "Think of the help-less women and children behind you, my friend," he said. "Come straight for the pipe!"

So there was nothing for the Lakota to do but take it, and to-gether they sat on the ground and smoked, making a long, long thing of the ceremony, while the Crazy Horse warriors rode back and forth behind their smoking man, circling and charging in a fine drilling until White Hat and some of the others were very im-patient. Finally someone saw four Indians riding over a little hill, far away.

"Crazy Horse!" the scouts cried out, pointing.

Yes, it was Crazy Horse, riding fast towards Spotted Tail agency. With him was Black Shawl and what looked like Shell Boy and the young warrior Kicking Bear, a brother of the Black Fox sitting there smoking so quietly with American Horse.

At White Hat's command thirty armed Indian scouts under No Flesh and twenty-five more under No Water, on the best horses, started after the Oglala chief, with two hundred of the white-man dollars offered to the man who got him. No Water took the lead, riding hard, but Crazy Horse had his own medicine way of re-treat, used so often against Snake and Crow. As usual, he ran his horses down hill and slowed them to a walk when climbing. So none of the scouts, not even No Water, got within shooting distance of the fleeing party all day. They saw them many times, the woman in the lead, the three men behind her, Crazy Horse hurrying her old mare along, Shell Boy and Kicking Bear riding with their guns across the horses, the only two men left of all the cloud of warriors the Oglala once led against Three Stars and Long Hair, but their guns were loaded and their hearts strong to help protect their man. and his Indian wife.

Towards the Spotted Tail country the scouts had to see Crazy Horse lengthen the ground between them, although No Water had left two horses dead along the trail and the third was white as from river foam, puffing under the sting of his rawhide whip; and as Crazy Horse reached the camp of Touch the Clouds, they saw the lodges begin to fall, the women making ready for flight while the warriors, painted and armed, rode out to meet the chasing scouts.

But not a shot was fired. No Water and the others managed to whip their worn-out horses to Spotted Tail agency, the Minne-conjous driving them hard, one warrior with a mighty lance making great sweeps and lunges at them, but the Brule scouts charged in to hold them off until No Water and his followers got through the stockade door.

Lee, the soldier chief, sent for Crazy Horse and then started out to meet him, taking the Brule agent and Louie Bordeaux along. They met the Indians coming in, several warriors in feathers and war paint. Ahead of them rode three men, on one side White Thunder, an agency Indian, on the other the tall, strong-faced Touch the Clouds, and between them the light-skinned man of the Oglalas, with not even a feather in his hair, no gun across his horse, only the folded red blanket. Behind him rode Black Crow, a Spotted Tail man, his hand ready on his rifle. But the warriors coming behind were armed too, and mostly northern Indians.

When they reached the Brule soldier place, Spotted Tail came riding up with several hundred followers. Angrily the two parties of warriors stopped in half circles opposite each other, threaten-ing, ready with guns and clubs and spears.

In the little bare place between them the soldier chief tried to make a talk with Crazy Horse, telling him he must go back to Fort Robinson. At this there was a roaring from the Minneconjous, challenged at once by the Brules, the warriors pushing hard towards each other. But all of them, even the friendlies, fell silent and moved back when Crazy Horse held up a hand, and the soldier chiefs, seeing this easy control of the angry warriors, spoke even better to him. He was a good man with his people and they would not see him hurt, Major Lee promised. Still the Oglala said nothing, but Spotted Tail had some words to make. With the scolding way the soldier chiefs once used against him he stood before his nephew.

"At my agency the sky is clear," he said, "and the air still and free from dust. I am chief here. Every Indian must obey me. You say you want to come here to live in peace. If you stay you must listen to me in all things. That is what I have to say." He made no talk of their relationship, or that Crazy Horse was a guest, and never that he thought this coming good or bad, but spoke like the whites, saying "you must, you must."

When the officers asked Crazy Horse to come to a soldier house he finally spoke his agreement, the first words he had made. There they asked him why he had left his camp and so the Oglala began to speak, softly, as though it had been a long time since he had known words at all.

He stayed with his people until a great party of scouts and soldiers came for him with wagon guns, and because he could not have the helpless ones hurt he went away. When he came in from the north he had offered the pipe to the great powers for everlasting peace. Now a few days ago he was asked to go fight the Nez Perces. It seemed they could not do this, for the promise to the powers was not to be forgotten. But finally he had said they would go and camp beside the soldiers and fight with them until the last Nez Perce was killed.

Yet it had not helped, for today the soldiers came to take him away, so he brought his sick wife to her relations here at Spotted Tail, where it was said there was peace, where he wanted all his people moved before he must leave them.

The soldier chiefs said his words were good, but that he must go to Robinson and tell these things to the officers there. If he did this they promised him no harm and would help him all they could to get his band transferred here. For the night they would give him into the hands of his friend, Touch the Clouds, and early to-morrow they would all start back to the agency.

So Crazy Horse went to sit as a guest among his Minneconjou friends and many came to lift the flap of his lodge in the darkness, some to whisper warnings of danger. "Ride!" they said, "ride north to Sitting Bull in the Grandmother's peaceful country."

But some came from the agency too, one saying Bordeaux had heard good words from the soldier chiefs. On the way in today Lee and the agent had looked back to Crazy Horse and talked seriously together, saying he was a strong young man, one who could become as great among his people in peace as he had been in war. He was not trained like the old chiefs in the harangue and the scheming or in working for power and advantage for himself, but was straightforward and dependable of tongue. His friend Touch the Clouds was a man of peace and honor. Together these two could lead their people far along the new road that runs beside the white man.

At his fire the worn-out man listened to all these voices and was silent, his hands moving uneasily upon each other, for his short pipe had been forgotten in the hurry of the morning. And across from him, on the woman's side, Black Shawl was silent too, thinking of that north country where Sitting Bull's people were, with the little snows already upon them. But the snow and the cold would seem good this night; no matter how bad the coughing, they would seem very good.

All through the darkness Crazy Horse sat in his blanket, and in the morning he was early at the soldier house, wanting his promise to go to Red Cloud given back to him. He wished the officers would go there to fix it for him and his people.

"It is told me something bad will happen—" was all he could say.

At last he saw that it had to be, so he agreed, but only if certain things were done. Neither he nor the soldier agent would take guns, the officer at Robinson should be told all that had been done here these two days, and that both Spotted Tail and the agent had agreed to let the northern people live among them if the soldier chief said it could be done. All this was promised and one thing more: Crazy Horse would be allowed to tell the soldier chiefs how his words at the council had been misinterpreted. He wanted them to understand he had said nothing of fighting white men. All he had wanted was peace.

Saying they would help him all they could, the party started, Lee, Bordeaux, Black Crow, and Swift Bear in the ambulance, and High Bear and Touch the Clouds along too. Behind them rode Crazy Horse, in dark blue shirt and leggings, one feather in his brown hair, his red blanket across his horse. With him were seven of his friends and some agency Indians.

But fifteen miles out many scouts from Spotted Tail came up and at Chadron Creek more, until there were over sixty, all in the soldier coats, and now, riding among these, Crazy Horse knew that he was already a prisoner.

Once he sent his horse fast over the top of a little hill, the scouts charging after him, as he had expected. He was not running away, he told them, just riding ahead to water his horse. But all the rest of the trail he remembered how it was to be alone that small time beyond the hill, with the earth, the sky, and the four great directions free about him as these things had been all his life until he let the sweet-talking of the agency people bring him to the white man's island. Then the scouts had come whooping over the rise, their guns in their hands, so once more he rode among the agency Indians, but back behind the ambulance, as the officer ordered.

When Crow Butte was coming near, Lee sent a note to White Hat, asking whether they should go to the fort or the agency, saying also the things they had promised Crazy Horse, particularly that Bradley let him tell his side of the trouble. There was an answer from White Hat, saying that Bradley wanted Crazy Horse brought to his office, but with nothing at all of the promises made.

The riding messengers looked like more scheming to Crazy

Horse, and as he neared the place thick with such things it seemed that he would need much strength there and so he tried to think of the man of his vision as he used to do when he went into a bad fight. But today all that seemed very long ago, and far away, while here, close behind him, was the great dust of many Indians coming. They were ahead, too, all along the trail, standing in dark bunches waiting for him. Those off to the sides, riding far away, might be his men, but they were so few, so very few. And only when he looked up to the bluffs could his heart escape the things of this day in its remembering that under that protecting wall a Frenchman once camped through a far-gone winter. Here the Oglalas had come to trade and Hump had taken the boy called Curly hunting for the little rabbits that lived in the rocks, and when he was hungry and tired from the snow they had stopped to rest, and roasted one for each on a long stick. Hump had let the boy turn them over the coals until the white meat was brown and juicy and the smell made him weak under his belt.

But in that day the country belonged to the Indians, all of it, and the friend with him then was a very great warrior, one who would have dropped his robe a hundred times before he agreed to walk this road of darkness.

As they reached the fort, He Dog came loping up, bareback, his war bonnet slapped hastily on his head. He pulled up beside Crazy Horse, shook hands with him and saw that he did not look right today, not as in those days of war when his medicine was very strong, but they rode with their horses together once more, their leggings touching, and Crazy Horse knew the anger between them was gone.

At the fort Little Big Man came walking important as the Indian police and, jerking Crazy Horse by the arm, said: "Come along, you man of no-fight. You are a coward!" The Oglala let it be said and went into an office with those from the ambulance. By now the open spaces between the buildings of the fort were filled with Indians, on one side the few who were still Crazy Horse warriors, on the other the agency scouts, with Red Cloud and American Horse at their heads, while all around them, clear back over the plain, were more Indians and horses and wagons hurrying in, making a rising noise like blood-smelling buffalo. But nowhere around was Woman's Dress, or the Grabber or White Hat or any of the others who had said so hard that Crazy Horse must be captured, nor was Spotted Tail there, although hundreds of Brules had come the long road.

While Crazy Horse and the others waited, Lee went to General Bradley. He told the officer of the wrong he believed had been done to the man of the Oglalas, and the promise he and Burke, the agent, had made that Crazy Horse should be heard, but Bradley said nothing could be done any more.

Nothing? Then it was really very bad?

Yes, the general agreed, very bad. Not even Crook could change the orders they had received. Not a hair of the chief's head would be harmed, but he must now be turned over to the officer of the day. "Say to him it is too late to have a talk."

So Major Lee put on a good face and came to Crazy Horse, telling him that night was almost here and General Bradley said it was too late for talking, but he should go with the little soldier chief and he would not be harmed.

"Hou!" the Indians said, and arose, Crazy Horse the last among them. But he shook friendly hands with the officer and went away with him, Little Big Man on the other side, two soldiers behind, some of the agency Indians hurrying ahead, seeming to know where to go. As they crossed to another building the warriors and the scouts pushing in on both sides raised a noise that became a roaring, and under it sounded the click of guns made ready to shoot.

Quietly, his blanket folded over his arm as though he were going to his lodge between two friends, Crazy Horse let himself be taken past a soldier walking up and down with a bayoneted gun on his shoulder and in through a door. Only then did he see the barred windows, the men with chains on their legs, and realize it was the iron house. Like a grizzly feeling the deadfall on his neck, the Indian jumped back, drawing the hidden gift knife to strike out around him, but Little Big Man grabbed his arms from behind. Trying to wrench free, Crazy Horse struggled into the open, dragging the stocky Indian through the door, his warriors crying out the warning: "He is holding the arms, the arms!" while on the other side the scouts raised their guns, Red Cloud and American Horse ordering: "Shoot in the middle; shoot to kill!" the officer of the day knocking the scout guns down with his sword as fast as they came up.

And between them the Indian, like a trapped animal, was heaving, plunging to get free, growling: "Let me go! Let me go!" as the angry bear growls, the knife flashing in the late sun. Then with a mighty jerk he threw himself sideways and Little Big Man had to drop one hand, blood running from a slash across his arm. But Swift Bear and other old Brule friendlies already had Crazy Horse, held him while the officer of the day tried to use his sword against him, yelling: "Stab him! Kill the son of a bitch!"

The guard came running up, lunged with his bayonet and, hitting the door, jerked the weapon free and lunged twice more. At the redness of the steel a noise of alarm, of warning rose from the watching Indians. Crazy Horse pulled at his old captors once more. "Let me go, my friends," he panted. "You have got me hurt enough."

And at these soft words all the Indians suddenly dropped their hands from him as though very much afraid. Released, Crazy Horse staggered backward, turned half around, and sank to the ground, his shirt and leggings already wet and blood-darkened.

The brightness of evening was fading from the top of Crow Butte and from all the sky over the upper White Earth country. The soldier fort at the foot of the bluffs settled into early darkness, rows of small yellow lights coming out in the windows before the evening star was clear. It seemed that every Indian was gone from Fort Robinson, even Woman's Dress, and the other scouts usually hanging around the soldiers. Most of the northern people had fled down along the river, waiting, afraid; the agency Indians gone back to their camps to get away from the trouble. At the fort the guard was heavy, many soldiers walking with guns on their shoulders, for it was known that there were Indians around under the darkness, both scouts and northern warriors, all watching the house called the adjutant's office, where it was said the great Lakota warrior lay, perhaps dying from the white man's bayonet.

No, not from a bayonet, not from the white man at all, some of the Red Cloud followers were saying through the camps. It was the knife of Crazy Horse himself, in his own hand, that hurt him in the fighting.

"Hurt him in the back?" others asked, even some friendlies, particularly those remembering the years of insults put upon them by the troublemaking Little Big Man, and now at last done carrying the night stories of the agency schemers. But many others were certain their Strange Man could not be dying. His medicine was too strong. He was only making what the whites called a fake, fooling the soldiers so he could get away. They said this behind the hand, and barely loud enough for their own ears, holding strong to the hope, some even going out to dig up the few guns long hidden against a day of need. Others were silent now that it was plain how much of this was Lakota work, with Woman's Dress, No Water, Little Big Man, and the half-Lakota Grabber all helping, and who could say how many more, for the long faces of the headmen around the agencies were suddenly well remembered. Even some of the friendlies were saying it was jealousy, the jealousy of Red Cloud and Spotted Tail for the following given Crazy Horse, that had started the stories saying he was to be made chief over all.

That was probably true, for who had told them besides the men who were owned by the agency chiefs? No white man that anyone ever heard. And where were these story-carriers tonight, others asked, and some went with guns to their lodges, but the fires were dark, even the women gone, none could tell where.

And many having to remember that they had helped the stories along covered their faces with their blankets and sat in silence, particularly after they heard that the soldier chiefs were saying it would be easy to move the Indians now.

Ahh-h, then it was true that the whites had picked this day to get rid of Crazy Horse so they could drive the people to the hated Missouri!

It seemed so, for at the fort a wagon had been ready since morning to take their chief down to the railroad and then to an iron house in a far place called Dry Tortugas, from which it was said no one returns.

Ahh-h, surely their Strange Man would have died locked away from his people. None had ever worked so much of his life for them. Even the friendlies who went north last winter remembered that they found him out alone in the hills, hoping for a sign to show how they could be saved.

And some who listened to the many good words being made tonight for the wounded man remembered that yesterday, even today, few, very few were on his side or the soldiers and the agency people would never have dared do this thing.

So the people sat around their darkened lodges, wandering in their minds like buffalo who have lost their leader. Of them all only He Dog had seen the man since he sank down into the dust before the guardhouse, with his warriors on one side, armed mostly with war clubs, and across from them the many agency scouts holding their soldier rifles, loaded with the ammunition issued today for the attack. And no one was running in to carry away the wounded man between them, not one of the dozen there who had been helped from the battlefield by him.

Before this, and before the shame of his own weakness, He Dog stood bowed a long time, his head down in sorrow, and when he could look again, he saw that all the Indians had fallen back and many, many soldiers had come up all around him, guns in their hands, their eyes in anger upon him. With his red agency blanket around him, the man waited, motionless, for whatever was to come.

Finally White Hat ran up from somewhere, saying he might go to Crazy Horse, and so He Dog went to the wounded man with the knife lying in the dust beside him and the dark patch of his blood that reflected the sacred sky. Stooping to speak, he saw that the Oglala was bad hurt and so he laid his red blanket over him and with arms folded stood at the feet of his friend.

Then Touch the Clouds came wading through the soldiers, parting them before him like grass with the barrel of his gun. He, too, saw how it was and waited beside He Dog for the army medicine man. And when the doctor was there, pulling the blood-soaked shirt from the wounds, one deep through the kidney, he looked to the two friends and made no word. So Touch the Clouds went to ask that the chief might be taken to a lodge of his people to die, but this, too, Bradley refused, not believing the doctor's word that the hurt was a bad one, but saying he could be put into the adjutant's office instead of the guardhouse. And when Touch the Clouds asked permission to stay with his cousin-friend, he was told he must give up his gun.

Quietly the tall Minneconjou looked down upon the white-man soldier. "You are many and I am only one, but I will trust you," he said.

Then they carried the wounded man to the place where he now lay, in the kerosene-lighted room under the red blanket on the floor, with only Touch the Clouds permitted to sit with him. Several times the white medicine man came with the sleeping water that quieted his moving and the low growling to the enemies Crazy Horse thought were about him. But none of them were there, and none of those who came to his lodge all the summer, talking this way and that, turning his face in as many directions as a *heyoka* dancer. The agent had not come to him, or White Hat or Bradley and Randall, or Three Stars, who was far away, getting ready to set up new forts in that north country and to make a hunt for himself, a hunt for buffalo and elk and big-horn sheep.

As the night lengthened, the stars turned towards midnight, and there was still no good sign to the watchers, no sign at all, many of the northern people lost their ears for the stories of hope and sat silent and dark in their blankets. Some of the women began to keen a little to themselves, afraid, for it was well known that their Strange Man could never be hurt by an enemy except when his arms were held, as the time that No Water shot him, and today— the arms always held by Little Big Man.

In the soldier house Touch the Clouds still sat beside the wounded man on the floor, with Worm there too now, his wrinkled old face half-covered with his blanket. When the father first came for permission to go to his son, the soldier chiefs asked for his bow and his knife. He knew why it was done but he gave them up without protest, for they would indeed be poor weapons to meet the sorrows of this day. Never could there be a gun strong enough or whites enough to kill if Crazy Horse died, never enough whites on all the earth to kill to make the heart of a father good for such a son gone.

And when Worm was brought to the bare, dusky room where Touch the Clouds was watching, he stooped over the wounded man, saying, "Son, I am here—"

But there was only the slow, heavy breathing of the medicine sleep and the feet of the soldier guard outside, walking up and down on the gravel, turning his face away from the shadow huddled against the wall, a shadow such as young Curly had once seen when another Lakota woman, the wife of Conquering Bear, watched the place of her wounded man.

So the night grew old and the fading moon arose, bringing a coldness into the soldier house. Gradually the breathing of the sleeping man changed. Once or twice he stirred a little and each time Worm stooped over him, but there was nothing. Then, slowly the eyes of the wounded warrior opened, moved guardedly over the strange room of his enemies.

"I am here," Worm said.

Now the son saw him. "Ahh-h, my father," he whispered. "I am bad hurt. Tell the people it is no use to depend on me any more now—"

For a while it seemed he would say more, then slowly his head seemed to settle back, the eyes opened wide, and one long brown braid slid to the floor. Gently Touch the Clouds replaced it, holding it on the breast of his friend with his strong hand. And in the yellow light of the lamp the two men wept, the tears like rain washing over live rocks, rocks in that old north country of the Powder and the Yellowstone, for the Strange Man of the Oglalas was dead.

White-Man Chronology

OF CRAZY HORSE COUNTRY

1849 Fort Laramie bought for military post.

1851 Great Fort Laramie Treaty Council, to establish roads and military posts and to bring peace to Plains tribes in return for annuities.

1854 Grattan Massacre, in Brule village, August 19, 1854.

1855 Battle of Blue Water, September 3, 1855.

1857 Sumner's expedition against Cheyennes, struck them July 29, 1857.

1861 Civil War draws soldiers from frontier posts.
Telegraph to California completed.

1863 Bozeman road through Powder River country established.

1864 Sand Creek massacre.

1865 Platte Bridge fight, July 25–6, 1865.
Powder River expedition under Connor.

1866 Forts Reno and Phil Kearny built on Bozeman trail.
Fetterman massacre at Fort Phil Kearny, December 21, 1866.

1867   Union Pacific Railroad through Sioux country.
        Wagon Box fight near Fort Phil Kearny, August 2, 1867.

1868   Attack on old Horsecreek station by Crazy Horse, March 19, 1868.
        Signing of Treaty of 1868.

1870   Sioux chiefs taken to Washington.

1872   Baker fight, August 14, 1872.

1873   Custer fight with Sioux at Yellowstone, August 11, 1873.

1874   Black Hills expedition, under Custer.

1875   Jenney expedition into Black Hills.
        Lone Tree council for sale of Black Hills.

1876   Reynolds fight, March 17, 1876.
        Rosebud battle, June 17, 1876.
        Custer massacre, June 25, 1876.
        Sibley scouts attacked, July 7, 1876.
        Battle of Slim Buttes, September 9, 1876.
        Miles's fight with Sitting Bull, October 21, 1876.
        Dull Knife fight, November 25, 1876.
        Sioux chiefs killed at Fort Keogh, December 1876.

1877   Miles strikes Crazy Horse, January 8, 1877.
        Crazy Horse surrenders, May 6, 1877.
        Railroad strike, summer 1877.
        Nez Perce outbreak, summer 1877.
        Crazy Horse killed, September 5, 1877.
        Sioux moved from Nebraska agencies to Missouri River, fall 1877.

Bibliography

(limited to the more important unpublished sources used)

✿

HINMAN-SANDOZ INTERVIEWS
1930–1, with Oglala Sioux who knew Crazy Horse

HE DOG, *brother-friend of Crazy Horse, approximately same age, came in with him, rode beside him on last day.*

LITTLE KILLER, *brother of Club Man, who married sister of Crazy Horse.*

RED FEATHER, *younger brother of Black Shawl, a wife of Crazy Horse.*

SHORT BULL, *youngest brother of He Dog.*

MRS. CARRIE SLOW BEAR, *daughter of Red Cloud.*

WHITE CALF, *government scout, 1876, saw the stabbing of Crazy Horse.*

✿

INTERVIEWS FROM RICKER COLLECTION, NEBRASKA STATE HISTORICAL SOCIETY

Judge E. S. Ricker, an early resident in northwest Nebraska and ten years an employee in the Indian Bureau, Washington, D. C., spent much of his later life collecting material on the Plains In-

dians, including the following interviews, in 1906–7, pertinent to Crazy Horse and his region, with the accompanying identifications:

Charles Allen, Pine Ridge agency, biographer of Red Cloud.

American Horse, Oglala chief.

Alexander Baxter.

Herbert Bissonnette, son of Joseph B.

Louis Bordeaux, son of Jim, born 1850, educated at Hamburg, Iowa, official interpreter at Spotted Tail in 1877 troubles.

Mrs. Julia Bradford, daughter of Hank Clifford.

Don Brown, with Crook, summer 1876.

John Burdick, with Stanley 1873 expedition.

Chips or Encouraging Bear, medicine man of No Water's camp.

The Reverend Mr. Cleveland, Episcopal minister at Spotted Tail Agency.

Mrs. Clifford.

Charles Clifford, son of Hank.

George W. Colhoff, member of 5th U. S. Volunteers, a galvanized Yankee regiment sent west to protect Union Pacific Railroad, 1865, stayed, married Sioux woman.

John Comegys, with Johnston's army of 1857, wintered with freight wagons at O'Fallon's Bluff.

General Augustus Whittemore Corliss, captain with Yellowstone expedition, 1873, sent to Red Cloud, 1874.

Cornelius A. Craven, scout for Carr, in charge of Red Cloud beef herd, 1875.

Sam Deon, came to upper Platte country 1847, lived much with Red Cloud.

Dr. Charles Eastman.

Moses Flying Hawk, half-brother of Black Fox.

Billy Garnett, son of Captain Richard B. Garnett, commanding officer at Fort Laramie in early fifties and an Oglala woman.

James Garvie, part Sisseton Sioux.

William Girton, five years student at Carlisle.

Mrs. Nettie Elizabeth Goings, half-sister of Frank Grouard, the Grabber.

Iron Hawk, northern Sioux with Crazy Horse.

Mrs. Nick Janis, widow of the early trader.

W. R. Jones, with Connor in 1864.

L. B. Lessert, called Ben Claymore, Clemow, or Clement, came to Laramie country in 1853.

William Denver McGaa.

Dave Mears, brother-in-law of Crook and his assistant chief packer in 1876.

Magloire Alexis Mousseau, working for American Fur Company spring 1850, to upper Platte country 1852, had Indian wife.

Big Bat Pourier, Frenchman, born St. Charles, Missouri, 1843, came to upper Platte country in boyhood, married sister of John Richard, Jr.

R. O. Pugh, at Red Cloud during first Black Hills council.

Red Cloud, Bad Face warrior and agency chief (unfortunately the great Sioux was almost blind by this time, and failing in health).

Red Hawk, as told to Nick Ruleau, was northern Indian.

Respects Nothing, out with northern Indians.

Nick Ruleau, early fur-trade employee.

Jack Russell, Denver 1863, later joined Richards on Platte, scout for Crooks starvation march 1876.

Frank Salaway, born in Idaho country, 1828, French-Indian, married Big Mouth's sister.

F. E. Server, around Crow agency 1872, sergeant in U. S. cavalry, eighteen years in the army.

John Shangrau, scout under Louis Richard with Crook, spring 1876, at Red Cloud when Crazy horse made prisoner, September 1877.

A. G. Shaw, to country 1862 with 11th Ohio Cavalry to protect overland stage from Laramie to South Pass under Colonel Collins, married a Sioux woman, living at Spotted Tail.

Shiveley, married a Crow woman, 1872.

Short Bull or Buffalo, as told to Dr. Walker, 1906.

Standing Bear, Oglala, in Custer battle.

Standing Soldier #1, scout sent to bring Crazy Horse back from Spotted Tail, 1877.

Richard C. Stirk, came to country 1870, charge of beef herd at time of Flagpole trouble at Red Cloud, scout for Merritt and Carr, summer 1876.

Mrs. Emma Stirk, sister of Little Bat Garnier.

George Stover, soldier at Fort Rice, 1866, lived at Red Cloud.

George Sword, born 1847, led the thirty Indians to Crazy Horse camp January 1877.

William H. Taylor, muleskinner with Crook, March 1876.

Clarence Three Stars, Sioux, grandson of Straight Foretop, Minneconjou who shot the Mormon cow, 1854.

Ben Tibbetts, with Custer in Washita campaign, etc., later butcher at Red Cloud.

Charles Turning Hawk, Sioux.

Henry Twist (Twiss), son of Major Twiss, Indian agent who went to live in north with the Oglalas.

Dr. J. R. Walker, physician at Pine Ridge agency eleven years.

Philip Wells, part Sioux.

John C. Whalen, with Cole, 16th Kansas Cavalry, 1865.

🙰

DOCUMENTS AND LETTERS

AGO Records, War Department, National Archives, Washington, Letter Books and Documents Files covering period 1849–1880, including:

> *Fort Laramie Letter Books and Document Files*
> *Medical History of the Post (Fort Laramie) to Fall 1877*
> *Sioux Expedition, 1856, Letter Book*
> *Camp Sheridan Letter Books, 1874 to 1878*
> *Department of the Platte Letter Books and Document Files*
> *Military Division of the Missouri Letter Books and Document Files, including Special Files on Sioux War, Powder River Expedition, Sitting Bull's Band, Fort McPherson, etc.*

Records of Indian Bureau, National Archives, Washington:

> *Document files of agencies to Sioux of Upper Platte*
> *Red Cloud agency Document Files, 1871–8*

Collins Correspondence, 1862–3, Letters Sent and Received, Fort Laramie and Upper Platte Stations, copies in Denver Public Library.

Bent Letters, George Bent to George Hyde, 1904–5, State Historical Society of Colorado.

🙰

MANUSCRIPTS

Bad Heart Bull Manuscript, prepared from picture history of Oglalas by Helen Blish, in Carnegie Institution.

Bettelyoun Manuscript, first draft, by Mrs. Susan Bettelyoun, daughter of Jim Bordeaux, early trader in Laramie region and niece of Swift Bear, Brule chief, in Nebraska State Historical Society.

Spring, Charles H.: "Campaign against the Sioux while Lieutenant Commanding B Co. 12th Mo. Volunteer Cavalry, Cole's Expedition," in Denver Public Library.

Notes

(Only unpublished material bearing on particularly controversial points or filling serious gaps in the published accounts is mentioned. Arrangement is roughly chronological.)

SHOOTING AND DEATH OF CONQUERING BEAR. Much of the Indian detail comes from the Salaway interviews, some from Clarence Three Stars and American Horse. The latter says the Brule chief died on the Running Water after calling the headmen about him and charging Man of Whose Horse the Enemy Are Afraid with the care of the Teton Lakotas.

SPOTTED TAIL'S ATTACK ON THE MAIL COACH. The consequences, including carrying the man in through the snow afoot, are based on the accounts given in the Fort Laramie Letter Books and in the Letter Book of the Sioux Expedition of 1856.

YOUNG CRAZY HORSE. Chips says the boy was known as The Light-Haired One. He Dog, who called him Curly, said he was born in 1838, but a checking of the old man's figures places the date about 1841–2. Still other sources say 1844. Verification of the events while Curly lived with the Brules, his part in the attack on the Omahas, and his later visit with the Cheyennes comes from the He Dog and the Mousseau interviews, the Bettelyoun manuscript and from my recollections of the Old Indian stories. The description of the fight that brought the boy his father's name is from He Dog and others. Young Curly's vision and subsequent dress, medicine, and demeanor are based on the He Dog, Garnett, and Chips interviews, my recollections, and the Blish notes, which agree that joining the Thunder Cult made little change in these things as the members went into battle in breechcloth and moccasins, with lightning marks on the face and hail spots on the horses to represent the storm powers. Descriptions of the mature Crazy Horse are from He Dog, Short Bull, Red Feather, Bordeaux, Garnett, Pourier, etc. Apparently no photograph was ever made of him. The picture often labeled Crazy Horse is of a small, very dark Indian, usually in a war bonnet. This is said to be the second husband of the Larrabee woman, who, according to the Blish notes, took the name of his noted predecessor, a not uncommon practice among the older Sioux.

OGLALA WINTER CAMPS, 1858–61. Pourier tells of leading Richard's pack-horse traders to the Oglala camps in the Wind River region in these years. For that reason Coutant's date for the big fight with the Snakes, June 1861, was chosen instead of Hebard's, the fall of 1866. The Oglalas were near the Snakes in 1861 and very far away in the fall of 1866, busy with the Bozeman Trail war.

CHIEFS SOCIETY AND SHIRT-WEARERS. The origin and duties as given are from the Blish notes, which agree in substance with Wissler. The story of the shirt-wearers made in 1865 is based on He Dog, American Horse, and Garnett, who were all there.

DIVISIONS OF THE NORTHERN OGLALAS, 1860's. These are taken from He Dog's accounts, verified by camp locations, war-party leaders, and so on.

SPOTTED TAIL'S DAUGHTER. Colhoff calls the reported love affair with an army officer a "silly story" and says that it was never heard around Laramie until after it appeared in a magazine. Sometimes a Captain Livingston is named as the man whom the Brule girl loved. According to Heitman he was wholly retired August 1862.

He went to Europe and died in 1865. When the girl died, in 1866, she was about seventeen.

ARMS AND AMMUNITION OF THE ARMY OF THE PLAINS, as reported by officers:

Enfield rifles are "entirely unfit" here; need breechloaders.—Collins, in letter of March 21, 1863.

The cavalry came up to Laramie with all kinds of arms or nothing. As much as possible was issued, September 25, 1866. The cavalry is going to Phil Kearny without proper arms, October 20, 1866.—Fort Laramie Letter Books.

No reserve supply of musket, carbine, or pistol ammunition is on hand at Fort Abraham Lincoln, July 8, 1876.—Military Division of the Missouri Document Files.

Metallic ammunition for rifles and carbines made prior to June 17, 1874 is liable to serious defects. Measures were taken to have it turned in to the arsenals about two years ago. Use at any post in the Department is forbidden, August 8, 1876.—Department of Platte Document Files. (Officers seemed reluctant to release the defective ammunition because replacements were often so tragically delayed.—Author.)

JOHN RICHARD, JR. Pourier, married to young Richard's sister, says John went to the hostiles after killing a soldier "over a loose woman." Garnett recalls that Richard slipped down to the officers now and then to plan for a pardon from President Grant if he could get the northern Oglala chiefs to go to Washington.

OGLALA LANCES given Crazy Horse and He Dog. The story as given is based on He Dog's accounts, the Blish notes, and my own recollections of the hero tales told of the bearers of these lances and the duties involved.

NO WATER TROUBLE. The story of Black Buffalo Woman is from the interviews with He Dog, Short Bull, Garnett, Chips, and others, and from the Blish notes. Evidently the officers at Camp

Robinson never understood this situation, perhaps knew nothing about it, for on the last day Lieutenant W. P. Clark seemed much surprised at the co-operation he got from one of the scout leaders he sent to catch the hostile chief. "Crazy Horse was promptly pursued and so earnestly that No Water who had charge of one party killed two ponies in his efforts to overtake and capture him," Clark says in a letter to the Commissioner of Indian Affairs and to General Crook. No Water later put in a claim against the government for the horses.

FRANK GROUARD, THE GRABBER. Garnett, whose sister married Grouard, heard Gallino, a Missouri River breed, call him Prazost (Ricker's spelling) at Red Cloud agency, saying that was Grouard's name when he lived up on the Missouri. Nick Janis told Garnett that he knew a former steamboat cook called Brazo (Ricker's later spelling), a colored man with several Indian wives, working for the Missouri traders. Mrs. Nettie Goings says she and Grouard were children of the same father, John Brazeau, a French creole employed by the American Fur Company at Fort Pierre and related to the Chouteaus and Picottes. Stover says Grouard told him he was a cousin of the mother of Frank Goings, a colored woman, and came from up near Apple River. (Indian relationship terms are flexible and translations vary.—Author.)

The account given of the Sibley scouts affair is based on the interviews with Pourier and others who were along. Pourier says Grouard was sick with venereal disease and kept getting off his horse and lying down. Stover agrees that Grouard became dissipated and a physical wreck around the forts. Louis Bordeaux and his sister, Mrs. Susan Bettelyoun, say that Grouard was afraid when Crazy Horse came in, left the agency soon afterward, and when he had to come back, gave false interpretations and lied to the officers to get the man who knew his past out of the way.

HOSTILES PLANNED TO SURRENDER, SPRING 1876. He Dog says he and the Cheyennes were making ready to come in when they were struck by Reynolds, March 17, 1876, but were so angered by the attack that they went to the Crazy Horse camp determined to stay out with him. "If it hadn't been for that attack by Crook on Powder River we would have come in to the agency that spring and there would have been no Sioux war," Short Bull says in his interview.

AGENCY IN THEIR OWN COUNTRY. Crook's promise of a northern agency appears in the interviews with Garnett, who was the interpreter at the council when the promise was made, and in those of a dozen others. Garnett says that the promise was repeated at a second council with Mackenzie and Clark present.

PEACE CHIEFS KILLED at Fort Keogh on the Tongue. Miles reported, December 17, 1876, that the day before five Minneconjou chiefs coming in under white flags were killed by the Crows at the fort. The Indians just behind them, twenty-five or thirty, fled. Later an Indian messenger said that Sitting Bull the Good from Red Cloud was among those shot.—Military Division of the Missouri Document Files. Short Bull says that eight men were sent to the Tongue fort to make a peace treaty, spoiled when five of them were killed.

RED CLOUD PROMISED REINSTATEMENT. Garnett, interpreter at the secret meeting of Lieutenant W. P. Clark and Red Cloud, gives the detailed story, verified later by the aggrieved Red Cloud when he was once more deposed, in the 1880's, this time by Agent McGillycuddy. That Little Wound, of the Bear Oglalas, helped the agent that day must have made this second great humiliation by the white man even harder to endure.

HOSTILES COAXED IN. Red Feather says that both the Sword and Spotted Tail delegations promised that the agents would give Crazy Horse rations and clothing and let him come back to his own country. He Dog insisted that they were very near Camp Robinson before they knew they would have to surrender. "Spotted Tail had laid a trap for us. Later on I found out he was telling the military things about Crazy Horse that were not so."

THE LARRABEE WOMAN. Pourier says Clark got Crazy Horse to take the young breed woman thinking this might mellow him towards the whites. A letter by Clark in the Document Files of the Department of the Platte speaks with some personal satisfaction about the alliance. Variants of Ricker's spelling are Larravee, Larrivee, Larivier, etc.

JEALOUSY OF THE AGENCY CHIEFS OVER THE HERO-WORSHIP OF CRAZY HORSE. Garnett, Pourier, Bordeaux, and others tell the story of the betrayal as it is given in the book. Eastman says Woman's Dress was in the service of the jealous chiefs, that Crazy Horse never plotted the death of Crook. He Dog and Red Feather agree. Shaw, living at the Brule agency, says Spotted Tail "bragged on" the Crazy Horse Indians but never on their chief and when asked about a conspiracy to kill the officers, he said: "Yes, there is a conspiracy but we will be the winners." Shaw thinks he was afraid that Crazy Horse would be the big man if he went to Washington. (The story of the misinterpretation and the falsehoods that ended in the death of Crazy Horse has been told in the *Nebraska History Magazine,* and also by Byrne, Standing Bear, Neihardt, and others.)

PROTESTS AGAINST THE FEAST AT CRAZY HORSE CAMP. The incident is based on a long letter to the Commissioner of Indian Affairs from Shopp, Special Agent, Indian Office, dated August 1, 1877. —Red Cloud Document Files. Shopp was at the council and was with Agent Irwin when the delegation came in the night.

ARREST AND DEATH OF CRAZY HORSE. Sheridan telegraphed Crook: ". . . I wish you to send Crazy Horse under proper guard to these Headquarters." September 5, 1877.—Military Division of the Missouri Letter Book. Bradley's report disposes of the dozens who claim to have been with Crazy Horse to the end: "His father and Touch the Clouds, chief of the San Arcs [*sic*] remained with him until he died." September 7, 1877.—Military Division of the Missouri Letter Book.

Glossary

In *Crazy Horse* Mari Sandoz uses only the English version of Indian names and only a few Lakota terms. When a Lakota name is known from historical sources, it is provided in the following format: the Anglicized form of the Lakota name, a phonemic transcription of the Lakota in italics and parentheses, and a literal gloss of the Lakota in single quotes. For example, Crazy Horse: Tašunke Witko (*thašʉ́ke witkó*) 'his horse is crazy'. When the English name is a literal gloss of the Lakota name, the literal gloss is omitted. The same format is used for Lakota terms. For a short overview of the Lakota language, see David S. Rood and Allan R. Taylor, "A Sketch of Lakhota, a Siouan Language," in *Handbook of North American Indians*, vol. 17, *Languages*, ed. Ives Goddard, 440–82 (Washington DC: Smithsonian Institution, 1996).

Cultural and Historical Terms

adoption: In Lakota society adoption was commonplace and relatively simple—usually a matter of addressing and responding with appropriate kin terms. Since being a relative was more a matter of social behavior than biology, an adoptee became a fully integrated member of the kinship network. *See also* hunka.

akicita: (*akíčhita*). The akicita were the "police force" of the Lakotas. One of the men's societies would be assigned to oversee a specific task, such as maintaining order in the camp circle or enforcing discipline during a camp move, communal buffalo hunt, or large war party. The badge of the akicita was a stripe of black face paint, and their punishments were swift and harsh. An offender might be whipped, or have his weapons broken, his wife's tipi cover slashed to shreds, or his horses killed.

animals: The Lakotas recognized that each kind of animal constituted a 'people' or 'nation' (oyate [*oyáte*]) with which they had a kinship relationship. Although animals would give themselves to the Lakotas for food or serve as helpers in spiritual contexts, their status as kinsmen required that they be treated with respect and honor.

arrow and hoop game: A boys' game in which the players tried to throw an arrow through a willow hoop rolling along the ground. The player who succeeded won all the arrows thrown.

Bad Faces: Itešiča (*itéšiča*). A band of the Oglalas.

Bannocks: A North Paiute–speaking group who lived in southern Idaho with the Shoshones (Snakes).

Bear people: The portion of the Oglalas who were relatives and followers of Chief Bull Bear, including his band, the Kiyuksas (*khiyúksa*) 'break in half', as well as the True Oglala band (Oglalaȟča [*oglálaȟča*]) and Red Water's band (Mnišana [*mnišána*] 'little red water'). After Bull Bear was killed by Red Cloud in 1841, the Bear people split from the rest of the Oglalas, moving gradually southeast from Fort Laramie and occupying the land between the Platte and Smoky Hill rivers. They were also identified as the Southern Oglalas. *See also* Smoke people.

Big Bellies: Tezi Tanka (*thezí tháka*). In the Red Cloud division of Oglalas, the chief's society or council elected seven chiefs (wičaša itančan [*wicháša itáčhą*]) to govern the people. These chiefs were known informally as "Big Bellies." Among the other Lakota groups, the Big Bellies were the chief's society or council itself. However, some contemporary Lakota sources identify the Big Bellies as the Silent Eaters (A'inila Wotapi [*á'inila wótapi*]), a multiband feasting society for retired warriors who would, after quietly dining on puppy and choice cuts of buffalo, engage in discussions of tribal politics and other issues.

Blackfeet: An Algonquian-speaking northern tribe whose territory extended from northwest Montana up into Canada. In the United States, they are usually called the Blackfoot.

Blackfoot: Sihasapa (*sihásapa*). One of the seven tribes of Lakotas. Not to be confused with the Algonquian-speaking Blackfoot tribe.

Black Robe: Šina Sapa (*šiná sápa*). The Lakota term for a Catholic priest and, by extension, Catholics in general.

Blue Clouds: Maȟpiyato (*maȟpíyatho*). The English translation of the Lakota name for the Arapaho Indians. The traditional territory of the Arapahos was in eastern Colorado. They were close allies of the Lakotas.

Bone-scrapers Society: The Elkhorn Scrapers. A Cheyenne warrior society.

breath feathers: The two downy plumes from under an eagle's tail.

brother-sister relationship: Once a brother and sister reached puberty, they would no longer speak to each other and would avoid being alone together. Despite this, they would remain close. A man would continue to provide meat to his sister even after her marriage, and she would make things for his children, often elaborately decorated.

Brulés: Sičaǧu (*sičháǧu*) 'burnt thighs'. One of the seven tribes of the Lakotas. The French term *brulé* 'burnt' is a partial translation of their Lakota name, said to be a reference to an incident in which several tribe members were burned in a prairie fire. The Brulés occupied the southeast range of Lakota territory.

buffalo berries: An evergreen shrub or bush that grows in the foot-hills and mountains. The ideal time to pick the berries is after a freeze, when the sour berries turn sweet. Women would beat the bushes with sticks, knocking the berries onto rawhides spread underneath.

Buffalo Calf Pipe: The sacred pipe of the Lakotas is the Buffalo Calf Pipe. During a time of famine long ago, the wakan beings sent a beautiful young woman, Woȟpe (*woȟpé*), to the Lakotas with the gift of the first pipe, establishing through it kinship between the buffalo and the people. She taught them how to pray with the pipe and established ceremonies for them. As she left the camp circle, Woȟpe transformed into a white buffalo cow. The Buffalo Calf Pipe brought unity and harmony to the Lakotas, and it has been in the possession of a keeper in the Sans Arc tribe through the generations.

Buffalo Sing: Tatanka Lowanpi (*thatháka lowápi*). When a girl reached puberty, her family might celebrate her transition to womanhood by sponsoring a Buffalo Sing for her. During the ceremony the girl would be instructed in the duties of womanhood, her hair would be braided like an adult woman's, the part painted with vermilion, and an eagle plume attached. Depending on the means of the family, a giveaway and feast would follow.

burial: *See* death scaffold.

camp circle: hočoka (*hóčhoka*) 'circular enclosure'. In their camps (wičoti [*wičhóthi*] 'place where humans dwell') the Lakotas erected their tipis in a circle, with an opening to the east as an entrance. The tipi doorways faced the center of the circle except for those at either side of the entryway, whose doorways faced east. In a tribal camp, each band of the tribe had a designated segment of the camp circle where band members erected their tipis. Similarly, in the large, multitribal camps, each tribe had its prescribed place around the circle.

Cheyennes: An Algonquian-speaking tribe, the Cheyennes were regarded as brothers by the Lakotas. By 1851 there were two divisions of Cheyennes: the Southern Cheyennes, who ranged through east Colorado and west Kansas, and the Northern Cheyennes, who moved from eastern Wyoming northward with the Lakotas into the Powder River basin.

chiefs: Each band had an itančan (*itáčhą*) 'leader, chief', who spoke for the people. A chief held his position by common consent; ideally he was a man who always put the welfare of the people ahead of his own, was generous, spoke and did no evil, and was self-controlled. However, a Lakota chief had no authority beyond persuasion and example.

chokecherry: A wild cherry (čanpa [*čhąphá*]) that grows on a shrub or small tree. Chokecherries have a very astringent, sour taste, but they sweeten following a frost or freeze.

chores: Boys were responsible for taking care of the horse herd when in camp. Girls would haul water or gather firewood.

circle: The Lakotas considered the circle to be sacred because it represented the natural world. Wanka Tanka had caused everything in nature to be round except stone: sun, sky, earth, moon, everything that breathed, everything that grew from the ground, even time—all were round. Reflecting this, the Lakotas made their tipis round, camped in a circle, sat in a circle at council, and made wide use of circles in sacred representation and decorative art.

cola: Sandoz's spelling of kola (*kholá*) 'friend', a word used only by men. A friendship between two men could be formalized into near-brotherhood.

communal hunt: wanasapi (*wanásapi*). In the fall the Lakotas would undertake a communal hunt to secure enough meat to dry for use in the winter. Scouts were sent out, and once they located a large buffalo herd, they reported back in a formal, ritualized manner. The entire camp would immediately move to intercept the buffalo. The actual hunt was conducted like a war party ambush. The hunters hid themselves until the buffalo were in the right spot, then charged the herd from two directions simultaneously. This confused the buffalo and kept them milling so that a larger number of animals might be killed. Hunters identified their kills by arrow markings.

coughing sickness: Tuberculosis.

council: In addition to a chief, each band had a council of respected adult men who discussed and decided all issues concerning the camp's welfare. All decisions had to be by consensus. Council decisions regarding camp movements or communal hunts would be implemented by appointed officials called wakičunza (*wakíčhuza*) 'deciders'. The wakičunza were older men of repute who would control all aspects of the move, including routes, daily distance, campsites, and security.

councilors: The shirt wearers.

coup: A war honor. To count coup originally referred only to the act of touching a fallen enemy in battle, but coups came to be awarded for other acts of bravery as well. In a complex system of ranked valor, certain actions won for the warrior the right to display distinctive paraphernalia, such as feathers, clothing, emblems, or paint designs, and to enjoy their attendant prestige. To be valid, a coup had to be witnessed and later sworn to by other warriors. On ritual occasions, a man would recite his coups as a way of validating his position. To have an enemy count coup on oneself was a humiliation.

courtship: Lakota standards of modesty and propriety made it difficult for young people to be alone together. Young men would stand wrapped in their blankets outside the tipis of young women or along the pathway the girls took to fetch water or firewood. When they would appear, the young men would try to entice their favorites to spend a few minutes with them. If a girl was willing, he would enfold the two of them in his blanket for as long as propriety allowed.

cradleboard: A flat board, often with a sunshade and decoration, to which a bundled baby would be secured. Cradleboards were designed to hang on trees, posts, or saddles, allowing a woman to work freely.

Crazy Dogs: A Cheyenne warrior society.

Crooked Lances: A Cheyenne warrior society.

crow: A dance bustle that included the body of a crow. It was used as a badge of office in certain men's societies.

Crow-Owners: Kaŋǵi Yuha (khaǧí yuhá). A Lakota men's society. The name refers to the dance bustle.

Crows: A Siouan-speaking tribe whose territory lay to the west of the Lakotas in Montana. When the Lakotas moved west into the Powder River basin, the Crows became their principal enemies.

death scaffold: Preferred interment was above ground. The body would be washed, dressed, and the face painted. Favorite weapons, work implements, or belongings would be wrapped with the body in a tanned skin tied with thongs. The body would be placed either on a scaffold platform beyond the reach of animals or in the branches of a tree. A horse might be killed for the use of the deceased in the next life. In contrast, the poor or socially insignificant would be buried in shallow graves covered with rocks.

Delawares: An eastern tribe dislocated westward by white encroachment and treaty. Groups eventually reached Wisconsin, Kansas, and Indian Territory (in present-day Oklahoma).

divorce: Both men and women had the right to 'throw away' (iȟpeya [*iȟpéya*]) a spouse. A man would move into another woman's tipi or a woman would place her husband's possessions outside of her tipi. A woman's new husband might send some horses to her previous husband to smooth things over.

"dog lifted its leg at your lodge, a": A Lakota metaphor for being cuckolded or having men try to seduce your wife. It was often used to express the burden of being a chief, for they were expected to ignore even such a personal provocation in favor of the peace and overall well-being of the community.

Dog Society: The Dog Men or Dog Soldiers. A Cheyenne warrior society.

double council lodge: tipi iyokiheya (*thípi íyokhiheya*) 'tipis joined together' or tiyotipi (*thiyóthipi*) 'lodge of lodges'. A double council lodge was a large lodge made of two tipi covers over two sets of adjoining poles. It would be erected in the center of the camp circle.

drying racks: Buffalo meat was preserved by drying. Women would cut the meat into thin sheets that were hung over wooden crosspieces to dry.

eagle catcher: The Lakotas caught eagles by digging a deep pit, covering it with a lattice of sticks and grass, and tying a rabbit or other animal to it as bait. The eagle catcher would hide in the pit below, and when an eagle landed on the bait, he would reach up, grab the eagle by the leg, drag it into the pit, and strangle it. The eagles were used to make regalia.

four: The number four was of particular significance to the Lakotas. They saw sets of four throughout nature, such as the four directions, the four winds, and the four seasons. In addition, shamans understood the wakan beings in sets of four. Thus, in ritual, ceremonial, or formal contexts actions were repeated four times or were attempted three times and only completed on the fourth.

Fox Society: Tokala (*thokhála*) 'kit fox'. A Lakota men's society.

generosity: Next to bravery, generosity was the virtue most admired by Lakotas. A reputation for generosity was a prerequisite for any leadership position and a necessity to retain it. Along with helping the poor, gifts would also be given to honor or express pride in a relative, as, for example, a father giving away horses to honor his son's first coup. *See also* giveaway.

giveaway: The distribution of gifts to mark a special occasion, as for a child's naming or a daughter's Buffalo Sing. A family would begin accumulating goods far in advance of the event, since the greater the number and value of the gifts, the greater the honor. A giveaway would also be conducted following a death. The relatives of the deceased would give away all of his or her possessions as part of the mourning process.

"grass houses, tribe who live in": Peẑi-Wokeya-Oti Kin (*pheẑí-wokhéya-othí kį*) 'the one who lives in a grass lodge'. The Shoshones.

Gros Ventres: An Algonquian-speaking tribe closely related to the Arapahos. Their territory was on the Canadian plains around the Saskatchewan-Alberta border and extended down to Montana.

hand game: hanpapa ečunpi (*hápapha ečhúpi*) 'moccasin game'. A gambling game in which one team concealed a small bone in the hand of a team member, and the other team had to guess the hand holding the bone. It was also played using four moccasins as hiding places. The game was accompanied by singing and drumming.

head-chief: The position of head chief of the Lakotas was established in the Treaty of 1851 at the insistence of the U.S. government, which wanted to have only one person to deal with as a representative of the Lakota people. The title had no standing among the Lakotas. No chief could exercise the kind of authority in his own band that the government envisioned for the position, let alone in another tribe.

herbs: The Lakotas had an extensive knowledge of plants and herbs useful for curing common ailments. Either a pežuta wičaša (*pežúta wičháša*) 'medicine man' or a pežuta winyan (*pežúta wíyą*) 'medicine woman' could administer these remedies.

heyoka: (*heyókha*). One who dreamed of wakinyan (*wakíyą*) 'the thunderbeings'. A man who had such a vision needed to participate in the Heyoka Ceremony; otherwise, he would be killed by lightning. Heyoka would often act in clownish ways, behaving or speaking the opposite of what was intended, but many were also great healers and warriors. *See also* thunder.

Heyoka Ceremony: The ceremony to initiate one who dreamed of the thunderbeings. During the ceremony, all of the heyokas acted as clowns, walking backward and making people laugh. The most notable aspect of the ceremony came when the heyokas would reach into a pot of boiling water to pick out pieces of dog meat without being burned.

Hidatsas: A horticultural and buffalo-hunting tribe at the confluence of the Missouri and Knife rivers. The Hidatsas and Crows at one time comprised a single group; beginning in the late 1600s, the two groups began to separate, a gradual process that was largely completed by 1750.

Hohes: The Lakota name for the Assiniboines. They were a closely-related Siouan-speaking tribe whose territory was north of the Lakotas and extended into the Canadian prairies.

honor place: čatku (*čhatkú*). The honor place in a tipi was at the back of the lodge, opposite the door. Similarly, in a camp circle it was on the west, opposite the entrance.

hunka: A relative adopted through the Hunka Ceremony (Hunka Alowanpi [*hųká alówąpi*] 'they sing over the *hųká*'). Those adopted in this way could thereafter paint a red stripe across their forehead as a mark of their honored status.

Hunkpapas: (*hųkpapha*) 'at the entrance head'. One of the seven tribes of the Lakotas. Their name is thought to be a reference to the tribe's assigned location in the camp circle. The Hunkpapas were one of the northern Lakota tribes.

Hunkpatila: (*hųkpathila*) 'little camp at the camp circle entrance'. A band of the Oglalas. Their name is a reference to their assigned place in the camp circle.

Indian police: The "Indian police" that Sandoz refers to was an informal group of six to twelve men (depending on circumstances) organized by the friendly chiefs to maintain order among the Indians at the agencies. It was not until 1879 that the formal, government-supported Indian Police Force was proposed for Pine Ridge Reservation.

Jenney Expedition: A scientific expedition into the Black Hills sponsored by the United States Geological Survey and led by Walter P. Jenney and Henry Newton. The expedition spent four months and twenty days during the summer of 1875 performing a complete geological and mineralogical survey of the region.

Kaws: Also known as the Kansa. The Kaws were a Siouan-speaking horticultural and buffalo-hunting tribe who lived in northern Kansas.

Lakota: (lakhóta), generally interpreted as 'feeling affection, friendly' or 'united, allied'. The self-designation of the Tetons.

lance bearers: Members of a men's society chosen because of their bravery to carry the society's decorated lances into battle. Lance bearers would advance toward the enemy and thrust their lance into the ground through a slit in the sash they wore, effectively immobilizing themselves. There they would fight until they were killed or released by another society member.

Loaf About the Forts: A band of Oglalas. Following the Treaty of 1851 and the establishment of annual distributions of annuity goods, some Lakotas chose to remain in the vicinity of Fort Laramie year-round. Other Lakotas began calling them Wagluȟe (wágluȟe) 'lives with wife's relatives', usually translated as 'Loafers'. Although they were originally from many different bands, the Loafers came to constitute a distinct band of Oglalas.

lodge: See tipi.

lodges, rolled up: In warm weather the Lakotas would roll up the bottom of their tipis to create a shaded, ventilated place, catch the cool evening breeze, or, in the case of ceremonies or councils, to allow the people outside to witness the activities.

Mandans: A horticultural and buffalo-hunting tribe near the confluence of the Missouri and Heart rivers in North Dakota.

marriage: In order to marry, a young man first had to prove himself on the warpath, ideally bringing back horses with which to "purchase" a bride. A suitor would bring one or more horses to the tipi of a woman's family in the hope that she would agree to marry him. For a woman, this was the most prestigious form of marriage, a matter of lifelong pride. A man of less means might, by mutual consent, move in with a woman's family or openly take her to live with his family. A woman could also go off with a man without the advice or consent of her relatives, but in doing so she would risk abandonment and a ruined reputation.

medicine: The power (wakan [*wakhą́*]) that a man received in a vision. A man's medicine was not unlimited but was restricted to a specific area or purpose, such as warfare, hunting, or healing a particular type of ailment or injury. To be effective, a man's medicine might require him to paint himself in specific patterns or symbols, wear or carry certain paraphernalia, sing particular songs (prayers), or observe taboos. This information would be conveyed to him as part of his vision.

medicine bundle: wopiye (*wóphiye*). A man's medicine bag was a pouch or bundle containing various objects of significance to his vision experience. A medicine bag was of use only to the dreamer.

Medicine-Lodge Ceremony: The Cheyenne version of the Sun Dance.

medicine man: An English term for a wičaša wakan (*wičháša wakhą́*) 'holy man', or shaman, who served as an intermediary between the wakan beings and the people. Shamans usually experienced a spontaneous dream or vision during which they would receive knowledge of how to heal certain ailments, locate game or people, or foresee future events. Shamans were called upon to cure only more serious illnesses or injuries.

Minneconjou: The historical spelling of Mnikowožu (*mnikhówožu*), one of the seven tribes of Lakotas. The significance of their name is not known. It is usually glossed as 'plant at water' or 'planters by the water', but this is probably a folk etymology.

moons: The Lakotas marked the passage of the year in moons. Moons had descriptive names indicative of recurring natural events, such as čanpasapawi (*čhąphásapawi*) 'moon when the chokecherries turn black' or ištawičayazanpiwi (*ištáwičhayaząpiwi*) 'moon of sore eyes' (from snowblindness).

mother, second: In Lakota kinship one's mother's sisters were also called "mother." Therefore one could have a second (or third, or fourth) mother.

mother-in-law: The relationship between a man and his mother-in-law was characterized by avoidance behavior. The two were never to speak to each other and were to avoid any circumstance where they would be alone together.

mourning: After a death, relatives of the deceased gave away their own possessions as well as those of the deceased, cut their hair, and wore ragged clothes. They slashed their arms or legs, would perhaps cut off a joint of a finger, and walked around camp wailing and bleeding. Eventually, others ended the mourning by taking the mourners to a dance, painting their faces, and dressing them in fine clothes.

murder, compensation for: When a Lakota killed another Lakota, the offender or his family would offer horses to the victim's family as compensation. A victim's family was expected to accept such compensation rather than disrupt the harmony of the camp by seeking revenge.

naming: Children were given a name four days after birth. Before announcing the child's name, the parents would have a feast and give presents to those attending. Infants could be named for their oldest living grandparent, a respected deceased grandparent, or in honor of a brave deed of the father. Successful young warriors might be given a new name commemorating some brave deed of their own. In some cases, a name was passed from father to son, often for several generations, as was the case with the Black Elk family.

Nez Perces: The French designation of a Sahaptin-speaking tribe who lived in eastern Oregon and Idaho. In 1877 a portion of the tribe under Chief Joseph resisted removal to a reservation, inflicted several defeats on the U.S. Army, and skillfully eluded capture before finally being caught.

No Bows: Itazipčo (*itázipčho*) 'without bows'. One of the seven tribes of the Lakotas. They are more familiarly known as Sans Arcs, the French rendering of their name.

No Clothes people: A reference to those Santees who fled Minnesota following the Dakota Conflict of 1862. They were pursued by the U.S. Army until they had no possessions left.

Oglalas: (*oglála*) 'scatter one's own'. One of the seven tribes of the Lakotas. The significance of the name is not known. The Oglalas occupied the southwest range of Lakota territory.

Omahas: A Siouan-speaking horticultural and buffalo-hunting tribe that lived along the Missouri River in northeastern Nebraska.

Otoes: A Siouan-speaking horticultural and buffalo-hunting tribe that lived along the Missouri River in southeastern Nebraska.

Oyukhpes: Oyuȟpe (*oyúȟpe*) 'unloaded'. A band of the Oglalas. Known in English as Thrown Down or Unloaded.

paints: Paints were made from shales and clays ground into powder. When used, the powder was mixed with water and animal fat.

parfleche: A container made of rawhide with a flap that could be tied closed. Parfleches were usually painted with colorful designs.

paunch boiling: Before the Lakotas had metal pots they cooked their meat in buffalo paunches. The paunch would be filled with water, and stones heated in the fire were added to boil the water.

Pawnees: A large, powerful horticultural and buffalo-hunting tribe and a traditional enemy of the Lakotas. The Pawnees occupied the Platte valley in central Nebraska.

Pawnee Scouts: A U.S. Army unit of Pawnee Indians recruited to serve as scouts in the wars against the Plains tribes.

pine bough shelter: The Plains tribes would place forked poles in the ground with pine bough crosspieces above to create shaded areas for work or relaxation.

pipe: čanunpa (*čhaŋúpa*). The pipe was the preeminent means of prayer, the direct link between Wakan Tanka and the people. White Buffalo Cow Woman herself was said to be present in the smoke as it rose upward, carrying the prayers of the people. As the pipe was filled, offerings were made to each of the four directions and to the sky and earth, thereby encompassing the whole of the universe in the bowl. Ordinarily, only men would smoke the pipe in ritual. *See also* Buffalo Calf Pipe.

Pipe Ceremony: Every religious ceremony, formal event, council, deliberation, or endeavor began with a Pipe Ceremony. The ritual filling, offering to the earth, sky, and the four directions, and communal smoking of the pipe sanctified what followed and precluded deception and insincerity.

pipe summons: A pipe would be sent around to summon participants to a council meeting. Similarly, a pipe would summon or invite other tribes or bands to the warpath.

pit drive: An old method of hunting in which herd animals, such as buffalo or antelope, would be driven over a cliff into a pit or into a confined area where they could be killed easily.

plum-pit game: A gambling game played by older women. A set consisted of six kansu (*khaŋsú*) 'plum stones' (each with a carved figure on one side), a tanpan (*thaŋpá*) 'basket', and usually one hundred čunwiyawa (*čhuŋwíyawa*) 'counting sticks'. A player would cast the plum stones from the basket and win counting sticks for each carved side showing.

polygamy: A man could marry more than one woman if he had the means to do so. Many such marriages occurred when a man married his wife's sister after she had been widowed. This was regarded as an ideal solution for both parties: as sisters, the two women would get along with each other, and the widow would have a man to hunt for her. It was also possible, but rare, for a woman to have more than one husband.

Pottawatomis: A tribe from the lower Great Lakes displaced by treaties to areas in Iowa, Kansas, and Indian Territory (in present-day Oklahoma).

red: Red was the honoring color and represented all things sacred. Individuals who went through ceremonies such as the Hunka Ceremony and Buffalo Sing were entitled to wear distinctive designs of red paint for the rest of their lives.

red willow bark: The dried bark of the red willow (čanšaša [*čhašáša*] 'red, red tree') would be mixed with tobacco for ceremonial smoking.

Rees: The Arikaras. They were a horticultural and buffalo-hunting tribe who dominated the Missouri River valley in South Dakota until they were decimated by smallpox. The Lakotas then forced them to retreat north.

relatives: Kinship (wotakue [*wótakuye*]) presented the most important obligations in social life. One's relatives were a social support network, and from the earliest age Lakota children were admonished to be good relatives. The widespread employment of adoption expanded Lakota kinship beyond biological relatedness; everyone, even outsiders, were potential relatives.

"sacred four times": *See* four.

Santees: The collective term for the four Sioux tribes who lived in southern and western Minnesota: Mdewakanton, Wahpekute, Wahpeton, and Sisseton. The term *Santee* is an anglicization of Isanyati (*isáyathi*) 'camp at knife', the name used by the Sioux groups on the Missouri River for these tribes. Following the Dakota Conflict of 1862 in Minnesota, many Santees fled westward onto the plains, and military campaigns to hunt them down sometimes led to clashes with other Sioux groups.

Saones: An early nineteenth-century Lakota tribe. The Saones broke into four separate tribes: the Sans Arcs, Two Kettles, Blackfeet, and Hunkpapas.

Seven Council Fires: In oral tradition the Očeti Šakowin (*očhéthi šakówį*) 'seven fireplaces' was a confederacy of all the Sioux tribes when they still lived in the woodlands and forests to the east. The seven tribes were the Mdewakanton, Wahpekute, Wahpeton,

Sisseton, Yankton, Yanktonais, and Titonwan. They spoke three
distinct but mutually intelligible dialects: Santee, Yankton/Yank-
tonais, and Lakota. There is no historical documentation that the
confederacy actually existed as a political entity. However, the
tradition demonstrates that the tribes understood themselves to
be one people.

shield dance: Possibly a reference to the dance of the Red Shield Society of the Cheyennes.

shirt wearers: wičaša yatapika (*wičháša yatápika*) 'praiseworthy men'.
Shirt wearers were active, younger men admired for their war
deeds and generosity who were appointed as leaders and councilors. They were given a hair-decorated shirt to signify their position, and they were expected to represent the ideals of a Lakota
man. The number of shirt wearers varied from tribe to tribe.

sitting: A proper Lakota woman would sit with her legs folded beneath
her to one side.

Slota: Slot'a (*slót'a*) 'to be slippery with grease'. The Lakota name for
the Métis. They were Canadian mixed-bloods who formed their
own indigenous communities and culture. Caravans of Métis
would travel down to Lakota territory in two-wheeled carts to
trade.

Smoke people: The followers of Chief Smoke. After the Oglalas were
divided by Red Cloud's killing of Bull Bear, the half of the tribe
aligned with Smoke drifted northward from Fort Laramie into
the headwater area of the Powder River. *See also* Bear people.

Snakes: A name for the Shoshone tribe who occupied western Wyoming and southern Idaho. They were enemies of the Lakotas.

snow snakes game: čanpaslohanpi (*čhąpáslohąpi*) 'they slide a stick'.
Each player had a thick, tapered stick about four feet long that he
would slide along the snow or ice; the longest throw won.

song: Most men possessed songs that were received in a vision and that
were relevant to that vision in ways only he understood. A man
would sing his songs before battle to activate his medicine or
invoke the power of his vision, during battle to call for assistance,
or simply as a daily ritual, such as greeting the rising sun.

Spider: Iktomi (*iktómi*). Spider was the trickster character of Lakota oral literature. He also played a role in their creation stories.

straightening stone: A stone with a hole bored through it used to straighten arrow shafts.

Sun Dance: Wiwanyag Wačipi (*wiwáyag wachípi*) 'sun-gazing dance'. The Sun Dance was the most important public religious ceremony of the Lakotas. Held when the tribe came together in midsummer, it celebrated tribal unity and was a prayer for the increase of the people and of the buffalo. During the four-day ceremony, authority in the camp rested with the medicine men. A man danced in the Sun Dance to fulfill a pledge made to the sacred powers (Wakan Tanka [*wakhą́ tháka*] 'great mystery') in a time of need, such as during battle or a child's illness.

Sun Dance pole: As part of the Sun Dance, an enclosed, circular dance space would be constructed and a cottonwood tree ritually selected and cut down. Several girls (virgins) and boys were given the honor of striking the first blows with the axe. The fallen tree was then trimmed, carried back to camp, and erected in the center of the dance arbor.

Sun Dance scars: Dancers were tethered to the Sun Dance pole or to buffalo skulls by skewers inserted under the flesh of their chest or back. They then had to tear themselves free of the skewers, usually through their own exertions but with help if necessary. Although women were not expected to dance, they too could make flesh offerings to help a relative fulfill his pledge. Sun Dance scars were a point of honor for Lakotas.

sun's way: The route that the sun travels is east, south, west, then north, so to go the sun's way around an obstacle or within a circular space, such as a camp circle, tipi, or sweatlodge, was to circle clockwise.

sweatlodge: The Sweatlodge Ceremony (Inikağapi [*iníkağapi*], freely translated as 'life renewal') was conducted in a low, dome-shaped lodge constructed of willows and covered with hides. Rocks were heated in a nearby fire and ritually deposited into a firepit in the center of the lodge. The door flap was closed, and incense,

followed by ladles of cold water, was poured onto the rocks, filling the chamber with steam. Prayers would then be offered by
the medicine man and the participants in turn. Participants in all
other ceremonies would first be purified in a sweatlodge.

Tetons: An anglicized version of the term titunwan (*thítųwą*) 'prairie
village', the name used by other Sioux groups to designate the
Lakotas.

thunder: The sound of thunder was the voice of the wakinyan (*wakį́yą*)
'thunderbeings', winged sacred beings who lived in the west.
Lightning was the flashing of their eyes. *See also* heyoka.

tipi: Lakota tipis were the property of women. They had a three-pole
base, with nineteen to twenty-one poles in total, including two to
control the wind flaps, which directed smoke out and could be
closed in bad weather. This framework was covered by twelve to
eighteen buffalo bull hides sewn together. A three- to four-foot-
high liner was tied to the poles to provide insulation. The liner
and the exterior were often painted with designs or depictions of
a man's vision or war deeds.

touch the pen: The act of signing a treaty. An Indian signer would touch
the end of the pen as a scribe marked an *X* after his name, thus
"confirming" his agreement. The Indians thought that this was
superfluous, since agreement had been reached during the council proceedings, but they complied to humor the whites. They
would learn later that not only were their words not recorded
in the treaty, but what was recorded did not always match their
understanding of the agreement.

travois: A transport device that consisted of a frame slung between
trailing poles fastened to the sides of a horse or dog.

Treaty of 1851: The Treaty of 1851, negotiated at Horse Creek near
Fort Laramie, was signed by most of the northern Plains tribes,
not just the Lakotas. It set down the boundaries of each tribe's
territory, the U.S. government apparently hoping (in vain) that
this would discourage tribal encroachments and conflicts. The
treaty included a provision that each tribe appoint a single head
chief to act for it in dealings with the United States, a concept

foreign to Plains Indian culture. Finally, it promised to provide the Indians with annuities of various manufactured goods for fifty years.

Treaty of 1868: The Treaty of 1868 created the Great Sioux Reservation, an area covering all of present-day South Dakota west of the Missouri River. The U.S. government pledged to prevent white intrusion into the reservation and to remove trespassers. In addition, the Lakotas retained the right to hunt in the Platte valley in northern Nebraska and in the Powder River basin in Montana. Finally, the government agreed that all future treaties would have to be approved by three-fourths of adult Lakota men.

True Oglalas: Oglalaȟča (*oglálaȟča*). A band of the southern Oglalas.

Two Kettles: O'ohenunpa (*o'óhenųpa*) 'two boilings'. One of the seven tribes of the Lakotas. Their name probably refers to two kettles of cooked food.

"two lances of the Oglalas": These are probably the crow-feathered lances of the Crow-Owners Society. One lance was red, the other blue, and both had the stuffed skin of a crow—feathers intact— fastened right below the spearhead. These lances were given to Crazy Horse and He Dog to carry into the battle with the Crows called When They Drove Them into Camp.

Utes: A large tribe whose territory extended from central Colorado west to the Great Salt Lake. They were enemies of the Lakotas.

vision quest: hanblečeyapi (*hąbléčheyapi*) 'they cry for a dream'. After puberty a young man usually undertook a vision quest. Under the guidance of a medicine man, he remained alone, fasting on an isolated hilltop for up to four days with nothing but a buffalo robe and a pipe, making himself pitiable before the sacred beings. A messenger might come to him, usually in animal form, offering him power in warfare or in curing. The medicine man would later help the dreamer interpret his vision and understand its requirements.

vision violation: If a man did not perform all that was required of him in his vision or if he violated some stricture he had been given, his power would fail him or he could be killed by his spirit helper.

wakan: (*wakhą́*) 'holy, sacred'. The animating force of the universe and the oneness of its being. Anything could be wakan.

Wanka Tanka: (*wakhą́ thą́ka*) 'great mystery'. The totality of the wakan power. It was a concept defined by its incomprehensibility, for it was simultaneously many and one. In stories the wakan beings of Wanka Tanka were personified with human characteristics.

war: Success in war was the preeminent means of attaining status, wealth, and influence for a Lakota man and, by extension, his female relatives. Any aspiration for a leadership position later in life required it. Thus, Lakota boys willingly spent their childhood training to become warriors. Warfare was broadly defined to include not just large-scale encounters between tribes but also raids by small groups for horses, scalps, or revenge. The common element in all cases was an emphasis on acquiring war honors through individual, often reckless, acts of bravery. The pursuit of war honors ensured that chiefs would have difficulty controlling their young men and that battle tactics would often be undermined by overeager warriors.

war leader: blotahunka (*blotáhųka*), sometimes translated as 'partisan'. Each band had a number of war leaders. In large war parties, the overall leader (blotahunka itančan [*blotáhųka itą́hą*]) would appoint a number of blotahunka to act as his lieutenants.

war paint: A warrior painted his face, body, and horse in accordance with the instructions he received in his vision. The pattern thus had a sacred dimension known only to him.

war party, return of: A successful war party would stop for the night within easy traveling distance of home so that the camp could be alerted to their return. With faces blackened and scalps and trophies held aloft, the warriors charged into camp singing. Men gave the scalps to their sisters and other female relatives, who would tie them to sticks and dance the Scalp Dance with them later that night.

wasna: (*wasná*). The Lakota name for pemmican, a mixture of grease, pounded dry meat, and pounded chokecherries, with perhaps some sugar. Wasna was carried by warriors on raids.

Wažaže: (*wažáže*) 'Osage'. Both the Oglalas and the Brulés had a band
    called Wažaže. The significance of the name is not known.
white buffalo: A white, or albino, buffalo was considered to be sacred.
    These rare animals were linked to White Buffalo Cow Woman,
    who had brought the gift of the sacred pipe from Wankan Tanka
    to the Lakotas. *See also* Buffalo Calf Pipe.
White Buffalo Cow Woman: Woȟpe (*woȟpé*). The wakan being who
    brought the pipe to the Lakotas. *See also* Buffalo Calf Pipe.
winter count: waniyetu iyawapi (*waníyetu iyáwapi*). In Lakota culture
    the passage of time was reckoned in winters (waniyetu [*waníyetu*]),
    and tribal history was maintained by means of winter counts. The
    winter count keeper painted on a skin a pictograph representing
    some event significant to the band that had occurred during the
    year. Thus, various winter counts often recorded different events
    for the same year. Each pictograph served as a mnemonic device
    for the keeper or for others, bringing events of each year to mind.
    Past years were referred to by their pictograph—for example,
    the Year (or winter) of Plenty Buffaloes. It is not known how or
    by whom the specific event to be depicted was selected.
woman feast: *See* Buffalo Sing.
Yanktonais: A Sioux tribe whose territory was east of the Missouri River
    in present-day North Dakota and South Dakota.

PLACE NAMES

Arrow Creek: A tributary of the Yellowstone River west of the Bighorn
    River.
Ash Creek: A small tributary of the Little Bighorn River.
Bad Lands: An arid area of eroded gullies, rock formations, and buttes
    east of the Black Hills along the White River.
Bear Butte: A prominent, isolated butte northeast of the Black Hills
    that was recognized as sacred by the northern Plains tribes.
Bear Lodge: The Lakota name for Devils Tower, a volcanic peak in the
    western Black Hills that was regarded as sacred by the Lakotas
    and other Plains tribes.

Beaver Creek: A tributary of the Platte River. (There are a number of streams in Lakota territory bearing this name, including one that flows into the Cheyenne River north of Fort Laramie, but the Platte River tributary is the one Sandoz is referring to.)

Belle Fourche River: A river beginning in the Big Horn Mountains and flowing north around the Black Hills, then east into the Cheyenne River.

Blue Water: A creek flowing south into the North Platte River southwest of the Sand Hills.

Bordeaux store: Located on the North Platte River about eight miles below Fort Laramie.

Bozeman Trail: A shortcut through the Powder River basin to the Montana goldfields. It was laid out in 1863 by John Bozeman and John Jacobs.

Bridger's road: The Bridger Trail. Established in 1864 as a safer alternative to the Bozeman Trail, the Bridger Trail left the North Platte River just west of present-day Casper, Wyoming, and headed northwest, staying west of the Big Horn Mountains and avoiding the Powder River basin hunting grounds.

Chalk Buttes: A rock formation ten miles southeast of present-day Ekalaka in the southeast corner of Montana.

Chugwater Creek: A stream flowing north into the Laramie River.

Cloud Peak: The highest peak of the Big Horn Mountains.

Crazy Woman Creek: A headwater of the Powder River in northeast Wyoming.

Crow Butte: A hill east of present-day Crawford, Nebraska.

Deer Creek: A creek emptying into the North Platte River about one hundred miles west of Fort Laramie at the site of present-day Glenrock, Wyoming.

Dry Fork: A creek flowing into the Powder River. It was the site of Fort Reno.

Fort Berthold: Established in 1845 as a trading post on the Missouri River below the mouth of the Little Missouri River. The fort was converted to an army post and renamed by General Alfred Sully in 1864.

Fort Kearney: Located on the south bank of the Platte River in central Nebraska from 1848 to 1871. The fort was an important army post and military depot on the Oregon Trail.

Fort Keogh: Located on the south bank of the Yellowstone River less than two miles above the mouth of the Tongue River in northeastern Montana. The fort was established in 1876 as a base of operations against the northern Indian tribes.

Fort Laramie: Located on the North Platte River at the mouth of the Laramie River. The site was first used in 1834 as a fur trading post named Fort William, later renamed Fort John. It was purchased by the army in 1849 to provide protection for settlers traveling along the Oregon Trail and renamed in honor of Jacques La Ramie, a local French fur trader.

Fort Phil Kearny: Established in 1866 on Piney Creek along the Bozeman Trail. It was abandoned in April 1868 in compliance with the Treaty of 1868.

Fort Reno: A Bozeman Trail fort built in 1865 on the east bank of the Powder River at the Dry Fork. It was abandoned in April 1868 in compliance with the Treaty of 1868.

Fort Rice: Located on the Missouri River ten miles north of the mouth of the Cannonball River. General Alfred Sully established the fort in July 1864 during his campaign against the Santee Sioux.

Fort Robinson: Established in March 1874 as Camp Robinson north of the White River near its confluence with Soldier Creek, two miles west of present-day Crawford, Nebraska. It was officially designated Fort Robinson in January 1878.

Good River: Wašte Wakpa (*wašté wakpá*). The Lakota name for the Cheyenne River.

Goose Creek: A headwater of the Tongue River near present-day Sheridan, Wyoming.

Grandmother's country: Unčiyapi tamakoče (*učíyapi thamákhočhe*). The Lakota name for Canada, referring to Queen Victoria.

Gratiot trading house: An American Fur Company trading post located on the North Platte River four or five miles below Fort Laramie.

Green River: Located in west-central Wyoming. From 1825 until 1840, it was the site of an annual trade rendezvous for traders, trappers, and Indians.

Hanging Woman Creek: A tributary of the Tongue River.

Holy Road: Čanku Wakan (*čhaŋkú wakhą́*). The Lakota name for the Oregon Trail.

Horse Creek: A creek that flows generally east, then north into the North Platte River some thirty miles below Fort Laramie.

Julesburg: A town on the South Platte River in the northeast corner of Colorado. Established in 1859 as a trading post by Jules Beni, Julesburg became an important station on the Overland Trail and a notorious center of vice.

Lance Creek: A headwater of the Cheyenne River northwest of present-day Lusk, Wyoming.

Lightning Creek: One of the headwaters of the Cheyenne River north of Fort Laramie.

Little Beaver Creek: A tributary of the Sweetwater River in central Wyoming.

Little Horn River: The Little Bighorn River. A tributary of the Bighorn River.

Little Powder River: A tributary of the Powder River.

Lodgepole Creek: A tributary of the Powder River.

Lodge Trail Ridge: Located near Fort Phil Kearny. It was the site of the Fetterman fight.

Lone Tree council place: Located on the White River about eight miles east of Red Cloud Agency and characterized by a large tree standing by itself. It was the site of the 1875 treaty negotiations in which the Allison Commission hoped to purchase the Black Hills from the Lakotas.

Medicine Water: The Lakota name for Lake De Smet, seven miles north of present-day Buffalo, Wyoming.

Milk River: A tributary of the Missouri River in northwest Montana.

North Platte River: A large river beginning in central Wyoming and flowing southeast across Nebraska into the Platte River.

Pa Sapa: (*pahá sápa*) 'black hills'. The Lakota name for the Black Hills.

Peno Creek: A stream near Fort Phil Kearny.

Piney Creek: A branch of the Powder River in the foothills of the Big Horn Mountains. It was the site of Fort Phil Kearny.

Platte Bridge stockade: Located on the North Platte River at present-day Casper, Wyoming. The stockade was established in 1858 at the site of a bridge built by Louis Guinard, also in 1858. In 1865 the stockade was renamed Fort Caspar in honor of Caspar Collins but was abandoned two years later. Both it and the bridge were subsequently burned down by Indians.

Powder River: The easternmost river flowing north into the Yellowstone River.

Powder River road: *See* Bozeman Trail.

Prairie Dog Creek: A creek in the lower Tongue River watershed.

Pumpkin Buttes: A range of four prominent mesas in present-day Campbell County, Wyoming, and the source of the Belle Fourche River.

Rawhide Buttes: Rocky heights south of present-day Lusk, Wyoming.

Rawhide Creek: A stream flowing south into the North Platte River about ten miles below Fort Laramie.

Republican River: A large river in southern Nebraska flowing east into the Missouri River.

Richard Bridge: A toll bridge across the North Platte River. Six miles east of Fort Caspar, it was built by a French trader named John Baptiste Richard Sr. The bridge operated from 1852 until 1865.

Rosebud Creek: A stream flowing north into the Yellowstone River between the Tongue and Bighorn rivers.

Running Water: The Niobrara River. It flows east across northern Nebraska from Wyoming to the Missouri River.

Sand Creek: A tributary of the Arkansas River southeast of Denver. At this location on November 29, 1864, a force of seven hundred soldiers (mostly volunteers) under Colonel John Chivington attacked a peaceful camp of Cheyennes and Arapahos under Chief

Black Kettle. Over 150 Indians were killed and mutilated, mostly old men, women, and children.

Shell River: The Lakota name for the North Platte River.

Shining Mountains: The Rocky Mountains west of the Big Horn Mountains.

Slim Buttes: A rock formation north of the Black Hills near present-day Reva, South Dakota.

Smoky Hill River: A river in central Kansas flowing east into the Kansas River.

Solomon River: A river in northern Kansas flowing east into the Kansas River.

Sweetwater: The Sweetwater River. The Oregon Trail left the North Platte River and followed the Sweetwater west to South Pass and over the Rocky Mountains.

Tongue River: A river flowing north to the Yellowstone River west of and parallel to the Powder River.

Warbonnet Creek: A tributary of the White River northwest of present-day Crawford, Nebraska.

Ward and Guerrier trading house: A trading post nine miles above Fort Laramie on the North Platte River. It was operated by Seth E. Ward and William Guerrier.

Washita River: A river in western Oklahoma flowing southeast into the Red River. At this location in November 1868, a force under Lieutenant Colonel George Armstrong Custer attacked the peaceful Cheyenne village of Chief Black Kettle, indiscriminately killing men, women, and children.

Whetstone Agency: Established in late 1868 on the Missouri River at Whetstone Creek, twenty-three miles above Fort Randall, as the new agency for the Brulé and Oglala tribes. The Lakotas were unaware that the 1868 treaty authorized this move, and even friendly Lakotas had to be forced to journey there under military threat. The agency became notorious for the whiskey ranches set up across the river. After continuous and bitter complaining, the Indians at Whetstone Agency were moved west in June 1871. The new Whetstone Agency was established at White Clay

Creek for Spotted Tail's Brulés, and a separate agency was created for the Oglalas. Whetstone Agency was later renamed Spotted Tail Agency.

White Earth River: Makasan Wakpa (*makhásą wakpá*). The Lakota name for the White River, which flows east through South Dakota into the Missouri River.

White Mountains: The Lakota name for the Big Horn Mountains.

White Stone Hill: Located east of the Missouri River near present-day Kulm, North Dakota. Here on September 3, 1863, General Alfred Sully, looking for Santees who had fled Minnesota following the Dakota Conflict of 1862, attacked a large encampment of peaceful Yanktonais Sioux, killing and capturing many women and children and destroying the Yanktonais' possessions and winter provisions.

Wind River: A tributary of the Bighorn River in west-central Wyoming.

Wolf Mountains: The Lakota name for the mountains surrounding the Tongue River valley.

PEOPLE

American Horse: Wašičun Tašunke (*wašíčhų thašų́ke*) 'white person horse'. Son of Sitting Bear of the True Oglala band. Nicknamed "Spider," American Horse (1840–1908) succeeded his father as band leader and was elected as a shirt wearer in 1868. He was married to a daughter of Red Cloud and joined him in 1871, becoming one of the agency chiefs. American Horse was a noted progressive on the reservation.

Ashes: Uncle of Crazy Horse.

Bad Face: Itešiča (*itéšiča*). The nickname of either Smoke's son (name lost) or his nephew Spotted Bear. It is said that his shrewish wife would loudly upbraid him for having a "bad face," and the people began referring to him—and eventually to his band—by that name.

Bad Heart Bull: Older brother of He Dog and nephew of Red Cloud.

He kept a winter count history of the Bad Faces. His son later drew a pictorial history of the Oglalas.

Bad Wound: Owešiča (*owéšiča*). Chief of the True Oglala band and leader of the Bear people. He was an advocate of peace and died in 1865.

Bear Coat: The Lakota name for Colonel Nelson A. Miles.

Bear Ribs: Bear's Rib. Hunkpapa. In 1856 Bear's Rib was appointed head chief of the Lakotas by General William S. Harney. He was killed by some Sans Arcs in May 1862 for accepting the annuities due under the 1851 treaty, even though he had been warned against doing so.

Beckwourth: James P. Beckwourth. Born in Fredricksburg, Virginia, Beckwourth (1798–1866) was a mulatto trapper and hunter who, by 1858, had joined the Crow Indians. He was with them when he died.

Big Bat: Baptiste Gene Pourier. Pourier (1842–1928) was born in St. Charles (in present-day Missouri); his mother was Sioux. He came west to work in the fur trade, and in 1859 he married Josephine Richard, the youngest daughter of John Richard Sr. Pourier also served as an interpreter and scout.

Big Leggins: Johnnie Bruguier. Bruguier (1849–98) was the son of a French father and Sioux mother. After attending the College of Christian Brothers in St. Louis, he served as the interpreter at Standing Rock Agency in 1875. On December 14, 1875, he killed a man and fled to the Black Hills, where for two months he lived in the lodge of Sitting Bull, acting as his personal interpreter and secretary. From 1876 until 1881 he worked as a guide and interpreter for Colonel Nelson A. Miles. He was killed by blows to the head from an unknown assailant.

Big Mouth: Itanka (*ithą́ka*). A member of the Loafer band. He had been a member of the Bad Faces band, but when they moved north to the Powder River in 1859, Big Mouth decided to stay at Fort Laramie, where he became a leader of the Loafer band. On October 27, 1869, at Whetstone Agency, a drunken Big Mouth tried to kill Spotted Tail and was himself shot and killed.

Big Partisan: Blotahunka Tanka (*blotáhuka tháka*) 'big war leader'. Although listed in 1845 as the chief of the Brulé Orphan band (Wablenica [*wablénica*]), after 1851 he was associated with the Corn band (Wagmeza Yuha [*wagméza yuhá*] 'owns corn'). He was the leader of the conservative members of the Corn band, those who wanted to continue to hunt and roam as in the past. In 1869 he joined Spotted Tail and ultimately settled on Rosebud Reservation.

Big Ribs: Oglala. A chief of the Loafer band. In 1866 he led a delegation of Loafers to the Powder River country in an effort to persuade the northern Oglala groups to meet with the Edmunds Commission and sign a new treaty.

Big Road: Čanku Tanka (*čhaků tháka*). Also known as Wide Trail. Big Road was a shirt wearer and chief closely allied with Crazy Horse. In 1877 he joined Sitting Bull in Canada rather than settle on the reservation, although he eventually returned to Pine Ridge Reservation.

Bissonnette: Joseph Bissonnette. Born in St. Louis, Bissonnette (1818–94) was an early fur trader on the upper Platte River. In 1875 he accompanied Red Cloud to Washington DC as an interpreter. He eventually settled on Wounded Knee Creek on Pine Ridge Reservation.

Black Buffalo Woman: Daughter of Red Cloud's brother. Black Buffalo Woman married No Water, the leader of the Badger Eaters (Ȟoka Yuta [*ȟoká yúta*]) band of Oglalas. They had three children. During the summer of 1870 she left her husband for Crazy Horse but returned to him shortly afterward.

Black Crow: Kanği Sapa (*kháği sápa*). Leader of a Brulé band. Black Crow was married to one of Spotted Tail's daughters. He had ambitions of being named head chief at Spotted Tail Agency and was later implicated in the 1881 assassination of his father-in-law.

Black Elk: Heȟaka Sapa (*heȟáka sápa*). A member of Big Road's band. His father's brother was Crazy Horse's paternal grandfather. Black Elk took part in the Fetterman fight in 1866 during which his right leg was crushed, crippling him for the rest of his life. He died in 1889 on Pine Ridge Reservation. *Black Elk* was a family name, and both his father and son were also named Black Elk. All of them were shamans. The life of his son, Nicholas Black Elk, is chronicled in *Black Elk Speaks* and *The Sixth Grandfather*.

Black Fox: Šungila Sapa (*šųǧíla sápa*). Oglala. Half brother of Kicking Bear and Flying Hawk. On September 4, 1877, after Crazy Horse had fled to Spotted Tail Agency, Black Fox commanded Crazy Horse's warriors when they met the force sent to arrest him, displaying courage that was admired by both sides of the confrontation. Later that year he fled to Canada rather than remain on the reservation. He was killed on his return to the United States in 1881 by members of an enemy tribe.

Black Kettle: Born around 1801, Black Kettle was a Southern Cheyenne chief and advocate of peace with the whites. On two occasions—at Sand Creek in 1864 and on the Washita River in 1868—his peaceful camp was attacked by army units, and most of the inhabitants were slaughtered. Black Kettle himself was killed on the Washita in 1868.

Black Moon: Hanwi Sapa (*hąwí sápa*). Hunkpapa chief, shaman, and ally of Sitting Bull. Black Moon was the leader of the Sun Dance held shortly before the Battle of the Little Bighorn. During the dance Sitting Bull had his famous vision of soldiers falling. Black Moon's son, also named Black Moon and called Hanwi Sapa Činčala (*hąwí sápa čhįčála*) 'young black moon', was killed in the battle.

Black Shawl Woman: Šina Sapawin (*šiná sápawį*). Wife of Crazy Horse. Black Shawl Woman (1843–1927) was the daughter of Old Red Feather, whose family maintained close kinship ties with Big Road's band. She married Crazy Horse in 1871 and gave birth to their only child, a daughter named They are Afraid of Her, who died in 1873.

Black Twin: Also known as Holy Bald Eagle. He was one of the last elected shirt wearers of the northern Oglalas. Black Twin was a traditionalist who bitterly opposed white encroachment onto

Lakota lands. He was held in such high esteem that many young warriors abandoned Red Cloud and the agency to join him. He passed away on the Powder River, probably in February 1876.

Bloody Knife: Born circa 1840 as the son of a Hunkpapa father and an Arikara mother, Bloody Knife was raised with the Lakotas. He was teased by other children, including a youthful Gall, until he and his mother moved back with the Arikaras in 1856. In 1865 Bloody Knife became a scout for the army and a favorite of George Armstrong Custer. He was killed at the Battle of the Little Bighorn in 1876.

Bordeaux: James Bordeaux. Bordeaux (1814–78) was born in St. Charles (in present-day Missouri) and came west as a trader for the American Fur Company. He married a Brulé woman, Huntkalutawin (*hųtkalutawį*) 'red loon woman', also known as Marie, and operated a trading house near Fort Laramie. He eventually settled on Rosebud Reservation.

Bordeaux, Louie: Louis Bordeaux. The third son of James Bordeaux and his Brulé wife, Louis (1849–1917) was frequently chosen by Lakota chiefs to be their interpreter on trips to Washington DC. He was the official interpreter at Spotted Tail Agency at the time of Crazy Horse's death. Bordeaux held various positions on Rosebud Reservation, where he lived until his death.

Boucher: Frank C. Boucher. A trader married to one of Spotted Tail's daughters. It was rumored that he traded guns and ammunition to the Lakotas in exchange for valuables looted from dead whites.

Bradley, General: Lieutenant Colonel Luther P. Bradley. Born in Connecticut, Bradley (1877–1910) attained the rank of brigadier general in the Civil War then accepted a commission as lieutenant colonel in the regular army. He served throughout the northern plains during the Indian wars, and he was commander of Camp Robinson at the time of Crazy Horse's death. Although Sandoz identifies him as "General Bradley," he was not a general at that time and retired as a colonel in 1886.

Brave Bear: Mato Ohitika (*mathó ohítika*). Chief of the Oyukpe band

(Oyuȟpe [*oyúȟpe*] 'unloaded'). He was the father of the shirt wearer Sword and a member of the 1870 delegation to Washington DC.

Brazeau: John Brazeau. A French Creole who worked for the American Fur Company. Some Lakotas claimed that he was the father of Frank Grouard (Grabber).

Bridger: Jim Bridger. Born in Richmond, Virginia, Bridger (1804–81) moved west and gained fame as a mountain man, trapper, trader, and guide.

Brown Hat: Wapoštangi (*waphóštągi*). Brulé. Later known as Baptiste Good Chief. A winter count keeper of the Brulé, his winter count was published in the *Tenth Annual Report of the Bureau of American Ethnology* (1893).

Brughier: *See* Big Leggins.

Bull Bear: Mato Tatanka (*mathó thatháka*). Chief of the Kiyuksa (*khiyúksa*) 'break in half' band. He was a rival of Smoke for overall leadership of the Oglalas in the 1830s. During a dispute in 1841, Bull Bear was killed by Red Cloud, a nephew of Smoke. After the killing, Bull Bear's followers, the Bear people, remained in the Platte River country, forming a southern division of the Oglala tribe.

Bull Head: Tatanka Pa (*thatháka phá*). Minniconjou band chief and maternal uncle of Crazy Horse.

Bull Tail: Tatanka Sinte (*thatháka sįté*). Brulé chief. Bull Tail spoke for the Lakotas at a council with Colonel S. W. Kearny at Fort John (later Fort Laramie) in 1845. He was the father of Iron Shell and died in 1854, right before the Grattan fight.

Burke: Captain Daniel W. Burke. In September 1877 Burke was in charge of the small army garrison named Camp Sheridan, attached to Spotted Tail Agency. He was not the Indian agent as identified by Sandoz. *See also* Lee.

California Joe: Moses E. Milner. Born in Kentucky, Milner (1829–76) came west as a trapper. He served as a scout and guide for the army, including generals George Armstrong Custer and Philip H. Sheridan, but his drinking lessened his effectiveness. He was murdered by "Red Dog" Tom Newcomb at Camp Robinson on October 29, 1876.

Carrington: Colonel Henry B. Carrington. In 1866, with a force of seven hundred infantry but no cavalry, Carrington (1824–1912) was ordered to build forts and organize a system of road patrols along the Bozeman Trail. His unexpected arrival at Fort Laramie in June startled and angered the Lakotas, who immediately abandoned the treaty negotiations taking place at the time.

Chips: Woptuȟ'a (*wóptuȟ'a*). A member of No Water's Bad Faces band. Chips (1836–1916) was the wičaša wakan (*wičháša wakhą́*) 'holy man' who provided Crazy Horse with wotawe (*wóthawe*), objects imbued with protective power. Chips claimed to be the only one who knew where Crazy Horse was buried. During the reservation years, Chips was a noted *yuwipi* man, one who performs ceremonies, finds lost objects, and receives answers through prayers.

Clark: William Philo Clark. A West Point graduate, Clark (1845–84) was assigned to the Second Cavalry in 1868. When reservation maintenance was transferred to the army in 1876, then-First Lieutenant Clark was named military agent of Fort Robinson and commander of the U.S. Indian Scouts. Clark was an expert on sign language and wrote a manual on the subject that was published after his sudden death in 1884.

Clifford, Hank: Clifford (1837–1906) was a freighter, trader, guide for the army, and, later, a fossil hunter. He married a Lakota woman, had seven children, and became a cattle rancher on Pine Ridge Reservation.

Club Man: Minneconjou. Club Man surrendered with Crazy Horse in 1877. He was married to Crazy Horse's sister, and they had eight children.

Cole: Colonel Nelson Cole. In the summer of 1865, Cole (1832–99) commanded the eastern wing of the three-prong Connor expedition into the Powder River basin. Cole's campaign suffered one disaster after another.

Collins, Caspar: Lieutenant Caspar Collins (1844–65) was the son of

Lieutenant Colonel William Collins, the commander of Fort
Laramie during the Civil War. The elder Collins was generally
sympathetic and friendly toward the Lakotas and maintained
good relations with them; Caspar was knowledgeable about the
Lakotas and well-liked by them. In the hostilities that followed
the Sand Creek massacre, he was killed at the battle at Platte
Bridge in July 1865.

Conquering Bear: Mato Wayuhi (*mathó wayúhi*) 'bear frightens away';
also translated into English as Frightening Bear and Brave Bear.
Chief of the Wažaže band of Brulés, Conquering Bear was appointed head chief of the Lakotas by Colonel David Dawson
Mitchell under the provisions of the 1851 treaty. He was killed at
the Grattan fight in 1854.

Crazy Horse: Tašunke Witko (*thašúke witkó*) 'his horse is crazy'. Crazy
Horse (1840–77) had been called His Horse Looking before
his father gave him his own name and took the name *Worm* for
himself. Crazy Horse's mother was a Minneconjou named Rattle
Blanket Woman, who may have been the paternal aunt of Touch
the Clouds. After Rattle Blanket Woman died in 1844 (perhaps
committing suicide in grief over the death of a relative), Worm
married two sisters of Spotted Tail, establishing Crazy Horse's
kinship with the Brulé leader.

Crook, George: An 1852 graduate of West Point, Brigadier General
George Crook (1828–90) was in command of the Department of
the Platte from 1875 until 1882. During his tenure he supervised
all of the major military campaigns against the Lakotas and the
other northern Plains tribes. He was called Three Stars by the
Lakotas, referring to the star on each shoulder and the one on
his hat.

Curly: The boyhood nickname of Crazy Horse.

Custer: George Armstrong Custer. Born in Ohio in 1839, Custer graduated from West Point in 1861. During the Civil War he attained
the rank of major general of volunteers, but he was forced to
revert to his prewar rank after the war's end. Custer was placed
in command of the Seventh Cavalry and participated in several

well-publicized campaigns in the West. He was killed near the Little Bighorn River in 1876.

Dark: A Cheyenne shaman. Dark was said to have the power to cause the enemy to fall dead or to make musket balls from the white men's guns fall harmlessly to the ground. After 1857 he was called Gray Beard. He was killed in 1875 while being transported to prison in Florida.

Deon, Peter A.: Also known as Samuel. Deon was a French Canadian from Montreal. He lived as a trader among the Lakotas beginning in the 1850s, working initially for the American Fur Company. He married a Lakota woman and lived with Red Cloud, who became his sponsor, protector, and friend.

Dull Knife: Cheyenne chief. Also known as Morning Star. Dull Knife (1808–83) fought at the Battle of the Little Bighorn. In November 1876 he and his band managed to escape a surprise attack by the army, although they had to abandon all of their possessions to do so. They surrendered in February 1877 and were transported to Indian Territory (in present-day Oklahoma). In September 1878 Dull Knife and Little Wolf escaped with their bands and set out for their homeland in the north. They separated on the North Platte, and Dull Knife's band was captured and taken to Fort Robinson. Dull Knife eventually rejoined the Cheyennes in Montana, where he died.

Dye: Brevet Brigadier General William Dye. Dye was commander of Fort Laramie in November 1868, when Red Cloud signed the Treaty of 1868.

Eubanks, Mrs.: Lucinda Eubanks. Born in Pennsylvania, by 1864 Eubanks (1840–1913) was married, the mother of two, and living at Little Blue River in Kansas. On August 7 of that year the Cheyennes raided the area, killing forty settlers and capturing a number of others, including Mrs. Eubanks and her children. She was traded to the Oglalas, spending time with Two Faces and Blackfoot. After nine months of captivity, the two chiefs took her to Fort Laramie, where she was released, and they were hanged.

Fetterman: Lieutenant Colonel William J. Fetterman. On December

21, 1866, Fetterman (1833–66) led a group of eighty men from Fort Phil Kearny to relieve a wood train under attack. He was under orders not to pursue any of the Indians, but he was lured away by Crazy Horse, and his entire force was killed.

Fitzgerald: Thomas Fitzgerald. Born in Ireland in 1799, Fitzgerald came to the United States at age sixteen. In 1822 or 1823 he began work in the fur trade, and by the 1840s he was acknowledged as the most famous guide in the Far West. In August 1846 he was appointed as the first Indian agent of the Upper Platte and Arkansas Agency, a position he retained until his death from pneumonia in Washington DC on February 7, 1854.

Flying By: Kinyan Iyaya (kįyą́ iyáya) 'one who flies when going'. Minneconjou. Son of Lame Deer. Flying By was a close ally of Crazy Horse following the Battle of the Little Bighorn.

Fontenelle: Lucien Fontenelle. Fontenelle (1800–ca. 1834) was a French trader for the American Fur Company and was married to an Omaha woman. His son Logan Fontenelle became a chief of the Omahas before being killed by a Brulé war party in 1855.

Four Horns: He Topa (hé tópa). Hunkpapa chief. The elder brother of Sitting Bull's father. Four Horns (ca. 1800–1887) preceded Sitting Bull into Canada, returning to the United States with him in 1881. After his release from prison in 1883, Four Horns settled on Standing Rock Reservation.

Fouts: Captain William D. Fouts, Seventh Cavalry. In June 1865 he was in charge of escorting the friendly Lakotas against their will to Fort Kearney; while en route the Lakotas escaped.

Gall: Pizi (pizí). Hunkpapa. Gall (1840–93) was a legendary warrior and a fierce opponent of the whites. His family was killed during the Battle of the Little Bighorn. Gall took his band to Canada but returned to the United States to surrender in 1880. Afterward, on Standing Rock Reservation, he joined the Episcopal Church and became a justice of the Indian Police Court.

Garnett, Billy: Garnett (1855–1929) was the son of an army officer, General Richard B. Garnett (killed in Pickett's Charge at Gettysburg), and an Oglala woman named Looks at Him. He was the interpreter for Agent James J. Saville at Red Cloud Agency from 1873 to 1876, worked for the army as a guide, interpreter, and as chief of Indian Scouts, and, after 1878, worked for the Indian Office in various positions. He settled on Pine Ridge Reservation.

Good Weasel: Itunkasan Wašte (*ithúkas' wašté*). Good Weasel was described as always being with Crazy Horse, perhaps as a war chief of one of the warrior lodges. He was part of the small war party led by Crazy Horse in 1870 in which High Back Bone was killed.

Grabber: The Lakota name for Frank Grouard.

Grass: Peži (*phežĭ*). Oglala. A chief of the Loafer band. Grass was once wounded and captured by soldiers near Platte Bridge. Expecting to be killed, he was instead taken to the post's hospital. After his recovery, he vowed never to fight the whites again. He signed the Treaty of 1868.

Grattan: Second Lieutenant John L. Grattan. After graduating from West Point, Grattan (1829–54) was posted to Fort Laramie. He was contemptuous of Indians and bragged about teaching them a lesson. On August 19, 1854, he volunteered to arrest the Minneconjou responsible for killing a settler's cow, an action that resulted in his and his men's deaths.

Grouard, Frank: Grouard claimed that he had been born in the Society Islands, the son of a missionary. The Lakotas believed that he was the son of a French Creole named John Brazeau and a Lakota woman. In 1869 he was either captured (according to him) by some northern Lakotas or he fled to them after getting into trouble at school. In 1873 he was hired by General George Crook as an army scout and interpreter at Fort Laramie. Grouard had a somewhat shady reputation, and rumors circulated that his mistranslation to General Crook somehow led to Crazy Horse's death.

Harney: Brigadier General William Harney. Called White Beard by the Lakotas. Harney (1800–1889) led the attack on Little Thunder's camp on Blue Water Creek in September 1855. The following March at Fort Pierre, in order to control the young warriors, he tried to convince some of the northern bands to adopt a military-style, authoritarian political system (the Senate rejected his plan). After the 1868 treaty, Harney was placed in charge of administering the Great Sioux Reservation.

He Dog: Šunka Bloka (*šúka bloká*) 'male dog'. A member of the Bad Faces band. His mother was a sister of Red Cloud. In 1865 He Dog (1840–1936) became a shirt wearer, and in 1870 he was elected to lead the powerful Crow Owners Society. He Dog was a lifelong friend and companion of Crazy Horse and surrendered with him. He settled on Pine Ridge Reservation.

High Back Bone: Čantku Wankatuya (*čhạtkú wạkátuya*) 'chest high up'; also translated as Hump. Minneconjou. High Back Bone was the war leader at the Fetterman and Wagon Box fights. He was killed by the Shoshones in 1870.

High Bear: Matho Wankatuya (*mathó wạkátuya*). Also known as Tall Bear. High Bear was the leader of a small band of Sans Arcs. He was a close ally of the Minneconjou Touch the Clouds, with whom he enlisted in the U.S. Indian Scouts in 1877. High Bear died on Cheyenne River Reservation in 1910.

Hinman: Rev. Samuel D. Hinman. An Episcopal priest and missionary. As a seminary student in 1860 in Minnesota, Hinman volunteered to establish the first Episcopal mission among the Sioux. Early in 1878 he was dismissed by Bishop William H. Hare on vague charges of immorality and fiscal irregularities, and though he won reinstatement from the church and libel damages from the courts, his missionary career was over. Both before and after his dismissal he served as an interpreter at treaty councils, but the Lakotas distrusted him, believing that he misled them and, at times, lied outright. He died in Minnesota in 1890.

His Horse Looking: The first adult name of Crazy Horse. It was given to him by his father after he was the first to ride a captured wild horse.

Hump: *See* High Back Bone.

Ice: A Northern Cheyenne shaman. Later known as White Bull. Ice (ca. 1837–1921) was said to have the power to cause the enemy to fall dead or to make musket balls from the white men's guns fall harmlessly to the ground. He made a war bonnet for Roman Nose that protected him during battle, but a woman serving food inadvertently violated one of the bonnet's taboos, and he was killed.

Inkpaduta: (*íkpaduta*) 'red end'. Santee. In 1857, in revenge for the killing of his family by white settlers, Inkpaduta (ca. 1797–1881) and a small group of warriors killed thirty-eight men, women, and children in what became known as the Spirit Lake (Iowa) Massacre. He took part in the Dakota Conflict of 1862, then fled west onto the plains, eluding all efforts to capture him. He was with Sitting Bull's Hunkpapa band on the Little Bighorn and fled with them to Canada, where he died.

Iron Plume: Sans Arc chief. Also known as American Horse. On September 9, 1876, Iron Plume's camp at Slim Buttes was surprised, and he was wounded and captured by elements of General George Crook's army. Crazy Horse rushed to the scene, but in the ensuing Battle of Slim Buttes he could not defeat Crook's army.

Iron Shell: Maza Pankeska (*máza phąkéska*). Brulé. A chief of the Orphan band (Wableniča [*wabléniča*]) and son of old Chief Bull Tail. Iron Shell was warlike and led his band north to join the northern Oglala groups in the Powder River country. He later settled on Rosebud Reservation.

Irwin, Dr.: Dr. James Irwin. Indian agent at Red Cloud Agency. He took charge on July 1, 1877, shortly after Crazy Horse had surrendered.

Janis, Antoine: Joseph Antoine Janis. Janis (1824–90) was born near St. Louis and came west in 1841, working for various traders before being appointed interpreter for Indian Agent Thomas Twiss. His wife was a member of Red Cloud's family, and he was often requested to interpret for Red Cloud. Janis died on Pine Ridge Reservation.

Janis, Nick: Nicholas Janis. Born near St. Louis, Janis (1827–1902) was a trader and trapper and the brother of Antoine Janis. Nicholas married Red Cloud's daughter (or niece) around 1851. Although he was a guide on Connors's 1865 expedition to the Powder River country, he remained one of Red Cloud's favorite and trusted interpreters, making several trips to Washington DC with him. He died on Pine Ridge Reservation.

Kelly, Mrs.: Fanny Kelly. On July 12, 1864, a force of Oglalas attacked the wagons of the Larimer and Kelly families about eighty miles west of Fort Laramie. Sarah Larimer and Fanny Kelly (1845–1904) were captured, along with some of their children. Kelly was sold to the Blackfeet Sioux; after five months in captivity, she finessed her way inside Fort Sully and was released. In 1871 she published *Narrative of My Captivity Among the Sioux Indians*. That same year she sued Sarah Larimer in a dispute over the authorship of Larimer's book. After several trials and appeals, the suit was settled in 1876.

Kicking Bear: Kicking Bear (1848–1904) was an Oglala by birth, but he became a Minneconjou band chief through his marriage to Woodpecker Woman, a niece of Minneconjou leader Big Foot. He was a close ally of his cousin Crazy Horse. Kicking Bear later became one of the leaders of the Ghost Dance among the Lakotas.

Lame Deer: Tȟáȟča Hušte (*tháȟča hušté*). Minneconjou chief. Lame Deer was a close ally of Crazy Horse. He and his band refused to settle at an agency, and he was killed near Rosebud Creek on May 7, 1877, by troops of Colonel Nelson A. Miles in the last conflict of the Sioux Wars.

Larimer, Mrs.: Sarah Larimer. On July 12, 1864, a force of Oglalas attacked the wagons of the Larimer and Kelly families about eighty miles west of Fort Laramie. Sarah Larimer and Fanny Kelly were captured, along with some of their children. Larimer and her son managed to escape on the second night, and they made it back to the Deer Creek telegraph station. In 1870 she published a purported account of her ordeal, entitled *The Capture and Escape: Or, Life Among the Sioux*, and was immediately sued by Fanny

Kelly over the authorship of her memoir. After several trials and appeals the suit was settled in 1876.

Larrabee, Joe: Joseph Larrabee (or Laravie) was a mixed-blood French trader living among the southern tribes of the Sioux and Cheyennes. With his first wife, a Southern Cheyenne woman known as Chi-Chi, Larrabee had four daughters, the second of which, Helen, was married to Crazy Horse for a brief time before his death.

Larrabee woman: Helen "Nellie" Larrabee (or Laravie). Daughter of Joe Larrabee and his Cheyenne wife. Nellie Larrabee was known among the Lakotas as Ištağiwin (*ištáǧiwį*) 'brown eyes woman'. She was married to Crazy Horse for a brief time before his death, following which she settled among Lip's Wažaže band of Brulés near Eagle Nest Butte.

Lean Elk: The Lakota name for John Richard Jr.

Lee: Lieutenant Jesse M. Lee. On January 11, 1877, he was appointed as acting Indian agent at Spotted Tail Agency, serving until July 1878. Sandoz identifies a man named Burke as the agent, but this is in error.

Little Bat: Baptiste Garnier. Little Bat (1854–1900) was born at Fort Laramie; his father was a trader, also named Baptiste. Making his living principally as a hunter, it was Little Bat who, in 1890, discovered Big Foot's camp, led the Seventh Cavalry to it, and accompanied them to Wounded Knee.

Little Big Man: Wičaša Tankala (*wičháša tȟákala*). Little Big Man was a close ally of his cousin Crazy Horse. In 1875, during a council with the Allison Commission negotiating the purchase of the Black Hills, he charged into the council area on horseback, naked, wearing a war bonnet, and carrying a rifle, and announced that he had come to kill the white men who wanted to take his land. He surrendered with Crazy Horse as one of the six principal men of the northern Oglalas but thereafter seemed to change his attitude. It was Little Big Man who held Crazy Horse's arms when he was stabbed and for whose death he came to be blamed.

Little Hawk: The name of Crazy Horse's uncle and of his younger brother. *Little Hawk* had originally been the name of the older man, but he gave it to Crazy Horse's younger brother. The young man was killed in 1870, and the uncle then reclaimed the name.

Little Thunder: Wakiyan Čik'a (*wakíyą čík'a*). By 1845 he was the leading man among the southern Brulés, and, following the death of Conquering Bear in 1853, head chief of all the Brulés. Little Thunder and Spotted Tail were convinced that the Lakotas could not defeat the Americans militarily, and they maneuvered to maintain their freedom of action without engaging in war. Little Thunder relinquished control of the Brulés to Spotted Tail in 1865 and died at Rosebud Agency in 1879.

Little Wolf: Little Wolf (ca. 1830–ca. 1906) was a noted chief of the Northern Cheyennes. Although he fought in many engagements before his surrender in 1877, he is best known for his escape from Indian Territory (in present-day Oklahoma). In September 1878 Little Wolf and Dull Knife escaped with their bands and set out for their homeland in the north. They separated on the North Platte River, with Little Wolf making an eastward arc. In March 1879 Little Wolf's band reached the vicinity of Fort Keogh in Montana, where they surrendered. They eventually settled on Tougue River Reservation in Montana.

Little Wolf: Šungmanitu Čikala (*šúgmanitu čík'ala*). Oglala. Little Wolf and his brother Lone Bear had kinship ties through their mother to the Bad Faces band and may have been cousins of Woman's Dress. Upon his surrender in 1877, Little Wolf enlisted as a U.S. Indian Scout. Woman's Dress later claimed that Little Wolf was the one who overheard Crazy Horse say he intended to kill General Crook, an accusation that Little Wolf denied.

Little Wound: Taopi Čikala (*tha'ópi čík'ala*). Son of Bull Bear. Little Wound became the chief of the southern Oglalas (the Bear people) following the death of his brother Bad Wound in 1865. He was generally friendly to whites but continued to make war on the Pawnees and other Indian tribes. In 1871 he was named an agency chief along with Red Cloud, whom he bitterly opposed for the rest of his life. He died in the winter of 1899.

Lone Bear: Mato Wažila (*mathó wažíla*) 'single bear'. Born around 1847, Lone Bear had kinship ties through his mother to the Bad Faces band of Oglalas and may have been a cousin of Woman's Dress. Lone Bear fought at the Battle of the Little Bighorn. Upon his surrender in 1877 he enlisted as a U.S. Indian Scout and was later transferred to the Pine Ridge Indian Police, in which he served for more than twenty years. Woman's Dress alleged that Lone Bear and his brother Little Wolf were the source of the information that Crazy Horse intended to kill General Crook.

Lone Horn: Hewažila (*hewážila*) 'single horn'. Lone Horn (ca. 1790–1875) was the chief of the Minneconjou tribe and was said to be an uncle of Crazy Horse. He was the father of Touch the Clouds and Spotted Elk, later known as Big Foot. Big Foot took his father's place as chief and was killed at Wounded Knee in 1890.

Long Chin: Ikuhanska (*ikhúhąska*). Brulé. Brother of Conquering Bear. After Conquering Bear was killed, Long Chin led a revenge attack on a mail wagon, for which he was imprisoned in 1855 for a year at Fort Leavenworth with his half-brother Red Leaf and Spotted Tail.

Long Face: The name taken by Crazy Horse's uncle after he gave his previous name, *Little Hawk*, to Crazy Horse's younger brother. After the young man's death, he reclaimed his original name.

Long Hair: The Lakota name for George Armstrong Custer.

Man Whose Enemies Are Afraid of His Horse: Tašunke Kokipapi (*thašúke khokíphapi*) 'his horse they fear it'. Known among the Oglalas as Our Brave Man. Man Whose Enemies Are Afraid of His Horse (1802–87) was the leader of the Hunkpatila band of Oglalas, part of the Smoke people, the northern division of Oglalas. In 1854 he was identified as head chief of the Oglalas. He remained the leader of the northern Oglalas well into the reservation period, even though the U.S. government regarded Red Cloud as more important. His son was Young Man Afraid of His Horse.

Miles: Nelson A. Miles. Miles (1834–1925) began his army career as a Civil War volunteer. As a colonel commanding the Fifth Infantry, he participated in the campaigns following Custer's defeat at the Little Bighorn. Later, during the Ghost Dance troubles, he was the commanding general of the Division of the Missouri, which included the Lakota reservations.

Mitchell: General Robert D. Mitchell. Mitchell (1823–1925) served as commander along the Overland Road on the Platte River from 1864 to 1865.

Moonlight: Colonel Thomas Moonlight. Moonlight was a cavalry officer and was made commander of Fort Laramie in 1865. When two Oglalas named Blackfoot and Two Face brought a captive, Mrs. Eubanks, to Fort Laramie, he ordered the Indians hanged. After only a few months in charge, Moonlight was mustered out of the service for incompetence.

No Flesh: Čoniča Waniča (*čhoníčha waničA*) 'lacks flesh'. Oglala band chief. Born around 1845, No Flesh enlisted in the U.S. Indian Scouts in 1877 and went to Washington DC that same year as part of the Oglala delegation. He settled on Pine Ridge Reservation.

No Water: Mni Waniča (*mní waničA*) 'lacks water'. Younger brother of Black Twin. No Water was the leader of the Badger Eaters (Ȟoka Yuta [*ȟoká yútA*]) band. He married Black Buffalo Woman and later shot Crazy Horse after she left No Water for him.

Pawnee Killer: Head warrior of Bad Wound's True Oglala band, then later of the southern Oglalas under Little Wound.

Provost, John: Son of a trader known as "Old Man Provost" and a Lakota woman. In 1879 he was hired as an interpreter at Red Cloud Agency.

Red Cloud: Maȟpiya Luta (*maȟpíya lútA*). A member of the Bad Faces band. In 1841 Red Cloud (1822–1909) killed Bull Bear, which created a split among the Oglala tribe. A renowned warrior and acknowledged war leader during the Powder River wars in the 1860s, Red Cloud later counseled the Lakotas to settle on the reservation following his visit to Washington DC in 1870. Although not a chief, Red Cloud was treated as one by whites, a fact that many Lakotas resented. Once at the agency, he was appointed as an agency chief.

Red Cloud, son of: Generally known as Jack Red Cloud. In 1876 Jack Red Cloud (1858–1918) left his father at the agency and joined the northern Oglalas. He fought in the Rosebud battle (where he lost the fancy rifle presented to his father by President Ulysses S. Grant) and at the Little Bighorn. He later became a Ghost Dance leader for a time. Although his father abdicated his chieftaincy to his son in 1903, Jack Red Cloud never exercised the authority that his father did.

Red Dog: Šunka Luta (*šúka lúta*). A chief of the Oyukhpe band of Oglalas. Red Dog was married to a sister of Red Cloud and maintained close association with the Bad Faces band. He was an orator and usually spoke for Red Cloud in negotiations with the U.S. government.

Red Feather: Oglala. Younger brother of Black Shawl, wife of Crazy Horse.

Red Leaf: Wapaša (*wapáša*). Brulé. Younger brother of Conquering Bear. In 1855 Red Leaf, his half-brother Long Chin, and Spotted Tail surrendered and were imprisoned for a year at Fort Leavenworth for their attack on a mail wagon. Red Leaf later became chief of the Wažaže band, who had moved north with the Oglalas. He was a close ally of Red Cloud, and he and his band settled at Red Cloud Agency until forced to move to Spotted Tail Agency in 1877 with the rest of the Brulés.

Richard: John Baptiste Richard Sr. Richard (pronounced "reeshar") was born in St. Charles (in present-day Missouri) in 1810 and married one of Red Cloud's sisters. In the 1830s Richard reportedly became the first trader to bring in liquor for the Indian trade. He built and operated a toll bridge over the North Platte River near Fort Caspar from 1852 until 1865. He was killed by Cheyennes along the upper Niobrara River in 1875.

Richard, John: Mixed-blood son of John Baptiste Richard Sr. He was called Lean Elk by the Lakotas. In 1869 he killed a soldier and fled north to hide out with the Oglalas. He was a favorite interpreter of Red Cloud, who requested that Richard accompany him to Washington DC in 1870. For his efforts in arranging the trip, Richard was promised a pardon by President Ulysses S. Grant. During a visit in May 1872, Richard shot his brother-in-law, an Oglala named Yellow Bear, and was immediately killed by Yellow Bear's relatives. (Note that this is not Chief Yellow Bear but another man.)

Roman Nose: *Roman Nose* was the name used by whites to refer to a noted Cheyenne warrior whose proper name was Sauts 'bat'. Roman Nose (1823–68) wore a protective war bonnet made for him by the medicine man Ice, but a woman serving him some food inadvertently violated one of its taboos, and he was killed at the battle on Arikaree Fork in 1868. There was a Minneconjou named Crow Nose who was also called Roman Nose by whites.

Salaway, Frank: Born in Idaho around 1828, Salaway was the son of a French trader and a mixed-blood woman. He worked for the traders in the Fort Laramie area.

Saville: Dr. James J. Saville. Indian agent at Red Cloud Agency from July 1873 until he was relieved in October 1875. Saville was charged with fraud, and although the investigation was inconclusive, he resigned on December 3, 1875.

Sitting Bear: Mato Iyotaka (*mathó íyotaka*). Chief of the True Oglala band. Sitting Bear was part of the delegation of Lakotas who visited Washington DC in 1870.

Sitting Bull: Tatanka Iyotaka (*thatháka íyotaka*). Hunkpapa. Sitting Bull's father was also named Sitting Bull, and he gave the name to his son after his first coup at age fourteen. Sitting Bull (1831–90) was a warrior and shaman and implacably opposed to whites and their culture. He took his followers into Canada in 1877 rather than surrender, but he finally returned in 1881. He was killed on December 15, 1890, on Standing Rock Reservation when Indian policemen tried to arrest him during the Ghost Dance troubles.

Sitting Bull: Tatanka Iyotaka (*thatháka íyotaka*). Oglala. Nephew of Little Wound. Sitting Bull was head warrior of his uncle's band. He was a conspicuous friend of the whites and often acted to protect agency property from other Lakotas. He was presented with a brass-mounted rifle by President Ulysses S. Grant during a trip to Washington DC in 1875. (The rifle, which Sitting Bull subsequently lost, is now at the Museum of the American Indian.) He was killed by Crows at Fort Keogh in December 1876.

Smoke: Šota (*šóta*). Oglala. Uncle of Red Cloud. Smoke was a rival of Bull Bear for leadership of the Oglalas in the 1830s. After Red Cloud killed Bull Bear in 1841, the followers of Smoke moved north, forming a northern division of the Oglala tribe. Although Smoke remained nominally chief, by 1850 he was content to remain in the vicinity of Fort Laramie, where he died in 1864.

Spotted Crow: Uncle of Crazy Horse.

Spotted Tail: Sinte Gleška (*sinté gleška*). Uncle of Crazy Horse. In 1855 Spotted Tail (1823–81) surrendered and was imprisoned for a year at Fort Leavenworth with his cousins Red Leaf and Long Chin for their attack on a mail wagon. After his release he was convinced that the Lakotas could not defeat the United States militarily, and he counseled diplomacy and negotiation rather than armed resistance. Around 1866 Spotted Tail was recognized as head chief by the Brulé tribe, a position he retained until his death, and he became a rival of Red Cloud for prominence. He was killed in 1881 on Rosebud Reservation by another Brulé named Crow Dog.

Stabber: Čapapi (*čhaphápi*). A member of the Brulé Wažaže band. After Chief Conquering Bear was killed in 1854, Stabber and his people drove Conquering Bear's family out of the Wažaže camp, apparently to demonstrate to the army that they had had no part in the Grattan incident. Stabber became chief of those Wažaže band members who were termed as "friendlies."

Stanley, Colonel: Colonel David S. Stanley. In 1873 Stanley led an expedition into Montana to aid and escort the Northern Pacific Railroad survey, locate sites for new military posts, make a scientific survey of the area, and subdue and intimidate the Indians. The party was protected by the Seventh Cavalry under Lieutenant Colonel George Armstrong Custer.

Straight Foretop: Minneconjou warrior. Also known as High Forehead. While visiting the Brulés in 1854, Straight Foretop shot a Mormon pioneer's straggling cow and precipitated a series of violent encounters between the Lakotas and the army. He was turned over to the army by his tribe in March 1856 but was then pardoned by General William Harney.

Swift Bear: Mato Oȟ'anko (*mathó oȟ'ákho*). Brother-in-law of trader Jim Bordeaux. Swift Bear was the leader of the portion of the Corn band (Wagmeza Yuha [*wagméza yuhá*] 'owns corn') who wanted to settle on the reservation and begin farming. On Rosebud Reservation Swift Bear was the second agency chief behind Spotted Tail. He died in 1909.

Sword: Miwakan (*míwakhą*). There were two men named Sword, both sons of Brave Bear of the Oyukhpe band of Oglalas. The elder Sword was a respected warrior, and he was elected as a shirt wearer in 1868. He died in 1876. Shortly after that, his brother Hunts the Enemy changed his name to Sword, becoming known as George Sword (1847–1910). Although raised in a traditional household, George Sword became a progressive following a visit to Washington DC in 1870. He is given credit for convincing Crazy Horse to come into the reservation. He became the head of the Indian Police on Pine Ridge Reservation in 1880.

Tall Bull: Southern Cheyenne warrior. Tall Bull was also chief of the Dog Soldiers. Following the Sand Creek massacre, the Southern Cheyennes began raiding white settlements and attacking wagon trains. Tall Bull was killed at the Battle of Summit Springs on July 11, 1869, effectively ending the power of the Southern Cheyennes.

Tesson, Joe: A trader married to a Lakota woman. He worked for the army as a scout.

They Are Afraid of Her: Daughter of Crazy Horse. She died in 1873 when she was about one year old.

Three Stars: The Lakota name for General George Crook. As a brigadier general, his uniform had a star on each shoulder and one on the hat.

Touch the Clouds: Maȟpiya Ičaȟtagya (*maȟpíya ičáȟtagya*). Minneconjou warrior and chief. Touch the Clouds (1836–1905) was a cousin and close ally of Crazy Horse. He was said to be seven feet tall. He and his followers settled on Cheyenne River Reservation.

Twiss: Major Thomas A. Twiss. Twiss (ca. 1802–71) graduated second in his class from West Point in 1826. He served as Indian agent at Upper Platte Agency from 1855 until 1861, when he was replaced by order of the new president, Abraham Lincoln. During his tenure he had married an Oglala woman named Wanikiyewin (*waníkhiyewį*) 'savior woman' and remained with his wife's people until his death.

Two Moons: Northern Cheyenne chief. He was an ally of Crazy Horse. Two Moons (ca. 1842–1917) led his camp to surrender at Fort Keough in 1877 following the battle at Wolf Mountain.

Warren, Lieutenant: Gouverneur Kemble Warren. After graduating second in his class at West Point in 1850, Warren (1830–82) joined the Corps of Topographical Engineers. During his time in the West, Warren conducted detailed mapmaking explorations of the Yellowstone and upper Missouri rivers, seeking out suitable sites for forts.

White Antelope: Noted Southern Cheyenne warrior and chief. White Antelope (ca. 1798–1864) sought to reach some accommodation with whites that would allow his people to remain in their traditional territory. He was killed at Sand Creek in 1864.

White Beard: The Lakota name for Brigadier General William Harney.

White Hat: The Lakota name for Lieutenant William Philo Clark.

Woman's Dress: Oglala. Son of Bad Face and grandson of Smoke. Woman's Dress (1846–1921) was alleged to have falsely warned General George Crook that Crazy Horse intended to kill him. In 1877 he enlisted in the U.S. Indian Scouts and later transferred to the Pine Ridge Indian Police. He died on Wounded Knee Creek.

Worm: Waglula (*waglúla*). Father of Crazy Horse. Worm (ca. 1811–81) was originally named Crazy Horse, as was his father. His first wife, the mother of Crazy Horse, was a Minneconjou named Rattle Blanket Woman. After her death in 1844, he married two sisters of Spotted Tail, one of whom was the mother of Little Hawk. After Crazy Horse was killed in 1877, Worm settled among the Brulés until his death.

Wyuse (or Yuse): Possibly the Lakota pronunciation of the last name of Auguste Lucien or Lucier (1814–54). Born in St. Charles (in present-day Missouri), he was a hunter and guide, married to a Lakota woman, and the father of two daughters. He was an army interpreter at Fort Laramie in 1853.

Yellow Bear: Mato Hinzi (mathó hízi) 'buckskin-colored bear'. A chief in the Oyukhpe band of Oglalas. Yellow Bear was an ally of Red Cloud and a member of the delegation that visited Washington DC in 1870. In 1877 he enlisted in the U.S. Indian Scouts with the rank of corporal.

Discussion Questions

The following questions are provided to help prompt discussion and further thinking about Crazy Horse.

Choose one or two of the defining events in Crazy Horse's life, and explain their importance. Similarly, select one or more of his significant relationships, and explain their influence on him or his life.

The term *medicine* seems to connote a wide range of meanings. We are often told that Crazy Horse has "strong medicine." Others also are described as having strong or weak medicine. Furthermore, medicine men may confer medicine, as the Cheyenne medicine man does on the warriors before their battle with the cavalry. From the various ways in which it is used, what do you think *medicine* means?

What are Crazy Horse's visions, and how do they inspire or guide him?

The Mormon cow incident occurs early in the book and seems to encapsulate many of the themes of Indian-white coexistence, as well as the confrontations to come. What do the incident's causes, misunderstandings, and eventual outcome foretell about the nature of the many upcoming conflicts?

The lack of consensus and unified leadership evidenced among the Lakotas reflects both the reality of political rivalries and Lakota cultural notions of leadership. In what respects do you feel the Lakotas' understanding of leadership is a benefit or a liability to them?

From the beginning of *Crazy Horse*, some of the Indians favor peace with the whites, and the number increases as the book progresses. What are some of the different reasons given for peaceful coexistence, and what underlying motives—positive or negative—are they founded upon?

Do the book's depictions of other great, well-known Indian leaders, such as Red Cloud and Sitting Bull, confirm, contradict, or simply supplement your previous knowledge of them?

How do the final few chapters of the book illustrate both the great power and great vulnerability of Crazy Horse?

There are many vivid depictions of Indian camps during both good and bad times, conveying the Indians' way of life, customs and rituals, the impact of white goods and encroachment, and contrasts between old agrarian routines and the hunting lifestyle the Plains Indians had practiced for several generations. What aspect or aspects of this picture do you find particularly memorable or interesting?

"The parfleches were full" or "the parfleches were empty" are statements repeated throughout the book, succinctly indicating prosperity or want in a Lakota village. How would you phrase a major indicator of economic or social well-being in contemporary U.S. society at the national, state, local, neighborhood, or family level?

How are the battles with enemy Indian groups, such as the Crows, different from the battles with the whites?

Lakota women "keen," sing "strong-heart songs," and, after the "unshirting" of Crazy Horse, mock the decision in song. What are some of the different functions women's singing serves?

How would you describe the cultural and domestic roles of, and relationships between, men and women in the Lakota groups? What differences in women's roles fascinate Crazy Horse during his visit to the Cheyennes?

At the conclusion of her foreword to *Crazy Horse*, Sandoz comments on the language of the book: "I have used the simplest words possible, hoping by idiom and figures and the underlying rhythm pattern to say some of the things of the Indian for which there are no white-man words, suggest something of his innate nature, something of his relationship to the earth and the sky and all that is between." Do you feel Sandoz uses language effectively to paint a vivid picture of the Indians? What examples did you find particularly powerful in suggesting the mindset or depicting the way of life of the Indians?

In the bibliography at the back of *Crazy Horse*, Sandoz lists the unpublished sources she consulted while writing the book. The first section consists of her own interviews with Oglalas who knew Crazy Horse, followed by the Ricker Collection interviews, which include a small number of Indian interviews conducted by various people. As you look through these lists, what other Indians mentioned in the main text but missing from the bibliography do you think would have been able to contribute valuable perspectives to the picture Sandoz has painted of Crazy Horse?

A NOTE ABOUT THE AUTHOR

In 1955 MARI SANDOZ received the National Achievement Award of The Westerners for having more books (four) than any other author, living or dead, on the list of One Hundred Best Books of the West. The Trans-Missouri Series, which is likely to stand as her central achievement, was conceived before the author was twenty. Two books of the series are still to be written: the first, which tells of the coming of iron and powder to stone-age man of the Great Plains, and the last—the story of oil in the Great Plains region. In addition to CRAZY HORSE, the published volumes are: *The Buffalo Hunters: The Story of the Hide Men*; *Cheyenne Autumn*; *Old Jules*; and *The Cattlemen: From the Rio Grande across the Far Marias*. Miss Sandoz also has written a half-dozen memorable novels of which the most recent are *The Horsecatcher* (1956) and *Son of the Gamblin' Man*. A selection of her short writings, HOSTILES AND FRIENDLIES, was published in 1959 by the University of Nebraska Press.